Frommer's®

POSTCARDS

FROM

BERMUDA

Horseshoe Bay Beach in Southampton Parish is one of Bermuda's finest places to enjoy sun and sand. See chapter 6. © Carl Purcell Photography.

Since visitors can't rent cars, your transportation options include mopeds and old-fashioned carriages. See chapter 3. Image above © Bob Krist Photography; image below © J. Barry O'Rourke/The Stock Market.

Jobson's Cove, one of the island's many secluded beaches. See chapter 6. © Bob Krist Photography.

Pink cottages are typical of the island's architecture. © Kindra Clineff Photography.

Bermuda is a great destination for sailing and boating. See chapter 6. Above, boats moored off Sandys Parish. © Bob Krist Photography.

In the Crystal Caves, you can take a guided tour through a network of subterranean lakes, caves, and caverns with dramatic formations of stalagmites and stalactites. See chapter 7. © Bob Krist Photography.

Bermuda is one of the world's top golf destinations. See chapter 6 for reviews of the top courses, plus details on the island's best tennis facilities. Photo above © Jay Thomas/International Stock; photo below © Carl Purcell Photography.

One of Bermuda's top attractions is the Botanical Gardens in Paget Parish. See chapter 7.
© Bob Krist Photography.

In St. George's Parish, you'll find Fort St. Catherine, first built in the 17th century. © *Bob Krist Photography.*

The island is full of colorful local characters . . . © *Bob Krist Photography.*

. . . and buttoned-up businessmen, who often don Bermuda shorts in warm weather.
© Catherine Karnow Photography.

Above: A guest room at Horizons and Cottages, one of the most upscale places to stay on the island.
Below: At Marley Beach Cottages, you can rent your own ocean-view cottage, complete with kitchen. See chapter 4 for complete reviews for both choices. Both images © Bob Krist Photography.

The sands at Warwick Long Bay. See chapter 6. © William Roy/The Stock Market.

You can learn more about the island's underwater world at the Bermuda Aquarium. See chapter 7. © Bob Krist Photography.

An aerial view of Hamilton Parish. See chapter 7. © Bob Krist Photography.

Hamilton, Bermuda's capital, is a great place for shopping and dining. © Ann Purcell Photography.

If it's too crowded at lovely Horseshoe Bay Beach, take one of the trails that wind through the park nearby; they'll lead you to more secluded cove beaches. See chapter 6. © Kindra Clineff Photography.

*St. George's Parish is full of lovely, secluded places to soak up the sun. See chapter 6.
© Michael Ventura/International Stock.*

*An amazing view from atop Gibbs Hill Lighthouse. See chapters 1 and 7. © M. Timothy
O'Keefe Photography.*

A touch of pink. © Bob Krist Photography.

The pool, golf course, and ocean views from the Southampton Princess. See chapter 4 for a complete review. © Howard Millard/The Viesti Collection.

Frommer's® 2000

Bermuda

by Darwin Porter
&
Danforth Prince

with Online Directory by Michael Shapiro

MACMILLAN • USA

ABOUT THE AUTHORS

A native of North Carolina, **Darwin Porter** was a bureau chief for the *Miami Herald* when he was 21, and later worked in television advertising. A veteran writer, he's the author of numerous best-selling Frommer's travel guides, notably to England, France, Germany, Italy, and the Caribbean. Working with Darwin is **Danforth Prince,** formerly of the Paris bureau of the *New York Times.* Both of these journalists discovered Bermuda during their various spring break College Weeks and have been frequent visitors ever since.

MACMILLAN TRAVEL

Macmillan General Reference USA, Inc.
1633 Broadway
New York, NY 10019

Find us online at **www.frommers.com**

Copyright © 1999 by Macmillan General Reference USA, Inc.
Maps copyright © 1999 by Macmillan General Reference USA, Inc.

ISBN 0-02-862992-2
ISSN 1069-3572

Editor: John Rosenthal
Production Editor: Robyn Burnett
Photo Editor: Richard Fox
Design by Michele Laseau
Staff Cartographers: John Decamillis, Roberta Stockwell
Page Creation by Sean Monkhouse

SPECIAL SALES

Bulk purchases (10+ copies) of Frommer's and selected Macmillan travel guides are available to corporations, organizations, mail-order catalogs, institutions, and charities at special discounts, and can be customized to suit individual needs. For more information write to Special Sales, Macmillan General Reference, 1633 Broadway, New York, NY 10019.

Manufactured in the United States of America

5   4   3   2   1

Contents

List of Maps

An Invitation to the Reader

In researching this book, we discovered many wonderful places—hotels, restaurants, shops, and more. We're sure you'll find others. Please tell us about them, so we can share the information with your fellow travelers in upcoming editions. If you were disappointed with a recommendation, we'd love to know that, too. Please write to:

Frommer's Bermuda 2000
Macmillan Travel
1633 Broadway
New York, NY 10019

An Additional Note

Please be advised that travel information is subject to change at any time—and this is especially true of prices. We therefore suggest that you write or call ahead for confirmation when making your travel plans. The authors, editors, and publisher cannot be held responsible for the experiences of readers while traveling. Your safety is important to us, however, so we encourage you to stay alert and be aware of your surroundings. Keep a close eye on cameras, purses, and wallets, all favorite targets of thieves and pickpockets.

What the Symbols Mean

✪ Frommer's Favorites
Our favorite places and experiences—outstanding for quality, value, or both.

The following abbreviations are used for credit cards:

AE	American Express	MC	MasterCard
DC	Diners Club	V	Visa
DISC	Discover		

Find Frommer's Online

Arthur Frommer's Budget Travel Online (www.frommers.com) offers more than 6,000 pages of up-to-the-minute travel information—including the latest bargains and candid, personal articles updated daily by Arthur Frommer himself. No other Web site offers such comprehensive and timely coverage of the world of travel.

The Best of Bermuda

Even some of its most diehard fans admit that Bermuda (like some beauty queens) is beautiful but dull. We prefer to think of it as "tranquil." If you're looking for exotic local color or sizzling rum-and reggae-filled nights, look farther south to the Caribbean.

But if you need to escape from the stress and strain of daily life, then make it Bermuda. The joint may not be jumping, but it's the most relaxing—and the safest—of all the foreign islands off the American coastline. Bermuda is a relatively hassle-free environment where you can concentrate on your tan, minus the hassles of aggressive vendors or worries about crime. As Mark Twain often said, "Sometimes a dose of Bermuda is just what the doctor ordered." This is the place to kick back and relax. If you're into sunning and swimming, it doesn't get much better than Bermuda between May and September. Pink sands and turquoise seas—it sounds like a corny travel poster, but it's for real.

Frankly, Bermuda is predictable, and its regular visitors wouldn't have it any other way. The tiny island chain has been hosting visitors for decades, and there aren't many secrets left to uncover. But those pink sandy beaches are just as inviting as ever, no matter how many times you return to their welcoming comfort.

Even to friends of Bermuda who make an annual pilgrimage to the island, though, the Bermudians can be a bit smug. They know that their landscape is more attractive than Chicago, New York, Los Angeles, or Miami, and they're not above reminding you. Bit of an imperial attitude, isn't it? Exactly.

There are those who claim that Bermuda has become Americanized. Look again. It has happened to islands much farther south than Bermuda, such as The Bahamas; but Bermuda remains stoically Bermuda, in open defiance to the gigantic cultural and economic power to its west. The island and its population steadfastly adhere to their British customs, even if at times that slavish devotion borders on caricature. (The afternoon tea ritual is pleasant enough, but the powdered wigs worn by lawyers and judges are a bit much—those things must get hot in a semitropical climate!) Some visitors find all the British decorum rather silly on a semitropical island that's closer to Atlanta than London. But many others find this stalwart commitment to British tradition on a remote island in the middle of the Atlantic colorful and quaint, forming part of the unique charm of the lovely, wonderful place that is Bermuda.

Bermuda

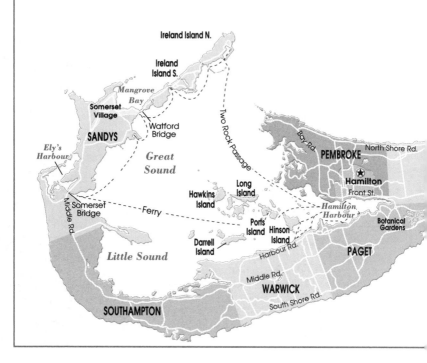

Quiet and romantic Bermuda is the best place in the world for a honeymoon—or to celebrate any occasion with your lover. You can walk its beaches on moonlit nights with little chance of getting mugged, as you might on San Juan's Condado.

If you're looking for some of the top golf courses in the world, Bermuda is your mecca. It's got the scenery, the state-of-the-art courses, and the British tradition of golfing excellence. Even the most demanding player is generally satisfied with the island's tee-off spots.

If you're a sailor, you'll find sailing the waters of Bermuda reason enough for a visit. Better yet, reason enough to be alive. The farther you go from shore, of course, the greater the visibility. Discovering your own hidden cove, away from the cruise-ship crowds, can make your day.

If you hate driving around British islands on the left side of the road, that's fine with Bermudians. You *can't* drive anyway, since they won't rent you a car. Bike your way around, or hop on a scooter and zip from one end of the island to the other.

We could go on and on with reasons to come to Bermuda, from exploring natural wonderlands to playing on choice tennis courts with gentle sea breezes and

warm sunshine. But we'll end here with a warning: If you're a demanding foodie, you'll find better dining on other islands, such as Martinique, although Bermuda has made much progress of late in its cuisine. If you want nightlife and glittering gambling casinos and all that jazz, head for San Juan. There is some nightlife in Bermuda, if you lean toward nursing a pint in a pub. It's always wise to bring along some good company (or a good book) to ensure a blissful night here.

So if you've decided that Bermuda sounds like the perfect place to relax, spend your vacation in peace and let us do the work. Below you'll find our carefully compiled list of the best that Bermuda has to offer, from beaches and dive sites to resorts, restaurants, and sightseeing—and nearly everything else you'll want to see and do in the course of your island getaway.

1 The Best Beaches

Most likely, your first priority on your Bermuda vacation will be to kick back at the beach. But which beach to choose? Hotels often have their own private stretches of sand, which we've described in each accommodation review to help you choose a place to stay (see chapter 4). There are many fine public beaches as well. Here are our picks for the top 10, arranged clockwise around the island, beginning with the south-shore beaches closest to the city of Hamilton. See chapter 6 for additional details on all of these beaches.

- **Elbow Beach** (Paget Parish): Pale pink sand stretches for almost a mile at Elbow Beach, one of the most consistently popular beaches in Bermuda. At least three hotels sit on the beach's perimeter. Because of the protective coral reefs that surround it, Elbow Beach is one of the safest on the island for swimming. During the Easter period, it tends to be packed with college students who invade Bermuda for College Weeks. **The Elbow Beach Hotel** (☎ 441/236-3535) offers facilities and rentals.

- **Astwood Cove** (Warwick Parish): At the bottom of a steep and winding road that intersects with South Shore Road, this beach is so remote that it's rarely overcrowded. Come here when you want to be alone. The trees and shrubbery of Astwood Park provide a verdant backdrop.

- **Warwick Long Bay** (Warwick Parish): This popular beach, on the southern side of South Shore Park, features a half-mile stretch of sand against a backdrop of scrubland and low grasses. Despite frequent winds, the waves are surprisingly small thanks to an offshore reef. Less than 200 feet offshore, a jagged coral island appears to be floating above the water.

- **Chaplin Bay** (Warwick and Southampton Parishes): At the southern extremity of South Shore Park, straddling the boundary between two parishes, this small but secluded beach almost completely disappears during storms or particularly high tides. An open-air coral barrier partially separates one half of the beach from the other.

- **Horseshoe Bay** (Southampton Parish): This is Bermuda's most famous beach, and it's one of the best for families. Unlike most island beaches, Horseshoe Bay has a lifeguard on duty from May to September—another reason families choose these sands over others. The **Horseshoe Bay Beach House** (☎ 441/238-2651) offers complete facilities, including rental equipment, to beachgoers.

- **Church Bay** (Southampton Parish): If you like to snorkel, this southwestern beach is for you. The relatively calm waters, sheltered by offshore reefs, harbor a variety of marine life. Sunbathers love to nestle in the beach's unusually deep pink sands.

- **Somerset Long Bay** (Sandys Parish): The waters off this beach are often unsafe for swimming, but its isolation will appeal to anyone who wants to escape the crowds. With about a quarter mile of sand, the crescent-shaped beach is ideal for strolling. The undeveloped parkland of Sandys Parish shelters it from the rest of the island.

- **Shelly Bay** (Hamilton Parish): On the north shore, you'll discover calm waters and soft pink sand—and you'll want for nothing else.

- **Tobacco Bay Beach** (St. George's Parish): A popular stretch of pale pink sand, this is the most frequented beach on St. George's Island. It offers lots of facilities, including equipment rentals and a snack bar.

- **John Smith's Bay** (Smith's Parish): The only public beach within Smith's Parish is long and flat, and boasts the pale pink sand for which the south shore is famous. There's usually a lifeguard on duty from May to September—a plus for families with children. Toilet and changing facilities are on-site.

2 The Best Outdoor Pursuits

See chapter 6 for more details on how to arrange any of these activities.

- **Golf:** Known for its outstanding golf courses, Bermuda attracts the world's leading golfers (and those who'd like to be). In the past, such luminaries as President Eisenhower, President Truman, and the duke of Windsor have hit the island's links. Rolling, hummocky fairways characterize the greens. Many avid golfers come to Bermuda to play all the courses; they call this "collecting courses." Some holes, such as Port Royal's notorious 16th, are from hell, as golfers say: Both the tee and the hole are placed high on cliff edges, with rich blue sea looming a dizzying 100 feet below. See "The Best Golf Courses," below, for our top picks.

- **Boating and Sailing:** Yachties around the world agree: Bermuda is one of the world's top boating and sailing destinations. Many people forget that Bermuda isn't just one island, but a series of islands (an archipelago, really) waiting to be discovered. With the fresh wind of the Atlantic blowing in your hair, you can set out upon your own voyage of discovery, perhaps sailing Great Sound with its tiny islets that take in Long Island and Hawkins Island. Tiny secluded beaches beckon frequently. Are you a novice at sailing? Try Mangrove Bay; it's protected and safer than some of the more turbulent seas.

- **Diving:** If you're happiest under the sea, Bermuda has what you're looking for. That includes the wrecks of countless ships that went aground in storm-tossed seas, underwater caves, rich reefs, and, during most of the year, warm, gin-clear waters. Among it all you'll find a kaleidoscope of coral and marine life that's the most varied in this part of the world. Many scuba experts cite Bermuda as one of the safest and best places to learn the sport. Depths begin at 25 feet or less but can reach 80 feet or more. Some wrecks are in about 30 feet of water, which puts them within the range of snorkelers. See also "The Best Dive Sites," below.

- **Biking:** Since you're not allowed by law to rent a car on Bermuda, you might as well hit the road on two wheels, even if you haven't been on a bike seat since you were a kid. Most of Bermuda isn't the world's greatest cycling terrain, with narrow roads and heavy traffic, but we suggest that you head for the Railway Trail, the island's premier bike path. The paved trail, which follows the former route of Bermuda's railway line, runs almost the entire length of the island.

- **Horseback Riding:** Because this sport is so restricted on Bermuda, it can be all the more memorable. Guiding a horse through the dune grass and oleander of the island, especially at South Shore Park, is an experience you won't want to miss. As you ride along beaches looking out over coral bluffs, you and your fellow riders may agree that while it may not be Kentucky, it's a pretty nice ride. Horseback-riding centers will guide you on trail rides through not only the best of the Bermuda countryside, but also beautiful hidden spots along the north coast.

3 The Best Dive Sites

The following are some of the most exciting shipwreck and coral reef dives. See chapter 6 for more information on diving in Bermuda.

- **The *Constellation:*** This 200-foot, four-masted schooner, which was en route to Venezuela in 1943, now lies in 30 feet of water off the northwestern side of the island, about 8 miles west of the dockyard. The true story of this ship inspired Peter Benchley to write *The Deep.*

The Baffling Bermuda Triangle

The area known as the Bermuda Triangle encompasses a 1½ million-square-mile expanse of open sea between Bermuda, Puerto Rico, and the southeastern shoreline of the United States. This bit of the Atlantic is the source of the most famous, and certainly the most baffling, legend associated with Bermuda.

Tales of the mysterious Bermuda Triangle persist, despite attempts by skeptics to dismiss them as fanciful. Below are just three of the most popular stories. Can they be true? See what you think:

- In 1881, a British-registered ship, the *Ellen Austin,* encountered an unnamed vessel in good condition sailing aimlessly without a crew. The *Austin's* captain ordered a handful of his best seamen to board the mysterious vessel and sail it to Newfoundland. A few days later, the two ships encountered each other again on the high seas. But to everyone's alarm, the crewmen who had transferred from the *Austin* were nowhere to be found—it was completely unmanned once again!
- Another tale concerns the later disappearance of a merchant ship called the *Marine Sulphur Queen.* It disappeared suddenly and without warning, and no one could say why. The weather was calm when the ship set sail from Bermuda, and everything onboard was fine, for no distress signal was received from the crew. In looking for explanations, some have held that the ship probably had a weakened hull that gave way, causing it to descend quickly to the bottom. Others attribute its loss to the mysterious forces that are behind all the stories.
- The most famous of all the legends occurred in 1945. On December 5, five U.S. Navy bombers departed from Fort Lauderdale, Florida, on a routine

- **The *Cristóbal Colón:*** This 480-foot Spanish luxury liner is the largest known shipwreck in Bermuda's waters; it ran aground in 1936 on a northern reef between North Rock and North Breaker. It now lies in 30 to 55 feet of water.
- **The *Hermes:*** This 165-foot steamer ship about a mile off Warwick Long Bay on the south shore, shipwrecked in 1985, lies in about 80 feet of water. Along with the *Rita Zovetta* and the *Tauton* (see below), the *Hermes* is a Bermuda favorite thanks to the incredible multicolored variety of fish—grouper, brittle starfish, spiny lobster, crabs, banded coral shrimp, queen angels, tube sponge, and more—that populate the waters around the ship.
- **L'Hermanie:** This first-class 60-gun French frigate was 17 days out of its Cuban port and heading back to France when it sank in 1838. The ship lies in 20 to 30 feet of water off the western side of the island, with 25 cannons still visible.
- **The *Marie Celeste:*** This paddle wheeler sank in 1964. Its 15-foot-diameter paddle wheel, located off the southern portion of the island, is overgrown with coral standing about 55 feet off the ocean floor.
- **The *North Carolina:*** One of Bermuda's most colorful wrecks, this English sailing bark foundered in 1879 and today lies in about 40 feet of water off the western portion of the island.
- **The *Rita Zovetta:*** A 360-foot Italian cargo ship, located in about 20 to 70 feet of water off the southern side of the island, ran aground off St. David's Island in 1924. This one's a favorite with underwater photographers, thanks to a kaleidoscope of fish that inhabit the area.

mission. The weather was fine; no storm of any kind threatened. A short time into the flight, however, the leader of the squadron radioed that they were lost, and then the radio went silent; all efforts by the ground to establish further communication proved fruitless. A rescue plane was dispatched to search for the squadron—but it, too, disappeared. The navy ordered a search lasting 5 days, but there was no evidence of any wreckage. To this day, the disappearance of the squadron and of the rescue plane remains a mystery as deep as the waters of the region.

How do those who believe in the Bermuda Triangle legend explain these phenomena? Some contend that the area is a time warp to another universe; others think the waters off Bermuda are the site of the lost kingdom of Atlantis, whose power sources still function deep beneath the surface of the water. Still others believe that there exists a perpetual focusing of laser rays upon the region from outer space, or that underwater signaling devices are guiding invaders from other planets, who have chosen the site for the systematic collection of human beings for scientific observation and experimentation. (Smacks of the *X-Files,* doesn't it?) Some, drawing upon the Book of Revelation, are fully persuaded that the Bermuda Triangle is really one of the gates to hell, the other lying midway between Japan and the Philippines, in the Devil's Sea.

No matter what your views on these mysteries, you're bound to provoke an excited response by asking residents what they think about it. On Bermuda, almost everyone has an opinion about the island's biggest and most fascinating legend of all: the baffling Bermuda Triangle.

- **South West Breaker:** This coral-reef dive off the south shore, about 1½ miles off Church Bay, has hard and soft coral decorating sheet walls at depths of 20 to 30 feet.
- **Tarpon Hole:** Located near Elbow Beach off the south shore, this dive's proximity to the Elbow Beach Hotel makes it extremely popular. The honeycombed reef here—one of the most beautiful off the coast of Bermuda—is known for its varieties of coral: yellow pencil, elkhorn, fire, and star coral.
- **The** *Tauton:* This popular dive site is a British Royal Mail steamer that sank in 1914. It lies in 10 to 40 feet of water off the northern end of the island; it's also home to scores of Bermuda's most colorful varieties of marine life.

4 The Best Golf Courses

See chapter 6 for more details on these courses.

- **Belmont Hotel Golf & Country Club** (Warwick Parish): This 18-hole, par-70, 5,777-yard course was designed in 1923 by Emmett Devereux, a Scotsman. It's been challenging golfers ever since, especially on its par-5 11th hole, a severe dogleg left with a blind tee shot. Trade winds play havoc with the listed lengths. Critics complain that the layout of the course is "maddening," yet they continue to return for new challenges. The grass is dense thanks to a modern irrigation system.

- **Castle Harbour Golf Club** (Hamilton Parish): This 18-hole, par-71, 6,440-yard course, designed by the noted golf architect Charles Banks, is known for its challenging tee shots. Trade winds sweeping in from the Atlantic make the course seem far longer than it actually is. Challenges abound, especially at the 2nd and 17th holes. As Bermuda courses go, you'll find fewer sand traps here. This is an expensive place to play, but much of the money collected goes toward its state-of-the-art maintenance.

- **Port Royal Golf Course** (Southampton Parish): This public golf course ranks among the very best on the island, public or private; in fact, it's rated as one of the greatest public courses in the world. Jack Nicklaus apparently agrees, since he likes to play here. Robert Trent Jones designed the 18-hole, par-71, 6,565-yard course along an ocean terrain. The 16th hole is the most famous in Bermuda; photos of it have appeared in countless golf magazines. Port Royal's greens fees are reasonable when compared with the more elitist courses on the island.

- **Southampton Princess Golf Club** (Hamilton Parish): This is an 18-hole, par-54, 2,684-yard course, with elevated tees, strategically placed bunkers, and an array of water hazards to challenge even the most experienced golfer. Regarding this course, one golfer commented, "You not only need to be a great player, but have a certain mountaineering agility as well."

- **St. George's Golf Club** (St. George's Parish): One of the island's newest courses—and one of its best—this 18-hole, par-62, 4,043-yard course was designed by the master himself, Robert Trent Jones. Within walking distance of historic St. George's, it lies on a windy headland at the northeastern tip of Bermuda. Although you'll enjoy panoramic vistas, your game is likely to be affected by Atlantic winds. The greens are the smallest on the island, at no larger than 24 feet across.

5 The Best Tennis Facilities

For further details, see chapter 6.

- **Southampton Princess** (Southampton Parish): This is Bermuda's premier destination for avid tennis players. Its tennis-court layout not only is the largest on the island but also is maintained in state-of-the-art condition. This deluxe hotel, one of the finest in Bermuda, offers 11 Plexipave courts. The courts are somewhat protected from the north winds, but swirling breezes may affect your final score.

- **Government Tennis Stadium** (Pembroke Parish): Although Bermuda has been known as the tennis capital of the Atlantic since 1873, players often complain that the trade winds swirling around the island affect their game, especially at courts near the water. That's why many prefer one of the inland courts, such as this government-owned stadium, which offers three clay and five Plexicushion courts (three illuminated for night play). The facility, which is north of Hamilton, requires players to wear proper tennis attire. On-site you'll find a pro shop, a ball machine, and a pro offering private lessons.

- **Port Royal Club** (Southampton Parish): Serious tennis is played right along with golf here, and these well-maintained courts are among the island's best. There are four Plexipave courts, and two are illuminated for night games. You can borrow racquets and balls if you didn't come prepared. Even golfing luminaries such as Jack Nicklaus have been spotted on these courts, which overlook the pink sands and blue waters of Whale Bay, one of the leading areas for fishing and boating in Bermuda.

- **Elbow Beach Hotel** (Paget Parish): A runner-up in the tennis sweepstakes, these courts don't stack up against those of the Southampton Princess. But some of America's leading collegiate tennis players use these courts during spring break College Weeks. During that time, you can often see future stars in action here. The first-class hotel offers five LayKold courts, one of which is reserved just for lessons, given by an on-site pro.

6 The Best Day Hikes

For more details, see chapter 6 and chapter 8.

- **The Bermuda Railway Trail** (Sandys Parish): Stretching for about 21 miles, this unique trail was created along the course of the old Bermuda Railway, which served the island from 1931 to 1948. Bermudians traveled on this train in lieu of cars, which weren't allowed on the island until the late 1940s. Armed with a copy of the *Bermuda Railway Trail Guide,* available at the various visitor centers, you can set out on your own, following the old rail route of what was called "Rattle and Shake." Most of the trail still winds along a car-free route, and you can do as much (or as little) of the route as your stamina allows.
- **From the Royal Naval Dockyard to Somerset** (Sandys Parish): Hikers can also take a 4-mile walk from the dockyard, the former center of the British navy on Bermuda, to Somerset Island. From the southern entrance to the dockyard, follow Pender Road for about half a mile, crossing Cut Bridge leading to Ireland Island South. After crossing Grey's Bridge, the route continues west along Watford Island until it crosses Watford Bridge, which eventually leads to Somerset Village in Sandys Parish. There are various sandy beaches along the route, perfect for pausing from your hike to stretch out on the sand awhile.
- **Spittal Pond Nature Reserve Tour** (Smith's Parish): This 60-acre unspoiled sanctuary is the island's largest nature reserve, home to both resident and migratory waterfowl. You can spot some 25 species of waterfowl here annually from November to May. Scenic trails and footpaths have been cut through the property. You can either explore on your own or take one of the guided hikes offered by the Department of Agriculture.

7 The Best Sailing

Bermuda is one of the major sailing capitals in the Atlantic. A great many sail-yourself boats are available for rent to qualified sailors. See chapter 6 for more information. The best outfitters include the following:

- **Blue Hole Water Sports** (Grotto Bay Beach Hotel, Hamilton Parish; ☎ 441/293-2915): Here you'll find a large selection of self-drive boats, such as a Sunfish, Boardsailer, kayak, Paddle Cat, or Sun Cat. Rentals are available for up to 8 hours.
- **Mangrove Marina** (Somerset Parish; ☎ 441/234-0914): This is the best place to rent a Boston whaler, which can hold three or four passengers, depending on its size—an ideal craft for exploring the uninhabited islands of Bermuda. This outfitter rents 13-foot whalers, along with a 30 HP, 15-foot Open Bowrider, which also accommodates four.
- **Pompano Beach Club Watersports Centre** (Southampton Parish; ☎ 441/234-0222): This is the best outfitter in this tourist-laden parish. Open from May to late October, it offers a variety of equipment, including the O'Brien

Windsurfer, which is suitable for one person (novice or experienced). Its fleet also includes other vessels that hold one or two people and can be rented for up to 4 hours: Dolphin paddleboats, Buddy Boards, Aqua-Eye viewing boards, Aqua Finn sailboats, and kayaks.

8 The Best Views

Bermuda is an incredibly scenic island, with lovely panoramas and vistas unfolding at nearly every turn. But not all views are created equal, and below are some of our personal favorites. See chapter 7 for additional suggestions.

- **Fort Scaur:** From Somerset Bridge in Sandys Parish, head for this fort atop the parish's highest hill. Walk the fort's ramparts, enjoying the vistas across Great Sound to Spanish Point. You can also gaze north to the dockyard to take in the fine view of Somerset Island. On a clear day, a look through the telescope will reveal St. David's Lighthouse, 14 miles away on the northeastern tip of the island. After taking in the fantastic view from the fort, you can stroll through the 22 acres of beautiful gardens.

- **Gibbs Hill Lighthouse:** For an even better view than the one enjoyed by Queen Elizabeth II (see below), climb the 185 spiral steps of the lighthouse itself. Built in 1846, it's one of the oldest cast-iron lighthouses in the world. From the top, you can relish what islanders consider the single-finest view in all of Bermuda. You can, that is, if the wind doesn't blow you away—be sure to hang onto the railing. In heavy winds, the tower actually sways; on certain days you may want to retreat in spite of the view.

- **The Queen's View:** At Gibbs Hill Lighthouse in Southampton Parish, a plaque designates the spot where Queen Elizabeth II paused in November 1953 to take in the view of Little Sound. You can admire that same view today, which includes Riddells Bay Golf Course and Perot's Island. (Although Ross Perot has a home in Bermuda, the island is not named for him, but for the father of William Bennett Perot, Bermuda's first postmaster.)

- **Warwick Long Bay:** This stretch of pristine pink sand—stretching for half a mile or so—makes this a dream beach of the picture-postcard variety. It's set against a backdrop of towering cliffs and hills studded with Spanish bayonet and oleander. A 20-foot coral outcrop, rising some 200 feet offshore and resembling a sculpted boulder, adds even more variety to this stunning beachscape.

9 The Best Historic Sights

See chapter 7 for more details.

- **Fort St. Catherine** (St. George's Parish): This fort—with its tunnels, cannons, and ramparts—towers over the beach where the shipwrecked crew of the *Sea Venture* first came ashore in 1609. The fort was completed in 1614, but extensive rebuilding and remodeling continued over the years, right up until the 19th century. The audiovisual presentation on St. George's defense system helps you better understand what you're seeing.

- **Fort Scaur** (Sandys Parish): Together with Fort St. Catherine, this was part of a ring of fortifications that surrounded Bermuda. Built by the British navy, the fort was supposed to protect the Royal Naval Dockyard from an attack that never materialized. During World War II, U.S. Marines were billeted nearby. Overlooking Great Sound, the fort offers some of the island's most dramatic scenery.

- **Royal Naval Dockyard** (Sandys Parish): This historic area was actually used by the British navy until 1951. Now restored as a major tourist attraction and multimillion-dollar cruise-ship dock, its centerpiece is the Bermuda Maritime Museum, the most important on the island. Constructed by convict labor, this 19th-century fortress today houses major exhibits on the island's nautical heritage.
- **St. Peter's Church** (St. George's Parish): This is the oldest Anglican house of worship in the Western Hemisphere. At one time virtually everybody was buried here, from governors to criminals; to the west of the church lies the graveyard of slaves. This is the site of the original church, which was built by the colonists in 1612. That church was destroyed in a hurricane in 1712, but some parts of the interior were salvaged. It was rebuilt on the same site in 1713.
- **Verdmont** (Smith's Parish): This 1770s mansion is situated on property once owned by William Sayle, founder and first governor of South Carolina. Filled with portraits, antiques, and china, the house offers a rare glimpse into a long-faded Bermudian life of style and grace. Resembling a small English manor house, it's the finest historic home in Bermuda.

10 The Best Places to Experience Old Bermuda

Although much of Bermuda is modern, the first settlers arrived here in 1609. The following places provide insights into the old Bermudian way of life, which has now largely disappeared. See chapter 7 for more details.

- **The Back Streets of St. George's** (St. George's Parish): The 17th-century stocks on King's Square in historic St. George's have been photographed by virtually every tourist to the island. But it's in the narrow back alleyways and cobblestoned lanes such as Shinbone Alley that you'll really discover the old spirit of this town. Arm yourself with a good map and wander at leisure through such places as Silk Alley (also called Petticoat Lane), Barber's Lane Alley (named for a former slave from South Carolina), Printer's Alley (where Bermuda's first newspaper was published), and Nea's Alley (former stamping ground of the Irish poet Tom Moore). Finally, walk through Somers Garden and head up the steps to Blockade Alley; on the hill is the aptly named Unfinished Cathedral.
- **The Royal Naval Dockyard** (Sandys Parish): Nothing recaptures the maritime spirit of this little island colony more than this sprawling complex of attractions on Ireland Island. Beginning in 1809, Britain began building this dockyard, perhaps fearing attacks on its fleet from warmongering Napoléon or greedy pirates. Convicts and slaves provided much of the labor that went into constructing a shipyard for the Royal Navy, which occupied it for almost 150 years. The shipyard closed in 1951, and the Royal Navy has little presence here today; but the Maritime Museum and other exhibits give you a good feel for a largely vanished era.
- **St. David's Island** (St. George's Parish): Though most of Bermuda looks pristine and proper—the old way of life largely replaced with pretty pink cottages and hotels—you'll still find some vestiges of rustic maritime life on St. David's. Some St. David's islanders never even bother to visit neighboring St. George's; to some locals, visiting the West End of Bermuda would be like a trip to the moon. St. David's Lighthouse has been a local landmark since 1879. To see how people actually used to cook and eat, you could drop by Dennis's Hideaway (see below); Dennis Lamb personifies the eccentricity of St. David's islanders, and his grubby place will give you an idea of how Bermudians used to eat before all that New York strip steak started arriving by plane.

11 The Best-Kept Secrets of Bermuda

- **Dining at Dennis's Hideaway** (St. George's Parish; ☎ 441/297-0044): At his small home on remote St. David's Island, Dennis Lamb is an unforgettable host. If you'd like to have dinner at his ramshackle place, call ahead for a reservation. Dennis will not only feed you his shark hash, mussel pie, or other seafood dishes, but also give you some insight into how life was on Bermuda long ago. When he's not tending his pots, cleaning fish, or throwing food to one of his yapping dogs, he might also share his philosophy of life with you. No ties allowed. See chapter 5 for further details.
- **Undersea Helmet Diving with Bermuda Bell Diving** (Smith's Parish; ☎ 441/292-4434): You can enjoy the greatest undersea walk on the island by participating in this adventure. Once an experienced guide has placed a helmet on your head, you'll descend the ladder of a boat to begin your guided underwater walk. Then, a wonderland will unfold before your eyes: the feeding of corals, the breathing of sponges, and an array of rainbow-hued fish. The walk is ideal for everyone 5 and over, including nonswimmers and those who wear glasses. See chapter 6 for more details.
- **Spelunking in Crystal Caves** (Hamilton Parish): A virtual spelunkers' paradise, Bermuda has the highest concentration of limestone caves in the world. These caves form one of the island's major natural wonderlands. Their surreal formations took millions of years to create, and the great stalactites and stalagmites have a Gothic grandeur. The best caves are Crystal Caves at Bailey's Bay. Discovered in 1907, these caves include the crystal-clear Cahow Lake. See chapter 7 for more information.

12 The Best Resorts for Honeymooners (& Other Lovers)

Bermuda has long been one of the world's favorite destinations for honeymooners. In fact, with all those honeymoon packages offered by hotels, ranging from deluxe resorts to guest houses, Bermuda attracts lovers of all kinds looking for a little peace, solitude, and seclusion.

Although some couples seek out small housekeeping cottages and guest houses, most seem to prefer a package offered by one of the splashy resort hotels. The following resorts feature not only romance, but also some of the best deals.

Note: It's a good idea to consult a travel agent for help in getting the best bargain. Before you call any of these hotels directly, see the section "Package Deals" in chapter 2. Full reviews of each of these hotels can be found in chapter 4.

- **Sonesta Beach Resort** (Southampton Parish; ☎ 800/766-3782 in the U.S., or 441/238-8122): You'll find champagne chilling in your room when you arrive—and it just gets better from there. To set the mood, the staff will arrange an introductory horse-and-buggy ride for you in the old Bermuda tradition. The following day, they'll give you a motor scooter for getting around. The sports director will also offer one free tennis or scuba lesson. The hotel is right on the beach; it's also a fully equipped, professionally staffed health spa. Honeymooners can dance to live music at the Boat Bay Club and Lounge, with its views of moonlit Boat Bay.
- **Grotto Bay Beach Hotel** (Hamilton Parish; ☎ 800/582-3190 in the U.S., 800/463-0851 in Canada, or 441/293-8333): This resort, which actively caters

to honeymooners, features everything from midnight swims at a private beach to cozy lovers' nests with private balconies overlooking the ocean. The honeymoon packages include romantic dinners and arrangements for cruises and walking tours, as well as optional champagne, fruit, and flowers.

- **Elbow Beach Hotel** (Paget Parish; ☎ **800/223-7434** in the U.S., or 441/236-3535): This hotel promises "marriages made in heaven." Its "Romance Packages" include daily breakfasts plus a romantic candlelit dinner for two in your room on the first night. Upon departure, newlyweds are presented with a copy of the *Elbow Beach Cookbook.*

- **Southampton Princess** (Southampton Parish; ☎ **800/223-1818** in the U.S., 800/268-7176 in Canada, or 441/238-8000): This hotel does everything it can to attract honeymooners seeking seclusion. Its honeymoon packages, which start at 4 days and 3 nights, include breakfast and dinner on a MAP "dine around plan," a bottle of champagne, a basket of fruit, admission to the exercise club, and even a special-occasion cake, plus a souvenir photo and watercolor print by a local artist.

- **Marriott's Castle Harbour Resort** (St. George's Parish; ☎ **800/223-6388** in the U.S. and Canada, or 441/293-2040): The island's largest beach resort might be the spot for a perfect honeymoon, since it offers seclusion for couples when they want it and a large range of activities and tours when they don't.

13 The Best Places to Stay with the Kids

Bermuda is more kid-friendly than anyplace else we can think of in the Caribbean or The Bahamas. It's a safe, clean environment in a politically stable country. Nearly all Bermuda hotels go the extra mile to welcome families with children, but these are our top choices. Turn to chapter 4 for full reviews of each hotel.

- **Southampton Princess** (Southampton Parish; ☎ **800/223-1818** in the U.S., 800/268-7176 in Canada, or 441/238-8000): From June through Labor Day, this hotel features the best children's program in Bermuda. Children under 16 stay free—and if the parents choose the MAP, kids also get free meals. With its many sports facilities, including two freshwater pools and 11 tennis courts, this Princess is definitely for families who enjoy the sporting life. The former Touch Club has been redesigned as Lenny's Loft, the social center for children's activities, and from there kids are taken on excursions around the island.

- **Sonesta Beach Resort** (Southampton Parish; ☎ **800/766-3782** in the U.S., or 441/238-8122): This luxurious resort offers one of the best family packages on the island. A maximum of four people, including two children, is accepted for the 4-day, 3-night packages; children eat free, and a second guest room is provided at 25% off the regular rate. A "Just Us Kids" activities program for ages 5 to 12 is held daily in summer, with pizza parties, unlimited free ice cream, and children's games, among other diversions; the "Just Us Little Kids" program entertains the 2- to 4-year-olds with a wading pool, a playroom, ice-cream parties, and other activities.

- **Grotto Bay Beach Hotel** (Hamilton Parish; ☎ **800/582-3190** in the U.S., 800/463-0851 in Canada, or 441/293-8333): With its excellent children's program in summer, this hotel attracts many families. Thanks to the 21 tropically landscaped acres, those who stay here usually don't mind its relative isolation across from the airport. The swimming pool has been blasted out of natural rock, and there are subterranean caves to explore. Beachside barbecues and a number of other activities make this a lively place.

- **Paraquet Guest Apartments** (Paget Parish; ☎ **441/236-5842**): Although some-what sterile and motel-like in character, these apartments are a good bet for fam-ilies looking for a bargain. Since nine of the units come equipped with kitchenettes, families often prepare their own meals here, which cuts down on Bermuda's high dining costs. There's also a budget restaurant on the premises.
- **Royal Palms Hotel** (City of Hamilton, Pembroke Parish; ☎ **800/678-0783** in the U.S., 800/799-0824 in Canada, or 441/292-1854): Although this hotel can't compete with the expensive children's programs at the large resorts, it does offer a cozy nest for families on a budget, who can enjoy communal life around the swimming pool. The hotel is also close to many island attractions. All the bed-rooms are spacious enough for families, and some minisuites are equipped with kitchenettes. Children under 16 are accepted for $25 a night; children 2 and under stay free.

14 The Best Hotel Bargains

See chapter 4 for full reviews of all these choices.

- **Astwood Cove** (Warwick Parish; ☎ **800/637-4116** in the U.S., or 441/236-0984): This place is definitely a good buy in pricey Bermuda. For families seeking a self-contained studio or suite apartment with a fully equipped kitchenette and a private porch or patio, this is a great choice. You prepare your own meals and use the hotel's English bone china and wine glasses. Studio partments have sofa beds that can accommodate a third person if necessary.
- **Loughlands** (Paget Parish; ☎ **441/236-1253**): Set on 7 acres of landscaped grounds, this guest house offers privacy, old-fashioned elegance, and plenty of Bermuda charm. Staying here is like living at a country house with attractively appointed bedrooms. There's a swimming pool, and arrangements can be made to participate in many other activities nearby, including golf, tennis, deep-sea fishing, and waterskiing.
- **Rosemont** (City of Hamilton, Pembroke Parish; ☎ **800/367-0040** in the U.S., 800/267-0040 in Canada, or 441/292-1055): This collection of housekeeping cottages near the Hamilton Princess has long been a family favorite, offering a central location at a good price. The site offers panoramic views of Hamilton Harbour and the Great Sound. Guests often prepare their own meals here to avoid relying on Bermuda's overpriced restaurants for every meal.
- **Sky-Top Cottages** (Paget Parish; ☎ **441/236-7984**): This cottage cluster stands close to Elbow Beach, on a hilltop overlooking the southern shoreline. It's one of the more moderately priced options for a cottage on the island. Each unit has a certain charm and character, and the property is well maintained. Each unit is named for a flower that grows in the garden, such as "Morning Glory," and each has a kitchenette.

15 The Best Restaurants

Admittedly, you don't come to Bermuda for fine cuisine. That said, there are quite a few places to enjoy a memorable meal. See chapter 5 for full reviews of each of the restaurants listed below.

- **La Coquille** (Pembroke Parish; ☎ **441/292-6122**): One of Bermuda's most sophisticated French restaurants enjoys a faithful following. Right in the heart of Bermuda, it presents a delectable French-inspired Mediterranean cuisine with such delights as a gratin of scallops in a saffron sauce, and a richly aromatic semi-boneless quail with wild boar sausages, served with porcini mushrooms, risotto, pancakes, and roasted pearl onions.

- **Black Horse Tavern** (St. George's Parish; ☎ 441/297-1991): When you crave good, hearty food served in a casual atmosphere, this is the place to come. Islanders fill up most of the tables at night, ordering shark hash or curried conch.
- **Fourways Inn Restaurant** (Paget Parish; ☎ 441/236-6517): In this 1700s Georgian house of cedar and coral stone, you'll dine as they did back in the plantation days, with traditional crystal, silver, and china. With the best piano music on the island playing in the background, introduce yourself to a bowl of Bermudian fish chowder, followed by your choice of French or Bermudian dishes.
- **Henry VIII** (Southampton Parish; ☎ 441/238-1977): The restaurant's mock Tudor decor is a bit corny, but this is a fun place to dine—and the food is really good. You'll get your fill of mussel pie (sometimes available) and such pub favorites as steak-and-kidney pie. Some diners actually manage to leave room for desserts like bananas flambé in dark mellow rum.
- **Tamarisk Dining Room** (Sandys Parish; ☎ 441/234-0331): This is an elegant and graceful enclave at the western tip of Bermuda. It's housed in one of the island's premier addresses for accommodations, Cambridge Beaches, and its staff fusses over its guests and presents them with a frequently changing international menu impeccably prepared. For your main course, you can't do better than the juicy tenderloin of beef with a grain mustard and blanched garlic sauce. The wine cellar is worthy of the menu.
- **Lobster Pot & Boat House Bar** (City of Hamilton, Pembroke Parish; ☎ 441/292-6898): If you don't find the local foodies at the restaurants we've discussed above, they'll surely be at this local favorite enjoying some of the island's best regional dishes. Black rum and sherry peppers might be the secret ingredients of their fish chowder, and their baked fish and lobster are sure to tempt your taste buds.
- **Newport Room** (at the Southampton Princess, Southampton Parish; ☎ 441/238-8000): Another part of the Southampton complex, this nautically decorated restaurant attracts an upscale crowd, especially yachties. The glistening teak decor makes it the most expensively furnished restaurant in Bermuda, and its French cuisine is worthy of the decor. The rack of lamb with mixed-nut crust is the stuff of which memories are made.
- **Tom Moore's Tavern** (Hamilton Parish; ☎ 441/293-8020): Reportedly, the Irish poet Tom Moore was a frequent visitor to this restaurant, which dates from 1652 and overlooks Walsingham Bay (hence its name). The menu, however, is no relic from the past—it's actually quite innovative. Duck is a specialty, as is Bermuda lobster, but who can forget the quail in puff pastry stuffed with foie gras?
- **Waterlot Inn** (at the Southampton Princess, Southampton Parish; ☎ 441/238-8000): In a historic inn and warehouse, this restaurant hosts the island's most famous Sunday brunch, but it's also an ideal choice for dinner. Everybody from Eleanor Roosevelt to Mark Twain has praised the Mediterranean cuisine here.

2 Planning a Trip to Bermuda

In this chapter, you'll find everything you need to plan your trip, from when to go to how to get the best package deals. Getting to Bermuda is now easier than ever, thanks to more-frequent flights from such gateway cities as New York, Boston, and Washington, DC We've also included information on the several cruise lines that sail to the island from spring until late autumn.

1 Visitor Information

Your best sources of all may be relatives, friends, or colleagues who have been to Bermuda, so ask around. For information sources once you're in Bermuda, see "Orienting Yourself: The Lay of the Land" in chapter 3.

THE BERMUDA DEPARTMENT OF TOURISM

IN THE UNITED STATES To receive a visitor information packet about Bermuda before you go, call ☎ **800/237-6832.**

To speak to a travel representative, contact the **Bermuda Department of Tourism** office nearest you: in New York at 205 E. 42nd St., New York, NY 10017 (☎ **212/818-9800,** Ext. 213); in Boston at 44 School St., Suite 1010, Boston, MA 02108 (☎ **617/742-0405**); and in Atlanta at 245 Peachtree Center Ave. NE, Suite 803, Atlanta, GA 30303 (☎ **404/524-1541**).

IN CANADA Contact the **Bermuda Department of Tourism** at 1200 Bay St., Suite 1004, Toronto, ON, Canada M5R 2A5 (☎ **416/923-9600**).

IN THE UNITED KINGDOM Contact the **Bermuda Department of Tourism** at 1 Battersea Church Rd., London SW11 3LY (☎ **0171/771-7001**).

SURFING THE WEB

The official Bermuda Web site is **www.bermudatourism.com.**

Beyond that, the Internet can provide lots of travel information. See the box later in this chapter on how to find great airfare bargains on the Web. **Yahoo** (www.yahoo.com), **Excite** (www.excite.com), **Lycos** (www.lycos.com), **Infoseek** (www.infoseek.com), and the other major Internet indexing sites all have subcategories for travel, country/regional information, and culture—click on all three for links to travel-related Web sites. One of the best hot lists for travel and destination information is **Excite's City Net** (www.city.net).

Other good clearinghouse sites for information are **Microsoft's Expedia** (www.expedia.msn.com), the **Internet Travel Network** (www.itn.com), and **TravelWeb** (www.travelweb.com).

Of the many, many online travel magazines, two of the best are **Arthur Frommer's Budget Travel Online** (www.frommers.com), written and updated by the guru of travel himself, and **Condé Nast's Epicurious** (www.epicurious.com).

As often as possible throughout this chapter, we've included specific Web sites along with phone numbers and addresses. The hotel reviews in chapter 4 also list Web sites so that you can pull up more information and perhaps pictures. *Important note:* Don't forget to check out the online directory at the end of this book; you'll find it an invaluable planning tool!

TRAVEL AGENTS

Travel agents can save you plenty of time and money by hunting down the best package deal or airfare. For the time being, most travel agents still charge you nothing for their services—they're paid through commissions from the airlines and other agencies they book for you. However, a number of airlines have begun cutting commissions, and increasingly agents are finding they have to charge you a fee to hold the bottom line. Some unscrupulous agents will offer you only the travel options that bag them the juiciest commissions. Shop around and ask hard questions. The best way to use a travel agent is to make preliminary decisions using this guide, and then go into your meeting as a smart and informed consumer.

If you decide to use a travel agent, make sure the agent is a member of the **American Society of Travel Agents** (ASTA), 1101 King St., Alexandria, VA 22314 (☎ **703/739-8739;** www.astanet.com). If you send a self-addressed, stamped envelope, ASTA will mail you the booklet *Avoiding Travel Problems* free.

2 Entry Requirements & Customs

ENTRY REQUIREMENTS

U.S. and Canadian citizens do not officially need a passport to enter Bermuda, but we strongly recommend that you carry one whenever you travel to a foreign country anyway.

Bermuda Immigration authorities require U.S. citizens to have in their possession any one of the following items: a birth certificate (or a certified copy of it accompanied by a photo ID), a U.S. naturalization certificate, a valid passport, a U.S. Alien Registration card, or a U.S. reentry permit. Go with the passport.

Canadian citizens must have a birth certificate (or a certified copy of it), a Canadian certificate of citizenship, or a valid passport plus proof of their Landed Immigrant status.

Bermuda Immigration authorities require visitors from the United Kingdom and Europe to show a valid passport.

All visitors must have a return or onward ticket in addition to their valid passport or original birth certificate. If you're staying in Bermuda longer than 3 weeks, you must apply to the **Chief Immigration Officer,** Government Administration Building, 30 Parliament St., Hamilton HM 12, Bermuda (☎ **441/295-5151**), for an extended stay.

It's a good policy to make copies of your most valuable documents before leaving home, including the inside page of your passport that has your photograph. You should also make copies of your driver's license, airline ticket, hotel vouchers, and any other type of identity card that might be pertinent. You should also make copies of any prescriptions you take. Leave one copy at home, place one copy in your luggage, and carry the original with you. The information on these documents would be extremely valuable if you were to experience a loss or theft abroad.

Passport applications are downloadable from the Internet sites listed below:

- **For Residents of the United States:** If you're applying for a first-time passport, you need to do it in person at one of 13 passport offices throughout the United States; a federal, state, or probate court; or at a major post office (though not all post offices accept applications; call the number below to find the ones that do). You need to present a certified birth certificate as proof of citizenship, and it's wise to bring along your driver's license, state or military ID, and Social Security card as well. You also need two identical passport-sized photos (2 in. by 2 in.), taken at any corner photo shop (not one of the strip photos, however, from a photo-vending machine).

  For people over 15, a passport is valid for 10 years and costs $60 ($45 plus a $15 handling fee); for those 15 and under, it's valid for 5 years and costs $40. If you're over 15 and have a valid passport that was issued within the past 12 years, you can renew it by mail and bypass the $15 handling fee. Allow plenty of time before your trip to apply; processing normally takes 3 weeks but can take longer during busy periods (especially spring). For general information, call the **National Passport Agency** (☎ **202/647-0518**). To find your regional passport office, call the **National Passport Information Center** (☎ **900/225-5674;** http://travel.state.gov).

- **For Residents of Canada:** You can pick up a passport application at one of 28 regional passport offices or most travel agencies. The passport is valid for 5 years and costs $60. Children under 16 may be included on a parent's passport but need their own to travel unaccompanied by the parent. Applications, which must be accompanied by two identical passport-sized photographs and proof of Canadian citizenship, are available at travel agencies throughout Canada or from the central **Passport Office, Department of Foreign Affairs and International Trade,** Ottawa, ON K1A 0G3 (☎ **800/567-6868;** www.dfait-maeci.gc.ca/passport). Processing takes 5 to 10 days if you apply in person, or about 3 weeks by mail.

- **For Residents of the United Kingdom:** To pick up an application for a regular 10-year passport (the Visitor's Passport has been abolished), visit your nearest passport office, major post office, or travel agency. You can also contact the **London Passport Office** at ☎ **0171/271-3000** or search its Web site at www.open.gov.uk/ukpass/ukpass.htm. Passports are £21 for adults and £11 for children under 16.

- **For Residents of Ireland:** You can apply for a 10-year passport, costing IR£45, at the Passport Office, Setanta Centre, Molesworth Street, Dublin 2 (☎ **01/671-1633;** www.irlgov.ie/iveagh/foreignaffairs/services). Those under age 18 and over 65 must apply for a IR£10 3-year passport. You can also apply at 1A South Mall, Cork (☎ **021/272-525**) or over the counter at most main post offices.

- **For Residents of Australia:** Apply at your local post office or passport office, or search the government Web site at www.dfat.gov.au/passports/. Passports are A$126 for adults and A$63 for those under 18.

- **For Residents of New Zealand:** You can pick up a passport application at any travel agency or Link Centre. For more info, contact the Passport Office, P.O. Box 805, Wellington (☎ **0800/225-050**). Passports are NZ$80 for adults and NZ$40 for those under 16.

CUSTOMS

Visitors may bring into Bermuda duty-free apparel and articles for their personal use, including sports equipment, cameras, 200 cigarettes, 1 quart of liquor, 1 quart of wine, and approximately 20 pounds of meat. Other foodstuff may be subject to duties. All imports may be inspected on arrival. Visitors entering Bermuda may also claim a duty-free gift allowance.

When you're ready to return home, U.S. Customs preclearance is available for all scheduled flights. Passengers leaving for the United States must fill out written declaration forms before clearing U.S. Customs in Bermuda. The forms are available at Bermuda hotels, travel agencies, and airlines.

Collect receipts for all your purchases. If a merchant suggests giving you a false receipt, misstating the value of your goods, beware: The merchant may be a Customs informer. You must also declare all gifts received during your stay abroad.

Compile a list of your more expensive carry-on items, and ask a U.S. Customs agent to stamp your list at the airport before your departure; this way, Customs won't think you've purchased the items overseas upon your return.

Returning **U.S. citizens** who have been away for 48 hours or more are allowed to bring back, once every 30 days, $400 worth of merchandise duty-free. You'll be charged a flat rate of 10% duty on the next $1,000 worth of purchases. Be sure to have your receipts handy. On gifts, the duty-free limit is $100. You cannot bring fresh foodstuffs into the United States; tinned foods, however, are allowed. For more information, contact the **U.S. Customs Service,** 1301 Constitution Ave. (P.O. Box 7407), Washington, DC 20044 (☎ **202/927-6724**) and request the free pamphlet *Know Before You Go.* It's also available on the Web at www.customs. ustreas.gov/travel/kbygo.htm.

U.K. citizens returning from a non-EC country such as Bermuda have a customs allowance of 200 cigarettes; 50 cigars; 250 grams of smoking tobacco; 2 liters of still table wine; 1 liter of spirits or strong liqueurs (over 22% volume); 2 liters of fortified wine, sparkling wine, or other liqueurs; 60cc (ml) of perfume; 250cc (ml) of toilet water; and £145 worth of all other goods, including gifts and souvenirs. People under 17 cannot have the tobacco or alcohol allowance. For more information, contact HM Customs & Excise, Passenger Enquiry Point, 2nd Floor Wayfarer House, Great South West Road, Feltham, Middlesex TW14 8NP (☎ **0181/910-3744;** from outside the U.K. 44/181-910-3744), or consult the Web site at www.open.gov.uk.

For a clear summary of **Canadian** rules, write for the booklet *I Declare,* issued by **Revenue Canada,** 2265 St. Laurent Blvd., Ottawa K1G 4KE (☎ **613/993-0534**). Canada allows its citizens a $500 exemption, and you're allowed to bring back duty-free 200 cigarettes, 2.2 pounds of tobacco, 40 imperial ounces of liquor, and 50 cigars. In addition, you're allowed to mail gifts to Canada from abroad at the rate of Can$60 a day, provided they're unsolicited and don't contain alcohol or tobacco (write on the package "Unsolicited gift, under $60 value"). All valuables should be declared on the Y-38 form before departure from Canada, including serial numbers of valuables you already own, such as expensive foreign cameras. *Note:* The $500 exemption can be used only once a year and only after an absence of 7 days.

The duty-free allowance in **Australia** is A$400 or, for those under 18, A$200. Personal property mailed back from Bermuda should be marked "Australian goods returned" to avoid payment of duty. Upon returning to Australia, citizens can bring in 250 cigarettes or 250 grams of loose tobacco, and 1,125 milliliters of alcohol. If you're returning with valuable goods you already own, such as foreign-made cameras, you should file form B263. A helpful brochure, available from Australian consulates or Customs offices, is *Know Before You Go.* For more information,

What Things Cost in Bermuda	BDS/US$
15-minute taxi ride	$12.50
Ferry from Hamilton to Ireland Island	$3.75
Local telephone call	.25
Double room at Elbow Beach Hotel (expensive)	$265.00
Double room at Rosemont (moderate)	$140.00
Double room at Salt Kettle House (inexpensive)	$100.00
Lunch for one at Whaler Inn (moderate)	$16.00
Lunch for one at Wickets Brasserie & Cricket Club (inexpensive)	$15.00
Dinner for one at Ascots (expensive)	$40.00
Dinner for one at La Trattoria (moderate)	$27.50
Dinner for one at Chopsticks Restaurant (inexpensive)	$20.00
Bottle of beer in a bar	$4.25
Coca-Cola in a cafe	$2.25
Cup of coffee in a cafe	$1.25
Glass of planter's punch in a restaurant	$5.00
Roll of ASA 100 color film, 36 exposures	$8.00
Admission to Bermuda Maritime Museum	$7.50

contact **Australian Customs Services,** GPO Box 8, Sydney NSW 2001 (☎ **02/ 9213-2000**).

The duty-free allowance for **New Zealand** is NZ$700. Citizens over 17 can bring in 200 cigarettes, or 50 cigars, or 250 grams of tobacco (or a mixture of all three if their combined weight doesn't exceed 250 grams); plus 4.5 liters of wine and beer, or 1.125 liters of liquor. New Zealand currency does not carry import or export restrictions. Fill out a certificate of export, listing the valuables you are taking out of the country; that way, you can bring them back without paying duty. Most questions are answered in a free pamphlet available at New Zealand consulates and Customs offices: *New Zealand Customs Guide for Travellers, Notice no. 4.* For more information, contact New Zealand Customs, 50 Anzac Ave., P.O. Box 29, Auckland (☎ **09/359-6655**).

3 Money

WHAT IT WILL COST

Time is money, and since Bermuda is less than a 2-hour flight from most cities on the U.S. East Coast, the savings begin even before you land on the island. A 4-day, 3-night vacation in Bermuda can actually include 4 days of vacation for the price of only 3 nights' accommodation. An 8:30am flight from New York gets you to Bermuda in time for lunch, with the whole afternoon to play.

The variety of accommodations—there are luxury resort hotels, small hotels, intimate guest houses, and cottage colonies—allows visitors to indulge their preferences and tastes regardless of budget. Although there are wide price differences, in general very expensive hotels get $200 or more a night for a double room. Expensive rooms generally range from $135 to $200; moderate, from $100 to $135. Some inexpensive rooms, under $100, are available.

The Bermuda Dollar, the U.S. Dollar & the British Pound

The Bermudian dollar is tied to the U.S. dollar and is valued on an equal basis: BD$1 = US$1. The British pound trades at an average of around 60 pence = US$1, or US$1.67 = £1. The chart below gives a rough approximation of conversion rates you're likely to find at the time of your trip. However, rates do fluctuate, so be sure to confirm the rate before you make transactions

U.S.$	U.K.£	U.S.$	U.K.£
0.25	0.15	15	9.00
0.50	0.30	20	12.00
0.75	0.45	25	15.00
1.00	0.60	50	30.00
2.00	1.20	75	45.00
3.00	1.80	100	60.00
4.00	2.40	150	90.00
5.00	3.00	200	120.00
6.00	3.60	250	150.00
7.00	4.20	300	180.00
8.00	4.80	350	210.00
9.00	5.40	400	240.00
10.00	6.00	500	300.00

Hotel costs also depend on what time of year you travel. If you're seeking major discounts—sometimes as much as 60% off the high-season rates—try visiting during the off-season, which, unlike in the Caribbean, is from November or December to March. (For more information, see "When to Go," below.) The off-season rates, which we've listed in this guide, are a bonanza for cost-conscious travelers, though you're not guaranteed that it will be warm enough to truly enjoy the beach.

Travel agents sometimes offer special packages, which can represent a substantial savings over regular hotel rates for families, golfers, tennis players, honeymooners, and others; for more information, see "Package Deals," below.

Dining out is an expensive undertaking in Bermuda. In the top places, you can end up spending as much as $60 to $80 per person for a meal, excluding wine. Even moderate to expensive restaurants are likely to charge $25 to $50 per person. Any dinner under $25 per person is considered inexpensive. Therefore, you might want to go for one of the package plans offered by most of the large resorts, which include meals—these can be real money savers. Other ways to reduce dining costs are to pack a picnic lunch, or to have your main meal in the middle of the day, at a pub.

To cut costs even more, families and others planning to stay for a week or more might opt for a housekeeping unit (efficiencies and apartments are available), a cottage with a kitchenette, or even a condominium (some condos are rented like timeshare units, when the owners aren't in residence).

In figuring your budget, be sure to consider transportation costs. Getting around the island isn't always easy, and since no rental cars are available on the island, you'll have to rely on Bermuda's local transportation. With the exception of taxis, which are very expensive, public transportation is efficient and inexpensive, saving you between $250 and $300, or even more, on the cost of a week's car rental. Options include the simple and comprehensive bus system, ferries, and bicycle or moped rentals; see "Getting Around," in chapter 3, for complete details. Once you reach a particular parish, you can reach many attractions on foot, and Bermuda becomes almost one vast walking tour.

In general, athletic and cultural activities, such as tennis, riding, guided tours, museums, and attractions, are also good values in Bermuda. Golfers will find that greens fees are comparable to or less than fees at other destinations. For example, Ocean View Golf and Country Club and St. George's Golf Club charge as little as $43 for 18 holes of golf. Bermuda is home to eight world-class golf courses with varying fees.

If you find the idea of unknown or extra costs intimidating, you might consider a package tour, where everything will be arranged for you. That way, you'll know the inclusive cost of your vacation before leaving home. For more information, see below.

CURRENCY

Legal tender is the Bermuda dollar (BD$), which is divided into 100 cents. It's pegged through gold to the U.S. dollar on an equal basis—BD$1 equals US$1.

U.S. currency is generally accepted in shops, restaurants, and hotels. Currencies from the United Kingdom and all other foreign countries are usually not accepted but can be easily exchanged for Bermuda dollars at banks and hotels. Banking and credit-card transactions in all foreign currencies are subject to exchange rates.

ATMS

ATMs are linked to a national network that most likely includes your bank at home. **Cirrus** (☎ 800/424-7787; www.mastercard.com/atm/) and **Plus** (☎ 800/843-7587; www.visa.com/atms) are the two most popular networks; check the back of your ATM card to see which network your bank belongs to. Use the 800 numbers to locate ATMs in your destination.

If you're traveling abroad, ask your bank for a list of overseas ATMs. Be sure to check the daily withdrawal limit before you depart, and ask whether you need a new personal ID number.

CREDIT CARDS

Credit cards are invaluable when you're traveling. They are a safe way to carry money, and they provide a convenient record of all your expenses. You can also withdraw cash advances from your credit cards at any bank (though you'll start paying hefty interest on the advance the moment you receive the cash, and you won't receive frequent-flyer miles on an airline credit card). At most banks, you don't even need to go to a teller; you can get a cash advance at the ATM if you know your PIN number. (If you've forgotten your PIN number or didn't even know you had one, call the phone number on the back of your credit card well before you leave home, and ask the bank to send it to you. It usually takes 5–7 business days, though some banks will provide the number over the phone if you tell them your mother's maiden name or pass some other security clearance.)

Almost every credit-card company has an emergency 800 number you can call if your wallet or purse is stolen. They may be able to wire you a cash advance off your credit card immediately, and in many places, they can deliver an emergency credit card in a day or two. The issuing bank's 800 number is usually on the back of the credit card (though of course that doesn't help you much if the card was stolen). The toll-free information directory will provide the number if you dial ☎ 800/555-1212. Citicorp Visa's U.S. emergency number is ☎ 800/336-8472. American Express cardholders and traveler's check holders should call ☎ 800/221-7282 for all money emergencies. MasterCard holders should call ☎ **800/307-7309.** The good news? There's not much theft on Bermuda.

Odds are that if your wallet is gone, the police won't be able to recover it for you. However, after you realize that it's gone and you cancel your credit cards, it is still worth informing the police. Your credit-card company or insurer may require a police report number.

TRAVELER'S CHECKS

Traveler's checks are something of an anachronism from the days before the ATM made cash accessible at any time. The only sound alternative to traveling with dangerously large amounts of cash, traveler's checks were as reliably accepted as currency, unlike personal checks, but could be replaced if lost or stolen, unlike cash.

These days, traveler's checks seem less necessary since ATMs abroad make it easy to access your bank account just as you would at home. But some travelers still prefer the security offered by traveler's checks.

You can get traveler's checks at almost any bank. **American Express** offers denominations of $10, $20, $50, $100, $500, and $1,000. You'll pay a service charge ranging from 1% to 4% of your total purchase. You can also get American Express traveler's checks over the phone by calling ☎ **800/221-7282;** by using this number, AmEx gold and platinum cardholders are exempt from the 1%. AAA members can obtain checks without a fee at most AAA offices. **Visa** offers traveler's checks at Citibank locations nationwide, as well as several other banks. The service charge ranges between 1.5% and 2%; checks come in denominations of $20, $50, $100, $500, and $1,000. **MasterCard** also offers traveler's checks. Call ☎ **800/ 223-9920** for a location near you.

If you opt to carry traveler's checks, be sure to keep a record of their serial numbers separate from the checks themselves so that you're assured a refund in event of an emergency.

4 When to Go

THE WEATHER

A semitropical island, Bermuda enjoys a mild climate; the term "Bermuda high" has come to mean sunny days and clear skies. The Gulf Stream, flowing between the island and North America, keeps the climate temperate. There is no rainy season and no typical month of excess rain. Showers may be heavy at times, but the skies clear quickly.

Bermuda, however, being farther north in the Atlantic than The Bahamas, is much cooler in winter. Springlike temperatures prevail from mid-December to late March, with the average temperature ranging from the low 60s to 70°F (17 to 21°C). Unless it rains, winter is fine for golf and tennis but not for swimming; it can be downright cool, and you may even need a sweater or a jacket. Water temperatures in winter are somewhat like the air temperature, ranging from about 66°F (19°C) in January through 75°F (24°C) in spring. Scuba divers or snorkelers will find the Caribbean waters appreciably warmer in winter. From mid-November to mid-December and from late March to April, be prepared for either spring or summer weather.

In summer, temperatures rarely rise above 85°F (29°C). There's nearly always a cool breeze in the evening, but some hotels have taken the precaution of installing air-conditioning. And local water temperatures can be as high as 86°F (30°C), which is actually warmer than many inshore and offshore Caribbean waters.

As a result, Bermuda's off-season is the exact opposite of that in the Caribbean. It begins in December and lasts generally until the first of March. In general, hotels quote their low-season rates—with discounts ranging from 20% to 60%—in winter. This is the time to go if you're traveling on a tight budget. During autumn and winter, many hotels also offer discounted package deals, and some hotels even close for a couple of weeks or months.

A look at the official chart on temperature and rainfall will give you a general idea of what to expect during your visit.

Bermuda's Average Daytime Temperatures & Rainfall

	Jan	Feb	Mar	Apr	May	June	July	Aug	Sept	Oct	Nov	Dec
Temp. (°F)	65	64	64	65	70	75	79	80	79	75	69	65
Temp. (°C)	19	18	18	19	21	24	26	27	26	24	21	19
Rainfall (inches)	4	5	4.6	3	3.9	5.2	4	5.3	5.3	6	4.5	3.9

THE HURRICANE SEASON

This curse of the Caribbean, The Bahamas, and Bermuda lasts officially from June to November, but don't panic—more tropical storms pound the U.S. mainland than Bermuda. It's also less frequently hit than islands in the Caribbean. Satellite forecasts are generally able to give adequate warning of any really dangerous weather, so precautions can be taken in time.

However, if you're concerned, you can call the nearest branch of the National Weather Service (it's listed under the U.S. Department of Commerce in the phone book). Radio and TV weather reports from the National Hurricane Center in Coral Gables, Florida, will also keep you posted.

To receive automated information about climate conditions in Bermuda, you can also contact the information service associated with The Weather Channel. It works like this: Dial toll free ☎ **800/WEATHER,** and listen to the recorded announcement. When you're prompted, enter the account number of a valid Visa or Master-Card. After the card's validity is approved, at a rate of 95¢ per query, punch in the name of any of 1,000 cities worldwide whose weather is monitored by The Weather Channel—in this case, Hamilton. The report that's delivered might help you in knowing what to wear and how to pack.

HOLIDAYS

The following public holidays are observed in Bermuda (those without a date change from year to year): New Year's Day (January 1), Good Friday, Easter, Bermuda Day (May 24), the Queen's Birthday (first or second Monday in June), Cup Match Days (cricket; Thursday and Friday preceding first Monday in August), Labor Day (first Monday in September), Christmas Day (December 25), and Boxing Day (December 26). Public holidays that fall on a Saturday or Sunday are usually celebrated the following Monday.

Bermuda Calendar of Events

January & February

✪ **Bermuda Festival.** Throughout January and February, the Bermuda calendar is jam-packed with such islandwide events as golf and tennis invitationals; an international marathon race; a dog show; open house and garden tours; and, of course, the Bermuda Festival, the 6-week International Festival of the Performing Arts, held in Hamilton, featuring drama, dance, jazz, classical and popular music, and other entertainment by the best international artists. Some tickets for the festival are reserved until 48 hours before curtain time for visitors. For details and a schedule for the 2000 festival, contact the Bermuda Festival, P.O. Box HM 297, Hamilton HM AX, Bermuda (☎ **441/295-1291;** www.bermudafestival.com).

- **The Bermuda International Marathon.** Featuring international and local runners, the marathon takes place the third weekend in January. For further information and entry forms, contact the **International Race Weekend Committee,** Bermuda Track and Field Association, P.O. Box DV 397, Devonshire DV BX, Bermuda (☎ **441/236-6086;** www.ontherun.bm).

March

✪ **Bermuda College Weeks.** This is an annual spring odyssey for at least 10,000 students who flock here every year (so it may not be the best time for the rest of you to come). These weeks began as Rugby Weeks in 1933, when rugby teams from Ivy League schools came to compete against British or Bermudian teams. "Where the boys are," to borrow the popular song title, led to "where the girls are," and a tradition was born.

The Department of Tourism issues a College Week Courtesy Card to those who have a valid college ID card. This becomes a passport to a week of free islandwide beach parties, lunches, boat cruises, dances, and entertainment, courtesy of the Bermudian government. Dates are arranged to coincide with U.S. college spring vacations. Contact your local Bermuda Department of Tourism office (see "Visitor Information," above) to obtain a list of this year's events.

- **Home and Garden Tours.** Each spring the Garden Club of Bermuda lays out the welcome mat at a number of private homes and gardens that are open to view. A different set of houses, all conveniently located in the same parish, is open every Wednesday during this springtime viewing. Normally a total of 20 homes participate in the program, many of them dating from the 17th and 18th centuries. The tourist office provides a complete listing of homes and viewing schedules. End of March to mid-May.

April

- **Beating Retreat Ceremony.** This ceremony of the Bermuda regiment and massed pipes and drums is presented once or twice per month, rotating among Hamilton, St. George's, and the Royal Naval Dockyard. The tourist office will supply exact times and schedules.

- **Peppercorn Ceremony.** His Excellency the governor collects the annual rent of one peppercorn for the use of the island's Old State House in St. George's. Mid-to late April (the date may vary, so call **800/223-6106** before you go).

- **Agriculture Exhibit.** Held over 3 days in late April at the Botanical Gardens in Paget, this event is a celebration of the agrarian and horticultural bounty of the Bermudas. In addition to prize-winning produce, the Agriculture Show provides a showcase for local arts and crafts. For more information, contact the **Department of Agriculture and Fisheries,** P.O. Box HM 834, Hamilton HM BX, Bermuda (☎ **441/236-4201**), or the **Bermuda Department of Tourism** (☎ **800/223-6106**).

✪ **International Race Week.** Scheduled every year during late April and early May, this yachting event pits equivalent vessels from seven classes of sailing craft against one another in a knockout, elimination-style event that's followed with avid interest by yachting enthusiasts around the world.

Other sailing contests are scheduled for alternate years, including the world's most famous wind-driven contest, the **Newport-to-Bermuda Race,** held in June. The record to date: a 56-hour transit. This year, the event is supplemented by October's

Match Racing, when pairs of identical sailing vessels, staffed by a rotating roster of teams from throughout the world, compete in elimination-style contests.

Unfortunately for spectators, the finish lines for the island's sailing races are almost always established several miles offshore. Afterward, however, boats tend to be moored in Hamilton Harbor; any vantage point on the harbor is good for watching the boats come in. Even better: Head for any of Hamilton's string of harborfront pubs, where racing crowds tend to celebrate their wins (or justify their losses) over pints of ale.

For information on all sailing events held off the coast of Bermuda, contact the **Sailing Secretary,** Royal Bermuda Yacht Club, P.O. Box HM 894, Hamilton HM DX, Bermuda (☎ **441/295-2214**), or (for those races originating off the U.S. coastline) the **New York Yacht Club,** 37 W. 44th St., New York, NY 10036 (☎ **212/382-1000**).

May

- **Bermuda Heritage Month.** Culminates on **Bermuda Day,** May 24, a public holiday that's Bermuda's equivalent to the United States's Independence Day. Bermuda Day is punctuated with parades through downtown Hamilton, dinghy and cycling races, and the Bermuda Half-Day Marathon (open only to residents of Bermuda). In addition to the Office of Tourism, any hotel in town can fill you in on the events planned for the year's biggest political celebration.

June

- **Queen's Birthday.** Her Majesty's birthday is celebrated by a parade down Front Street in Hamilton. First or second Monday in June.
- **Marion to Bermuda Race.** For details, see the entry for "International Race Week," under April, above.
- **Marine Science Day.** Lectures, hands-on demonstrations, and displays for adults and children, by the **Bermuda Biological Station.** The date varies but is usually mid-month; call ☎ **441/297-1880** for exact schedule and more information.

August

- **Cup Match and Somers Days (also known as the Cup Match Cricket Festival).** Compared by many to the United States's Thanksgiving ritual, this annual event celebrates the year's bounty with Bermuda's most illustrious cricket match. Cricketers from the East End (St. George's Cricket Club) play off against those from the West End (Somerset Cricket Club), with lots of attendant British-derived protocol and hoopla. Advance ticket reservations aren't necessary, as virtually everybody buys them at the gate on match day; they'll run only about $10 each. The event is held on Thursday and Friday before the first Monday in August. For more information, call ☎ **800/223-6016.**

September

- **Labor Day.** This public holiday features a host of activities; it's also the ideal time for a picnic. Climax of the day is a parade from Union Square in Hamilton Bernard Park. Held the first Monday in September.

October

- **Match Racing.** For details on this international sailing event, see the entry for "International Race Week," under April, above.

November

- **The Opening of Parliament.** Traditional ceremony and military guard of honor connected with the opening of Parliament by His Excellency the governor as the Queen's personal representative. In anticipation of the entry of MPs into Parliament at 11am, crowds begin gathering outside the Cabinet Building around 9:30 or 10am. Spectators traditionally include lots of schoolchildren being trained in civic protocol, as well as nostalgia buffs out for a whiff of British-style pomp. November 6.

- **World Rugby Classic.** Former international rugby players compete with Bermudians at the **Bermuda National Sports Club** (☎ **441/236-6994**). Mid-November.
- **Guy Fawkes Day.** Small annual celebration with a minifair starts with the traditional burning of the Guy Fawkes effigy at the Keepyard of the Bermuda Maritime Museum, Royal Naval Dockyard, at 4:30pm. November 7.
- **Remembrance Day.** A small parade is held, with Bermudian police, British and U.S. military units, Bermudians, and veterans' organizations taking part. November 11.
- **Invitation Tennis Weeks.** More than 100 visiting players vie with Bermudians during 2 weeks of matches. Unlike at Wimbledon—this event's role model—virtually everyone buys tickets at the gate. For information, contact the **Bermuda Lawn Tennis Association,** P.O. Box HM 341, Hamilton HM BX, Bermuda (☎ **441/296-0834**).

December

- **Bermuda Goodwill Tournament.** Pro/amateur foursomes from international golf clubs play more than 72 holes on four of Bermuda's eight courses during golfing activity. Anyone who wants to compete must pass the stringent requirements of the sponsors and may appear by invitation only. Spectators are welcome to watch the event from the sidelines free. For more information, contact the **Bermuda Goodwill Golf Tournament,** P.O. Box WK127, Warwick WK BX, Bermuda (☎ **441/238-3118**). Early December.

5 Planning an Island Wedding or Honeymoon

GETTING MARRIED IN BERMUDA

Couples who would like to get married in Bermuda must file a "Notice of Intended Marriage" form with the Registry General, accompanied by a fee of $176 (in the form of a bank draft or money order, not a personal check). The draft should be made out to "The Accountant General" and should be mailed or delivered in person to the **Registry General at the Government Administration Building,** 30 Parliament St., Hamilton HM 12, Bermuda (☎ **441/297-7709**). "Notice of Intended Marriage" forms can be obtained from the Bermuda Department of Tourism offices in Atlanta, Boston, Chicago, and New York (see "Visitor Information," above). If either of the prospective marriage partners has been married before, that person will need to attach a photocopy of the final divorce decree to the "Notice of Intended Marriage."

Once the "Notice of Intended Marriage" is received, it will be published, including names and addresses, once in any two of the island's newspapers. Assuming that there is no formal objection, the registry will issue the license 15 days after receiving the notice. Since airmailing your completed notice to Bermuda will take an additional 6 to 10 days, make your plans accordingly. The marriage license will be valid for 3 months.

HIRING A WEDDING CONSULTANT

Many hotels can help make wedding arrangements, from reserving the church and clergy to hiring a horse and buggy, ordering the wedding cake, and securing a

Cut the Cake

Custom dictates that Bermudians have two wedding cakes: a plain pound cake covered with gold leaf for the groom, and a tiered fruit cake covered with silver leaf and topped off with a miniature cedar tree for the bride. The tiny tree is planted on the day of the wedding to symbolize the hope that the marriage will grow and mature like the tree. The rest of the first tier of the bride's cake is frozen until the christening of the first child.

photographer. Bermuda weddings range from simple ceremonies on the beach to large-scale extravaganzas for 100 guests and up at the Botanical Gardens. Other sites include churches or yachts.

The following island wedding consultants can discuss your options with you and arrange all the details: **The Wedding Salon,** 51 Reid St., P.O. Box HM 2085, Hamilton HM HX, Bermuda (☎ **441/292-5677;** fax 441/292-2955; e-mail: barbara.whitecross@gte.net); and **The Bridal Suite,** Parkside Building, 3 Park Rd., Suite 7, Hamilton HM 09, Bermuda (☎ **441/292-2025;** fax 441/296-2070; e-mail: wedding@ibl.bm). Packages range from $1,000 to as much as $15,000, depending on what you want.

Certain hotels will also arrange weddings, including the Belmont Hotel Golf & Country Club, the Elbow Beach Hotel, Marriott's Castle Harbour Resort, the Sonesta Beach Resort, and both of the Princess hotels; see chapter 4, "Accommodations," for contact information. If you're staying at one of the small hotels, it's better to go through one of the island's wedding consultants.

HONEYMOONING IN BERMUDA

There are good reasons why Bermuda hosts more than 23,000 honeymooners and second honeymooners each year: It offers an ideal environment for couples, whether they prefer an active schedule or a relaxing one. Many of Bermuda's hotels, from luxurious resorts to intimate cottage colonies, offer special honeymoon packages. Typically, these include airfare, accommodations, meal plans, champagne upon arrival, flowers in your room, and special discounts at local attractions and restaurants. See "The Best Resorts for Honeymooners (& Other Lovers)," in chapter 1, for the best of these packages. For other options, consult your travel agent or call the hotels listed in chapter 4 directly and inquire about packages.

6 Spa Vacations

Full-fledged spa facilities are available at the **Sonesta Beach Resort,** Southampton (☎ **800/766-3782** in the U.S., or 441/238-8122; www.sonesta.com). Designed in the European style, it offers the same health-and-fitness programs you'd find in an American spa. Some of the treatments offered include Ionithermie, the inch-reducing treatment from Europe; deluxe facial care from Paris; ancient forms of therapeutic and relaxing massage such as aromatherapy, reflexology, and Swedish massage. Some people check into the hotel on calorie-controlled 4-, 5-, or 7-day programs. Clients are usually kept busy every day from 8:30am to 7pm with such activities as aerobics, skin and body care, supervised indoor and outdoor stretching exercises, massages, facials, and beauty regimens. Clients are allowed, however, free time for themselves.

The facilities are also available to hotel guests or outsiders who would like only selected treatments rather than the full spa experience. The up-to-date accoutrements include Universal gym equipment, saunas, steam baths, and massage rooms. The staff conducts daily exercise classes, which outsiders can join for a fee. Each procedure is priced separately for nonpackage participants. For after-workout pick-me-ups, there's a beauty salon adjacent to the health spa. Half- or full-day packages are sold to nonguests of the hotel.

For more details on Sonesta Beach Resort, including high-season, off-season, and MAP rates, see "Resort Hotels" in chapter 4.

7 Health & Insurance

STAYING HEALTHY

If you need medical attention while in Bermuda, finding a doctor or getting a prescription filled is no real problem. See "Fast Facts: Bermuda" in chapter 3 for specific locations and addresses of pharmacies. In an emergency, call **King Edward VII Hospital,** 7 Point Finger Rd., Paget Parish (☎ **441/236-2345**), and ask for the emergency department. A private doctor, **Dr. Gordon Campbell,** Sea Venture Building, Parliament Street, Hamilton (☎ **441/295-8106**), will treat colds, the flu, and other medical problems.

Limit your exposure to the sun, especially during the first few days of your trip and, thereafter, from 11am to 2pm. Use a sunscreen with a high protection factor and apply it liberally. Remember that children need more protection than adults do.

If you worry about getting sick away from home, you may want to consider **medical travel insurance** (see the following section on travel insurance). In most cases, however, your existing health plan will provide all the coverage you need. Be sure to carry your identification card in your wallet.

If you suffer from a chronic illness, consult your doctor before your departure. For conditions such as epilepsy, diabetes, or heart problems, wear a **Medic Alert Identification Tag** (☎ 800/825-3785; www.commedicalert.org), which will immediately alert doctors to your condition and give them access to your records through Medic Alert's 24-hour hotline. Membership is $35, plus a $15 annual fee.

Pack prescription medications in your carry-on luggage. Carry written prescriptions in generic, not brand-name, form, and dispense all prescription medications from their original labeled vials. Also bring along copies of your prescriptions in case you lose your pills or run out.

If you wear contact lenses, pack an extra pair in case you lose one.

Contact the **International Association for Medical Assistance to Travelers (IAMAT)** (☎ 716/754-4883 or 416/652-0137; www.sentex.net/~iamat). This organization offers tips on travel and health concerns abroad.

INSURANCE

There are three kinds of travel insurance: trip-cancellation, medical, and lost-luggage coverage. **Trip-cancellation insurance** is a good idea if you have paid a large portion of your vacation expenses up front, say, by paying for a package or cruise. The other two types of insurance, however, don't make sense for most travelers. Rule number one: Check your existing policies before you buy any additional coverage.

Your existing health insurance should cover you if you get sick while on vacation (though if you belong to an HMO, you should check to see whether you are fully covered when away from home). If you need hospital treatment, most health-insurance plans and HMOs will cover out-of-country hospital visits and procedures, at least to some extent. However, most make you pay the bills up front at the time of care, and you'll get a refund after you've returned and filed all the paperwork. Members of **Blue Cross/Blue Shield** can now use their cards at select hospitals in most major cities worldwide (☎ **800/810-BLUE** or www. bluecares.com /blue/bluecard/wwn for a list of hospitals). For independent travel health-insurance providers, see below. Your homeowner's insurance should cover stolen luggage. The airlines are responsible for $1,250 on domestic flights if they lose your luggage; if you plan to carry anything more valuable than that, keep it in your carry-on bag.

The differences between travel assistance and insurance are often blurred, but in general the former offers on-the-spot assistance and 24-hour hotlines (mostly oriented toward medical problems), whereas the latter reimburses you for travel problems (medical, travel, or otherwise) after you have filed the paperwork. The coverage you should consider will depend on how much protection is already contained in your existing health insurance or other policies. Some credit- and charge-card companies may insure you against travel accidents if you buy plane, train, or bus tickets with their cards. Before purchasing additional insurance, read your policies and agreements carefully. Call your insurers or credit/charge-card companies if you have any questions.

Some credit cards (American Express and certain gold and platinum Visas and MasterCards, for example) offer automatic flight insurance against death or dismemberment in case of an airplane crash.

If you do require additional insurance, try one of the companies listed below. But don't pay for more than you need. For example, if you need only trip-cancellation insurance, don't purchase coverage for lost or stolen property. Trip-cancellation insurance costs approximately 6% to 8% of the total value of your vacation. Among the reputable issuers of travel insurance are the following:

- **Access America,** 6600 W. Broad St., Richmond, VA 23230 (☎ **800/284-8300**) **Travel Guard International,** 1145 Clark St., Stevens Point, WI 54481 (☎ **800/ 826-1300**)
- **Travel Gaurd International, Inc.,** 1145 Clark St., Stevens Point, WI 54481 (☎ **800/826-1300**)
- **Travel Insured International, Inc.,** P.O. Box 280568, East Hartford, CT 06128 (☎ **800/243-3174**)
- **Columbus Travel Insurance,** 17 Devonshire Square, London EC2M 4SQ (☎ **0171/375-0011** in Londo n; www.columbusdirect.com/columbusdirect)
- **International SOS Assistance,** P.O. Box 11568, Philadelphia, PA 11916 (☎ **800/523-8930** or 215/244-1500), strictly an assistance company
- **Travelex Insurance Services,** P.O. Box 9408, Garden City, NY 11530-9408 (☎ **800/228-9792**)

Medicare covers U.S. citizens traveling only in Mexico and Canada. Companies specializing in accident and medical care include these:

- **MEDEX International,** P.O. Box 5375, Timonium, MD 21094-5375 (☎ **888/MEDEX-00** or 410/453-6300; fax 410/453-6301; www. medexassist. com)
- **Travel Assistance International** (Worldwide Assistance Services, Inc.), 1133 15th St. NW, Suite 400, Washington, DC 20005 (☎ **800/821-2828** or 202/828-5894; fax 202/828-5896)
- **The Divers Alert Network (DAN)** (☎ **800/446-2671** or 919/684-2948), for scuba divers

8 Tips for Travelers with Special Needs

TIPS FOR TRAVELERS WITH DISABILITIES

A disability shouldn't stop anyone from traveling. There are more resources out there than ever before. *A World of Options,* a 658-page book of resources for travelers with disabilities, covers everything from biking trips to scuba outfitters. It costs $45 ($30 for members) and is available from **Mobility International USA,** P.O. Box 10767, Eugene, OR 97440 (☎ **541/343-1284,** voice and TDD; www.miusa.org). Annual membership for Mobility International is $35, which includes their quarterly newsletter, *Over the Rainbow.* In addition, **Twin Peaks Press,** P.O. Box 129, Vancouver, WA 98666 (☎ **360/694-2462**), publishes travel-related books for people with disabilities.

The **Moss Rehab Hospital** (☎ **215/456-9600**) has been providing friendly and helpful phone advice and referrals to travelers with disabilities for years through its **Travel Information Service** (☎ **215/456-9603;** www.mossresourcenet.org).

You can join **The Society for the Advancement of Travel for the Handicapped (SATH),** 347 Fifth Ave., Suite 610, New York, NY 10016 (☎ **212/447-7284;** fax 212-725-8253; www.sath.org), for $45 annually, $30 for seniors and students, to gain access to their vast network of connections in the travel industry. They provide information sheets on travel destinations, and referrals to tour operators that specialize in traveling with disabilities. Their quarterly magazine, *Open World for Disability and Mature Travel,* is full of good information and resources. A year's subscription is $13 ($21 outside the U.S.).

Travelers with disabilities may also want to consider joining a tour that caters specifically to them. One of the best operators is **Flying Wheels Travel,** 143 West Bridge (P.O. Box 382), Owatonna, MN 55060 (☎ **800/535-6790**). They offer various escorted tours and cruises, with an emphasis on sports, as well as private tours in minivans with lifts.

You can obtain a copy of *Air Transportation of Handicapped Persons* by writing to Free Advisory Circular No. AC12032, Distribution Unit, U.S. Department of Transportation, Publications Division, M-4332, Washington, DC 20590.

Vision-impaired travelers should contact the **American Foundation for the Blind,** 11 Penn Plaza, Suite 300, New York, NY 10001 (☎ **800/232-5463**), for information on traveling with seeing eye dogs.

IN THE UNITED KINGDOM

RADAR (Royal Association for Disability and Rehabilitation), Unit 12, City Forum, 250 City Rd., London EC1V 8AF (☎ **0171/250-3222;** fax 0171/250-0212; www.radar.org.uk), publishes holiday "fact packs"—three in all—that sell for £2 each or £5 for a set of all three. The first pack provides general information, including planning and booking a holiday, insurance, finances, and useful organization and holiday providers. The second outlines transport and equipment, transportation available when going abroad, and equipment for rent. The third deals with specialized accommodations.

TIPS FOR GAY & LESBIAN TRAVELERS

Think twice before planning a gay holiday in Bermuda. Although many gays live in and visit Bermuda, the colony has rather repressive antihomosexual laws. Relations between homosexuals, even between consenting adults, are subject to criminal sanctions, carrying a maximum sentence of 10 years in prison. Even attempted contacts among homosexuals, at least according to the law, can be punished with up to 5 years in prison.

If you want really happening gay beaches, bars, or clubs, consider heading to Miami, Key West, or Puerto Rico.

TIPS FOR SENIORS

Don't be shy about asking for discounts, but always carry some kind of identification, such as a driver's license, that shows your date of birth. Also, mention the fact that you're a senior citizen when you first make your travel reservations. For example, many hotels offer seniors discounts.

Members of the **American Association of Retired Persons (AARP),** 601 E St. NW, Washington, DC 20049 (☎ **800/424-3410** or 202/434-2277), get discounts not only on hotels but on airfares and car rentals too. AARP offers members a wide range of special benefits, including *Modern Maturity* magazine and a monthly newsletter.

The **National Council of Senior Citizens,** 8403 Colesville Rd., Suite 1200, Silver Spring, MD 20910 (☎ **301/578-8800**), a nonprofit organization, offers a newsletter six times a year (partly devoted to travel tips) and discounts on hotel and auto rentals; annual dues are $13 per person or couple.

Mature Outlook, P.O. Box 9390, Des Moines, IA 50306 (☎ **800/336-6330**), began as a travel organization for people over 50, though it now caters to people of all ages. Members receive discounts on hotels and receive a bimonthly magazine. Annual membership is $19.95, which entitles members to discounts and, often, free coupons for discounted merchandise from Sears.

Golden Companions, P.O. Box 5249, Reno, NV 89513 (☎ **702/324-2227**), helps travelers 45-plus find compatible companions through a personal voice-mail service. Contact them for more information.

Another helpful publication is *101 Tips for the Mature Traveler,* available from Grand Circle Travel, 347 Congress St., Suite 3A, Boston, MA 02210 (☎ **800/ 221-2610** or 617/350-7500; fax 617/346-6700).

Another of the hundreds of travel agencies specializing in vacations for seniors is **Grand Circle Travel,** 347 Congress St., Suite 3A, Boston, MA 02210 (☎ **800/ 221-2610** or 617/350-7500). Many of these packages, however, are of the tour-bus variety, with free trips thrown in for those who organize groups of 10 or more. Seniors seeking more independent travel should probably consult a regular travel agent. **SAGA International Holidays,** 222 Berkeley St., Boston, MA 02116 (☎ **800/343-0273**), offers inclusive tours and cruises for those 50 and older. SAGA also sponsors the more substantial "Road Scholar Tours" (☎ **800/621-2151**), which are fun but with an educational bent.

Although all the **specialty books** on the market are U.S.-focused, three do provide good general advice and contacts for the savvy senior traveler. Thumb through *The 50+ Traveler's Guidebook* (St. Martin's Press), *The Seasoned Traveler* (Country Roads Press), or *Unbelievably Good Deals and Great Adventures That You Absolutely Can't Get Unless You're Over 50* (Contemporary Books). Also check out your newsstand for the quarterly magazine *Travel 50 & Beyond.*

TIPS FOR FAMILIES

Several books on the market offer tips to help you travel with kids. Most concentrate on the United States, but two, *Family Travel* (Lanier Publishing International) and *How to Take Great Trips with Your Kids* (The Harvard Common Press), are full of good general advice that can apply to travel anywhere. Another reliable tome, with a worldwide focus, is *Adventuring with Children* (Foghorn Press).

Family Travel Times is published six times a year by TWYCH (Travel with Your Children; ☎ 888/822-4388 or 212/477-5524) and includes a weekly call-in service for subscribers. Subscriptions are $40 a year for quarterly editions. A free publication list and a sample issue are available when you call.

TIPS FOR STUDENTS

The Bermuda Department of Tourism tolerates, but does not actively encourage, the hordes of students that head to Bermuda every year during spring break. Partly as a means of putting a respectable spin on things, they offer Spring Break Sports Programs for sports teams from the mainland, as well as Spring Break Arts Programs. Inquire with the tourism office for details.

9 Package Deals

Before you start your search for the lowest airfare, you may want to consider booking your flight as part of a package that also includes your accommodations. It's often possible to save serious money by going this route.

Package tours are not the same thing as escorted tours. They are simply a way to buy airfare and accommodations at the same time. For popular destinations like Bermuda, they are a smart way to go, because they save you a lot of money. In many cases, a package that includes airfare, hotel, and transportation to and from the airport will cost you less than just the hotel alone would have, had you booked it yourself. That's because packages are sold in bulk to tour operators—who resell them to the public at a cost that drastically undercuts standard rates.

Packages, however, vary widely. Some offer a better class of hotels than others. Some offer the same hotels for lower prices. Some offer flights on scheduled airlines, whereas others book charters. In some packages, your choice of accommodations and travel days may be limited. Some packages let you choose between escorted vacations and independent vacations; others will allow you to add on just a few excursions or escorted day trips (also at lower prices than you could locate on your own) without booking an entirely escorted tour. Each destination usually has one or two packagers that are cheaper than the rest because they buy in even greater bulk. If you spend the time to shop around, you will save in the long run. Use the reviews in this guide to choose your hotel wisely.

The best place to start your search is the travel section of your local Sunday newspaper. Also check the ads in the back of national travel magazines such as *Travel & Leisure, National Geographic Traveler,* and *Condé Nast Traveler.*

Liberty Travel (☎ 888/271-1584; www.libertytravel.com) has many local branches nationwide. One of the biggest packagers in the Northeast, Liberty

A Timesaving Tip

Shopping around for the right package can be time-consuming. To speed up the process, call **TourScan Inc.,** P.O. Box 2367, Darien, CT 06820 (☎ 800/962-2080 or 203/655-8091; fax 203/655-6689; www.tourscan.com). Its computerized list provides both hotel and air package deals not only to Bermuda, but also to The Bahamas and the Caribbean. This organization usually has a whole range of offerings so that you can pick and choose from what's out there. Its *Island Vacation Catalog,* which costs $4 and is issued twice yearly, contains complete details (your $4 will be refunded if you book a tour). If you decide to take a tour, you can either book it directly through TourScan or use any travel agent.

usually boasts a full-page ad in Sunday papers. You won't get much in the way of service, but you will get a good deal. **American Express Vacations** (☎ 800/241-1700; www.leisureweb.com) is another option. Check out its **Last Minute Travel Bargains** site, offered in conjunction with **Continental Airlines** (www.americanexpress.com/travel/lastminutetravel/default.asp), with deeply discounted vacation packages and reduced airline fares that differ from the E-Savers bargains that Continental e-mails weekly to subscribers. **Northwest Airlines** offers a similar service. Posted on Northwest's Web site every Wednesday, its **Cyber Saver Bargain Alerts** offer special hotel rates, package deals, and discounted airline fares.

Another good resource is the airlines themselves, which often package their flights together with accommodations. Your options include **American Airlines FlyAway Vacations** (☎ 800/321-2121), **Delta Dream Vacations** (☎ 800/872-7786), and **US Airways Vacations** (☎ 800/455-0123).

The biggest hotel chains and resorts also offer package deals. If you already know where you want to stay, call the resort itself and ask if they can offer land/air packages.

10 Flying to Bermuda

From North America's East Coast, you can be in Bermuda in approximately 2 hours. If you're coming from the United Kingdom, it'll take you about 7 hours to arrive from London.

American Airlines (☎ 800/433-7300; www.aa.com) flies to Bermuda nonstop twice a day from New York's JFK Airport. Departures are timed to coincide with dozens of connecting flights from elsewhere throughout North America.

Delta (☎ 800/241-4141; www.delta-air.com) offers daily nonstop service to Bermuda from both Boston and Atlanta. The Boston flight departs in the morning (around 9am), whereas the Atlanta flight leaves around noon, late enough to allow connections from most of the other cities within Delta's vast network.

Continental Airlines (☎ 800/231-0856; www.flycontinental.com) offers daily nonstop service to Bermuda from New Jersey's Newark Airport year-round.

US Airways (☎ 800/428-4322; www.usair.com) offers nonstop flights from Philadelphia and Baltimore year-round, plus nonstop flights seasonally from New York (November 6 to May 6). There's also a flight from Charlotte with a stopover in Philadelphia but with no change of plane.

Air Canada (☎ 800/776-3000 in the U.S., or 888/247-2262 in Canada; www.aircanada.ca) offers daily nonstop flights from Toronto to Bermuda, with frequent connections into Toronto from virtually every other city in Canada. The flight departs around 9am, permitting convenient connections from both Montréal and Québec City. The airline also offers Saturday nonstop flights to Bermuda from Halifax leaving at noon.

The airline of choice for visitors from the United Kingdom is **British Airways** (☎ 0141/222-2345 in Britain; www.britishairways.com); it flies between London's Gatwick Airport and Bermuda about three times a week year-round. No other airline flies nonstop between Britain and Bermuda.

Most airlines offer the best deals on tickets ordered at least 14 days in advance, and that includes stopovers in Bermuda of at least 3 days. You'll often need to stay over on a Saturday night to keep fares down. Airfares fluctuate according to the season but tend to remain competitive among the companies vying for shares of the lucrative Bermuda run.

Peak season (summer) is the most expensive time to go; low season (usually mid-September or early November until mid-March) offers less-expensive fares.

The airlines that fly to Bermuda seldom offer a shoulder (intermediate) season. Because most aircraft flying from North America to Bermuda are medium-size, there's space for only two classes of service: first class and economy.

To give you some idea of the fares, we checked with American when researching this book. They were offering round-trip flights from New York starting at $339 Monday to Thursday in low season and at $550 in high season. Fares for travel in both directions between Friday and Sunday entail a surcharge of around $50. Round-trip first-class fare was the same regardless of the season, beginning at $952.

FLYING FOR LESS: TIPS FOR GETTING THE BEST AIRFARES

Package deals are the number-one way to save, but most accommodations featured in packages are the bigger resort hotels. Especially if you prefer to rent a cottage or stay in a more intimate place, you may wind up booking your airfare separately.

Consolidators, also known as bucket shops, are a good place to find low fares. Consolidators buy seats in bulk from the airlines and then sell them back to the public at prices below even the airlines' discounted rates. Their small boxed ads usually run in the Sunday travel section at the bottom of the page. Before you pay a consolidator, however, ask for a record locator number and confirm your seat with the airline itself. Be prepared to book your ticket with a different consolidator—there are many to choose from—if the airline can't confirm your reservation. Also be aware that bucket-shop tickets are usually nonrefundable or rigged with stiff cancellation penalties, often as high as 50% to 75% of the ticket price.

Council Travel (☎ 800/226-8624; www.counciltravel.com) and **STA Travel** (☎ 800/781-4040; www.sta.travel.com) cater especially to young travelers, but their bargain-basement prices are available to people of all ages. **Travel Bargains** (☎ 800/AIR-FARE; www.1800airfare.com) was formerly owned by TWA but now offers the deepest discounts on many other airlines, with a 4-day advance purchase. Other reliable consolidators include **1-800-FLY-CHEAP** (www.1800flycheap.com); **TFI Tours International** (☎ 800-745-8000 or 212/736-1140), which serves as a clearinghouse for unused seats; and "rebaters" such as **Travel Avenue** (☎ 800/333-3335 or 312/876-1116) and the **Smart Traveller** (☎ 800/448-3338 in the U.S. or 305/448-3338; www.smarttraveller@juno.com), which rebate part of their commissions to you.

TIPS FOR FLYING IN COMFORT

- You'll find the most leg room in a bulkhead seat, in the front row of each airplane cabin. Consider, however, that you will have to store your luggage in the overhead bin, and you won't have the best seat in the house for the in-flight movie.
- When you check in, ask for one of the emergency-exit-row seats, which also have extra leg room. They are assigned at the airport, usually on a first-come, first-served basis. In the unlikely event of an emergency, however, you'll be expected to open the emergency-exit door and help direct traffic.
- Ask for a seat toward the front of the plane. You'll be one of the first to disembark after the gangway is in place.
- When you make your reservation, order a special meal if you have dietary restrictions. Most airlines offer a variety of special meals: vegetarian, macrobiotic, kosher, and meals for the lactose intolerant among them.
- Wear comfortable clothes and dress in layers. The climate in airplane cabins is unpredictable. You'll be glad to have a sweater or jacket to put on or take off as the temperature on board dictates.

Cyber Deals for Net Surfers

It's possible to get some great deals on airfare via the Internet. Grab your mouse and surf before you take off—you could save a bundle on your trip. Always check the lowest published fare, however, before you shop for flights online. And see the online directory at the end of this book for even more helpful advice about making the Web work for you!

Arthur Frommer's Budget Travel (www.frommers.com) Home of the *Encyclopedia of Travel* and *Arthur Frommer's Budget Travel* magazine and daily newsletter, this site offers detailed information on 200 cities and islands around the world, and up-to-the-minute ways to save dramatically on flights, hotels, and cruises. Book an entire vacation online and research your destination before you leave. Consult the message board to set up "hospitality exchanges" in other countries, to talk with other travelers who have visited a hotel you're considering, or to direct travel questions to Arthur Frommer himself. The newsletter is updated daily to keep you abreast of the latest breaking ways to save, to publicize new hot spots and best buys, and to present veteran readers with fresh, ever-changing approaches to travel.

Microsoft Expedia (www.expedia.com) The best part of this multipurpose travel site is the "Fare Tracker." You fill out a form on the screen indicating that you're interested in cheap flights from your hometown, and, once a week, they'll e-mail you the best airfare deals on up to three destinations. The site's "Travel Agent" will steer you to bargains on hotels, and with the help of hotel and airline seat pinpointers, you can book everything right online. This site is even useful once you're booked. Before you depart, log on to Expedia for maps and up-to-date travel information, including weather reports and foreign exchange rates.

The Trip (www.thetrip.com) This site is really geared toward the business traveler, but vacationers-to-be can also use The Trip's exceptionally powerful fare-finding engine, which will e-mail you every week with the best city-to-city airfare deals for as many as 10 routes. The Trip uses the Internet Travel Network, another reputable travel-agent database, to book hotels and restaurants.

E-Savers Programs Several major airlines offer a free e-mail service known as E-Savers, via which they'll send you their best bargain airfares on a regular basis. Here's how it works: Once a week (usually Wednesday), or 7whenever a sale fare comes up, subscribers receive a list of discounted flights to and from various destinations, both international and domestic. Here's the catch: These fares are usually available only if you leave the very next Saturday (or sometimes Friday night) and return on the following Monday or Tuesday. It's really a service for the spontaneously inclined and travelers looking for a quick getaway. But the fares are cheap, so it's worth taking a look. If you have a preference for certain airlines (in other words, the ones you fly most frequently), sign up with them first.

- Pack some toiletries for long flights. Airplane cabins are notoriously dry places. Take a travel-size bottle of moisturizer or lotion to refresh your face and hands at the end of the flight. If you wear contact lenses, bring eye drops.
- If you're flying with a cold or chronic sinus problems, use a decongestant 10 minutes before ascent and descent, to minimize pressure buildup in the inner ear.
- If you're flying with kids, don't forget a deck of cards, toys, extra bottles, pacifiers, diapers, and chewing gum to help them relieve ear-pressure buildup during ascent and descent.

11 Cruising to Bermuda

Cruise ships tie up at three harbors in Bermuda—St. George's in the east end, the Royal Naval Dockyard in the west end, and Hamilton Harbour at the city of Hamilton. While the cruise experience isn't for everyone, it's very appealing to some people, and is certainly a carefree, all-inclusive vacation. You can sail from the east coast of the United States to Bermuda in a little over a day, then spend a few full days (usually three) moored at the island, exploring and enjoying during the day then returning to the ship at night. It's convenient and comfortable—like having a luxury hotel and restaurant that travels with you.

Of course, that's also its major disadvantage. Most cruisers don't get to know the real Bermuda as well as those who stay in hotels ashore. Cruise-ship passengers generally eat all their meals aboard the ship, for instance—mainly because they've already paid for the meals as part of their cruise price—and so miss out on sampling the various cuisines of Bermuda's restaurants. They also rarely get to meet and interact with Bermudians the way land-based visitors do.

WHICH CRUISE LINE IS FOR YOU?

If you've decided a Bermuda cruise is right for you, you need to choose your cruise line. Some lines want their passengers to have a total vacation—one filled with activities from sunup to sundown. Others see time at sea as a period of tranquillity and relaxation, with less emphasis on organized activities. The cruise lines listed here offer regularly scheduled Bermuda sailings. See the section that follows for tips of getting a good deal on the price.

- **Celebrity Cruises** (☎ 800/437-3111 or 305/539-6000)   Noted for modern, state-of-the-art, large but not mammoth cruise ships and for its exceptional cuisine and service, Celebrity is unpretentious but classy, several notches above mass market but still competitively priced. Cabins are roomy and well-equipped, and the decor of its ships in general is elegantly modern, eschewing the glitz of some of its competitors. Celebrity attracts a broad range of passengers, including families drawn by the line's children's programs. Its *Zenith* sails 7-night Bermuda itineraries from New York between April and October, spending two and four nights in either Hamilton or St. George's, and in some cases, at a combination of the two. Runs from other east coast cities are interspersed throughout the season.
- **Norwegian Cruise Line** (☎ 800/327-7030)   NCL operates two roughly equivalent medium-size ships that visit Bermuda in the summer. The *Norwegian Crown* spends early spring and late autumn traveling between Port Canaveral, Florida, and Montréal, stopping at Bermuda and historic ports along the Eastern Seaboard en route. Between April and October, it makes an ongoing series of circular 7-day itineraries between New York City and Bermuda's biggest ports (Hamilton and St. George's), spending 2 days in each city. The *Norwegian Majesty* makes Bermuda runs from Boston between April and October, allowing 4 days "shore leave" in St. George's. Despite their relatively small sizes, NCL's ships offer a great roster of activities and sports, both of the active and spectator variety—both ships have sports bars with links to ESPN, so you won't miss the big game.
- **Princess Cruises** (☎ 800/421-0522)   Princess has the small, 1970-vintage liner *Pacific Princess* on Bermuda itineraries. One of the ships used in the original *Love Boat* TV series, the vessel is old and small, but beloved. About a quarter the size of the newer ships in Princess's fleet, and carrying about a third as many passengers, it looks more like a ship than the huge floating resorts of today, and offers a more intimate experience. Something important for fans of the TV series to

note: The cabin sets used in the show were *massive* compared to the real accommodations available on the ship (and, for that matter, compared to the accommodations on *any* ship).

- **Royal Caribbean Cruises, Ltd.** (☎ **800/327-6700**)   Royal Caribbean sails its 1,600-passenger *Nordic Empress* on Bermuda runs from New York between May and October. The ship, built in 1990, has compact but well designed cabins and a wide variety of entertainments, including a casino, a health spa, a children's program, and much more. Its onboard atmosphere is a little more high-energy than Celebrity and Princess, and roughly comparable to NCL. Stopovers include 2 days in St. George's and 2½ days in Hamilton Harbour.

HOW TO GET THE BEST DEAL ON YOUR CRUISE

Cruise lines operate like airlines, setting rates for their cruises and then selling them in a rapid-fire series of discounts, offering almost whatever it takes to fill their ships. Because of this, great deals come and go in the blink of an eye, and most are only available through travel agents.

If you've got a travel agent you trust, leave the details to him or her. If not, try contacting a travel agent who specializes in booking cruises. Some of the most likely contenders include the following: **Cruises, Inc.,** 5000 Campuswood Dr. E., Syracuse, NY 13057 (☎ **800/854-0500** or 315/463-9695); **Cruise Fairs of America,** Century Plaza Towers, 2029 Century Park E., Suite 950, Los Angeles, CA 90067 (☎ **800/456-4FUN** or 310/556-2925); **The Cruise Company,** 10760 Q St., Omaha, NE 68127 (☎ **800/289-5505** or 402/339-6800); **Kelly Cruises,** 1315 W. 22nd St., Suite 105, Oak Brook, IL 60523 (☎ **800/837-7447** or 630/990-1111); **Hartford Holidays Travel,** 129 Hillside Ave., Williston Park, NY 11596 (☎ **800/828-4813** or 516/746-6670); and **Mann Travel** and **Cruises American Express,** 6010 Fairview Rd., Ste. 104, Charlotte, NC 28210 (☎ **800/849-2301** or 704-556-8311).

A FEW MONEY-SAVING TIPS

- **Book Early:** You can often receive considerable savings on a 7-day cruise by booking early. Ask a travel agent or call the cruise line directly.
- **Book an Inside Cabin:** If you're trying to keep costs down, ask for an inside cabin (meaning one without a window). They're often the same size and offer the same amenities as the more expensive outside cabins, and if you're planning on only using the space to sleep, who needs natural light during the day?
- **Take Advantage of Senior Discounts:** The cruise industry offers some discounts to seniors (usually defined as anyone 55 years or older), so don't keep your age a secret. Membership in AARP, for example, can net you substantial discounts; always ask your travel agent about these types of discounts when you're booking.
- **Don't Sail Alone:** Since cruise lines base their rates on double occupancy of cabins, solo passengers usually pay between 150 and 200 percent of the per person rate. If you're traveling alone, most lines have a program that allows two solo passengers to share a cabin, thus bringing their rates back down to normal.

12 Tips on Accommodations

TIPS FOR SAVING ON YOUR HOTEL ROOM

The *rack rate* is the maximum rate a hotel charges for a room. It's the rate you'd get if you walked in off the street and asked for a room for the night. We've listed rack rates in this guide, but especially at the big resorts, hardly anybody pays these prices. There are many ways around them.

- **Don't be afraid to bargain.** Get in the habit of asking for a lower price than the first one quoted. Most rack rates include commissions of 10% to 25% or more for travel agents, which many hotels will cut if you make your own reservations and haggle a bit. Always ask politely whether a less-expensive room is available, or whether any special rates apply to you. You may qualify for corporate, student, military, senior citizen, or other discounts. Be sure to mention membership in AAA, AARP, frequent-flyer programs, or trade unions, which may entitle you to special deals as well.

- **Rely on a qualified professional.** Certain hotels give travel agents discounts in exchange for steering business their way, so if you're shy about bargaining, an agent may be better equipped to negotiate discounts for you.

- **Dial direct.** When booking a room in a chain hotel, call the hotel's local line, as well as the toll-free number, and see where you get the best deal. A hotel makes nothing on a room that stays empty. The clerk who runs the place is more likely to know about vacancies and will often grant deep discounts in order to fill up.

- **Remember the law of supply and demand.** Resort hotels are most crowded and therefore most expensive on weekends, so discounts are usually available for mid-week stays. To the contrary, business hotels in downtown locations are busiest during the week; expect discounts over the weekend. Avoid high-season stays whenever you can; planning your vacation just a week before or after official peak season can mean big savings.

- **Avoid excess charges.** Find out before you dial whether your hotel imposes a sur-charge on local or long-distance calls.

- **Consider a suite.** If you are traveling with your family or another couple, you can pack more people into a suite (which usually comes with a sofa bed), and thereby reduce your per-person rate. Remember that some places charge for extra guests, some don't.

- **Book an efficiency.** A room with a kitchenette allows you to grocery shop and eat some meals in. Especially during long stays with families, you're bound to save money on food this way.

- **Investigate reservation services.** These outfits usually work as consolidators, buying up or reserving rooms in bulk and then dealing them out to customers at a profit. They do garner special deals that range from 10% to 50% off; but remember, these discounts apply to rack rates, inflated prices that people rarely end up paying. You're probably better off dealing directly with a hotel, but if you don't like bargaining, this is certainly a viable option. Most of these services offer online reservation services as well. Here are a few of the more reputable providers:

  Accommodations Express (☎ **800/950-4685;** www.accommodationsexpress. com); **Hotel Reservations Network** (☎ **800/96HOTEL;** www.180096HOTEL. com); **Quikbook** (☎ **800/789-9887,** includes fax-on-demand service; www. quikbook.com); and **Room Exchange** (☎ **800/846-7000** in the U.S., 800/ 486-7000 in Canada).

  Online, try booking your hotel through **Arthur Frommer's Budget Travel** (www.frommers.com), and save up to 50% on the cost of your room. **Microsoft Expedia** (www.expedia.com) features a "Travel Agent" that will also direct you to affordable lodgings.

LANDING THE BEST ROOM

Somebody has to get the best room in the house. It might as well be you.

Always ask for a corner room. They're usually larger, quieter, and closer to the elevator. They often have more windows and light than standard rooms, and they don't always cost more.

When you make your reservation, ask if the hotel is renovating; if it is, request a room away from the renovation work. Many hotels now offer nonsmoking rooms; if smoke bothers you, by all means ask for one. Inquire, too, about the location of the restaurants, bars, and discos in the hotel—these could all be a source of irritating noise. If you aren't happy with your room when you arrive, talk to the front desk. If they have another room, they should be happy to accommodate you, within reason.

Getting to Know Bermuda

Settling into Bermuda is relatively easy. First-timers soon learn that Bermuda isn't one island, as is commonly thought, but a string of islands linked by causeways and bridges—at least the 20 or so that are inhabited. The other islands can be reached by boat.

Unlike many islands in the Caribbean (including the Dominican Republic) that are dotted with poverty-stricken slums, Bermuda is a prosperous island characterized by neat, trim houses that are a source of great pride to their owners. There won't be a casino at your megaresort—in fact, Bermuda has no casinos at all—and you'd better have your fill of Big Macs before you leave home. There are some fast-food joints, but nothing in comparison with those on the U.S. mainland, or even those in The Bahamas. There's a sense of order in Bermuda, and everything seems to work efficiently, even when the weather is hot.

1 Arriving

BY PLANE

Planes arrive at the **Bermuda International Airport,** at Kindley Field Road, St. George's (☎ **441/293-2470**), 9 miles east of Hamilton and about 17 miles east of Somerset at the far western end of Bermuda.

The flight from most East Coast destinations, including New York, Raleigh/Durham, Baltimore, and Boston, takes about 2 hours, so most U.S. travelers won't have jet lag on arrival (unless you've come from farther west to catch a connecting flight in one of these cities). Even flights from Atlanta take only 2½ hours; from Toronto it's still less than 3 hours.

After clearing Customs (see "Entry Requirements & Customs," in chapter 2, for details), you can pick up tourist information at the airport before heading out to your hotel. Since you aren't allowed to rent a car in Bermuda, and buses don't allow passengers to board with luggage, you must rely on a taxi or minivan to reach your hotel.

LEAVING THE AIRPORT BY TAXI OR MINIVAN

More than 600 taxis are available in Bermuda, and cabbies meet all arriving flights. Taxis, which are regulated by meter, are allowed to carry a maximum of four passengers. If you and your travel companion have a lot of luggage, you will need the taxi all to yourselves, of course. Including a tip of 10% to 15%, it costs from about $20 to $28 to reach a destination in Hamilton. Since you're already near

---

❓ Did You Know?

- More than 23,000 couples honeymoon in Bermuda each year.
- Bermudians imported the idea of moon gates, large rings of stone used as garden ornaments, from Asia centuries ago. Walking through a moon gate is supposed to bring good luck.
- William Shakespeare's 1610 play, *The Tempest*, was inspired by this mysterious island.
- Somerset Bridge is the world's smallest drawbridge. Only 22 inches wide, the opening is just large enough for a ship's mast to pass through.
- Bermuda has more golf courses per square mile than any other place in the world; there are eight of them on the island's approximate 21 square miles.
- The first game of tennis in the western hemisphere was played in Bermuda by Sir Brownlow Gray, the island's chief justice, in 1873.
- With the arrival of spring comes the blossoming of Bermuda's Easter lilies, first brought to the island from Japan in the 18th century.
- Bermuda has no billboards: There is a ban on outdoor advertising and neon signs.

St. George's, the fare there is about $20, or $16 to Tucker's Town. To the south-shore hotels, the charge is likely to be $26 to $30.

To the West End, site of many more resorts, the charge is more than $45. Fares go up 25% between 10pm and 6am, as well as all day on Sundays and holidays. Luggage carries a surcharge of 25¢ per piece. Expect to pay about $4 for the first mile and $1.40 for each additional mile. There are several authorized taxi companies on the island, including **Radio Cab** (☎ 441/295-4141), **C.O.O.P.** (☎ 441/292-4476), **B.T.S.L.** (☎ 441/295-8294), and **Sandys** (☎ 441/234-2344).

It would be cheaper for a party of four to call a minivan and split the cost among themselves. You should arrange one before you arrive in Bermuda by contacting **Bermuda Hosts,** 2 Kindley Field Rd., St. George's CR 04 (☎ 441/293-1334). This outfit can arrange to have a minivan waiting for your flight. If you're only two people (rather than four), you can ask a waiting minivan at the airport if it has room to take on two extra passengers. Trips cost about $60. If you split the cost four ways, it's much cheaper than having a taxi all to yourself. Bermuda Hosts can provide transportation for golfers and can also arrange sightseeing tours.

BY CRUISE SHIP

This is the easiest way to arrive in Bermuda. The cruise-ship staff presents you with a list of tour options long before you arrive in port; almost everything is done for you, unless you opt to make your own arrangements. (If you take an independent taxi tour, it will be far more expensive than an organized tour.) Most passengers book shore excursions when they reserve the cruise.

Seven-day cruises out of New York spend 4 days at sea, with 3 days in port. Most cruise ships arrive in the traditional port of Hamilton, the capital of Bermuda and its chief commercial and shopping center. If shopping is more important to you than sightseeing, be sure that your cruise ship docks here.

If you're more interested in historic Bermuda, make sure that your ship is scheduled to anchor at St. George's, at the eastern tip of the island. With its narrow lanes and old buildings and streets, St. George's has been called the island's equivalent of

Colonial Williamsburg in Virginia. Although St. George's has a few shops and boutiques, this isn't the primary place to come for shopping. Depending on the cruise line, its schedules, and the current tides, some cruise ships will dock at both St. George's and Hamilton while in Bermuda. Ships often plan to dock at St. George's but find that they cannot do so because of the tides.

It's not too likely that you'll disembark at Somerset, which is at the western end of the island and farthest away from Bermuda's major attractions. If you do, the West End has its own charm and sightseeing appeal; it is, after all, home of the Royal Naval Dockyard, one of the major attractions in Bermuda. In a shopping mall at the dockyard, craft stores and museums exist side by side.

Whatever port you dock at, you can avail yourself of the waiting taxis near your ship, or rent a moped or bicycle (see "Getting Around," below) and do some touring and shopping on your own.

2 Orienting Yourself: The Lay of the Land

For administrative purposes, the islands of Bermuda are divided into several **parishes,** all named for shareholders of the original 1610 Bermuda Company. They're listed below as they are geographically organized, from the western end of the island to the eastern.

SANDYS PARISH

In the far western part of the archipelago, Sandys (pronounced "Sands") Parish encompasses the islands of **Ireland, Boaz,** and **Somerset.** This parish (named for Sir Edwin Sandys, a major shareholder of the 1610 Bermuda Company) is centered around Somerset Village. Somerset Island, site of Somerset Village, pays tribute to Sir George Somers of Sea Venture fame; Sandys Parish is often called Somerset.

Some visitors to Bermuda head directly for Sandys Parish and spend their entire time here; they feel that the far western tip, with its rolling hills, lush countryside, and tranquil bays, is something special. (This area has always stood apart from the rest of Bermuda: During the U.S. Civil War, when most Bermudians sympathized with the Confederates, Sandys Parish supported the Union side.) Sandys Parish has areas of great natural beauty, including **Somerset Long Bay,** the biggest and best public beach in the West End, which the Bermuda Audubon Society is developing into a nature preserve, and **Mangrove Bay,** a protected beach right in the heart of **Somerset Village.** Try to walk around the old village; it's filled with typically Bermudian houses and shops. On Somerset Road is the **Scaur Lodge Property;** this typical Bermuda steep-shoreline hillside is open daily at no charge.

If you want to be near the shops, restaurants, and pubs of Hamilton, you may want to stay in a more central location and visit Sandys Parish on a day trip. However, it's the parish's very isolation that forms part of its charm for those who prefer tranquillity and unspoiled nature to shopping for cashmeres or lingering over an extra pint in a pub. This is the perfect parish for couples seeking privacy and romance away from the crowds.

Visitor Information on the Island

You can get answers to most of your questions at the **Visitors Service Bureau** at the Ferry Terminal, Hamilton (☎ **441/295-1480**); **King's Square,** St. George's (☎ **441/297-1642**); or the **Royal Naval Dockyard** (☎ **441/234-3824**). During the summer, the other Visitors Service Bureau locations are open Monday to Saturday from 9am to 2pm; off-season they're open Monday to Saturday from 9am to 4pm.

The Parishes in Brief

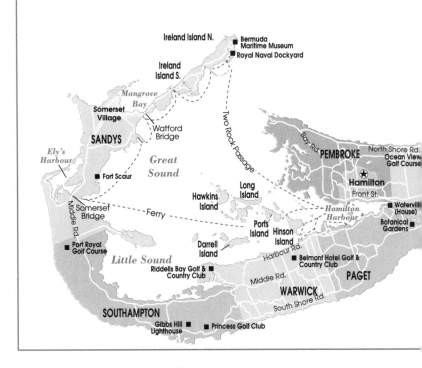

An advantage of staying here is that the parish has several points for embarkation for various types of sea excursions. Sandys also has some of the most elegant places to stay in Bermuda. You can commute to Hamilton by ferry service, although this is a bit time-consuming, especially if your days in Bermuda are limited.

SOUTHAMPTON PARISH

Going east, Southampton Parish (named for the third earl of Southampton) is a narrow strip of land opening at its northern edge onto Little Sound and on its southern shore onto the Atlantic Ocean. It stretches from Riddells Bay to Tucker's Island and is split by Middle Road.

If dining at waterfront restaurants and staying at big resort hotels are part of your Bermuda dream, then Southampton is your parish; it's the site of such famed resorts as the Southampton Princess and the Sonesta. Southampton is also the best place to stay if you plan to spend a great deal of your time on the wide, pink sandy beaches for which the island is fabled. Among its jewels is **Horseshoe Bay,** one of Bermuda's most attractive public beaches, with changing rooms, a snack bar, and space for parking.

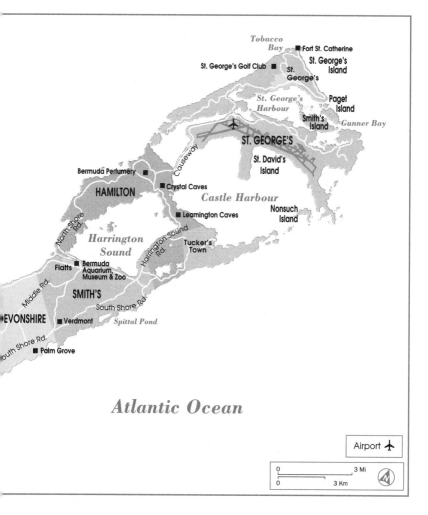

Southampton lacks the intimacy and romance of Sandys, but it's got a lot of razzle-dazzle going for it. It's great for a golfing holiday. If you like to sightsee, you can easily occupy 2 days of time just exploring the many attractions of the parish. It also has more nightlife than Sandys, especially at the Sonesta, Southampton Princess, and Henry VIII—but not as much as in Hamilton, of course.

WARWICK PARISH

Named in honor of another shareholder in the Bermuda Company, the second earl of Warwick, this parish lies in the heart of Great Bermuda Island. Like Southampton, it is known for its long stretches of pink sands. Along the south shore is **Warwick Long Bay,** one of Bermuda's best public beaches. Warwick also boasts parklands bordering the sea, winding country roads, two golf courses, and a number of natural attractions. This area is Bermuda's best for horseback riding, which is the finest means for seeing pastoral Bermuda up close.

Warwick is the preferred choice of those visitors who seek cottage or apartment rentals, where they can do some of their own cooking to cut down on Bermuda's out-rageous food prices. The parish is not strong on restaurants; one of its disadvantages is that you'll have to travel a bit if you like to dine out. Nightlife is also very spotty here; just about the only action you'll find after dark is at hotel lounges. This parish is for tranquillity seekers; but because of its more central location, it doesn't offer quite the seclusion Sandys does.

PAGET PARISH

East of Warwick Parish, Paget Parish lies directly south of the capital city of Hamilton, separated from it by Hamilton Harbour. Named after the fourth Lord Paget, it has many residences and historic homes; it's also the site of the 36-acre **Botanical Gardens.** But it's the parish's south-shore beaches—the best on the chain of islands—that draw visitors here in droves. In spring, the Elbow Beach Hotel is the center of most College Weeks activities. Paget Parish is also the site of **Chelston,** on Grape Bay Drive, the official residence of the U.S. consul general, situated on 14½ acres of landscaped grounds; it's open only during the Garden Club's open-houses-and-gardens program in the spring (see "Calendar of Events," in chapter 2, for details).

This is one of the best parishes in which to stay in Bermuda, because it is filled with excellent accommodations, including Elbow Beach Hotel. It's close enough to the city of Hamilton for an easy commute, but also far enough away to escape the hordes. Since public transportation is all important in Bermuda (you can't rent a car), Paget is a good place to situate yourself; it's also got some of the best and most convenient ferry connections and bus schedules. There are docks at Salt Kettle, Hodson's, and Lower Ferry; you can even "commute" by ferry to Warwick Parish or Sandys Parish to the west. If you'd like to bike, Paget is also ideal for that, because its terrain is relatively flat and the parish is filled with many rural lanes or streets lined with old Bermuda mansions. Hikers will find many small trails bordering the sea.

If you don't like to stay at the big resort hotels like Elbow, you'll find many cottages to rent here and several little guest houses with cute names like Salt Kettle and Pretty Penny. Unlike Warwick, Paget has a number of fine dining choices. Elbow Beach offers the most places to dine, but other fine choices include Fourways Inn and Paraquet. Most of the parish's nightlife centers around Elbow Beach.

There are no particularly noteworthy disadvantages to staying in Paget, other than overcrowded beaches during spring break, when Paget becomes the most rollicking good-time spot on the island, and in summer, when too many cruise ships arrive at Hamilton.

PEMBROKE PARISH

This parish (named after the third earl of Pembroke) is home to one-quarter of Bermuda's population. It is home to the capital **city of Hamilton,** Bermuda's only full-fledged city, which opens at its northern rim onto the vast Atlantic Ocean and on its southern side onto Hamilton Harbour; its western border is on Great Sound. Hamilton is the first place passengers arriving aboard cruise ships will see when they drop anchor in Hamilton Harbour.

This parish is not exactly for those seeking a tranquil holiday. Pembroke not only boasts the island's greatest population density, but it also is overrun with the most visitors. The little city is especially crowded when cruise ships are in the harbor, and the stores and restaurants become overrun. Yet for those who like to pub-crawl English style, like to shop until they drop, and prefer to be near the largest concentration of dining choices, Pembroke—the city of Hamilton in particular—is without equal.

Whether or not you stay in Pembroke, try to fit a shopping stroll along Front Street into your itinerary, if only for window-shopping. The area also boasts a number of sightseeing attractions, most of which can be easily reached on foot, so you don't have to depend on taxis, bikes, or scooters (which can get to be a bit of a bore after a while). Nightlife, such as it is, is the finest on the island. Don't expect splashy Las Vegas–type revues, however; instead, think restaurants, pubs, and small clubs.

DEVONSHIRE PARISH

Lying east of Paget and Pembroke Parishes, near the geographic center of the archipelago, Devonshire Parish (named for the first earl of Devonshire) is green and hilly. It has some housekeeping apartments, a cottage colony, and one of Bermuda's oldest churches, the **Old Devonshire Parish Church,** which dates from 1716. The parish is traversed by three of Bermuda's major roads: the aptly named South Shore Road, Middle Road, and North Shore Road. As you wander its narrow lanes, you can, with some imagination, picture yourself in the original county of Devon, in England.

Golfers flock to Devonshire to play the links at the **Ocean View Golf Course.** Along North Shore Road, near the border of Pembroke Parish, is **Devonshire Dock,** long a seafarer's haven. During the War of 1812, British soldiers came to Devonshire Dock to be entertained by local women. Today, fishers still bring in such catches as grouper and rockfish at the dock, so you can shop for dinner if you're staying at a nearby cottage with a kitchen.

Devonshire has a number of unspoiled nature areas. At the **arboretum** on Montpelier Road, you'll discover one of the most tranquil oases in Bermuda. This open space, created by the Department of Agriculture, Fisheries, and Parks, is home to a wide range of Bermudian plant and tree life, especially conifers, palms, and other subtropical trees. Along South Shore Road, west of the junction with Collector's Hill, is the **Edmund Gibbons Nature Reserve.** This portion of marshland, owned by the National Trust, provides living space for a number of birds and rare species of Bermuda flora.

Devonshire is one of the sleepy residential parishes of Bermuda, known for its hilly interior, beautiful landscape, and fabulous estates bordering the sea. There's little sightseeing to do here; all those stunning private estates aren't open to the public, so unless you get a personal invite, you're out of luck. But the parish is right in Bermuda's geographic center, so it's an ideal place to base yourself if you'd like to see many of Bermuda's attractions in both the West End and the East End. However, there are two major drawbacks: With a few notable exceptions, the parish has very few places to stay and almost no dining choices.

SMITH'S PARISH

Named for Sir Thomas Smith, another member of the Bermuda Company, this parish faces the open sea on both its northern and its southern borders. To the east is Harrington Sound; to the west, bucolic Devonshire Parish.

The parish encompasses **Flatts Village,** one of the most charming parish towns of Bermuda (reached by bus no. 10 or 11 from Hamilton). It was a smugglers' port for about 200 years and also served as the center of power for a coterie of successful "planter politicians" and landowners; their government ranked in importance second only to that of St. George's, then the capital. People gathered at the rickety Flatts Bridge to "enjoy" such public entertainment as hangings; if the offense was serious enough, victims were drawn and quartered here. From Flatts Village, you'll have panoramic views of both the inlet and Harrington Sound.

At the top of McGall's Hill is St. Mark's Church, based on the same designs used for the Old Devonshire Parish Church.

Finding an Address

The island chain of Bermuda doesn't follow a system of street addresses too rigidly. Most hotels, even in official government listings, don't bother to include street addresses, although they do include post-office boxes and ZIP codes. It's just assumed that everybody knows where everything is, which is fine if you've lived in Bermuda all your life. But if you're a first-time visitor, you should get a good map before setting out—or don't be shy about asking directions, since most people are very helpful.

Most of the establishments you'll be seeking are on some street plan. However, some places use numbers in their street addresses, whereas others—perhaps their neighbors—don't. The actual building number is not always important, since a building such as a resort hotel is likely to be set back so far from the main road that you couldn't see its number anyway. It's far better to look for a sign indicating, for example, the Sonesta Beach Hotel than for a street number. Cross streets will also aid you in finding an address.

Most visitors view Smith's Parish as a day trip or a half-day trip, although there are places to stay here, such as the Pink Beach Club and Cottages. Dining choices are extremely limited, however, unless you stick to the hotels. Again, if you're seeking lots of nighttime diversion, you'll have to go to another parish. Because Smith's is the location of the Spittal Pond Nature Reserve, many nature lovers prefer to locate here over one of the more overpopulated parishes, such as Southampton and Pembroke. Basically, Smith's Parish is for the connoisseur who'd like serenity and tranquillity but not at the celestial prices charged at the "cottages" of Sandys.

HAMILTON PARISH

Not to be confused with the city of Hamilton (which is in Pembroke Parish), Hamilton Parish lies directly north of Harrington Sound, opening onto the Atlantic. It's bordered on the east by St. George's and on the southwest by Smith's Parish. Named for the second marquis of Hamilton, the parish ropes itself around Harrington Sound, a saltwater lake stretching some 6 miles. On its eastern periphery, it opens onto Castle Harbour.

The big attractions here are the **Bermuda Aquarium,** the **Crystal Caves,** and **Leamington Caves.** Scuba diving and other water sports are very popular in the area.

Around **Harrington Sound,** the sights differ greatly from those of nearby St. George's (see below)—more action, less history. Some experts believe that back in some prehistoric era, Harrington Sound was a cave that fell in. Its gateway to the ocean is through an inlet at Flatts Village (see "Smith's Parish," above). However, it is believed that there are underwater passages as well, since several deep-sea fish have been caught in the sound.

For the best panoramic view of the north shore, head for **Crawl Hill,** the highest place in Hamilton Parish, just before you come to Bailey's Bay. Crawl is a corruption of the word *kraal*, which is where turtles were kept before slaughter. **Shelly Bay,** named for one of the passengers of the Sea Venture, is the longest beach along the north shore. The **Hamilton Parish Church,** reached by going down Trinity Church Road, stands on Church Bay; built as a one-room structure in 1623, it has been much altered over 3½ centuries.

At Bailey's Bay, **Tom Moore's Jungle** consists of wild woods. The poet Tom Moore is said to have spent many hours writing poetry under a still-standing calabash tree here. Since the jungle is now held in private trust, permission must be obtained to enter it. It's much easier to pay your respects to the Romantic poet by going to Tom Moore's Tavern (see "Hamilton Parish" in chapter 5).

In spite of the major resorts here, such as Grotto Bay Beach Hotel, most visitors come here for sightseeing instead of lodging. We have to agree: In our judgment, Hamilton is a better place to go exploring for a day or half day. You're better off staying elsewhere; if you stay here you'll spend a great deal of your holiday time commuting into either Hamilton or St. George's. Bus no. 1 or 3 from Hamilton will get you here in about an hour.

St. George's Parish

At Bermuda's extreme eastern end, this historic parish encompasses several islands. The parish is flanked by Castle Harbour on its western and southern edges and divided into two major parts, **St. George's Island** and **St. David's Island,** by St. George's Harbour. St. David's Island is linked to the rest of Bermuda by the Severn Bridge. Those who inhabit this most easterly part of Bermuda are longtime sailors and fishers. St. George's Parish also includes **Tucker's Town** (founded in 1616 by Governor Daniel Tucker) on the opposite shore of Castle Harbour.

Settled in 1612, the **town of St. George's** was once the capital of Bermuda, losing that position to Hamilton in 1815. The town was settled 3 years after Admiral Sir George Somers and his shipwrecked party of English sailors came ashore in 1609 (Admiral Somers died in Bermuda in 1610, and his heart was buried in the St. George's area, while the rest of his body was taken home to England for burial). Founded by Richard Moore, of the newly created Bermuda Company, and a band of 60 colonists, St. George's was the second English settlement in the New World (Jamestown, Virginia, was the first). Named after England's patron saint, it has a coat of arms depicting St. George and the dragon.

Almost 4 centuries of history come alive here; generations upon generations of sailors have set forth from its sheltered harbor. St. George's even played a role in the American Revolution: Bermuda depended on the American colonies for food, and when war came, the food supply became dangerously low. Although Bermuda was a British colony, the loyalties of its people were divided, since many Bermudians had relatives living on the American mainland. A delegation headed by Colonel

Finding Your Way

We've included bulleted maps throughout this book to help you locate Bermuda's accommodations, restaurants, beaches, and sights. There's also a handy full-color foldout map in the back of the book.

The Bermuda Department of Tourism publishes a free ***Bermuda Handy Reference Map.*** This tiny pocket map, distributed by the tourist office and available at most hotels, has on one side an overview and orientation map of Bermuda highlighting its major attractions, golf courses, public beaches, and hotels. It does not, however, pinpoint individual restaurants unless they are attached to hotels. On the other side is a detailed street plan of the city of Hamilton, indicating all its major landmarks and service facilities, such as the ferry terminal and the post office. There's also a detailed map of the Royal Naval Dockyard, the West End, and the East End, plus tips on transportation—ferries, taxis, buses—and other helpful hints, such as a depiction of various traffic signs. For exact locations of visitor centers where you can pick up a copy of the *Bermuda Handy Reference Map* for yourself, see "Visitor Information on the Island" under "Orienting Yourself: The Lay of the Land," above.

Henry Tucker went to Philadelphia to petition the Continental Congress for food and supplies, for which Bermuda was willing to trade salt. George Washington had a different idea, however. He needed gunpowder, and a number of kegs of it were stored at St. George's. Without the approval of the British/Bermudian governor, a deal was consummated that resulted in the gunpowder's being trundled aboard American warships waiting in the harbor of Tobacco Bay under cover of darkness. In return, the grateful colonies supplied Bermuda with food.

Although St. George's still evokes a feeling of the past, it's actively inhabited. However, when cruise ships are in port, it's likely to be overrun with visitors. Many people prefer to visit St. George's at night, when they can walk around and enjoy it in relative peace and quiet. You won't be able to enter any of the sightseeing attractions, but they're of minor importance anyway. After dark, there's a mood of enchantment that settles over the place: It's like a storybook village.

Would you want to live here for a week? Probably not. Several chains, including Club Med, have tried and failed to make a go of it here. Accommodations are extremely limited, although there are a number of restaurants (many of which, frankly, are mediocre). For history buffs, there's no place in Bermuda to top St. George's. But for a parish to base yourself in, you might do better in the more centrally located and activity-filled Pembroke or Southampton Parishes. Once you've seen the glories of the town of St. George's, which you can do in a day, you're really isolated at the easternmost end of Bermuda for the rest of your stay. As for nightlife, you can always go to a pub on King's Square.

3 Bermuda in a Nutshell: Suggested Sightseeing Itineraries for 1 to 5 Days

After you've landed in Bermuda, you may be eager to start exploring right away, especially if your time is short. Below is a suggested itinerary for the first 5 days. A week's visit will let you break up your sightseeing trips with time to relax on the beach, go boating, or engage in some of the other outdoor pursuits available on the island, such as golf, scuba diving, or boating. Hitting the beach is obviously the number-one priority for most visitors—but you don't need us to tell you how to schedule your time in the sun!

IF YOU HAVE 1 DAY

If you have only 1 day for sightseeing, we suggest you spend it in the historic former capital of **St. George's,** a maze of narrow, alleyway-like streets with quaint names: Featherbed Alley, Duke of York Street, Petticoat Lane, Old Maid's Lane, Duke of Kent Street. You can spend a day exploring British-style pubs, seafood restaurants, shops (several major Hamilton stores have branches here), old forts, museums, and churches. You'll even see stocks, a ducking stool, and a pillory, all used generations ago to humiliate wrongdoers.

And what would a day in Bermuda be without time spent on the beach? **Elbow Beach** and **Warwick Long Bay** are among the most appealing spots to catch some sand.

IF YOU HAVE 2 DAYS

Day 1 Spend Day 1 as indicated above.

Day 2 Devote this day to sightseeing and shopping in the city of Hamilton. Since it's likely that you'll be staying in one of the hotels in Paget or Warwick, a ferry from either parish will take you right into the city. For many visitors, Hamilton's shops are its most compelling attraction. Try to time your visit to avoid the arrival of cruise ships; on those days, the stores and restaurants in Hamilton can really get crowded.

If you took our advice and went to the beach yesterday, try a different one today. After all, Bermuda isn't just about sightseeing and shopping—it's about those marvelous pink sands too.

IF YOU HAVE 3 DAYS

Days 1–2   Spend your first and second days as outlined above.

Day 3   On your third day, take the ferry from Hamilton across Great Sound to Somerset. Carry your cycle on the boat—you'll need it later (see "Getting Around," below, for details on rentals). You'll be let off at the western end of Somerset Island in Sandys Parish, where you'll find the smallest drawbridge in the world. It's easy to spend an hour walking around Somerset Village. Then, head east until you reach a beach on Long Bay, along the northern rim of the island.

There are several places for lunch in Sandys Parish (see chapter 5). The **Somerset Country Squire Tavern,** a typical village inn near the Watford Bridge ferry stop at the western end of the island, is one of the best.

After lunch, we suggest crossing Watford Bridge to **Ireland Island,** home of the **Maritime Museum.** On your way back to Somerset Bridge and the ferry back to Hamilton, you might take the turnoff to Fort Scaur; from **Scaur Hill,** you'll have a commanding view of Ely's Harbour and Great Sound. If you don't want to go through Somerset again, the ferry at Watford Bridge will take you back to Hamilton.

IF YOU HAVE 4 OR 5 DAYS

Days 1–3   Spend your first 3 days as outlined above.

Day 4   Make this a beach day. Head for **Horseshoe Bay Beach** in the morning. Spend most of your time there, exploring hidden coves in all directions. You can have lunch right on the beach at a concession stand. In the afternoon, visit **Gibbs Hill Lighthouse.** After a rest at your hotel, sample some Bermudian nightlife.

Day 5   To conclude your stay, head for **Flatts Village,** which lies in the eastern sector of Smith's Parish. Explore the **Bermuda Aquarium,** the **Zoological Garden,** and the **Natural History Museum;** consider an undersea walk (see "Walking Underwater," in chapter 6).

Have lunch at the **Palmetto Hotel and Cottages,** and then visit **Elbow Beach.** Make sure you've purchased any duty-free liquor you care to take back with you. After relaxing over afternoon tea at one of the hotels, arrange to see an island show that evening.

4 Getting Around

Driving is on the left, and the national speed limit is 20 m.p.h. in the Bermuda countryside, 15 m.p.h. in busier areas. Cars are limited to one per resident family—and visitors are not allowed to rent cars at all. You'll rely on taxis, bikes, motorized bicycles called "putt-putts," or maybe even a romantic, colorful fringe-topped surrey.

BY TAXI

There are always dozens of taxis roaming the island, and virtually every hotel, restaurant, and shop in Bermuda is happy to call one for you. The hourly charge is

$20 for one to four passengers. A luxury tour van accommodating up to six passengers is $42 an hour. If you want to use one for a sightseeing tour, the minimum is 3 hours. When a taxi has a blue flag on its hood (locals call it the "bonnet"), the driver is qualified to serve as a tour guide. Because these drivers are checked out and tested by the government, you should use this type of driver if you plan to tour Bermuda by taxi. "Blue-bonnet" drivers charge no more than regular taxi drivers.

For a radio-dispatched cab, call **Radio Cabs Bermuda** (☎ **441/295-4141**).

BY CYCLE & SCOOTER

Bermuda is the only Atlantic island that restricts car ownership to local residents. Part of the reason for this is the notoriously narrow roads, with their narrow or nonexistent shoulders and hundreds of blind curves. These factors, coupled with frequent rainfalls and the British-inspired custom of driving on the left, would probably lead to traffic chaos if every newcomer were allowed to take to the local roads in a rented car.

The resulting dependence on cabs, or rented motor scooters, mopeds, and bicycles, is simply a fact of Bermudian life that newcomers quickly accept as part of the island's charm. Although it's inconvenient not having a car at your disposal, the island's tourist brochures make it all seem just wonderful: A happy couple bicycling or mopeding their way around Bermuda on a sunny day, putt-putting their way at slow speeds (no more than 20 m.p.h., the maximum speed allowed by law for any motorized vehicle) across the island.

But what these brochures don't tell you is that the roads are too narrow, and the Bermudians themselves (who are likely to own cars, and pay dearly for the privilege) feel that the road is theirs. Sometimes it starts raining almost without warning; but the skies usually clear rapidly, and the roads dry quickly. During inclement weather, scooter riders are likely to be edged sometimes disturbingly close to the shoulder; and in the aftermath of rainstorms, they'll almost certainly be splattered with water or mud. Many accidents occur on Bermuda's slippery roads after a rain, especially involving those not accustomed to using a motor scooter.

Who should rent a moped or scooter, and who should avoid them altogether? Frankly, the answer depends on your physical fitness and the time of day. Even the most stiffly starched of you might find a wind-whipped morning ride from your hotel to the beach or tennis courts invigorating and fun, but dressed to the nines in anticipation of a candlelit dinner, you'd find the experience horrifying. And although the putt-putters can be a lot of fun on a sunny day, the machines can be dangerous and capricious after dark and, of course, whenever you've had too many daiquiris. Not everyone is fit enough. Visitors on mopeds have a high accident rate, with at least some of the problems derived from the English custom of driving on the left.

Considering the hazards, we usually recommend that reasonably adept sports enthusiasts rent a moped for a day or two's use during daytime. But for evening outings, we firmly believe that a taxi is the way to go.

What are the requirements for renting a motorbike? You must be 16 or older. Some of these vehicles are big enough for two cozy adults. Helmets are required to protect you from possible spills, and rental companies must provide them. Know in advance that on a hot day, they're uncomfortable. But, what the heck—you'll be at the beach soon enough anyway.

What's the difference between a moped and a motor scooter? They're basically alike, with equivalent maximum speeds and horsepower. Mopeds, however, have larger wheels than scooters, thereby allowing riders fewer shocks as they traverse bumps in the road. And while most (but not all) mopeds are designed for one rider, scooters are available for either a single passenger or two passengers riding in tandem. Frankly, many visitors rent one or another of the machines and never really understand the differences between the two.

There are quite a few gas stations (called "petrol stations" here). Once you "tank up" your motorbike, chances are you'll have plenty to get you to your destination; for example, one tank of gas in a motorbike will take you from Somerset in the west to St. George's in the east.

Among the rental companies listed below, there's a tendency toward price-fixing. It's usually a waste of time to shop around for a better deal. Rental fees across the island tend to be roughly equivalent. Mopeds for one rider rent for $33 for the first day, $57 for 2 days, and $74 for 3 days. Scooters for two riders cost $42 for 1 day. You must use a major credit card as your means of payment; it serves as a deposit in case of damage or theft. You must also purchase a one-time insurance policy priced at $15. The insurance is valid for the entire length of the rental.

You can rent either mopeds or 50cc scooters at **Wheels** (☎ **441/292-2245**), which has two convenient locations along Front Street in Hamilton and one at Flatts Village, as well as locations at the following resorts: the Princess, the Sonesta Beach Resort, Coral Beach Cottages, the Stonington Resort, White Sands Hotel and Cottages, and Horizons and Cottages.

You can also find comparable prices at **Marriott's Castle Harbour Resort** (☎ **441/293-0007**) and **Concord Cycle Shop,** Southampton Princess (☎ **441/238-3336**).

One of the best rental deals on the island is offered by **Eve's Cycle Livery,** 114 Middle Rd., Paget Parish (☎ **441/236-6247**). Named after a now-legendary matriarch who founded the company more than 40 years ago, Eve's rents men's and women's pedal bicycles (usually 10- to 12-speed mountain bikes, well suited to the island's hilly terrain) for $20 for the first day, $15 for the second day, and $10 for the third day. A $20 deposit is required. The shop is within a 10-minute taxi ride (or a 20-min. leisurely cycle) west of Hamilton. The company also rents a variety of scooters for between $42 and $60 for the first day, depending on the model, with successively lower prices for each additional day.

At **Oleander Cycles Ltd.,** Valley Road, P.O. Box 114, Paget Parish (☎ **441/236-5235**), scooters and mopeds are reliable and well maintained. There are other locations, on Gorham Road in Hamilton (☎ **441/295-0919**), and at Middle Road in Southampton (☎ **441/234-0629**). All locations are open daily from 8:30am to 5:30pm. Rentals require a $20 deposit and a supplemental charge of $15 for an insurance policy effective for the duration of your rental, or until you cause any damage to your rented vehicle.

BY BICYCLE

Looking for a more natural means of locomotion than a putt-putt? You can also rent bikes at most cycle liveries (see "By Cycle & Scooter," above), but for cyclists who don't work out 6 hours a day, pedaling a bike up those steep hills can be a bit of a challenge. Prices range from $10 to $15 a day, depending on your steed's brand name and degree of stylishness. (See "Biking," in chapter 6, for more details.)

BY BUS

You can't rent a car. Taxis are expensive. Horse-drawn carriages aren't really a viable option. You may not want to ride a bicycle or a motorbike. What's left for getting around Bermuda? Buses, of course.

All major routes are covered by the bus network, and nearly all hotels, guest houses, and restaurants have bus stops close by. There's even a do-it-yourself sightseeing tour by bus and ferry, and regularly scheduled buses go to most of the destinations that interest visitors in Bermuda—but be prepared for waits. And some buses don't run on Sundays and holidays, so be sure to find out about bus schedules for the trip you want to make.

Bermuda is divided into 14 zones of about 2 miles each. The regular cash fare for up to three zones is $2.50, or $4 for more than three zones. Using tokens, the fare is $2.25 for up to three zones, or $3.75 for more than three zones. Children 5 to 16 years pay $1 for all zones; those 4 and under go free. *Note:* You must have the exact change or tokens ready to deposit in the fare box as you board the bus, because drivers do not make change.

You can purchase tokens at subpost offices or at the **Central Bus Terminal** on Washington Street in Hamilton, where all routes, except Route 6, begin and end. The terminal is just off Church Street, a few steps east of City Hall. You can get there from Front Street or Reid Street by going up Queen Street or through Walker Arcade and Washington Mall.

If you plan to travel a lot around Bermuda, you might want to purchase a booklet of 15, 14-zone tickets for $24, or 15, 3-zone tickets for $15. For children, 15 tickets cost $6, regardless of the number of zones. You can also purchase passes that allow travel for 1 day to 1 month. A 1-day pass costs $10, a 1-week pass is $34, and a pass allowing travel for 1 month is $40.

For more information on bus service, call ☎ **441/292-3854.**

In the east, **St. George's Mini-Bus Service** (☎ **441/297-8199**) operates a minibus service around St. George's Parish and St. David's Island. The basic fare is $2. Although buses depart from King's Square in the center of St. George's, they can also be flagged down along the road. Service is year-round daily from 7:30am to 10pm. The service also offers historical tours of St. George's; the cost is $18 per person for the 1-hour tour.

BY FERRY

One of the most interesting means of getting around is via the government-operated ferry service. Ferries crisscross Great Sound between Hamilton and Somerset, charging $3.75 fare one way; they also take the harbor route, going from Hamilton to the parishes of Paget and Warwick, where so many hotels are concentrated. The ride from Hamilton to Paget costs only $2.25; children from 5 to 16 pay $1 (those 4 and under ride free). Motorcycles are allowed on the Hamilton-to-Somerset run; you must pay $3.75 for your cycle, however. Bicycles can be carried on free.

For ferry service information, call ☎ **441/295-4506** in Hamilton. Ferry schedules are posted at each landing, and they are also available at the Ferry Terminal or the Central Bus Terminal in Hamilton. Most hotels will also give you a timetable if you ask.

BY HORSE-DRAWN CARRIAGE

Once upon a time, this was the only way a tourist had to get around Bermuda. Before 1946 (when automobiles first came to the island), horses were the principal means of transportation. But the allure and appeal of the horse-drawn carriage has waned so much that only about a dozen are left. The drivers often seem a little bored hauling you around and don't take you to any unusual places, but along routes both the driver and the horses know only too well. You might find it a nice diversion if you try it once or twice, or if you book one of these four-wheeled rigs for a chauffeured tour of the island's midriff, but you won't miss out on a lot if you skip a ride.

Island-Hopping on Your Own

Most first-time visitors think of Bermuda as one island, when in fact it's a small archipelago. Many of the islands that make up the chain are uninhabited. If you're a bit of a skipper, you can explore them on your own. With a little guidance and armed with the proper maps, you can discover these islands as well as out-of-the-way coral reefs and hidden coves that seem straight of that old Brooke Shields B-movie, *The Blue Lagoon.*

For this boating adventure, rent a Boston whaler with an outboard engine. The romantic-sounding name of these small but sturdy boats reveals their origins: Such boats were once used by New Englanders in their pursuit of Moby Dick. Of course, it's important to exercise caution, remembering that Bermuda itself was found by the English in 1612 only after the *Sea Venture,* en route to the Jamestown Colony, was wrecked off the Bermuda coast.

In the East End, you can explore protected Castle Harbour, which is almost completely surrounded by islands forming a protected lake. If you stop to do some fishing, snapper is your likely catch. (Visitors who rent condos or apartments often take their catch of the day back to their kitchenette to prepare for dinner.) To avoid often-powerful swells, drop anchor on the west side of Castle Harbour, near Castle Harbour Golf Club and Tucker's Town. Then, head across Tucker's Town Bay to Castle Island and Castle Island Nature Reserve. In earlier days, Castle Island was fortified to protect Castle Harbour from enemy attack. In 1612, Governor Moore ordered a fort built there, the ruins of which remain today.

In the West End, it's best to begin your exploration by going under Somerset Bridge into well-protected Ely's Harbour. To the north, you can visit Cathedral Rocks before making a half-circle to Somerset Village; from here, you can explore the uninhabited islands off of Mangrove Bay.

You can rent a 13- to 15-foot Boston whaler—and pick up some local guidance—at **Mangrove Marina Ltd.,** at the end of Cambridge Road, Mangrove Bay, Somerset (☎ **441/234-0914**); **Blue Hole Water Sports,** at Grotto Bay Beach Hotel, Hamilton Parish (☎ **441/293-2915**); and **Rance's Boatyard,** Crow Lane, in Paget Parish (☎ **441/292-1843**). Charges begin at $60 for 2 hours; half-day rentals go from $85, and full-day rentals cost from $140.

Drivers congregate on Front Street in Hamilton, adjacent to the No. 1 passenger terminal near the cruise-ship docks. A single carriage (accommodating one to four passengers) drawn by one horse costs $40 for 30 minutes. An additional 30 minutes costs another $20. If you want to take a ride lasting more than 3 hours, the fee is negotiable. Unless you make special arrangements for a night ride, you aren't likely to find any carriages after 4:30pm. Contact **Terceira's Stables** at ☎ **441/236-3014.**

Fast Facts: Bermuda

American Express   The AmEx representative in Hamilton, **Meyer Agencies,** 35 Church St. (P.O. Box 510), Hamilton HM 12 (☎ **441/295-4176**), provides complete travel service, traveler's checks, and emergency check cashing.

Banks   Bermuda has three banks, all with their main offices in Hamilton:

The Bank of Bermuda Ltd., 6 Front St., Hamilton (☎ **441/295-4000**), has branches on Church Street, Hamilton; on Par-la-Ville Road, Hamilton; at King's Square, St. George's; and in Somerset.

The Bank of N.T. Butterfield & Son, Ltd., 65 Front St., Hamilton (☎ 441/295-1111), has several branches throughout the island, including one at St. George's and another at Somerset.

The Bermuda Commercial Bank Ltd. is at 44 Church St., Hamilton (☎ 441/295-5678).

All banks and their branches are open Monday to Thursday from 9:30am to 3pm, and on Friday from 9:30am to 4:30pm. All banks are closed Saturday, Sunday, and public holidays.

In addition, many of the big hotels will cash traveler's checks, and ATMs are all around the island.

Bookstores Bermuda Book Store (Baxters) Ltd., Queen Street, Hamilton (☎ 441/295-3698), stocks everything that's in print about Bermuda, including titles on gardening, flowers, local characters, poets, and other topics; some are available only through this store. There are also many English publications not easily obtainable in the United States, as well as a fine selection of children's books. You can also buy maps and prints here, as well as that beach novel you forgot to bring. Open Monday to Saturday from 8:30am to 5pm.

Business Hours Most businesses are open Monday to Friday from 9am to 5pm. Stores are generally open Monday to Saturday from 9am to 5pm; several shops open at 9:15am and close at 5pm. A few shops are also open in the evening, but usually only when big cruise ships are in port.

Car Rentals There are no car-rental agencies in Bermuda. For tips on available modes of transportation, see "Getting Around," earlier in this chapter.

Climate See "When to Go," in chapter 2.

Crime See "Safety," below.

Currency Exchange Because the U.S. dollar and the Bermudian dollar are on par, both currencies can be used (it's not necessary to convert U.S. dollars into Bermudian dollars). However, Canadian dollars and British pounds must be converted into local currency because of their differing valuations. For more information, see "Money," in chapter 2.

Customs For details on what you can bring into Bermuda and what you can carry home, see "Entry Requirements & Customs," in chapter 2.

Dentists For dental emergencies, call **King Edward VII Hospital**, 7 Point Finger Rd., Paget Parish (☎ 441/236-2345), and ask for the emergency department. They maintain lists of dentists on call for dental emergencies. One well-recommended dentist you might consider calling directly is **Dr. David Roblin**, Outerbridge Building, Pitts Bay Road, Pembroke Parish(☎ 441/292-7676).

Doctors In an emergency, call **King Edward VII Hospital**, 7 Point Finger Rd., Paget Parish (☎ 441/236-2345), and ask for the emergency department. A private doctor, **Dr. Gordon Campbell**, Sea Venture Building, Parliament Street, Hamilton (☎ 441/295-8106), will treat colds, the flu, and other medical problems.

Documents Required See "Entry Requirements & Customs," in chapter 2.

Driving Rules Visitors cannot rent cars. In the case of motor-assisted cycles, you must be age 16 or over to operate such vehicles. All cycle drivers and passengers must wear safety helmets that are securely fastened. Driving is on the left side of the road, and the speed limit is 20 m.p.h., 15 m.p.h. in busy areas.

Drug Laws Importation of, possession of, or dealing in unlawful drugs (including marijuana) is illegal in Bermuda; there are heavy penalties for infractions. Customs officers, at their discretion, may conduct body searches for drugs or other contraband goods.

Drugstores   In Hamilton, try **Bermuda Pharmacy,** in the Russell Eve Building, Church Street West, next to the bus terminal in Hamilton (☎ 441/295-5815). It's open Monday to Saturday from 8am to 6pm. Under the same ownership is the **Phoenix Drugstore,** 3 Reid St. (☎ 441/295-3838), open Monday to Saturday from 8am to 6pm, and Sunday 12 to 6pm.

In Paget Parish, you can go to **Paget Pharmacy,** 130 South Shore Rd. (☎ 441/236-7275), open Monday to Saturday from 8am to 8pm and on Sunday from 10am to 6pm. At 49 Mangrove Bay, the **Somerset Pharmacy** in Somerset Village (☎ 441/234-2484) is open Monday to Friday from 8am to 7pm, Saturday from 8am to 6pm, and Sunday from 11am to 4pm.

Electricity   Electricity is 110 volts AC (60 cycles). American appliances are compatible without converters or adapters. Visitors from the United Kingdom or other parts of Europe will need to bring a converter.

Embassies & Consulates   The **American Consulate General** is at Crown Hill, 16 Middle Rd., Devonshire (☎ 441/295-1342). They do not keep general business hours—rather, they have hours for specific services. It would be advisable to call before you go to find out if they're open for whatever service you need. Canadians can refer to the **Canadian Consulate General** (Commission to Bermuda), 1251 Avenue of the Americas, New York, NY 10020 (☎ 212/596-1600). Britain doesn't have an embassy or a consulate in Bermuda.

Emergencies   To call the police in an emergency, dial **911;** if you need to reach the police but it's not an emergency, dial ☎ 441/295-0011. To report a fire, dial 911; to summon an ambulance, call 911. For Air-Sea Rescue, dial ☎ 441/297-1010.

Etiquette   Well-tailored Bermuda shorts are acceptable on almost any occasion, and many men wear them with jackets and ties at rather formal gatherings. However, on such formal occasions, they must be accompanied by knee socks. Aside from that, Bermudians are rather conservative in their attitude toward dress—bikinis, for example, are banned more than 25 feet from the water. Men are usually required to wear a jacket to dinner.

Eyeglass Repair   **Argus Optical Company** (Henry Simmons, OD), Melbourne House, Parliament Street, Hamilton (☎ 441/292-5452), works with both prescription glasses and contact lenses. Hours are Monday to Friday from 9am to noon and 1 to 4:45pm.

Gasoline   Mopeds take a mixture of oil and gas, and there's always a separate pump at gasoline stations for these vehicles. Honda scooters require regular unleaded gasoline. The typical touring biker needs about one refill per week. Both Honda scooters and mopeds are rented with full tanks. Gasoline stations are conveniently situated around the island, and gas for cycles is $3 to $4 per gallon.

Holidays   See "When to Go," in chapter 2.

Hospitals   **King Edward VII Memorial Hospital,** 7 Point Finger Rd., Paget Parish (☎ 441/236-2345), has a highly qualified staff and Canadian accreditation.

Hotlines   Call ☎ 441/236-0224, ext. 226 or 227, for a consultation on psychiatric problems, but only Monday to Friday from 8:45am to 5pm. After 5pm, call ☎ 441/236-3770; you'll be connected to one of two island hospitals, either the Bermuda Psychiatric Hospital's outpatient clinic or (in the evening) St. Brendan's Hospital. Either can help with life-threatening problems, personal crises, or referral to a proper medical specialist.

Information   For information before you go, see "Visitor Information," in chapter 2; once you're on the island, see "Orienting Yourself: The Lay of the Land," earlier in this chapter.

Legal Aid   The U.S. consulate will inform you of your rights (limited) and offer a list of attorneys. However, the consulate's office cannot interfere with Bermuda's law-enforcement officers. One useful hotline in an emergency—useful for questions about U.S. citizens arrested abroad—is the **Citizens' Emergency Center** of the Office of Special Consular Services in Washington, DC (☎ 202/ 647-5225). They can also tell you how to send money to U.S. citizens arrested abroad.

Liquor Laws   Bermuda sternly regulates the sale of alcoholic beverages. The legal drinking age is 18, and most bars close at 1am. Some nightclubs and hotel bars can serve liquor until 3am. Many bars are closed on Sunday.

Hard liquor is sold in specialty stores selling liquor, beer, and wine. Although it's legal for grocery stores to sell hard liquor, beer, and wine, most grocery stores limit their inventories just to beer and wine. Alcohol can't be sold on a Sunday. You can bring beer or other alcohol to the beach legally, as long as your party doesn't get too rowdy and you generally stay in one spot. (The moment you actually *walk* on the beach or the streets with an open container of liquor, it's illegal. The thinking behind this law is apparently that roaming gangs of loud, obnoxious drunks are more dangerous and disruptive than sedentary gangs of loud, obnoxious drunks.)

Mail   Regular mail can be deposited in the red pillar boxes on the streets. You'll recognize them by the monogram of Queen Elizabeth II. The postage rates for airmail letters up to 10 grams and for postcards is 65¢ to the United States and Canada, 80¢ to the United Kingdom. Airmail letters and postcards to the North American mainland can take 5 to 7 days, and to Britain possibly a little longer. Often visitors return home before their postcards arrive.

Newspapers/Magazines   One daily newspaper is published in Bermuda, the *Royal Gazette.* Three weekly papers, the *Bermuda Sun,* the *Bermuda Times,* and the *Mid-Ocean News,* are issued on Friday. Major U.S. newspapers, including the *New York Times* and *USA Today,* and magazines such as *Time* and *Newsweek* are delivered to Bermuda on the day of their publication on the mainland. *This Week in Bermuda* is a weekly guide published for tourists.

Passports   See "Entry Requirements & Customs," in chapter 2.

Pets   If you want to take your pet with you to Bermuda, you'll need a special permit issued by the director of the **Department of Agriculture, Fisheries, and Parks,** P.O. Box HM 834, Hamilton HM CX, Bermuda (☎ 441/236-4201). Animals arriving without proper documents will be refused entry and will be returned to the point of origin, since there are no quarantine facilities in Bermuda. Some guest houses and hotels will allow you to bring in small animals, but others will not; so be sure to inquire about this in advance. You should always check to see what the latest regulations are before attempting to bring a dog or another pet into Bermuda, including Seeing Eye dogs.

Photographic Needs   If you want to buy a camera or film, or develop either Kodak or Fuji film, try **Stuart's,** 5 Reid St., near the corner of Queen Street (☎ 441/295-5496), Hamilton's leading camera store. Film can be developed in-house in about 3 hours (sometimes within 1 hour for a surcharge). Open Monday to Saturday from 9am to 5pm.

Police   In an emergency, call **911;** otherwise, call ☎ 441/295-0011.

Post Offices   The General Post Office, at 56 Church St., Hamilton (☎ **441/ 295-5151**), is open Monday to Friday from 8am to 5pm and on Saturday from 8am to noon. Post-office branches and the Perot Post Office, Queen Street, Hamilton, are open Monday to Friday from 9am to 5pm. Some post offices are closed for lunch from 11:30am to 1pm. Airmail service for the United States and Canada closes at 9:30am in Hamilton, leaving daily. See also "Mail," above.

Radio & TV   News is broadcast on the hour and half hour over AM stations 1340 (ZBM), 1230 (ZFB), and 1450 (VSB). The FM stations are 89 (ZBM) and 95 (ZFB). Tourist-oriented programming, island music, and information on activities and special events are aired over AM station 1160 (VSB) daily from 7am to noon.

The television channel, 10 (ZBM), is affiliated with America's Columbia Broadcasting System (CBS).

Rest Rooms   Hamilton and St. George's provide public facilities, but only during business hours. In Hamilton, toilets are located at City Hall, in Par-la-Ville Gardens, and at Albouy's Point. In St. George's, facilities are available at Town Hall, Somers Gardens, and Market Wharf. Outside of these towns, you'll find rest rooms at the public beaches, at the Botanical Gardens, in several of the forts, at the airport, and at service stations; but often you'll have to use the facilities in hotels, restaurants, and wherever else you can find them.

Safety   Bermudians are generally peaceful people, not given to violence. To be sure, the island has experienced racial tensions in the past, but right now relations between its white and black residents seem to be harmonious, as blacks assume a greater role in Bermuda's affairs.

Crimes, violent or otherwise, against tourists are rare, but don't be lulled into a false sense of security. Crime does exist in Bermuda, as it does in any society. Take care to protect your valuables, especially when you're at the beach. Lock your moped each time you leave it. If you bring very valuable items with you to Bermuda (this is not advisable), place them in your hotel safe and never leave them carelessly in your room.

Smoking   Tobacconists and other stores carry a wide array of tobacco products, generally from either the United States or England. Prices vary but tend to be high. At most tobacconists you can buy classic cigars from Havana, but you must enjoy them on the island, since they can't be taken back to the United States. Smoking in public places (such as restaurants) is generally permitted, but check first before lighting up. Movie theaters set aside a section for nonsmokers.

Taxes   Visitors to Bermuda are levied a Passenger Tax before departing from the island. For those who leave by air, the tax, collected at the airport, is $20 for adults or children (children under 2 are exempt). For those who leave by ship, the tax, collected in advance by the cruise-ship company, is $60 (children under 2 are exempt).

All room rates, regardless of the category of accommodation or the plan under which you stay, are subject to a government tax of between 6% (for simple guest houses) to 7.5% (for the large majority of Bermuda's conventional hotels).

Taxis   See "Getting Around," earlier in this chapter.

Telephone/Telegrams/Telexes/Faxes   Worldwide direct-dial phone, fax, and cable service is available at **Cable & Wireless Office,** 20 Church St., Hamilton (opposite City Hall). Prepaid phone cards may be purchased and used islandwide, and calling cards may be used from selected call boxes. Hours are Monday to Saturday from 9am to 5pm. For information, call ☎ **441/297-7022,** 24 hours.

Cable & Wireless, in conjunction with the Bermuda Telephone Co., provides international direct dialing (IDD) to more than 150 countries. Country codes and calling charges may be found in the latest edition of the Bermuda telephone directory. Telephone booths are available at the Cable & Wireless office, and customers can either prepay for their calls or purchase cash cards in $10, $20, and $50 denominations. Cash-card phone booths are available at numerous locations around the island. Making international calls with cash cards can be a lot cheaper than using the phone at your hotel, which might impose stiff surcharges. To make a local call, deposit 20¢, either Bermudian or U.S. Hotels often charge from 20¢ to $1 for local calls.

Special phones have also been installed at passenger piers in Hamilton, St. George's, and the dockyard that will connect you directly with an AT&T, Sprint, or MCI operator in the United States, thus permitting you to make collect or calling-card calls.

Telephone Directory   All Bermuda telephone numbers appear in one phone book, revised annually. The helpful yellow pages lists, in the back, all the goods and services you are likely to need.

Time   Bermuda is 1 hour ahead of Eastern standard time. Daylight saving time is in effect from the first Sunday in April until the last Sunday in October, as it is in the United States.

Tipping   In most cases, a service charge is added to your hotel and/or restaurant bill. In hotels, this is in lieu of tipping the various individuals such as the bellhop, maids, and restaurant staff (for meals included in a package or in the daily rate). Check for this carefully to avoid double-tipping. Otherwise, a 15% tip for service is customary. Taxi drivers usually get 10% to 15%.

Tourist Offices   See "Visitor Information," in chapter 2, and "Visitor Information on the Island," under "Orienting Yourself: The Lay of the Land," earlier in this chapter.

Transit Information   For information about ferry service, call ☎ **441/ 295-4506.** For bus information, call ☎ **441/292-3854.**

Useful Telephone Numbers   For time and temperature, call ☎ **977**-1. To learn "What's On in Bermuda," dial ☎ **974.** For medical emergencies or the police, dial ☎ **911.** If in doubt during any other emergency, dial ☎ **0** (zero), which will connect you with either your hotel's switchboard or the Bermuda telephone operator.

Water   Tap water is generally safe to drink.

Weather   This might be an all-important consideration for your Bermuda plans. In addition to consulting the newspaper and the radio, you can call ☎ **977** at any time of the day or night for a forecast covering the next 24-hour period.

Accommodations 4

Bermuda offers a wide choice of lodgings, ranging from small, casual guest houses to large, luxurious resorts. You'll find that facilities vary greatly in size and amenities within each category.

CHOOSING THE ACCOMMODATION THAT'S RIGHT FOR YOU

Accommodations in Bermuda basically fall into five categories:

- **Resort Hotels:** These generally large properties are Bermuda's best, offering many facilities, services, and luxuries—but also charging the highest prices, especially in summer. The lowest rates, usually discounted about 20%, are in effect from mid-November to March. The large resorts usually have their own beaches or beach clubs, along with swimming pools; some even have their own golf courses. It's cheaper to choose the modified American plan (MAP) rates (including breakfast and dinner) than to order all your meals à la carte. However, if you go the MAP route, you'll be confined to the same dining room every night and miss the opportunity to sample different restaurants.
- **Cottage Colonies:** This uniquely Bermudian option typically consists of a series of bungalows constructed around a clubhouse, which is the center of social life, drinking, and dining. The cottages, usually scenically arranged on landscaped grounds, are designed to provide maximum privacy and are typically equipped with kitchenettes for preparing light meals. In many of the cottage colonies, breakfast isn't available; you can either go out for breakfast or buy supplies the night before and prepare your own morning meal. Most of the colonies have either their own beaches or swimming pools.
- **Small Hotels:** For those who absolutely hate megaresorts, this option might be for you. Bermuda's small hotels offer the intimacy of an upscale bed-and-breakfast, but with considerably more facilities than you'd get at a B&B. At a small hotel, you'll feel more connected to the island and its people. Another plus? They're often cheaper than the big resorts.
- **Housekeeping Units:** These cottage or apartment-style accommodations (often called efficiencies in the U.S.) are generally situated on landscaped estates, around a main clubhouse. All of them offer kitchen facilities (perhaps a full and well-equipped

Bermuda's Hotels at a Glance

	Access for disabled	Directly beside the beach	On-site swimming pool	Restaurant on premises	Cable TV in bedroom	Fitness facilities	Access to golf nearby	On-site tennis courts	Convention facilities	Welcomes children	Childcare facilities	On-site spa facilities	Access to water sports	Accepts credit cards	Air-conditioned bedrooms	Live on-site entertainment	Wharf or marina facilities
Angel's Grotto	•			•		•			•			•	•	•		·	
Ariel Sands Beach Club		•	•	•			•	•		•	•		•	•	•	•	
Astwood Cove			•							•					•		
Barnsdale Guest Apartments			•		•					•				•	•		
Cambridge Beaches		•	•	•		•	•	•	•			•	•		•	•	•
Clear View Suites & Villas	•	•	•	•	•		•	•	•	•	•			•	•		
Dawkin's Manor			•	•						•				•	•		
Edgehill Manor			•		•					•					•		
Elbow Beach Hotel	•	•	•	•	•	•	•	•	•	•	•	•	•	•	•	•	
Fourways Inn			•	•	•		•		•					•	•		
Greenbank Guest House										•			•	•	•		•
Greene's Guest House			•		•		•			•					•		
Grotto Bay Beach Hotel	•	•	•	•	•	•	•	•	•	•	•		•	•	•	•	•
Hamiltonian Hotel & Island Club			•		•			•		•				•	•		
Harmony Club		•	•	•		•	•						•	•	•		
Hillcrest Guest House														•	•		
Horizons and Cottages			•	•			•	•		•	•				•	•	
Little Pomander Guest House	•				•		•			•			•	•	•		
Loughlands			•				•	•		•					•		
Marley Beach Cottages		•	•		•		•			•			•	•	•		
Marriott's Castle Harbour Resort	•		•	•	•	•		•	•	•	•		•	•	•	•	
Mermaid Beach Club		•	•	•						•			•	•			

	Access for disabled	Directly beside the beach	On-site swimming pool	Restaurant on premises	Cable TV in bedroom	Fitness facilities	Access to golf nearby	On-site tennis courts	Convention facilities	Welcomes children	Childcare facilities	On-site spa facilities	Access to water sports	Accepts credit cards	Air-conditioned bedrooms	Live on-site entertainment	Wharf or marina facilities
Newstead Hotel			•	•			•	•		•	•		•	•	•	•	•
Oxford House, The					•					•				•	•		
Palmetto Hotel & Cottages			•	•			•		•	•	•		•	•	•	•	•
Paraquet Guest Apartments				•	•		•			•					•		
Pink Beach Club & Cottages		•	•	•			•	•	•	•	•		•	•	•	•	
Pompano Beach Club		•	•	•		•	•	•	•	•	•		•			•	•
Princess, The (Hamilton)	•		•	•	•	•	•	•	•	•	•	•	•	•	•	•	•
Reefs, The		•	•	•	•		•	•	•	•	•	•	•	•		•	•
Rosedon			•		•					•				•			
Rosemont			•		•					•	•			•	•		
Royal Heights Guest House			•		•					•				•	•		
Royal Palms Hotel			•	•	•					•			•	•			
St. George's Club	•	•	•	•	•		•	•	•	•	•	•		•	•	•	
Salt Kettle House						•				•			•		•		•
Sandpiper Apartments			•		•					•				•	•		
Sky-Top Cottages						•				•				•	•		
Sonesta Beach Resort	•	•	•	•	•	•	•	•	•	•	•	•	•	•	•	•	
Southampton Princess	•	•	•	•	•	•	•	•	•	•	•	•	•	•	•	•	•
Stonington Beach Hotel		•	•	•			•	•	•	•	•		•	•	•	•	
Surf Side Beach Club		•	•	•	•		•		•	•			•	•	•		
Waterloo House			•	•				•	•			•	•	•	•	•	
White Sands Hotel & Cottages		•	•	•	•		•			•	•		•	•	•		

Bermuda Accommodations

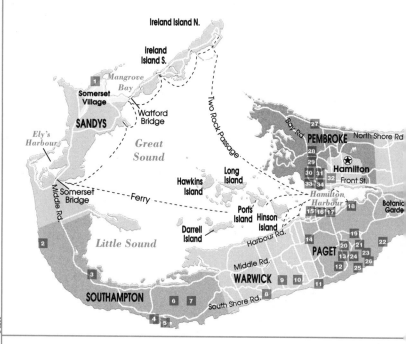

Angel's Grotto 38
Ariel Sands Beach Club 35
Aunt Nea's Inn at Hillcrest 43
Barnsdale Guest Apartments 23
Cambridge Beaches 1
Clear View Suites & Villa 36
Dawkin's Manor 13
Edgehill Manor 29
Elbow Beach Hotel 25
Fourways Inn 14
Greenbank Guest House 15

Green's Guest House 3
Grotto Bay Beach Hotel 41
Hamiltonian Hotel & Island Club 27
Harmony Club 19
Hillcrest Guest House 44
Horizons and Cottages 12
Little Pomander Guest House 18
Loughlands 21
Marley Beach Cottages 9
Marriott's Castle Harbour Resort 40
Mermaid Beach Club 8

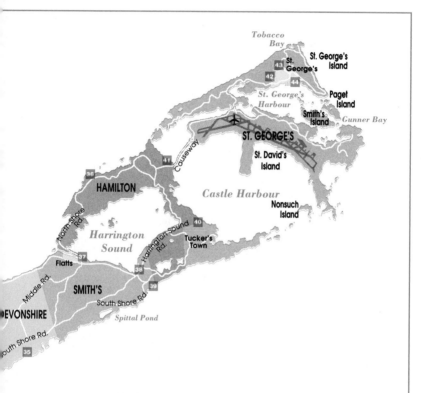

Atlantic Ocean

Airport ✈

| 0 | | 3 Mi |
| 0 | | 3 Km |

Newstead Hotel **17**

The Oxford House **32**

Palmetto Hotel & Cottages **37**

Paraquet Guest Apartments **24**

Pink Beach Club & Cottages **39**

Pompano Beach Club **2**

The (Hamilton) Princess **33**

The Reefs **4**

Rosedon **31**

Rosemont **30**

Royal Heights Guest House **6**

Royal Palms Hotel **28**

St. George's Club **42**

Salt Kettle House **16**

Sandpiper Apartments **10**

Sky-Top Cottages **20**

Sonesta Beach Resort **5**

Southampton Princess **7**

Stonington Beach Hotel **26**

Surf Side Beach Club **11**

Waterloo House **34**

White Sands Hotel & Cottages **22**

kitchen, but at least a kitchenette where you could whip up snacks and break-fast). Most offer minimal daily maid service.

- **Guest Houses:** These are Bermuda's least expensive accommodations. The larger guest houses are old Bermuda homes in garden settings. Generally, they've been modernized and have comfortable guest rooms. Some of them have their own swimming pools. A number of these guest houses are small, modest places, offering breakfast only; you may share a bathroom with other guests. If you stay in a guest house, you may have to "commute" to the beach.

Another option is renting a villa or vacation home. Renting a villa is like renting someone's home. At some you're entirely on your own; others provide maid service. Most tend to be on or near a beach. This is generally an expensive option.

Private apartments offer fewer frills than either villas or condos; the buildings housing the apartments may not have swimming pools, or even a front desk to help you. They're available with or without maid service.

Cottages, or cabanas, offer the most independent lifestyle in this category of vaca-tion accommodations, since they're entirely self-catering. Some open onto a beach, whereas others are clustered around a communal swimming pool. Most of them are fairly basic, consisting of just a simple bedroom plus a small kitchen and bathroom. For the peak summer season, you should make your cabana reservations at least 5 or 6 months in advance.

Several U.S. and Canadian agents can arrange these types of rentals. You might try **Rent-a-Home International,** 7200 34th Ave. NW, Seattle, WA 98117 (☎ **206/789-9377;** fax 206/789-9379; www.rentavilla.com), which specializes in condos and villas. They can arrange bookings for a week or longer.

RATES & RESERVATION POLICIES

The rates we've listed throughout this chapter are "rack rates"—that is, the rate you'd be quoted if you walked in off the street. These are helpful largely for pur-poses of comparison. Especially at the big resorts, almost no one ever pays the rack rates. By booking a package deal that includes airfare or by just asking for packages and discounts at the hotel when you make your reservation, you can usually do much better. (The rates we've given are much more likely to be accurate at the small hotels and guest houses.) Before you book anything, read the section "Package Deals," in chapter 2.

All room rates, regardless of the meal plan you've chosen, are subject to a 7.5% Bermuda tax, which will be tacked onto your bill. A service charge (ranging from 10% to 15%) is also added to your room rate in lieu of tips; remember that service charges do not cover bar tabs. Third-person rates (for those occupying a room with two other people) are lower, and children's tariffs vary according to their age. The rack rates we've listed in this chapter include tax and service charge unless otherwise noted. However, we strongly encourage you to confirm what the rates include when you make reservations, to avoid any misunderstanding. Hotels usually quote you the full rate you'll pay upon check-out; they don't want misunderstandings, either.

Bermuda's high season is spring and summer—the opposite of the Bahamian and Caribbean high season. Most of Bermuda's hotels start charging their high-season rates in March (Easter is the peak period) and bring their rates down again around mid-November. A few hotels have year-round rates, and others charge in-between, or "shoulder," prices in spring and autumn. If business is slow, many smaller places will shut down in winter.

You may see some unfamiliar terms and abbreviations used by Bermuda's hotels to describe their rate plans. **AP** (American Plan) includes three meals a day (sometimes called full board). **MAP** (Modified American Plan), sometimes called half-board, includes breakfast and dinner. **BP** (Bermuda Plan) includes a full American or English breakfast. **CP** (Continental Plan) includes only a continental breakfast (basically bread, jam, and coffee) in the room rate. **EP** (European Plan) is always cheapest, because it offers only the room, no meals.

Following is a rough guideline to the price ranges we've used, based on rates for standard double rooms with no meals included in high season (April to October), unless otherwise noted. Rates exclude government tax and service charges. In general, hotels are **very expensive** if they offer double rooms for $225 and up (and we do mean *up*). Hotels listed as **expensive** generally ask between $175 and $225 for a double; **moderate** rooms go for $125 to $175. Anything under $125 for a double qualifies as **inexpensive.**

Note that prices aren't uniform in several of the larger, older resorts, which tend to offer a wide range of rooms. For instance, one guest at the Elbow Beach Hotel might be paying a price that can be categorized as "moderate," whereas another might be booked at a "very expensive" rate—it all depends on your room assignment. So even if you can't pay $200 a night, it might be worth a call to see if a cheaper room is available.

Members of the Bermuda Hotel Association require 2 nights' deposit within 14 days of confirming a reservation; full payment 30 days before arrival; and notice of cancellation 15 days before scheduled arrival, or your deposit will be forfeited. Since some smaller hotels and other accommodations levy an energy surcharge, you should inquire about this when you make your reservations.

BOOKING LAST-MINUTE ACCOMMODATIONS

If you didn't have time to reserve a room before going to Bermuda, head to the **Visitors Service Bureau** at the airport (☎ **441/293-0030**). Located near Customs clearance and open from 10:30am to 5pm, the bureau can help you make a reservation. Unless you have a specific hotel reservation and a return airplane ticket, you will not be allowed to proceed beyond this point.

1 Resort Hotels

With their wealth of amenities, the big resort hotels can keep you so occupied that you may not feel the need to leave the premises (but make sure you resist the urge and venture out!). The large hotels typically have their own beaches or beach clubs and swimming pools; some even have their own golf courses. Most of these hotels also boast such luxury services and facilities as porters, room service, planned activities, sports facilities (such as tennis courts), shops (including bike shops), beauty salons, bars, nightclubs, entertainment, and taxi stands.

VERY EXPENSIVE
SOUTHAMPTON PARISH
✪ Sonesta Beach Resort

South Shore Rd., Southampton Parish (P.O. Box HM 1070), Hamilton HM EX, Bermuda. ☎ **800/766-3782** in the U.S., or 441/238-8122. Fax 441/238-8463. www.sonesta.com. 441 units. A/C MINIBAR TV TEL. May–Aug $280–$440 double, from $650 suite; Sept 1–Nov 15 and Apr $250–$400 double, from $650 suite; Nov 16–Mar $130–$250 double, from $350 suite. MAP (breakfast and dinner) $55 extra per person in high season, $45 in winter. Discount honeymoon and family packages available. AE, DC, MC, V. Bus: 7.

The Sonesta is Bermuda's only major luxury resort boasting access to three beaches, including Church Bay, 5 minutes away by bike. As a full-service hotel, only Elbow

Beach outclasses it. Built in the shape of a crescent, the resort is located on 25 acres of prime seafront property, curving along the spine of a rocky peninsula whose jagged edges provide ocean views. It boasts ample lengths of oceanside walkways. Those who are seeking Bermudian charm and character would probably prefer Cambridge Beaches, but spa-goers, honeymooners, and water-sports and beach buffs like this resort a lot. The resort also caters to families.

Shaped like a circle and flanked by limestone cliffs and sandy beaches, the bay fronting the Sonesta was used long ago by gunpowder smugglers, and later by rum-runners, who loved its well-camouflaged entrance. Encircled with palm-covered cabanas and bars and with a soft sandy bottom, the bay looks like a small corner of Polynesia transported onto the sands of Bermuda.

The resort was last renovated in 1996. Each room, equipped with a private terrace, offers a flowery kind of charm. Rooms are adorned with thick carpeting, high-quality light woods, louvered closets with private safes, and such extras as irons and ironing boards, along with electronic locks. Bathrooms are generous in size with tiled tub areas, hair dryers, and thick towels. Some open onto garden views, whereas more-expensive units front ocean or beach views. Some accommodations are set aside for nonsmokers and those with disabilities.

Dining/Diversions: The hotel has three restaurants, including Lillian's, an elegant restaurant serving northern Italian cuisine. There's also the bistro-style Boat Bay Club, as well as the Sea Grape, which offers alfresco dining overlooking Boat Bay. Both Lillian's and the Sea Grape are worthy choices, even if you're not staying at the hotel (see chapter 5 for complete reviews). Overall, the food is perfectly good here, if not truly gourmet or as excellent as that at the Southampton Princess. You'll never go thirsty at the Sonesta, since each of the three restaurants has a separate bar of its own. The one at the BBC (Boat Bay Club) is particularly fun, thanks to live entertainment almost every night: calypso music, jazz, merengue, or at least a deejay. There's also a jukebox and a row of big-screen TVs in Splits, the hotel's sports bar.

Amenities: The most complete spa facilities on the island, including massage and a range of beauty treatments (see "Spa Vacations," in chapter 2, for more details), outdoor swimming pool, indoor swimming pool, diving center for snorkelers and scuba divers, six tennis courts (two illuminated for night play), full-time tennis pro, room service, laundry, baby-sitting, children's program from May 1 until Labor Day.

✪ Southampton Princess

101 South Shore Rd. (P.O. Box HM 1379), Hamilton HM FX, Bermuda. ☎ **800/223-1818** in the U.S., 800/268-7176 in Canada, or 441/238-8000. Fax 441/238-8968. www.cphotels.ca. E-mail: reservations@cphotels.ca. 626 units. A/C TV TEL. Apr 9–May 1 and Sept 7–Nov 14 $290–$425 double; Nov 15–Apr 8 $165–$215 double; May 2–Sept 6 $330–$465 double. Suite from $540 in summer, from $320 off-season. AE, DC, MC, V. Private ferry from the Hamilton Princess.

This Princess, even more than the Hamilton Princess, deserves to be called royal, especially after its $2.5 million renovation. Sitting atop Bermuda's highest point, overlooking the ocean and bay and with its own good beach right in front of the hotel, it's the largest and most luxurious property on the island. It more than justifies its membership in "The Leading Hotels of the World." Several of its restaurants serve the best food of any Bermuda hotel, and its sports and facilities are among the island's finest. But even with all this praise, we don't think it's the place for those who want an intimate romantic hideaway; in fact, its biggest drawback is that it's a favorite with conventions and tour groups.

The hotel is decorated in an 18th-century English style, and all of its furnishings are well upholstered. The public rooms, situated on three floors, are connected by baronial staircases. The plush guest rooms are arranged in wings that radiate more or less symmetrically from a central core. This design gives each luxurious bedroom a private veranda with a sweeping view of the water; suites have a minibar. Bedrooms are generally spacious, with one king or two double beds. Most bathrooms are modest but contain thick towels and hair dryers. (The only complaint we've ever heard is from someone who checked in next door to a couple who "appeared to be in training for the Sex Olympics" and truly regretted not having more soundproofing!) Recently created was the Newport Club, a concierge service wing in the hotel, offering extra service and a private lounge equipped by a staff. This club offers a complimentary continental breakfast, newspapers, and the use of a fax and VCR.

Dining/Diversions: The Southampton Princess's cuisine is among the island's finest—so much so that we recommend several of the resort's restaurants even if you're not staying here (see chapter 5 for details). In general, it's all continental fare that's consistently pleasing. In an operation this large and with a catering so vast, especially when the house is packed with tour groups, it's hard to keep an eye on quality, but the Southampton Princess does admirably well. This is a mammoth operation, but the hotel has wisely broken down its dining into smaller and more intimate enclaves: One dining rooms is Windows on the Sound, a three-tiered palace that seems to combine London's Mayfair of the 1930s and New York's late, great Rainbow Room; through 20-foot-high arched windows, you can see the islands of Great Sound while you dine. Other choices include Wickets Brasserie & Cricket Club, Newport Room, Rib Room Steak House, Whaler Inn, and Waterlot Inn (see chapter 5 for more details). Nightlife is more staid here than at the Sonesta, and not every restaurant has a bar that's open to nondiners (the Waterlot Inn and the Whaler Inn do). The Lobby Lounge has live music, usually a jazz combo, beginning at 8pm; and the Neptune Club functions after 9:30pm either as a bar with live music or as a disco with recorded music.

Amenities: Guests who never want to leave enjoy a self-contained village of bars, restaurants, shops, and athletic facilities. Everyone's favorite pool is a re-creation of a Polynesian waterfall, with streams of heated water spilling from an artificial limestone cliff. You can swim here even during cold weather, thanks to the greenhouse constructed above. If you crave the salty waters of the sea, the hotel's beach is sheltered in a jagged cove, flanked by cliffs and studded with rocky outcroppings lashed by the tides. A shuttle bus transports guests to and from various hotel facilities, and hotel ferryboats make runs along Little Sound into Hamilton. Private beach club; outdoor pool; indoor pool; dive shop; par-3, 18-hole golf course; tennis; fitness center with spa facilities; room service; laundry; baby-sitting; beauty salon; moped rental; massages; children's program in summer.

The hotel runs a well-publicized **Dolphin Quest Interactive Program** that offers in-the-water encounters with Atlantic bottlenose dolphins on the beach. Within a 2-acre holding pen that's between 4 and 12 feet deep and separated from the open sea with underwater netting, the hotel keeps seven dolphins. There are four "Dolphin Experiences" scheduled each day (year-round, weather permitting, at 9 and 11am, and at 2 and 4pm), in which up to 10 swimmers (wearing conventional bathing suits in summer, wet suits in winter) cavort in the water with the dolphins for just under 30 minutes. People tend to take tons of pictures and buy lots of souvenirs (T-shirts saying "I played with the dolphins"). The price for adults is $85, for children under 16 it's $75. In winter, it's easy to get a slot, but in summer, there's so much demand that the hotel has a lottery system. Is all this cruel to the dolphins? The staff is rigorous about protecting and caring for the dolphins; the overall atmosphere is playful and light-hearted; and the dolphins have a largish area (2 acres) to swim in. But we can't help worrying that the continued contact with hordes of people and the dolphins' separation from their natural habitat must have something of a traumatizing effect on these beautiful animals. You decide for yourself.

PAGET PARISH

✪ Elbow Beach Hotel

60 South Shore Rd. (P.O. Box HM 455), Hamilton HM BX, Bermuda. ☎ **800/223-7434** in the U.S., or 441/236-3535. Fax 441/236-8043. 329 units. A/C MINIBAR TV TEL. Apr 10–Nov 1 $265–$445 double; from $520 suite; off-season $290–$340 double; from $425 suite. Packages available. Children 12 and under stay free when sharing rooms with adults. AE, DC, MC, V. Bus: 1, 2, or 7.

Elegant and commanding, this is the best full-service resort on the island, though it lacks the intimacy and local charm you'd find at a smaller place. Following a $42 million sprucing up—and that is one massive renovation—Elbow Beach reopened in February of 1999. The renovations have added a decidedly upscale colonial English gloss to the hotel, with miles of expensive chintzes and piles of reproduction antiques. It's very impressive. Elbow Beach appeals to vacationers who like everything under one roof (or at least on-site). Another advantage is the proximity to Hamilton, which is only 10 minutes away by taxi. It's set in 50 acres of gardens with its own quarter-mile pink-sand beach on the south shore. Long gone are the days when rowdy college students descended on this place as a party site at Easter.

You can choose from a wide array of rooms or suites, from bedrooms with balconies overlooking the water to duplex cottages; some lanai rooms overlook the pool and the Atlantic, whereas others are surfside. Many bedroom walls are draped in silk; bathrooms are Italian marble, and plumbing has been brought completely up-to-date. Bathrooms contain thick towels, hair dryers, and robes. The most spacious units are situated in low-rise buildings on terraces leading to the sands; the least desirable rooms open onto a heavily trafficked corridor on the lobby floor.

Dining/Diversions: The cuisine here has never been better; a culinary team—a sort of "dream team" in the kitchen—has been brought in to wake up the taste buds of diners. The current chefs have worked at some of the grandest dining rooms of the world, ranging from Atlanta's Ritz-Carlton to the restaurants of California's Wolfgang Puck. All guests, including those on MAP, may choose dinner at either of the hotel's two restaurants—each enjoys an ocean view—or from one outdoor theme party nightly. The main dining room, The Seahorse Grill, is the most formal of the restaurants. At Café Lido, the resort's beachfront restaurant, the kitchen focuses on seafood with a Mediterranean accent. The resort also participates in a "dine around" program with several Hamilton restaurants; hotel guests can eat at a participating restaurant and charge their meals to the resort.

After dinner, festivities continue with "bamboo dancing," or limbo. Every Sunday, a lively Elbow Beach Party and barbecue is held on the resort's pink-sand beach, featuring music and entertainment.

Amenities: Five all-weather tennis courts (two lit for night play), a large swimming pool, game room, health club with exercise room and whirlpool, water sports (including deep-sea fishing and windsurfing), room service, baby-sitting, laundry, beauty salon, moped rental, children's program.

Package Deals

Refer to the "Package Deals" section of chapter 2 before you call these resorts yourself. Buying a package is really the way to go; you can save hundreds of dollars over what you'd pay if booking your hotel and airfare separately.

PEMBROKE PARISH (CITY OF HAMILTON)
The Hamilton Princess
76 Pitts Bay Rd. (P.O. Box HM 837), Hamilton HM CX, Bermuda. ☎ **800/223-1818** in the U.S., 800/268-7176 in Canada, or 441/295-3000. Fax 441/295-1914. 413 units. A/C TV TEL. Apr 18–Nov 13 $225–$375 double, $1,150 suite. Off-season $165–$250 double, from $265 suite. MAP $55 per person in summer, $45 in off-season. AE, DC, MC, V. Bus: 7 or 8.

This hotel, which is often said to resemble a wedding cake, is situated just a short distance from downtown Hamilton, on the edge of Hamilton Harbour. This location is ideal save one major drawback: There is no nearby beach. The closest, Elbow Beach, is a 20-minute taxi ride or 45-minute bicycle ride from the hotel. The easily accessible ferry delivers guests to the Southampton Princess, however, and sun lovers can get their fill at the sandy stretch there. The lack of a beach at the Hamilton Princess hasn't kept the glitterati away: Often called the Hamilton Princess, this is the hotel of choice for Hollywood and European movie stars, as well as the yachting set, having hosted a roster of visitors ranging from Mark Twain to Michael Jackson (quite a stretch!).

Opened in 1887 and named for Princess Louise (Queen Victoria's daughter), this Princess is far more staid than its cousin in Southampton (see above) and doesn't even attempt to offer the roster of activities available at Elbow Beach, so the young and the restless might want to book elsewhere. This is the flagship of the Princess Hotel chain, and it's certainly the one with the most history: British intelligence officers stationed here during World War II worked to crack secret Nazi codes.

The colonial core is flanked by modern wings, each of which is pierced with row upon row of balconied loggias. The property was designed around a concrete pier that extends into the harbor, near which lies a Japanese-style floating garden. The botanical theme is repeated in the lobby. In 1996, management renovated the well-decorated guest rooms and public salons, making a good property even better. Many of the rooms have private balconies; each was designed "to create the feeling that you'd choose the same kind of bedroom if you owned a home here." Most of the tiled bathrooms are generous in size, with good towels and hair dryers. Some 40% of the guests are repeat visitors.

Dining/Diversions: The hotel has a wide array of bars and restaurants. For a complete look at what kind of food to expect, see the reviews of the Tiara Room, Harley's, and the Colony Pub Steak House in chapter 5; also see The Gazebo Lounge in chapter 10.

Amenities: Frequent ferryboat service to and from the Southampton Princess, weather permitting; laundry; room service; baby-sitting; heated freshwater swimming pool; unheated saltwater swimming pool; water-aerobics classes; dive shop (an independent concessionaire); moped rental; access to tennis, sailing, white-sand beaches, and golf at the Southampton Princess. The hotel's fitness center, usually open daily from 6am to 9pm, features an exercise room with extensive exercise equipment, massage area, saunas, and showers.

HAMILTON PARISH
✪ Marriott's Castle Harbour Resort
2 South Rd. (P.O. Box HM 841), Hamilton HM CX, Bermuda. ☎ **800/223-6388** in the U.S. and Canada, or 441/293-2040. Fax 441/293-8288. 420 units. A/C TV TEL. Apr–Oct $239–$310 double, suites from $900; Nov–Mar $99–$135 double, suites from $700. MAP (breakfast and dinner) $52 extra per person. AE, DC, MC, V. Bus: 1.

All the conventions and groups that book here find a completely self-contained resort, almost rivaling the Southampton Princess or Elbow Beach—and Castle Harbour has a more traditional Bermudian feel and is the best hotel for sports on the island. It has access to two small nearby beaches, plus a private beach on the south shore.

Originally built in the 1920s of coral blocks on a hilltop overlooking Castle Harbour and Harrington Sound, this property had fallen into disrepair before Marriott undertook a $60 million renovation late in 1986 (rooms were renovated again from 1995 to 1996). The public areas are some of the most elegant on the island. The most glamorous room in Bermuda is the 18th-century salon, which is straight out of an English country house: Filled with copies of Chippendale and Queen Anne furniture and sheathed with mahogany paneling, it's a showplace. Adjacent is an elegant dining room, with chinaware duplicating the original 1920s Castle Harbour china. The 250 acres of prime real estate surrounding the resort are maintained by at least 50 gardeners.

Several buildings house accommodations on the property. The guest rooms are typically furnished with good replicas of traditional English furniture. Rooms have good mattresses and such extras as hair dryers, massaging showerheads, and good-size vanities to spread out your stuff. Towels are thick and the housekeeping is excellent. Some accommodations are reserved for nonsmokers and those with disabilities. Most accommodations also have balconies or private terraces.

Dining/Diversions: The hotel has five restaurants: the Mikado (reviewed in chapter 5), the more formal Windsor Room, the Golf Club Grill, Café Cascade, and the Terrace Café. The food is consistently good here—not innovative, but simply delicious dishes, prepared with some of the best ingredients available in Bermuda. The cafe food here is more for convenience than culinary fanfare. For after-dark entertainment, there's a disco, Blossoms.

Amenities: Massages, laundry, baby-sitting, room service, beauty salon, well-equipped and upgraded health club (free to guests), 18-hole Castle Harbour Golf Course, six tennis courts, three pools (one Olympic size), full water-sports complex.

EXPENSIVE
HAMILTON PARISH

✪ Grotto Bay Beach Hotel

11 Blue Hole Hill, Hamilton CR 04, Bermuda. ☎ **800/582-3190** in the U.S., 800/463-0851 in Canada, or 441/293-8333. Fax 441/293-2306. 201 units. A/C TV TEL. Apr–Oct $195–$210 double; Nov–Mar $95–$97 double. Suites from $350 year-round. MAP (breakfast and dinner) $48 extra per person. AE, MC, V. Bus: 1, 3, 10, or 11.

This resort, unattractively located across from the airport, appeals to young couples and families who don't expect all the activities of a resort like Elbow Beach. The sprawling, 21-acre property is made up of 11 three-story (no elevator) balconied buildings with sea views. If you're assigned a room far from the main building, you may think you've been sentenced to Siberia. All accommodations, which were last renovated in 1996, are equipped with safes and average-size bathrooms with hair dryers and good-sized towels. The best rooms are directly on the beach, though they're at the bottom of a serpentine flight of about 30 masonry steps—no big deal for guests of average fitness but a drawback for anyone with limited mobility, who might opt for ocean-view, but not ocean-fronting, rooms instead.

The resort (named after its subterranean caves) is lushly planted with tropical fruit trees. A sandy but mediocre beach nearby offers a view of an unused series of railroad pylons, leading onto forested Coney Island across the bay. From the seaside, the airy public areas look like a modernized version of a mogul's palace, with big windows, thick white walls, and three peaked roofs with curved eaves.

Dining/Diversions: The restaurant serves pretty fair if unremarkable continental cuisine, enlivened by fresh seafood. That about sums it up. There's also a poolside restaurant that offers lunch and theme barbecues. Nightly live entertainment is provided in the Rum House Lounge, and a handful of other bars are on the property. Afternoon tea is served every day, and there's a daily happy hour.

Amenities: The swimming pool, which has been blasted out of natural rock, is ringed with serpentine edges, much like a grotto. Nature walks, twice-weekly "cave crawls," daily cave swims, complete program for children in summer, frequent tennis clinics, daily Jazzercise in the Rum House Lounge before breakfast, scavenger hunts, communal croquet near the bar, fish feeding, bridge competitions, organized activities for teenagers, laundry, room service, baby-sitting, excursion boat, small health club, scuba diving, snorkeling, swimming pool with swim-up bar, Jacuzzi, four tennis courts (two lit for night play), and nearby golf course.

2 Small Hotels

In contrast to the sprawling luxury and first-class resort hotels are Bermuda's more intimate, informal small hotels. Many of them have their own dining rooms and bars, and some even have their own beaches or beach clubs; all of them offer pools and patios.

VERY EXPENSIVE
SOUTHAMPTON PARISH

✪ Pompano Beach Club
36 Pompano Beach Rd., Southampton SB 03, Bermuda. ☎ **800/343-4155** in the U.S. and Canada, or 441/234-0222. Fax 441/234-1694. www.pompano.com. E-mail: Pompano@ ibl.bm. 54 units. A/C TV TEL. May 1–Nov 14 $360–$390 double, from $370 suite. Apr $295–$325 double, $305 suite. Off-season $230–$260 double, from $240 suite. Packages available. Rates include MAP (breakfast and dinner). AE, MC, V. Hamilton ferry to Somerset.

This place is for those seeking a personal, friendly welcome—something impossible to come by at a megaresort. It attracts both younger and older couples who want privacy and tranquillity; golfers especially like this place. The Pompano Beach Club was Bermuda's first fishing club when it opened on the southwest shore in 1956; today, it's one of the most delightful smaller hotels on the island, owned and operated by the Lamb family, who give it lots of personality. The setting is lovely, perched on the side of a limestone hill, virtually surrounded by the Port Royal Golf Club and opening onto a beach. Years ago, stepped terraces were cut in the hill to accommodate the "Pompano pink" buildings of this well-maintained property.

From the terraced beach below the clubhouse, water lovers can walk waist-deep along a clean sandy bottom for the length of 2½ football fields before reaching deep water. The renovated accommodations provide great water views; each of the hillside villas scattered over the landscaped property is equipped with either a balcony or a terrace. Accommodations are decorated in a tropical motif, often with rattan pieces, and contain such extras as private safes, irons and ironing boards, robes, and hair dryers. All of them have good, firm mattresses and thick towels.

Dining/Diversions: The cuisine served in the Cedar Room is international. In general, the food is first-rate here, prepared by chefs who try to bring as much variety to the menu as they can; a team of five prepares each dish. Menus change daily, so you never get bored, even if you dine here nightly: One evening we were treated to a terrific dish of shrimp sautéed in a coconut ginger sauce, the next night we enjoyed a freshly made pasta that evoked some of the finest of Italy. The hotel has one of the island's best pastry chefs (if you can get the recipe for that delectable peach mousse, be sure to send it to us). The hotel also maintains a dine-around plan with four other small Bermuda hotels. Mealtime is relatively informal; jackets and ties for men are required only 3 nights a week. There's also a British-style pub where you can watch the sun set over the ocean.

Amenities: Freshwater heated swimming pool, ocean and poolside Jacuzzi, four all-weather tennis courts (two lit), fitness center, on-site moped rental, easy access to the government-owned Port Royal Golf Course, Sunfish and Windsurfer rentals, laundry, baby-sitting.

The Reefs

56 South Shore Rd., Southampton SN 02, Bermuda. ☎ **800/742-2008** in the U.S. and Canada, or 441/238-0222. Fax 441/238-8372. www.thereefs.bm. E-mail: reesbda@ibl.bm. 75 units. A/C TEL. Apr 18–Nov 6 $348–$418 double, $378–$968 suite. Off-season $226–$296 double, $256–$646 suite. Rates include MAP (breakfast and dinner). AE, MC, V. Bus: 7.

Not as refined, but also not as stuffy, as Horizons or Cambridge Beaches, The Reefs is one of the most state-of-the-art inns on the island, with top-notch maintenance, first-class personal service, and unmatched ocean views. This "lanai colony" on Christian Bay is arranged along a low coral ridge; the cluster of salmon-pink cottages faces a private beach of pink-flecked sand surrounded by palm trees and jutting rocks. The lanais are decorated in rattan and island colors, and all come with private sundecks and ocean views. The decor is bright and cheerful, with florals and striped fabrics complementing rattan pieces. Accommodations have private safes, good firm beds, and small bathrooms with separate dressing areas and dual basins.

Dining/Diversions: You can dine either in the plant-filled Terrace Dining Room or alfresco under the swaying palms at Coconuts. In the more formal main dining room, the staff is attentive. Continental and North American cuisine is the focus here. The chefs concentrate on bringing out the food's natural flavors; they don't overpower your taste buds with extra sauces and gimmicks. You'll find classic favorites such as Black Angus filet mignon, juicy prime rib, and rack of lamb. We like their wine list, especially those excellent but well-priced Chilean bottles we're becoming increasingly fond of. If you want to let your hair down a bit, opt for Coconuts instead; there's no finer or more romantic spot in Bermuda for an alfresco sunset dinner than this beach terrace. The chefs here use the world for inspiration, from Thailand to the United States. Their codfish cakes are without equal on the island. If you're game for wahoo, order it grilled here; there's usually nothing better among the catch of the day. The main clubhouse, with its beam-ceilinged lounge, offers entertainment 7 nights a week in summer, ranging from calypso to pub-style sing-along favorites.

Amenities: Kidney-shaped swimming pool, situated on a ledge with an ocean view; two all-weather tennis courts; moped and mountain-bike rental; fitness center; laundry; baby-sitting.

PAGET PARISH

Harmony Club

South Shore Rd. (P.O. Box 299), Paget PG BX, Bermuda. ☎ **888/427-6664** or 441/236-3500. Fax 441/236-2624. www.harmonyclub.com. E-mail: harmby@ibl.bm. 68 units. A/C TV TEL. Mar–Apr and Nov $425–$435 double; May–Oct $575 double; Dec–Feb $415 double. Rates include all meals and drinks, activities, taxes, and service. AE, DC, MC, V. Bus: 7, 8, or 27. No children under 18 accepted.

This is Bermuda's only all-inclusive hotel—you'll know exactly what your vacation will cost in advance. It's for couples only; however, the couple can be any combination of gender or age (over 18). Elbow Beach, the closest beachfront, is a 15-minute walk or a 5-minute scooter ride away. Named after the circa 1830 home of a 19th-century merchant that stood on the site, this hotel retains only a few vestiges of its original historic core but tries to keep the friendly informality of a private home. It was renovated in 1997.

The accommodations, furnished in Queen Anne style, are located in a series of rambling pink-sided wings that encircle formal gardens with gazebos. Those near the road tend to be somewhat noisy. Units are generous in size with sitting areas and double or king beds with firm mattresses along with oversize closets. Bathrooms have tub/shower combinations and sport good towels.

Dining/Diversions: If you stay here, you're locked into dining here for all your meals, since you're paying for an all-inclusive plan. The chefs are competent if not dazzling. However, there's such a wealth and variety of food here that you're almost certain to find something you like. Evening meals are served by candlelight on fine china and crystal in the Casuarina. A full English tea is served every afternoon; there are also weekly cocktail parties and entertainment 6 nights a week.

Amenities: Laundry, moped rental, freshwater swimming pool, whirlpool, two tennis courts, Jacuzzis, two saunas, unlimited use of a double-seat motor scooter (one per couple) during a week's stay. Putting green on-site, and free greens fees at nearby Belmont golf course.

Newstead Hotel

27 Harbour Rd. (P.O. Box PG 196), Paget PG BX, Bermuda. ☎ **800/468-4111** in the U.S. and Canada, or 441/236-6060. Fax 441/236-7454. 50 units. A/C TV TEL. Apr 1–May 31 $303–$395 double; June 1–Jan 4 $326–$415 double; Jan 5–Mar 31 $285 double. Suite $390–$450 year-round. Rates include MAP (breakfast and dinner). AE, MC, V. Ferry from Hamilton.

Overlooking Hamilton Harbour, the Newstead is a Bermudian landmark, attracting an older crowd of mainly repeat visitors who wouldn't think of staying anywhere else. The original house accommodated only 12 guests when it opened in 1923, but today there's room for 107 visitors. Owned by a local family, this is one of the very best small resorts in Bermuda. The place is dignified and refined—definitely not for hell-raisers.

Part of the property, Lyndham, was the former home of Sir Richard and Lady Fairey; long ago, it expanded to include several adjoining properties, comprising what is now a waterfront resort on a flowering hillside. The ancestral home has become the social hub. The setting is traditional, with drawing rooms, a library, and lounges, furnished in part with English antiques. It's a true country-house flavor, accented with many informal touches. Traditionalists prefer old-fashioned rooms of the main house, but you can also opt for up-to-date comforts in the more contemporary bungalows. All the accommodations have traditional decor, including gleaming brass and polished woods. Most rooms have twin beds and tiled bathrooms, complete with dressing area; the newer units are also equipped with double sinks. The least desirable rooms in the main house have older bathrooms and may be subject to street noise. The most luxurious option is the modern poolside units, with furnished terraces, comfortable sitting rooms, and king-size beds.

The hotel opens onto its own beach, and guests also have access to Coral Beach Club, a 15- to 20-minute walk away, or a 10-minute bike jaunt. From the estate, it's a 10-minute ferry ride to Hamilton.

Dining/Diversions: The Harbour Room is solid and reliable, with respectable cuisine. You get straightforward fare here, not innovation—just what the guests coming here are looking for. Fresh, quality ingredients are used whenever possible, and chefs concentrate on good cookery instead of theatrical flair. MAP guests can either dine here or participate in the dine-around plan involving two other hotels. There's an outdoor terrace, where you can enjoy waterside barbecue buffets, rum-swizzle parties, calypso music, and dancing, according to the season. Newstead also operates Brellas, a casual dining spot overlooking Hamilton Harbour.

Amenities: Swimming pool (you can also swim from two private docks), sauna room, two clay tennis courts, guest privileges at the Coral Beach Tennis Club, on-site putting green, use of the 9-hole mashie golf course at Horizons, room service, laundry, baby-sitting.

Stonington Beach Hotel

South Shore Rd. (P.O. Box HM 523), Hamilton HM CX, Bermuda. ☎ **800/447-7462** in the U.S. and Canada, or 441/236-5416. Fax 441/236-0371. www.bermuda.best.com/StoBeach/. E-mail: bav@triton.bercol.bm. 64 units. A/C TV TEL. May 1–Oct 31 $398–$440 double; Nov 1–Apr 15 $246–$280 double; Apr 16–30 $346–$385 double. Rates include MAP (breakfast and dinner). AE, MC, V. Bus: 7.

This place near Elbow Beach is operated by the Hospitality and Culinary Institute of Bermuda, whose headquarters and classrooms are located atop a nearby knoll. It's a bit offbeat, but, training ground or not, it's still a good choice, with a gracious atmosphere and welcoming service. Stonington is smart, neat, modern, angular, almost corporate looking, lacking softness and a sense of tradition, which some visitors will like more than others. Some of the employees are students who are supervised by a professional international staff. The students are likely to be more helpful than many battle-trained, jaded personnel in the hotel field, but if you're looking for mistakes you'll no doubt find them.

A lamplit drive leads you through the greenery and up to the buff-colored facade, where you'll follow a stucco passageway to an inner octagonal courtyard graced by a palm tree. The reception area is high-ceilinged, its dark pine beams alternating with white plaster. The accommodations are situated in four outlying buildings; a complete renovation was done in 1994. The rooms are comfortably spacious, equipped with either a wide balcony or a patio offering ocean views. Done in blue and yellow, the rooms have ceiling fans, small refrigerators, and love seats that could serve as an extra folding bed. You reach the hotel's sandy beach via steps cut through foliage and limestone.

Dining/Diversions: The library, with its glowing fireplace, is most inviting, as is the restaurant and bar, the Norwood Room (see chapter 5 for a complete review). In the unlikely event you don't like the food served here, the hotel has a dinner exchange program with four surrounding properties (so you can check in with the knowledge that you won't be trapped every night on MAP in the same dining room if it doesn't suit you).

Amenities: Freshwater swimming pool, two tennis courts, business center, access to a nearby fitness center, room service, laundry, baby-sitting.

White Sands Hotel & Cottages

55 White Sands Rd., Paget Parish PG BX, Bermuda. ☎ **800/548-0547** in the U.S., 800/228-3196 in Canada, or 441/236-2023. Fax 441/236-2486. www.white-sands-bermuda-co. E-mail: wsands@ibl.bm. 40 units. A/C TV TEL. Apr 1–Nov 15 $301–$356 double; Nov 16–Mar 31 $226–$266 double. Rates include MAP (breakfast and dinner). AE, MC, V. Bus: 7 or 8.

For years, honeymooners and families have sought out this rather British hotel, which still evokes the period when it was built, the 1950s, although it's constantly being upgraded and improved. Comprising a compound of salmon-colored buildings amid terraced gardens, it's just a short walk downhill to a wide, semiprivate beach with exceptionally fine sand at Grape Bay. Of all the hotels on Bermuda's south shore, this one is the closest to Hamilton—just a 10-minute ride by taxi or bus.

The rooms are furnished with wall-to-wall carpeting, large closets, small refrigerators, a radio, a coffeemaker, and comfortable beds with firm mattresses. Each room is spacious, airy, and bright, and generally decorated with modern furniture. Especially noteworthy is tower room 222, whose five oversized windows provide an

Accommodations in the City of Hamilton

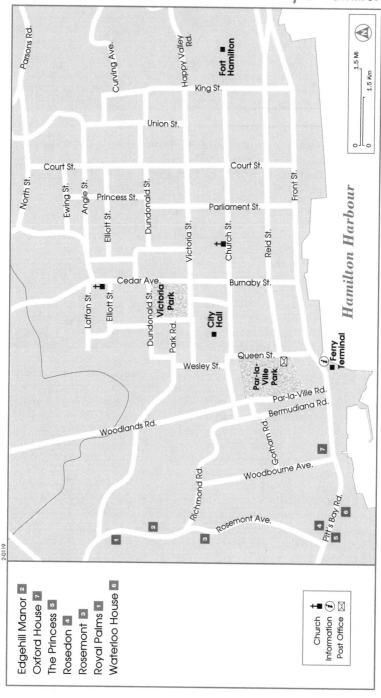

Edgehill Manor 2
Oxford House 7
The Princess 5
Rosedon 4
Rosemont 3
Royal Palms 1
Waterloo House 6

Church ✝■
Information ⓘ
Post Office ⊠

2-0119

77

eagle's-nest view of the surrounding shoreline. In addition to the rooms in the main building, there are several two- and three-bedroom cottages.

Dining/Diversions: Much of the food here is what you'd expect at an upscale British hotel—solid, reliable fare, not daring at all, but consistently prepared with decent ingredients. There's a convivial atmosphere in the eating and drinking facilities here that seems to make the sometimes-bland fare have more zest. A formal but relaxed dining room, The Captain's Table, is outfitted in a colonial English motif. Lunch is served at the Terrace Club poolside restaurant. There's also an English-inspired pub, the Sandbar.

Amenities: Room service at breakfast and dinnertime (8 to 8:45am and 7 to 8:30pm); baby-sitters available with advance notice; a heated freshwater swimming pool; easy access to tennis, golf, and water-sports facilities at nearby south-shore hotels; moped rentals.

PEMBROKE PARISH (CITY OF HAMILTON)
Waterloo House

Pitts Bay Rd. (P.O. Box HM 333), Hamilton HM BX, Bermuda. ☎ **800/468-4100** in the U.S. and Canada, or 441/295-4480. Fax 441/295-2585. www.bermudasbest.bm. E-mail: waterloo@ibl.bm. 30 units. Apr–Nov $260–$450 double, from $500 suite; Dec–Mar $190–$310 double, from $400 suite. Rates include full breakfast; MAP (breakfast and dinner) $36 extra per person. AE, MC, V. Bus: 1, 2, 10, or 11.

On the edge of Hamilton Harbour in Pembroke Parish (just on the outskirts of town) is this enlarged and remodeled private home (ca. 1910). Terraced gardens descend to the water in the Italian Riviera style; behind salmon-colored walls, the gardens are filled with palms, magnolias, poinsettias, urns overflowing with ivy, a splashing fountain, and white wrought-iron garden furniture shaded with fringed parasols.

Inside, the drawing room is furnished with English antiques and decorative tile floors. The bedrooms vary in size and decoration; each evokes the feeling of a country-house guest room. Most guest rooms and public areas were upgraded in 1997. A newer wing offers small studios and twin-bedded units. All rooms have firm mattresses and generous towels. The highest prices are charged for the five cottages, which have living and dining areas and refrigerators (though no kitchens).

Dining/Diversions: The main dining room, overlooking the terrace and harbor, is graced with Queen Anne chairs (for a complete review, see chapter 5). On the lower terrace level is a bar lounge with Moorish arches, English armchairs, and handwoven pillows. You can enjoy afternoon tea on the lawn at the water's edge.

Amenities: There are nooks for drinks and sunbathing around the property, and shade trees stand at the edge of an open-air, freshwater swimming pool. You'll also find a private dock, a waterside barbecue area, and a terrace for rum-swizzle parties. The hotel isn't on a beach, but guests enjoy privileges at the members-only Coral Beach and Tennis Club, 4 miles from Hamilton, where the pink sands and protected waters create some of the best swimming conditions on the island.

EXPENSIVE
PAGET PARISH
Rosedon

Pitts Bay Rd. (P.O. Box HM 290), Hamilton HM AX, Bermuda. ☎ **800/742-5008** in the U.S. and Canada, or 441/295-1640. Fax 441/295-5904. E-mail: rosedon@ibl.bm. 43 units. TV TEL. Apr–Nov $188–$260 double; off-season $138–$198 double. Rates include full breakfast and afternoon tea. Extra person $35. AE, MC, V.

If you shun megahotels (such as the Hamilton Princess across the street), Rosedon may appeal to you. Housed in a stately 1906 mansion, it's big on local charm and character. The staff is helpful, polite, and a real pleasure to be around. Although its rates are rather high for what it is—basically, an overblown guest house—it has its fans. Business travelers often stay here because of its proximity to Hamilton.

Rosedon resembles a colonial-era plantation Great House, with a pristine white exterior and royal-blue shutters. The house is surrounded by extensive gardens and lawns. Look for the loquat tree, a Bermuda trademark; other shrubs include hibiscus, banana plants, and bird of paradise. Once occupied by an English family, this was the first house in Bermuda with gaslights. The formal entry hall is dominated by an open staircase and a midway landing window; there are two antique-filled lounges. You can sit on a flagstone terrace under parasol-shaded tables around a large temperature-controlled pool.

The individually decorated bedrooms come with private bathrooms and refrigerators. The modern veranda rooms in the back, called lanai suites, open onto a pool; there are also air-conditioned colonial-style rooms in the main house.

Dining/Diversions: The honor system prevails at Nigel's Bar. The full breakfast included in the rates is good and plentiful, with plenty of variety even if you stayed a week. It can also be delivered to your room. There's afternoon tea, but no restaurant, so you'll have to eat your meals out.

Amenities: You'll find access to tennis courts, and free round-trip shuttle service to the sands at Elbow Beach (10 min. away), plus a swimming pool.

SMITH'S PARISH

Palmetto Hotel & Cottages

Harrington Sound Rd. (P.O. Box FL 54), Flatts FL BX, Bermuda. ☎ **800/982-0026** in the U.S., or 441/293-2323. Fax 441/293-8761. 42 units. A/C TEL. Apr–Oct $170–$190 double, $210 cottage; off-season $140–$160 double, $180 cottage. Rates include continental breakfast. MAP $32 per person per night. Special packages available. AE, MC, V. Bus: 10 or 11.

The Palmetto, located on Harrington Sound about 4½ miles east of Hamilton, is especially popular among couples and young families. This was once the ancestral home of the Tucker family, whose son, Teddy, became famous in the 1950s for dredging up treasures from 17th-century wrecked ships. The exteriors of the main building, the cottages, and the outbuildings are pink; the main building's reception area is paneled in Bermuda cedar. There are 26 double rooms in the main building; the remaining units are in separate cottages, all providing views of the water. The guest rooms are attractively furnished in a bright, cheerful resort style, with tropical furnishings. They contain twin beds with firm mattresses, along with tiled bathrooms that are average in size but supplied with generous towels. Some of the bathrooms have showers only (no tubs). The more expensive units have refrigerators.

There's a raised beach beside the sound, with access for both swimming and snorkeling in the sandy-bottomed bay. The hotel also provides transportation to two nearby beaches, one on the south shore and one on the north shore, both just 5 minutes away.

Dining/Diversions: Dinner can be taken on an à la carte basis or booked for your entire stay at the MAP rate; MAP is a much better value if you don't mind eating all your meals at the hotel. The Inlet Restaurant overlooks the moon gate, which frames a view of Harrington Sound (see chapter 5 for a complete review). The Ha' Penny Pub is a darkly intimate hideaway with big windows behind the dark-grained bar. Afternoon tea is served.

Amenities: Transportation to nearby beaches, laundry service, baby-sitting, swimming pool overlooking the water.

MODERATE
Pembroke Parish (City of Hamilton)

Hamiltonian Hotel & Island Club

Langton Hill (P.O. Box HM 1738), Hamilton HM GX, Bermuda. ☎ **800/441-7087** or 441/295-5608. Fax 441/295-7481. 32 1-bedroom units. A/C TV TEL. Apr–Nov $156 double. Off-season $88 double. AE, MC, V.

Set on a hill less than a mile northwest of Hamilton, this is a quiet, relatively simple hotel that markets its rooms as timeshare units. Don't expect a particularly cozy reception—think of it as an anonymous getaway from the pressures of urban life, with no particular facilities for dining or partying. Accommodations are divided among four pink-sided, stone-roofed apartment-style buildings, and are clean, comfortable, and well maintained, with good beds and average-size bathrooms. A small corner within each of them contains a microwave, small refrigerator, coffeemaker, and toaster—by no means a comprehensive kitchen, but fine for whipping up a snack. There are three tennis courts on the premises (two of which are lit for night play), and a swimming pool set on a plateau about 15 steps uphill from the rest of the complex.

3 Cottage Colonies

These accommodations are uniquely Bermudian. Each colony has a main clubhouse with a dining room, lounge, and bar, plus its own beach or pool. The cottage units, spread throughout landscaped grounds, offer privacy and sometimes luxury. Most have kitchenettes suitable for beverages and light snacks, but not for full-time cooking.

If you were a travel agent, and three women showed up named Brooke Astor, Barbara Walters, and Goldie Hawn, you'd book them as follows: the blue-blooded, aristocratic Astor into Cambridge Beaches; the media star and social denizen Walters into Horizons; and the actress/producer/comeback kid Hawn into Ariel Sands.

VERY EXPENSIVE
Sandys Parish

Cambridge Beaches

30 Kings Point Rd., Sandys MA 02, Bermuda. ☎ **800/468-7300** in the U.S., 800/463-5990 in Canada, or 441/234-0331. Fax 441/234-3352. www.cambridgebeaches.bm. 105 units. A/C TEL. Apr 16–Oct $400–$560 double, $600 suite, $1,275 cottage for 4; Nov–Feb $255–$360 double, $415 suite, $825 cottage for 4; Mar–Apr 15 $330–$465 double, $500 suite, $1,025 cottage for 4. Rates include MAP (breakfast and dinner). MC, V. Bus: 7.

With an ambience even more refined than that at Horizons and a selection of five private palm-fringed beaches, Cambridge Beaches attracts rich honeymooners, old-money families who live off stocks and bonds, and Vanity Fair couples who seek privacy, pampering, and plenty of facilities. If you're a first-time visitor, the clubby atmosphere here may make you feel like an outsider. No doubt about it, Cambridge Beaches is numero uno in Bermuda for snob appeal, followed by Horizons. Saudi royalty, who could afford to stay anywhere, naturally elect Cambridge Beaches when in Bermuda. If you bring your children (that is, those under 5), make sure they show up with a nanny—it's a house rule.

On a peninsula overlooking Mangrove Bay in Somerset, the colony's 25 acres of semitropical gardens and green lawns occupy the entire western tip of the island. Everything is centered around an old sea captain's house. The main lounges are tastefully furnished with antiques; the dominant feeling here is that of a country estate. Scattered throughout the gardens are nicely furnished, pink-and-white units, some of which are nearly 300 years old and retain their distinct Bermudian architectural features, but with an added British starchiness. All of the cottages (some of which were once private homes) are conservatively furnished and color-coordinated, and come with sun-and-breakfast terraces, generally with unobstructed views of the bay and gardens. A cottage can comfortably house four. One-fourth of the rooms are refurbished annually.

The colony also boasts a wealth of water-sports programs, equipment, and facilities, including a full marina with Boston whalers and various sailboats available for both self-piloted rentals and guided sailing excursions.

Dining/Diversions: Dining is in the excellent and very pricey Tamarisk Dining Room (see chapter 5 for a complete review), or on the terrace, where barbecues are sometimes held. There's also an informal lounge, the Port O' Call Pub, with nightly entertainment during the high season.

Amenities: Three all-weather tennis courts; putting green; Robert Trent Jones–designed golf course, Port Royal, just minutes away; temperature-controlled pool. Water sports include windsurfing with instruction, canoeing, kayaking, snorkeling, and fishing (equipment is available); parasailing, sailing, and snorkeling trips, plus glass bottom–boat excursions and fishing voyages are available. Adjacent to the colony are two bone-fishing flats. The full-service European-style spa features exercise equipment, whirlpool, massages, steam, sauna, and hair dressing, plus 50-odd types of skin, beauty, and relaxation treatments. Room service, laundry.

PAGET PARISH

Horizons and Cottages

33 South Shore Rd., Paget PG, Bermuda. ☎ **800/468-0022** in the U.S. and Canada, or 441/236-0048. Fax 441/236-1981. 46 units. A/C TEL. Mar 15–Jan 4 $310–$720 double; off-season $236–$540 double. Rates include MAP (breakfast and dinner). No credit cards. Bus: 2 or 7.

Both of Bermuda's top cottage colonies—Cambridge Beaches and Horizons—are popular with a well-heeled crowd, and each is characterized by subdued sophistication, though Horizons is perhaps a touch less snobbish. At Horizons, families with big bank accounts predominate in summer, and there's a mature repeat clientele in winter; trust-fund honeymooners are likely to show up year-round. Sometimes the atmosphere here is like a discreet house party, with fellow guests regularly being introduced. You might find more privacy, anonymity, and seclusion at Cambridge Beaches.

Horizons and Cottages have at their core a converted manor farm (ca. 1690), where the traditional ambience remains. A Relais & Châteaux member, Horizons is situated on a 25-acre estate with terraced gardens and lawns, atop a hill overlooking Coral Beach, a 10-minute walk away; this lack of a beach might be a serious drawback for some visitors (especially at these prices). The reception rooms of the manor house have old Bermudian architectural details, as well as antiques from England and the Continent; several drawing rooms have open fireplaces.

All guest units are handsomely furnished with Italian terra-cotta tile floors, scatter rugs, traditional tray ceilings, and ceiling fans. Accommodations all have separate dressing areas, as well as private terraces overlooking the ocean. Some units are split-level. Minibars and TVs are available on request. Medium-size tiled bathrooms are furnished with hair dryers, oversize mirrors, and thick towels.

Dining/Diversions: The main dining room, the Middleton Room, serves French *cuisine naturelle,* using all fresh products. The food, especially the tender steak and fresh seafood dishes, is exceptional for Bermuda, although the chefs at

---

ⓘ Family-Friendly Accommodations

Elbow Beach Hotel *(see p. 70)*   Children stay free in parents' room at this hotel, one of the best full-service resorts on the island. Your best bet is the "Family Value Package," which includes accommodations, transfers, daily breakfast buffet, and a host of activities and extras; inquire about it when you book.

Grotto Bay Beach Hotel *(see p. 72)*   A longtime family favorite, this hotel features a heavily discounted "Family Special" for two adults and two children under 16, requiring a minimum stay of 4 nights.

Southampton Princess *(see p. 68)*   This giant resort offers the best children's program on the island, including parties and reliable baby-sitting services. Children 16 and under stay free in a room with one or two adults and receive a complimentary breakfast and dinner daily.

Sandpiper Apartments *(see p. 87)*   Families looking for a moderately priced vacation might check in here. Some of the units have living/dining areas with two double pull-out sofa beds that will work for kids. Each unit is also equipped with a kitchen where Mom and Dad can prepare simple meals to cut down on the high cost of dining out in Bermuda.

Rosemont *(see p. 88)*   Rosemont caters to families, and each of its units contains a kitchen. Some of the rooms can be joined together to accommodate larger broods. Baby-sitting can also be arranged.

Cambridge Beaches seem to work more magic. See chapter 5 for a full review. You can enjoy lunch on the terrace; in the evening, it's transformed into an entertainment area, with informal dancing and often calypso music. Lunch and dinner, by reservation, can be exchanged at Newstead and Waterloo House.

Amenities: 9-hole golf course, 18-hole putting green, tennis courts, heated freshwater swimming pool, room service, laundry, baby-sitting.

DEVONSHIRE PARISH

Ariel Sands Beach Club

34 South Shore Rd., Devonshire (P.O. Box HM 334), Hamilton HM BX, Bermuda. ☎ **800/468-6610** in the U.S., or 441/236-1010; call collect from Canada. Fax 441/236-0087. www.arielsand.bm. E-mail: ariel@ibl.bm. 47 units. A/C TV TEL. May–Oct $340–$720 double; Nov–Mar $200–$510 double; Apr $230–$550 double. Rates include breakfast. MAP (breakfast and dinner) $40 extra per person. AE, MC, V. Bus: 1.

Secluded at the ocean's edge, with a sandy beach just a 2-minute walk away, Ariel Sands has long been one of the best cottage colonies in Bermuda. This is a quiet place, much in demand by well-heeled families looking for a summer retreat. The grounds are well landscaped, with flowering trees and coconut palms; one of the most original sculptures on the island is the namesake resort's stainless-steel statue of Ariel (created by Seward Johnson, Jr.), who dances like a water sprite on the surf. The hotel is owned by the mother of actor Michael Douglas (and ex-wife of film legend Kirk Douglas).

The resort was last refurbished in 1996. In chilly weather, a double-hearth fireplace warms a reception lounge and a conservatively attractive bar area. The smallish accommodations, with private entrances, offer a simple but attractive decor of white walls, Bermudian flower paintings, and bentwood furniture; most have private porches as well. The art in many of the private and public rooms here is based on themes from *The Tempest,* and guest rooms have names such as Miranda's Cabana, Sea Nymph, and Prospero. Room interiors, including the upholstery, have been saturated in cool pastel shades, including periwinkle blue and pistachio green, colors that are unmistakably Bermudian. Accents include straw matting on terra-cotta floors, walls adorned with local shells and coral, and glossy white Chinese Chippendale bamboo furnishings.

Dining/Diversions: Very respectable international cuisine is served in Calibans. Think country-club dining room—not exceptional, but decently prepared—and that's a pity, since Devonshire Parish doesn't have great restaurants. During the season, a local calypso band often entertains.

Amenities: Oval freshwater pool, rectangular saltwater pool whose waters are replenished daily by the tides, three tennis courts (two lit for night games), room service (at mealtimes only), laundry, baby-sitting.

SMITH'S PARISH
Pink Beach Club & Cottages
South Shore Rd. (P.O. Box HM 1017), Hamilton HM DX, Bermuda. ☎ **800/355-6161** in the U.S., or 441/293-1666. Fax 441/293-8935. www.pinkbeach.bm. E-mail: info@pinkbeach.bm. 91 units. A/C TEL. Apr 1–Nov 15 $350–$495 double; off-season $260–$350 double. Rates include MAP (breakfast and dinner). AE, MC, V. Closed Dec 14–Mar 2. Bus: 1.

This remotely located cottage colony, the largest on Bermuda, doesn't have the opulence or flair of Cambridge Beaches or Horizons, but it does attract an affluent international crowd. Its 16-acre garden setting is graced with bay grape trees and hibiscus bushes, and its pink cottages are surrounded by two private south-shore beaches. The staff, among the best on the island, includes many people who have been with Pink Beach since it began in 1947. The cottages range from studios with combination bedroom/sitting rooms, bathroom, and patio to full units with living room and terrace. Contemporary furnishings, fully equipped kitchens, and plush carpeting add to the allure of the place, along with medium-size combination bathrooms and generous towels. The more expensive units contain two double beds and bathrooms with hair dryers.

Dining/Diversions: The heart of the colony is the pink-painted limestone clubhouse, with its natural-wood dining room, where "backyard" vegetables and fresh seafood are used for the international cuisine. Every table provides a view of the ocean and the south-shore breakers. You might spot the occasional celeb dining here. The food is well-prepared if not outstanding. The chefs strive for variety, but you might find dining here every night a bit monotonous if you're booked in on MAP. Breakfast here is a special treat; request it the night before and a maid will arrive to serve you on your private terrace.

Amenities: Large saltwater pool, sun terrace, two tennis courts, laundry, baby-sitting. There are two championship golf courses just 2 minutes away from the hotel.

ST. GEORGE'S PARISH
St. George's Club
Rose Hill (P.O. Box GE 92), St. George's GE BX, Bermuda. ☎ **441/297-1200.** Fax 441/297-8003. www.stgeorgeclub.bm. 69 cottages. A/C TV TEL. Apr–Oct $350 cottage for up to 4, $550 cottage for up to 6; Nov–Mar $175 cottage for up to 4, $250 cottage for up to 6. AE, DC, MC, V. Bus: 6, 8, 10, or 11.

Far less stuffy than the cottage colonies listed above, this resort, encompassing 18 acres atop Rose Hill (off York Street), features clusters of traditionally designed Bermudian one- and two-bedroom cottages that were completely renovated in

1996. A family or two or three couples traveling together can afford these cottages and bring the price down to more reasonable level. A shuttle bus takes guests to the beach club at Achilles Bay, about a 2-minute ride away. The complex functions primarily as a timeshare property; units are rented to the public when the owners are not using them. The cottages come with private balconies or patios, comfortable living and dining areas, fully equipped kitchens, and bathrooms with sunken tubs and marble vanities; they have views of the ocean, the pool, or the golf course.

Dining/Diversions: The colony's elegant restaurant, Margaret Rose, is open to the public; it's among the finest dining rooms in the whole East End. The Sir George Pub is also a popular rendezvous spot.

Amenities: Laundry, baby-sitting, three freshwater swimming pools (one is heated), and three all-weather tennis courts (two can be lit at night). Golfers receive preferential tee time at reduced rates on the adjacent Robert Trent Jones–designed 18-hole golf course. There's a convenience store, the Ample Hamper, at the clubhouse.

MODERATE
HAMILTON PARISH
Clear View Suites & Villas

Sandy Lane, Hamilton Parish. ☎ **800/468-9600** in the U.S. or Canada, or 441/293-0484. Fax 441/293-0267. www.bermuda-online.com/clearview.htm. 30 units. A/C TV TEL. Year-round rates $156–$214 double. MAP $37 extra per person per day. AE, DC, MC, V. Bus: 10 or 11.

Set adjacent to a grassy and rock-strewn patch of seafront, Clear View offers units that feature kitchenettes and a good deal of privacy. Set midway between Hamilton and St. George's, it's a cluster of one- and two-story concrete buildings erected during the 1970s, with between two and six units each, and each of which is painted a soft shade of Bermuda pink. Inside, the decor includes summery, pastel-colored upholsteries, tiled surfaces, and big windows. Prices vary according to whether you get a sea view. The centerpiece of the resort is a white-sided farmhouse, site of the establishment's restaurant and bar. You can swim in the ocean here if you want, but there's no sandy beachfront. Most guests head a mile west to the sands of Shelly Bay Beach. There are a swimming pool and a tennis court on the premises, and a small art gallery that displays the works of local painters. Ruth Paynter, and to a lesser degree her husband, Gerald, arrange art classes that are popular among the island's community of retirees.

4 Housekeeping Units

Housekeeping apartments, Bermuda's efficiency units, vary from modest to superior. Most are equipped with kitchens or kitchenettes and provide minimal daily maid service. Housekeeping cottages, which are all air-conditioned and have fully equipped kitchens or least kitchenettes, offer privacy and casual living either on or close to a beach.

VERY EXPENSIVE
WARWICK PARISH
Mermaid Beach Club

South Shore Rd. (P.O. Box WK 250), Warwick WK BX, Bermuda. ☎ **800/441-7087** in the U.S. and Canada, or 441/236-5031. Fax 441/236-8325. 50 units (26 with kitchens). A/C TEL. Apr–Oct $236 double, $276–$390 apt with kitchenette; off-season $130 double, $150–$260 apt with kitchenette. AE, MC, V. Bus: 7.

Unlike some of Bermuda's stiff, snobby resorts and hotels, this place is informal, attracting both older and younger couples who want to have a good time without having to dress up too often. Set beside a curved shoreline that has both rocky cliffs and a sandy beachfront, this complex is made up of two-story cement-sided buildings, the outgrowth of a beach club founded in the 1940s. All units were built with patios or balconies overlooking the sea. Bedrooms are simple and summery, decorated with pastel colors and rattan furniture. The units with kitchenettes will be fine for whipping up salads and sandwiches but are too small for anything more ambitious. You'll need to take a cab or ride a moped to pick up groceries (there's a minimart in a Shell gas station that's a 15-min. walk, or a 2-min. ride by moped from the hotel, and a more substantial market that's about an 8-min. moped ride away).

Dining/Diversions: There are a snack bar and a main bar (outfitted in a nautical theme), plus a restaurant called the Jolly Lobster (as the name suggests, it offers pretty straightforward but fresh seafood).

Amenities: A curved swimming pool is situated on a terrace above the beach. There's also a bike-rental shop.

PAGET PARISH
Fourways Inn

1 Middle Rd. (P.O. Box PG 294), Paget PG BX, Bermuda. ☎ **800/962-7654** in the U.S. and Canada, or 441/236-6517. Fax 441/236-5528. 10 units. A/C MINIBAR TV TEL. Apr–Oct $230 double, $325–$555 suite; off-season $150 double, $190–$340 suite. Extra person $40. Rates include continental breakfast; MAP (breakfast and dinner) $42.50 extra per person. AE, MC, V. Bus: 8. No children under 16 accepted.

This posh little place really feels like a secret hideaway. Pink-sided, airy, and stylish, these Bermudian cottages were erected in the well-maintained gardens of one of the best restaurants on the island, the Fourways Inn Restaurant (see chapter 5). The sands of Elbow Beach and Mermaid Beach lie within a 15-minute walk (or a 5-min. scooter ride). The main building is a former private home dating from 1727. Each of five suites consists of two bedrooms, a patio, a private safe, a fully equipped kitchenette, conservatively comfortable furniture, satellite TV, and lots of extra touches. Their kitchenettes here are more viable than those at Mermaid Beach, but still, they're better suited to sandwiches and snacks than anything too ambitious. There's a medium-sized grocery store across the road.

Amenities: Communal heated swimming pool.

EXPENSIVE
WARWICK PARISH
Marley Beach Cottages

South Shore Rd. (P.O. Box PG 278), Warwick PG BX, Bermuda. ☎ **800/637-4116** in the U.S., or 441/236-1143. Fax 441/236-1984. www.bermudahotels.com. E-mail: ejensen@ibl.bm. 13 cottages. A/C TV TEL. Apr 15–Oct $180–$260 double; Mar 15–Apr 14 and Nov 1–Jan 2 $145–$200 double; Jan 3–Mar 14 $105–$155 double. Extra person $28. No credit cards. Bus: 2 or 7.

If you're two couples traveling together, this may be your best bargain. These pink-walled cottages accommodating four were erected on a steep but beautifully landscaped plot of land atop a low cliff on the south shore, near Astwood Park, that was used for scenes in *The Deep* and *Chapter Two*. More recently, part of another film, *Bermuda Grace*, was shot there. Three narrow beaches lie at the bottom of the slope that leads to the sea. It's not the most ideal place for children, since there's little for them to do, other than enjoy the pool or beach. Parents who do bring the kids are also warned to keep a close eye on them, because of the steep drop-off to the beaches below. We wouldn't recommend this place for anyone with mobility problems who might have a problem with the steps leading down the cliff to the ocean (guests of reasonable fitness won't mind a bit).

The spacious cottages offer sea views from the patio and come with fully equipped kitchens and hibachis. Each cottage has both a suite and a studio apartment, which you can rent as one unit or two, depending on your needs. Guests can either eat out or prepare their own meals. You can either personally place a phone order to a local grocery that delivers, or give a handwritten list to the staff, who'll phone in your order. There's no delivery charge for orders over $20.

Amenities: Curved, heated freshwater swimming pool, and whirlpool.

Surf Side Beach Club

South Shore Rd. (P.O. Box WK 101), Warwick WK BX, Bermuda. ☎ **800/553-9990** in the U.S., or 441/236-7100. Fax 441/236-9765. www.bermuda.bm/surfside. E-mail: surf@ibl.bm. 37 units. A/C TV TEL. Apr–Oct $185–$215 double, $260–$325 for up to 4; off-season $115–$145 double, $170–$220 for up to 4. Extra person $25. Off-season discounts available for extended stays. AE, MC, V. Bus: 7.

The Surf Side Beach Club is terraced into a steeply sloping hillside that descends, after passing through gardens, to a crescent-shaped sweep of private beachfront. (The steps down to the beach may be hard for mobility-impaired guests to manage.) The property was redesigned nearly 25 years ago and still maintains a varied array of flowering trees and panoramic walkways. The stonemasons added several lookout points in the garden, where visitors can see grouper and other fish swimming among the distant rocks of the shallow sea.

Accommodations consist of one-bedroom apartments near the terrace pool, as well as other lodgings in hillside buildings. The self-contained units are simple and sunny, outfitted in bright colors and comfortable accessories. Each has a fully equipped kitchenette (English china, wineglasses, even salt and pepper shakers), and a local grocery accepts phone orders and will deliver right to your unit (with no charge for orders over $20). The apartments also have private balconies or patios; some have sitting rooms as well. Ten units are equipped with showers only, the rest with tub/shower combos.

Dining/Diversions: For those who need an occasional break from preparing their own meals, there is also a small cafe that serves breakfast and lunch during the high season. The beach club recently launched a new restaurant and bar, Palms, with a menu, both American and international, that is changed daily.

Amenities: Pool and hot tub, fitness center, sauna, and laundry facilities.

MODERATE
WARWICK PARISH

✪ Astwood Cove

49 South Shore Rd., Warwick WK 07, Bermuda. ☎ **800/637-4116** in the U.S., or 441/236-0984. Fax 441/236-1164. 20 apts. A/C TEL. Apr 1–Nov 15 $120–$150 double; Nov 16–Mar 31 $80–$94 double. No credit cards. Bus: 7.

Nigel (Nicky) and Gabrielle (Gaby) Lewin own this homestead, which was built in 1720 on a dairy farm. The house bears the name of the three Astwood sisters (Maude, Ada, and Mary), who stipulated in their will that it should always carry their moniker. The apartment complex enjoys a peaceful setting, overlooking lightly wooded meadows and the south shore. The closest large beach, Long Bay, is a quarter of a mile away; however, Astwood's Beach and Mermaid Beach are only a 3-minute stroll from the complex.

Each of the 20 self-contained, air-conditioned units has a shower (no tubs), free local calls, a ceiling fan, and a terrace or porch. Some units have sitting rooms, and all have kitchens or kitchenettes equipped with English china. Most of the kitchens are generously proportioned units with conventional stoves, microwaves, and the basic accessories you'd need to prepare a real meal. A few of the smaller units, however, have just microwaves and stovetop burners, so ask when you reserve if you're planning to cook. There's a minimart less than 2 miles away. A competing grocery store, somewhat farther away, will deliver orders over $20. A building was added in 1985 with a communal terrace and pavilion, a TV, and an exercise machine. Additional features include a sauna, a freshwater swimming pool, and gas-fired barbecue grills.

Sandpiper Apartments

South Shore Rd. (P.O. Box HM 685), Hamilton HM CX, Bermuda. ☎ **441/236-7093.** Fax 441/236-3898. www.bda.hotel.ibl.bm. 14 units. A/C TV TEL. Apr–Oct $130 double, $170–$200 suite for 3 or 4; off-season $78 double, $93–$106 suite for 3 or 4. AE, MC, V. Bus: 7.

Built in 1979 and frequently upgraded, this apartment complex is a bargain for Bermuda. Nine of the units are studios for one or two people: each has two double beds in the bedroom, a small bathroom, and a fully equipped kitchenette that would suffice for making simple meals. Five of the units are made up of a bedroom (with king-size or twin beds), a kitchen, a bathroom, and a living/dining area with two double pull-out sofa beds. All the apartments come with radios, balconies, and daily maid service. The Sandpiper is only minutes away from restaurants and the supermarket. The closest beach is 500 yards away; there are an outdoor whirlpool and a swimming pool for relaxation, as well as gardens for lounging on the property.

PAGET PARISH

Barnsdale Guest Apartments

2 Barnes Valley. Paget PG03. Bermuda. ☎ **441/236-0164.** Fax 441/236-4709. www.bermudamall.com E-mail: barnsdal@ibl.bm. 7 units. A/C TV TEL. Summer $130 double; $155 triple; $185 quad. Off-season $90 double; $100 triple; $120 quad. AE, MC, V. Ferry to Hamilton.

This small apartment complex may not be cozy, but you'll get a clean, fairly priced hideaway. It's a neutrally decorated, unremarkable, modern-looking building. If you like to feel anonymous and independent when you're on vacation, it'll suit you. The setting lies within a 15-minute scooter or taxi drive of Elbow Beach, on a 1-acre site in a quiet residential neighborhood overlooking a banana grove. The peach and green-trimmed concrete structure sits on grounds that feature a rectangular swimming pool and a barbecue pit. Furnishings are durable but unexciting. All units have attractive, well-accessorized kitchenettes where you can actually prepare a moderately ambitious meal. There's a grocery store, with its own liquor department, within a 2-minute walk.

✪ Paraquet Guest Apartments

South Shore Rd. (P.O. Box PG 173), Paget PG BX, Bermuda. ☎ **441/236-5842.** Fax 441/236-1665. 12 apts. A/C TV. Apr–Oct $137.50 double without kitchen, $176 double with kitchen; Nov–Mar $126.50 double without kitchen, $148.50 double with kitchen. No credit cards. Bus: 7.

If you're looking for a bargain and are happy with clean but rather motel-like accommodations, this is the place for you. This buff-colored collection of Bermudian houses, landscaped into a gentle knoll, is a 5-minute walk from Elbow Beach, and a 10-minute bus ride from Hamilton. Built in the mid-1970s, the complex is owned by the Portuguese-born Correia family. Nine of the units are equipped with kitchenettes that are attractive and compact but efficient, filled with the basic cooking equipment you'd need to prepare a meal. There's a grocery store within 50 yards of the hotel, making shopping easy. All units have maid service and functional modern furniture. The focal point here is the decently priced restaurant, Paraquet Restaurant; see chapter 5 for a complete review.

PEMBROKE PARISH (CITY OF HAMILTON)

✪ Rosemont

41 Rosemont Ave. (P.O. Box HM 37), Hamilton HM AX, Bermuda. ☎ **800/367-0040** in the U.S., 800/267-0040 in Canada, or 441/292-1055. Fax 441/295-3913. E-mail: rosemont@ ibl.bm. 37 units. A/C TV TEL. Apr–Nov $140–$220 double; Dec–Mar $110–$114 double. Rates do not include service and taxes. MC, V.

Rosemont is a cluster of gray-walled cottages, each with a large veranda, set on a flowered hillside near the Hamilton Princess. Two of the cottages were formerly private homes, built in the 1940s; the rest are more modern structures constructed within the past 15 years or so. The harbor, with its passing ships, is visible from the raised terrace beside the small L-shaped swimming pool. The business travelers, families, and older couples who frequent Rosemont come for the peace and tranquillity. The policy here is to "keep it quiet," so the hotel usually doesn't accept college students or large groups.

Each of the well-furnished rooms is equipped with a kitchen; we find some of the units a little on the dark side, though. As many as three rooms can be joined together to suit families. The hotel also has three suites with private entrances and better furnishings. There's no restaurant on the premises; everybody cooks in. A grocery store is close by, downtown Hamilton is just 10 minutes away, and Elbow Beach is a 15-minute scooter or taxi ride away. Upon request, the hotel will arrange a motor-scooter rental. Laundry and baby-sitting can also be arranged.

SMITH'S PARISH

Angel's Grotto

P.O. Box HS 81, Smith's HS BX, Bermuda. ☎ **800/550-6288** in the U.S. and Canada, or 441/293-1986. Fax 441/293-4164. www.morbey.com/angelsgrotto. E-mail: angelsg@ibl.bm. 7 apts (all with kitchenettes). A/C TV TEL. Apr–Nov 15 $120–$200 double; off-season $105–$160 double. AE, MC, V. Bus: 3.

These housekeeping cottages are among the best in Bermuda and are preferred by couples. Following recent renovations, they're now better than ever. Situated on 1½ acres of seafront property overlooking Harrington Sound, this complex consists of three white-sided structures, originally built as a private home in the 1940s. Later, it functioned as a disco and nightclub, with the large seafront terrace the site of long-ago dance parties. The property has been owned by Daisy Hart since 1981. Each unit contains an air-conditioned bedroom, a combination living room/dining area, and a well-equipped kitchen. (There's a convenience store with a small selection within a 3- to 4-min. walk, and a full-fledged supermarket within a 7-min. moped or taxi ride.) Those units that overlook the water are slightly more expensive. The coastline adjacent to the complex is too rocky for swimming, but the pink sands of John Smith's Bay on the south shore are a 5-minute walk away.

INEXPENSIVE

PAGET PARISH

✪ Sky-Top Cottages

65 South Shore Rd. (P.O. Box PG 227), Paget PG BX, Bermuda. ☎ **441/236-7984.** Fax 441/232-0446. www.bermuda.com/skytop. E-mail: skytop@bermuda.com. 11 units. A/C TV TEL. Mar 16–Nov 15 $100–$130 double; winter $80–$115 double. Extra person $25 in summer, $15 off-season. Children under 12 $10. Off-season weekly and monthly discounts available. MC, V. Bus: 7.

In case you want to be welcomed there.

We're here to see that you're always welcomed at establishments everywhere. That's why millions of people carry the American Express® Card – for peace of mind, confidence, and security, around the world or just around the corner.

do more

Cards

And in case you'd rather be safe than sorry.

We're here with American Express® Travelers Cheques. They're the safe way to carry money on your vacation, because if they're ever lost or stolen you can get a refund, practically anywhere or anytime. To find the nearest place to buy Travelers Cheques, call 1 800 495-1153. Another way we help you do more.

do more

Travelers Cheques

Set on a hilltop above Paget's southern shoreline, opposite the Elbow Beach Hotel, this collection of cottages offers a great deal. The comfortable, secluded accommodations are contained in four cozy cottages, all of which have been upgraded and refurbished by the property's new owners, Andrea and John Flood. Each of the units has a fully equipped kitchen and a small private terrace. On all sides of the property, emerald-colored lawns are dotted with shrubs and trees; everywhere there are lovely views of the sea. There are few social activities here, except an occasional rainy-day party to cheer everybody up, but a warm sense of camaraderie is present. It's just a 5-minute walk to Elbow Beach, and a 10-minute ride by cab, bus, or moped to Hamilton.

5 Guest Houses

Bermuda's guest houses are usually comfortable old converted manor houses in garden settings. Some have pools and terraces; the smaller ones offer fewer facilities and are much more casual, often outfitted with simple, lived-in furniture. Most guest houses serve only breakfast. Those accommodating fewer than 12 guests are usually private homes. Some have housekeeping units, whereas others offer shared kitchen facilities for guests to prepare snacks.

EXPENSIVE
PEMBROKE PARISH (CITY OF HAMILTON)
✪ **Royal Palms Hotel**

24 Rosemont Ave. (P.O. Box HM 499), Hamilton HM CX, Bermuda. ☎ **800/678-0783** in the U.S., 800/799-0824 in Canada, or 441/292-1854. Fax 441/292-1946. www.royalpalms.bm. E-mail: rpalms@ibl.bm. 25 units. A/C TV TEL. Apr–Nov 15 $180–$240 double; off-season $135–$160 double. Extra person $40. Children under 16 $25, children under 3 free. Rates include continental breakfast. AE, MC, V. Bus: 1, 2, 10, or 11.

Located just a 5-minute walk from Hamilton, the family-owned and -managed Royal Palms is one of the most sought-after small hotels on the island, thanks to the care and restoration work of a brother-sister team, Richard Smith and Susan Weare. The exact year of the house's construction isn't known, but it's at least a century old. It's a fine example of Bermudian architecture, with coral-colored walls, white shutters, and a white roof, plus a wraparound front porch with rocking chairs and armchairs. Nearby residents often walk by the Royal Palms' garden to admire the marigolds and zinnias. The closest beach is Elbow Beach, a 10-minute taxi or scooter ride or a 30-minute walk away.

What had formerly been the living rooms, parlors, and bedrooms of a grand private house were converted into guest rooms. Today, each room is spacious, sunny, and comfortably furnished. Rich fabrics have been used throughout, and most units have high ceilings and tall windows. Each accommodation is equipped with a teakettle or coffeemaker, and many have small refrigerators. In the mews next to the hotel are four additional units, some with kitchen facilities.

Dining/Diversions: Cozy public areas include Ascots (see chapter 5), which serves both European and Bermudian cuisine, and a bar surrounded by a terrace.

Amenities: Freshwater pool.

MODERATE
SOUTHAMPTON PARISH
Royal Heights Guest House

Lighthouse Hill (P.O. Box SN 144), Southampton SN BX, Bermuda. ☎ **441/238-0043.** Fax 441/238-8445. 7 units. A/C TV. Apr–Nov $145 double, $195 triple; off-season $125 double,

$175 triple. Rates include continental breakfast. $50 extra for children under 12 to stay in parents' room. AE, MC, V. Closed late Nov to Mar. Bus: 7 or 8.

Set at the top of a steeply inclined driveway near the summit of Lighthouse Hill, this guest house is convenient to the Southampton Princess, with its varied nightlife and dining options. This is a modern, turquoise-trimmed building, whose two wings embrace the front entryway. Guests are welcome to gather in the living room of the owners, Russel Richardson and his wife, Jean, who are happy to suggest activities to you. Each of the spanking-clean bedrooms is equipped with a balcony and comfortable furniture. Horseshoe Bay, the closest beach, is a 5-minute taxi or scooter ride, or a 15-minute walk away. You can watch ships passing by on Great Sound while you float in the swimming pool.

PAGET PARISH

Dawkin's Manor

29 St. Michael's Rd. (P.O. Box PG34), Paget PG BX, Bermuda. ☎ **441/236-7419.** Fax 441/236-7088. 8 units. A/C TV TEL. Summer $120 double without kitchenette, $140 double with kitchenette, $160 suite for 2 with kitchenette. Off-season $85 double without kitchenette, $95 double with kitchenette, $105 suite for 2 with kitchenette. AE, MC, V.

Set within a quiet residential neighborhood a 5-minute walk from Elbow Beach, this peach-colored Bermudian inn is well maintained by Jamaica-born Celia Dawkins. Originally built in the 1930s and expanded massively since Ms. Dawkins bought the place in the early 1990s, it offers clean, eggshell-colored bedrooms that are simple and unpretentious. The rooms sometimes serve as home to off-island lecturers conducting short-term classes at nearby Bermuda College. Even the simplest rooms contain microwaves and coffeemakers; the more elaborate accommodations contain kitchens that are bigger than those you'll find in lots of other rental properties, suitable for bona fide cooking. There's a grocery store within a 2-minute walk from the hotel, and a swimming pool and a garden are on the premises.

✪ Loughlands

79 South Shore Rd., Paget PG 03, Bermuda. ☎ **441/236-1253.** 19 units. A/C. Mar 15–Nov 14 $125 double; off-season $85 double. Rates include continental breakfast. No credit cards. Bus: 2 or 7.

Built in 1920, Loughlands is the stately former residence of the president of the Staten Island Savings Bank in New York, who bestowed his name, Lough, on the estate. Loughlands was purchased in 1973 by Stanley and Mary Pickles, who sold their large country house in Cornwall, England, and shipped many of their antiques to what is now the largest guest house in Bermuda. Situated on 9 acres of landscaped grounds in the center of the island, it's plantation chalk-white, and its entry hall bears a large portrait of Queen Victoria. The bedrooms at Loughlands are handsomely decorated, some with high-post beds and antique chests.

On the grounds are a swimming pool and a tennis court. At breakfast, you'll enjoy such Bermudian treats as citrus fruit or bananas and homemade preserves. Elbow Beach, the closest beach, is an 8-minute walk or a 3-minute bike ride away.

PEMBROKE PARISH (CITY OF HAMILTON)

Edgehill Manor

Rosemont Ave. (P.O. Box HM 1048), Hamilton HM EX, Bermuda. ☎ **441/295-7124.** Fax 441/295-3850. www.bermuda.com/edgehill. E-mail: edgehill@bermuda.com. 9 units. A/C TV. Mar 16–Nov 15 $116–$138 double; off-season $94–$106 double. Rates include continental breakfast. $16 extra for children under 12 to stay in parents' room. No credit cards. Bus: 7 or 8.

Just outside the city limits and a 15-minute walk to the nearest beach, in a quiet residential area that's nevertheless convenient to Hamilton's restaurants and shopping,

Edgehill Manor just might become your "little home in Bermuda." Painted green, it was built around the time of the American Civil War and still exudes an old-fashioned, homey quality, attracting a rather middle-aged clientele. Your landlady is British-born Bridget Marshall, who continues the tradition of serving English tea in the afternoon. Although each unit has its own style, all come with small balconies or patios; three are equipped with kitchenettes. Ms. Marshall's continental breakfast, she is proud to say, is "all home baked."

✪ The Oxford House

Woodbourne Ave. (P.O. Box HM 374), Hamilton HM BX, Bermuda. ☎ **800/548-7758** in the U.S., 800/272-2306 in Canada, or 441/295-0503. Fax 441/295-0250. 12 units. A/C TV TEL. Mar 16–Nov 30 $150 double; off-season $137 double. Rates include full breakfast. AE, MC, V.

The Oxford House is one of the best and most centrally located guest houses in Hamilton, lying about a 10-minute scooter ride or a 30-minute walk from Elbow Beach. Possibly the only property in Bermuda constructed specifically as a guest house, it's located on a side street that leads into Front Street, near the Bermudiana Hotel.

The guest house was built in 1938 by a doctor and his French wife, who requested that some of the architectural features follow French designs. The white-and cream-colored entrance portico is flanked by Doric columns, corner mullions, and urn-shaped balustrades. Inside, a curved stairwell sweeps upward to spacious, well-furnished bedrooms, each named after one of Bermuda's parishes. There's even an upstairs sitting room, bathed in sunlight. Each bedroom evokes the feeling of a private home, with high ceilings, dressing areas, and a coffeemaker. The Bermudian breakfast might include a fresh fruit salad made with oranges and grapefruit grown in the yard. Your gracious host is Welsh-born Ann Smith.

ST. GEORGE'S PARISH

Aunt Nea's Inn at Hillcrest

1 Nea's Alley (P.O. Box GE 96), St. George's GE BX, Bermuda. ☎ **441/297-1630.** Fax 441/297-1908. 11 units. A/C. Apr–Oct $120–$170 double, $180–$225 suite. AE, MC, V. Bus: 1, 3, 6, 10, or 11.

This inn has been upgraded and vastly improved, and it is the only true B&B inn in historic St. George's. This early 18th-century house stands on the rise of a hill off Old Maid's Lane. Three beaches with great water sports are within a 10-minute walk of the hotel. (In 1804, the Irish poet Thomas Moore roomed here for several weeks. He developed a passion for Nea Tucker next door and consequently wrote several romantic verses for her.)

Each room is uniquely furnished with four-poster beds constructed of tropical hardwoods or wrought iron, and complementary armoires and accent pieces. Four of the rooms have whirlpools. Owners Delaey and Andrea Robinson have given the rooms charming names such as "Green Turtle" and "Queen Conch" that represent many of the natural treasures of Bermuda.

Hillcrest Guest House

1 Old Maid's Lane (P.O. Box GE 96), St. George's GE BX, Bermuda. ☎ **441/297-1630.** Fax 441/297-1908. 10 units, 1 cottage. A/C. $120–$135 double; $125 cottage. AE, MC, V. Rates include continental breakfast. Bus: 1, 3, 6, 10, or 11.

This yellow-and-green clapboard-sided house is one of the most envied historic homes in St. George's. Built in the 18th century, and frequently expanded, most recently in 1997, it began a tradition of accepting out-of-towners in 1914, when descendants of its present owner opened the house to victims of sea wrecks living temporarily (and often indigently) in Bermuda. Set on a hill, with a veranda whose view sweeps out over the town and the harbor, it began its role as a full-fledged guest house in the 1970s. In 1997, its interior received a massive upgrade, propelling it into the forefront of the island's glamorous B&Bs. Legend associates the place with Tom Moore, who lived here during his celebrated courtship of Nea, who occupied a still-standing pink house in nearby Nea's lane. Look for an interior loaded with Bermudian and Virginia cedar, Oriental carpets, four-poster beds, and heirloom family portraits. The staff, directed by Rachel Grant, is helpful in pointing out opportunities for local swimming, snorkeling, golfing, and shopping. Bedrooms don't have private phones or TVs. Breakfast is the only meal served.

INEXPENSIVE
SOUTHAMPTON PARISH
Greene's Guest House

71 Middle Rd. (P.O. Box SN 395), Southampton SN BX, Bermuda. ☎ **441/238-0834.** Fax 441/238-8980. 8 units. A/C TV TEL. $100 double. Rates include a full breakfast. No credit cards. Bus: 7 or 8.

The exterior of this guest house overlooking Great Sound (owned by Walter "Dickie" Greene and his wife, Jane) appears well maintained, clean, and unpretentious. A look on the inside reveals pleasant and conservatively furnished rooms, which are more impressive than you might have initially supposed. The entryway is flanked by a pair of lions resting on stone columns. The tables of the dining room, which can be closed off from the adjacent kitchen by a curtain, are set with a full formal dinner service throughout the day. Wall-to-wall carpeting covers the floors of the entrance lobby, as well as the spacious and well-furnished living room; guests are free to use this room, as well as the sun-washed terraces in back. There's a swimming pool in the back garden. Whale Bay Beach lies 3 minutes away by bus, or a 10-minute walk away.

Each bedroom is equipped with an ironing board and iron, a coffeemaker, and a refrigerator. Facing the sea is a cozy bar where guests record their drinks on the honor system. Dinner is available in the dining room if requested in advance. The regular Bermuda bus going to and from Hamilton stops at the front door.

PAGET PARISH
Greenbank Guest House

17 Salt Kettle Rd. (P.O. Box PG 201), Paget PG BX, Bermuda. ☎ **800/637-4116** in the U.S., or 441/236-3615. Fax 441/236-2427. www.bermudamall.com/greenbank. E-mail: grebank@ibl.bm. 11 units. A/C TEL. Apr–Nov: $125–$145 waterside cottage with kitchen for 2; $230 waterside apt with kitchen and 2 bathrooms for 4; $105 garden apt with kitchen for 2; $195 gardenside apt with kitchen for 4; $105 standard double. Off-season: $100–$120 waterside cottage with kitchen for 2; $200 waterside apt with kitchen and 2 bathrooms for 4; $80 garden apt with kitchen for 2; $170 garden apt with kitchen for 4; $75 standard double. Extra person $25 year-round. AE, MC, V. Ferry from Hamilton.

This guest house stands at the water's edge in Salt Kettle, just across the bay from Hamilton, a 10-minute ferry ride away. It's an old Bermuda home, hidden under pine and palm trees, with shady lawns and flower gardens. The oldest section dates from the 1700s; the manager welcomes guests in an antique-filled drawing room. The atmosphere is relaxed, and service is personal.

Greenbank offers accommodations with private entrances and kitchens, in either waterside or garden-view cottages. The guest house has a private dock for swimming; there's also a charter operation on the property for renting motorboats and sailboats. The nearest beach is world-famous Elbow Beach, but it's a 15-minute taxi or moped ride away.

Little Pomander Guest House

16 Pomander Rd. (P.O. Box HM 384), Hamilton HM BX, Bermuda. ☎ **441/236-7635.** Fax 441/236-8332. 6 units. A/C TV TEL. Apr 1–Oct 31 $115 double; off-season $85 double. Rates include continental breakfast. AE, MC, V. Bus: 1, 7, or 8.

This guest house is a pink-sided Bermuda home that once served as the annex to what is now a privately operated tennis club across the street. Little Pomander can trace its history and foundations back to the 1630s. The grassy lawn stretches a short distance down to the rocky shoreline, where you can see the cruise ships anchored in Hamilton Harbour. The bedrooms have been tastefully outfitted with floral prints and alpine-style curtains by decorator Irene Trott, who, along with her daughters, owns the inn. Each of the three apartments has a full kitchenette, but even the conventional bedrooms have microwave ovens and refrigerators. The closest beach is Elbow Beach; it's a 5-minute scooter ride or a 15-minute walk away.

Salt Kettle House

10 Salt Kettle Rd., Paget PG 01, Bermuda. ☎ **441/236-0407.** Fax 441/236-8639. 8 units (4 with kitchenettes). A/C. Mar–Dec 1 $50 per person double, $55 per person cottage; Dec 2–Feb $42 per person double, $45 per person cottage. Rates include full breakfast. No credit cards. Hamilton ferry to Salt Kettle (3-min. walk from ferry stop).

The core of this guest house is a 200-year-old cottage that was enlarged over the years. In the late 1970s, another cottage was custom-built on the lot's only remaining space. Today, the compound is a cheerful architectural hodgepodge that's informal and secluded, situated on a narrow peninsula that juts into Hamilton Harbour. You can watch the ships going in and out of the harbor and can swim in a cove outside. Four cottages are equipped with kitchens, and the guests staying in the main house also have use of a fully equipped kitchen. The guest lounge has cable TV. The owner-manager is Mrs. Hazel Lowe.

5

Dining

Wahoo steak, shark hash, mussel pie, fish chowder laced with rum and sherry peppers, Hoppin' John (black-eyed peas and rice), and the succulent spiny Bermuda lobster (called guinea-chick) await you in Bermuda. Trouble is, you'll have to search hard to find these offbeat dishes, since many hotels and a large number of restaurants serve typical international resort cuisine.

Bermudian food has improved in recent years, but dining out is not a major reason people come to the island. Both American and British dishes are common. Truly innovative gourmet fare often isn't—although the prices would make you think you're getting something really special. Bermuda dining is generally more expensive than dining in the United States and Canada. Because virtually everything except fish must be imported, restaurant prices are more comparable to those in Europe than to those in America. As we updated this year's guide, we found that restaurant prices have remained fairly stable, although slight price increases are expected in the year 2000. The feeling is that the prices were almost more than the market could handle, so chefs have been trying to hold the line as much as possible.

In general, it's not a good idea to order meat very often; it has been flown in, and you can't be sure how long it has been held in storage. Whenever possible, it's best to stick to local food; for a main course, that usually means fish. The seafood is generally excellent, especially Bermuda rockfish—that is, when local fishers have caught something that day. Sometimes waters are too rough for fishing. Therefore, a lot of the fish served in Bermuda restaurants is imported frozen from the U.S. mainland; you may want to ask before you order. To find the dishes that are truly worthy, you'll have to pick and choose your way carefully through the menu—and that's where we come in.

Most restaurants, at least the better ones, prefer that men wear a jacket and tie after 6pm; women usually wear casual, chic clothing in the evening. Of course, as most of the world dresses more and more casually, Bermuda's dress codes have loosened up a bit—but this is still a more formal destination than many other islands. It's always wise to ask when you're reserving a table. During the day, no matter what the establishment, be sure to wear a cover-up—don't arrive for lunch sporting a bikini.

Because of the absence of inexpensive transportation on the island, many travelers on a budget eat dinner at their hotels to avoid adding transportation expenses to an already pricey dinner. If you like to dine around and you're concerned about cost, either find a hotel that offers a variety of dining options or stay at one in or near Hamilton. This way, you can walk to and from restaurants in town.

BERMUDA'S BEST DINING BETS

You'll find Bermuda's best sushi at the **New Harbourfront Restaurant & Sushi Bar** in Hamilton; the best steaks at the **Colony Pub Steak House** at the Hamilton Princess; the best Chinese and Thai at **Chopsticks Restaurant** in Hamilton; the best sandwiches at **Fourways Pastry Shop** in Hamilton; the best British pub grub at **Hog Penny** in Hamilton; the best Bermudian cuisine at **M. R. Onions** in Hamilton; the best French food at **Fourways Inn Restaurant** in Paget Parish; the best pasta at **Pasta Pasta** in St. George's; the best ice cream at **Bailey's Ice Cream & Food D'Lites Restaurant** in Hamilton Parish; and the best pizzas at **Portofino** in Hamilton. Our favorite for brunch is the **Waterlot Inn** in Southampton Parish.

For details on all of these restaurants, see below for full reviews (all restaurants are listed geographically under "City of Hamilton" or by parish).

1 From Rockfish to Island Rum: Dining, Bermuda Style

For years, Bermuda wasn't an island of grand cuisine; the food was too often bland, lacking in flavor. In recent years, however, there has been a notable change. Bermuda currently shares in the revived interest in fine cuisine that has swept across America. Chefs seem better trained than ever, and many top-notch (albeit expensive) restaurants dot the archipelago, from Sandys Parish in the west to St. George's Parish in the east. Italian food is currently much in vogue; the Chinese have also landed. (On the other side of the coin, fast food has also arrived in Bermuda, including KFC.)

In recent years, some Bermudians have shown an increased interest in their heritage, and many traditional dishes and recipes have been revived and published in books devoted to Bermudian cookery (not a bad idea for a souvenir).

Today, Bermuda imports most of its food from the United States. As the population grows, less and less land is available for farms on the island. But lots of people still tend their own gardens; at one Bermudian home, we were amazed at the variety of vegetables grown on just a small plot of land, including sorrel (from which a good-tasting soup is made), oyster plants, and Jerusalem artichokes.

Most meat is imported, so you're usually better off ordering fish from a Bermudian menu. However, you can't assume that all fish is fresh, either; much of it, too, is imported from such stateside markets as Boston.

WHAT'S COOKING?

SEAFOOD   Any local fisherman will be happy to tell you that more species of both shore and ocean fish—including grunt, angelfish, yellowtail, gray snapper, and the ubiquitous rockfish—are found just off Bermuda's coastline than are found in any other place.

Rockfish, which is similar to the Bahamian grouper, appears on nearly every menu. As pulled from the ocean, it weighs anywhere from 15 to 135 pounds (or even more). Steamed, broiled, baked, fried, or grilled, rockfish is a challenge to any

Bailey's Ice Cream
  & Food D'Lites Restaurant 19

Black Horse Tavern 22

Café Lido 14

Dennis's Hideaway 23

Fourways Inn Restaurant 11

Freeport Gardens 2

Frog & Onion 1

Grandview Restaurant 5

Halfway House 16

Henry VIII 7

Il Palio 4

Inlet Restaurant 17

Lillian's/The Sea Grape 6

Middletown Room 12

Mikado 21

Newport Room 9	Tamarisk Dining Room 3
Norwood Room 15	Tio Pepe 8
Paraquet Restaurant 13	Tom Moore's Tavern 18
Pawpaws Restaurant & Bar 10	Waterlot Inn 9
Pirates Landing 1	Whaler Inn 9
Rib Room 9	Wickets Brasserie & Cricket Club 9
Somerset Country Squire Tavern 4	Windsor Room 21
Swizzle Inn 20	

97

chef. There's even a dish known as "rockfish maw," which we understand only the most old-fashioned cooks (there are still a handful left on St. David's Island) know how to prepare. It's the maw, or stomach, of a rockfish, stuffed with a dressing of forcemeat and simmered slowly on the stove. If you view dining as an adventure, you may want to try it.

The most popular dish on the island is **Bermuda fish chowder.** Waiters usually pass around a bottle of sherry peppers and some black rum, which you lace your own soup with; it adds a distinctive Bermudian flavor.

Shark isn't as popular on Bermuda as it used to be. Many traditional dishes, however, are still made from shark, including hash. Some people still use shark liver oil to forecast the weather; it's said to be more reliable than the nightly TV forecast. The oil is extracted at a specific time, then poured into a small bottle and left in the sun. If the oil lies still, fair weather can be predicted; if, however, droplets form on the sides of the bottle, expect foul weather.

The great game fish to order in Bermuda is **wahoo,** which is found in local waters. If it's on the menu, we recommend that you go for a wahoo steak. When properly prepared, it's superb.

The **Bermuda lobster** (or "guinea chick," as it's known locally) has been called a first cousin of the Maine lobster and is in season only from September to March. Its high price tag has led to overfishing, forcing the government at times to issue a ban on its harvesting. In those instances, lobster is imported from elsewhere.

Occasionally, you can still get a good **conch stew** at one of Bermuda's local restaurants. **Sea scallops,** though still available, have become increasingly rare. **Mussels** are cherished in Bermuda; one of the most popular and traditional mussel dishes is Bermuda-style mussel pie.

FRUITS & VEGETABLES   In both restaurants and Bermudian homes, **Portuguese red-bean soup**—the culinary contribution of the farmers who were brought to the island to till the land—precedes many a meal.

The **Bermuda onion** figures in many Bermudian recipes, including onion pie. Bermuda-onion soup, an island favorite, is usually flavored with Outerbridge's Original Sherry Peppers.

Today, Bermudians grow more **potatoes** than any other vegetable; the principal varieties are the Pontiac red and the Kennebec white potatoes. The traditional Sunday breakfast of codfish and banana cooked with potatoes is still served in some homes.

"Peas and plenty" is a Bermudian tradition. Black-eyed peas are cooked with onions and salt pork, with rice sometimes added. Dumplings or boiled sweet potatoes may also be added at the last minute. Another peas-and-rice dish, called **Hoppin' John,** is eaten either as a main dish or as a side dish with meat or poultry.

Both Bermudians and Bahamians share the tradition of **Johnny Bread,** or **Johnnycake,** a simple pan-cooked cornmeal bread. Fishermen on their boats would make it over a fire in a box filled with sand to keep the flames from spreading to the craft itself.

The **cassava,** once an important food in Bermuda, is now used chiefly as an ingredient in the traditional Christmas cassava pie. Another dish with a festive holiday connection is **sweet-potato pudding,** traditionally eaten on Guy Fawkes Day (first week in Nov).

Bermuda grows many **fresh fruits,** including strawberries, Surinam cherries, guavas, avocados, and, of course, bananas. Guavas are made into jelly, which in turn often goes into making the famous Bermuda syllabub, traditionally accompanied by Johnnycake.

WHAT TO WASH IT ALL DOWN WITH

For some 300 years, **rum** has been the drink of Bermuda. Especially popular are Bacardi (the company's headquarters are in Bermuda) and Demerara rum (also known as black rum). The rum swizzle is the most famous cocktail in Bermuda.

For decades, the true Bermudian has preferred a drink called **"Dark 'n Stormy."** Prepared with black rum and ginger beer (pronounced *burr*), it's been called the national drink of the island; you might want to give it a try.

An interesting drink is loquat liqueur, now exported. It can be made with loquats, rock candy, and gin, or more elaborately with brandy instead of gin and the addition of such spices as cinnamon, nutmeg, cloves, and allspice.

You'll also find all the name-brand alcoholic beverages in Bermuda, but prices on such mixed drinks as scotch and soda can run high, depending on the brand.

LOCAL DINING CUSTOMS

The most delightful custom on Bermuda is the English ritual of **afternoon tea.** Many local homes and hotels have maintained the tradition for visitors to enjoy.

In hotels, the typical afternoon tea is served daily from 3 to 4pm. Adding a contemporary touch, tea is often served around a swimming pool, with guests partaking of the ritual in their bathing suits—a tolerated lapse from the usual formal code that governs social functions on the island.

In its more formal observance, tea is served at a table well laid with silver, crisp white linen napery, and fine china, often imported from Britain. Finger sandwiches made with thinly sliced cucumber or watercress, or scones and strawberry jam, usually accompany the tea.

Like the British, Bermudians also enjoy a good sociable **pub lunch.** There are several pubs in Hamilton, St. George's, and elsewhere on the island. For the visitor, a pub lunch—say, fish-and-chips or shepherd's pie; a pint or two of ale; and animated discussion about politics, sports, or the most recent royal visit—is an experience to be cherished, here as much as in any city or town in Britain.

Another favorite meal of the typical Bermudian is **Sunday brunch.** Your hotel is likely to feature a big buffet at that time.

2 Restaurants by Cuisine

AMERICAN

M. R. Onions (City of Hamilton; *M*)

BERMUDIAN

Black Horse Tavern (St. George's Parish; *M*)
Fisherman's Reef (City of Hamilton; *M*)
Fourways Inn Restaurant (Paget Parish; *VE*)
Hog Penny (City of Hamilton; *I*)
M. R. Onions (City of Hamilton; *M*)
Paraquet Restaurant (Paget Parish; *I*)
Pawpaws Restaurant & Bar (Warwick Parish; *M*)

Swizzle Inn (Hamilton Parish; *I*)
White Horse Tavern (St. George's Parish; *M*)

BRITISH

Frog & Onion (Sandys Parish; *I*)
Henry VIII (Southampton Parish; *E*)
Hog Penny (City of Hamilton; *I*)
Somerset Country Squire Tavern (Sandys Parish; *M*)
Swizzle Inn (Hamilton Parish; *I*)

CHINESE

Chopsticks Restaurant (City of Hamilton; *I*)

Key to abbreviations: *VE* = Very Expensive   *E* = Expensive   *M* = Moderate   *I* = Inexpensive

CONTINENTAL

Chancery Wine Bar (City of Hamilton; *M*)

Henry VIII (Southampton Parish; *E*)

Little Venice (City of Hamilton; *M*)

Monte Carlo (City of Hamilton; *E*)

The Norwood Room (Paget Parish; *E*)

Pawpaws Restaurant & Bar (Warwick Parish; *M*)

The Tiara Room (City of Hamilton; *VE*)

Tom Moore's Tavern (Hamilton Parish; *VE*)

DELI/LIGHT BITES

Bailey's Ice Cream & Food D'Lites Restaurant (Hamilton Parish; *I*)

Fourways Pastry Shop (City of Hamilton; *I*)

The Hickory Stick (City of Hamilton; *I*)

Pink's (City of Hamilton; *I*)

FRENCH

Ascots (City of Hamilton; *E*)

La Coquille (City of Hamilton; *E*)

Fourways Inn Restaurant (Paget Parish; *VE*)

Newport Room (Southampton Parish; *VE*)

Red Carpet Bar and Restaurant (City of Hamilton; *M*)

Tom Moore's Tavern (Hamilton Parish; *VE*)

INDIAN

The Bombay (City of Hamilton; *I*)

INTERNATIONAL

Black Horse Tavern (St. George's Parish; *M*)

Botanic Garden (City of Hamilton; *I*)

The Colony Pub (City of Hamilton; *M*)

Front Street Terrace (City of Hamilton; *I*)

Grandview Restaurant (Southampton Parish; *I*)

Green Lantern (City of Hamilton; *I*)

Halfway House Restaurant & Bar (Hamilton Parish; *I*)

Inlet Restaurant (Smith's Parish; *E*)

The Middleton Room (Paget Parish; *E*)

Monty's (City of Hamilton; *I*)

Pirates Landing (Sandys Parish; *M*)

The Porch (City of Hamilton; *M*)

Red Carpet Bar and Restaurant (City of Hamilton; *M*)

Tamarisk Dining Room (Sandys Parish; *E*)

Waterloo House (City of Hamilton; *VE*)

Wickets Brasserie & Cricket Club (Southampton Parish; *I*)

Windsor Dining Room (Hamilton Parish; *M*)

ITALIAN

Ascots (City of Hamilton; *E*)

Il Palio (Sandys Parish; *M*)

La Trattoria (City of Hamilton; *M*)

Lillian's (Southampton Parish; *E*)

Little Venice (City of Hamilton; *M*)

Monte Carlo (City of Hamilton; *E*)

New Harbourfront Restaurant & Sushi Bar (City of Hamilton; *E*)

Pasta Basta (City of Hamilton; *I*)

Pasta Pasta (St. George's Parish; *I*)

Portofino (City of Hamilton; *I*)

Primavera (City of Hamilton; *M*)

Red Carpet Bar and Restaurant (City of Hamilton; *M*)

San Giorgio (St. George's Parish; *M*)

Tio Pepe (Southampton Parish; *M*)

Windsor Dining Room (Hamilton Parish; *M*)

JAPANESE

Mikado (Hamilton Parish; *VE*)

MEDITERRANEAN

Café Lido (Paget Parish; *E*)

Harley's (City of Hamilton; *M*)

La Coquille (City of Hamilton; *E*)

Monte Carlo (City of Hamilton; *E*)

Waterlot Inn (Southampton Parish; *VE*)

PACIFIC RIM

The Sea Grape (Southampton Parish; *E*)

SEAFOOD

Dennis's Hideaway (St. George's Parish; *M*)

Fisherman's Reef (City of Hamilton; *M*)

Lobster Pot & Boat House Bar (City of Hamilton; *M*)

New Harbourfront Restaurant & Sushi Bar (City of Hamilton; *E*)

Somerset Country Squire Tavern (Sandys Parish; *M*)

Whaler Inn (Southampton Parish; *E*)

Wharf Tavern (St. George's Parish; *M*)

STEAKS/SEAFOOD

Carriage House (St. George's Parish; *M*)

Freeport Gardens (Sandys Parish; *I*)

Port O'Call (City of Hamilton; *M*)

The Rib Room (Southampton Parish; *E*)

SUSHI

Mikado (Hamilton Parish; *VE*)

New Harbourfront Restaurant & Sushi Bar (City of Hamilton; *E*)

TEX-MEX

Rosa's Cantina (City of Hamilton; *I*)

3 Sandys Parish

The following restaurants are all located on Somerset Island.

EXPENSIVE

✪ Tamarisk Dining Room

At Cambridge Beaches, 30 Kings Point Rd. ☎ **441/234-0331**. Reservations required. Main courses $10–$15 at lunch; fixed-price 5-course dinner $55. No credit cards. Daily 12:30–2:30pm and 7–9pm. Bus: 7. INTERNATIONAL.

The kitchen at Tamarisk has recently reached new heights. There's been a new focus on offering classic cuisine of a high order and impeccable service. Situated within Bermuda's first cottage colony, the traditionally styled dining room—with its limed wood, impressive columns, and beamed ceiling—reminds us of an upscale country club. In warm weather, sliding-glass doors extend the dining area onto a rambling, eastward-facing terrace that overlooks the bay. Although Princess Margaret has dined here in the past, today you'll find groups of lawyers and business leaders, especially after dark.

At lunch you're likely to find a menu offering platters of chicken-macadamia salad, a signature pita-bread sandwich (stuffed, California-style, with chicken salad, avocado slices, and bean sprouts), and some of the best cheeseburgers in the parish. The dinner menu changes frequently, but nearly always includes a juicy tenderloin of beef with a grain mustard and blanched garlic sauce; "cushions" of lamb served with a Stilton mousse soufflé, red wine sauce, and lentils; and a flavorful thyme-and-garlic roasted monkfish floating on a bed of ratatouille.

MODERATE

Il Palio

64 Main Rd. ☎ **441/234-1049**. Reservations required. Main courses $16–$28. AE, DC, MC, V. Tues–Sun 6–10pm. Bus: 8. ITALIAN.

Named after the famous horse race in Siena, Italy, and located in the center of Somerset, this restaurant serves some of the best pizzas on the island. Of course, the regular and classic Italian cuisine—everything from steak Diane to roast duckling with a zesty green peppercorn sauce—is also quite good. The emphasis is on the tried-and-true, such as fettuccine Alfredo or tender slices of sautéed veal; among the best choices are the pasta primavera and the ground meat- and spinach-filled cannelloni.

We also recommend the fresh fish, especially the selection that's sautéed with bits of garlic to which pine nuts, capers, and well-seasoned tomato sauce are added. If you arrive early, you can enjoy a drink in the downstairs bar.

Pirates Landing

Royal Naval Dockyard. ☎ **441/234-5151.** Reservations accepted but usually not necessary. Lunch from $8; main courses $14.50–$24 at dinner; early dinner special (6–7pm) $22. AE, DC, MC, V. Daily 11:30am–4pm and 6–10pm. Closed Feb. Bus: 8 or ferry from Hamilton. INTERNATIONAL.

Overlooking the Great Sound, this restaurant has a widely diverse menu that pleases most diners. The seating, at pine tables and chairs, is comfortable, and the costumed serving staff is helpful. It's a little hokey, but especially after a rum punch or two, everyone seems to have fun and get into the spirit of it. Most visitors, who come for lunch, sample the standard soups, burgers, pastas, and even grilled specialties. The gyros on pita are spicy delights, especially the 6-inch gyro pizza made with fresh vegetables, pepperoni, and mozzarella.

At night the kitchen shines brighter, with its chefs searching abroad for inspiration. Some of the unusual dishes include a lamb and spinach curry and dolphin (mahimahi) pizzaiola in a tangy tomato base with mixed herbs. Savory grills include thin slices of veal in olive oil and lemon dressing, and there's a nightly pasta selection. Some of the more flavorful dishes include strips of chicken prepared Asian style, seasoned with ginger and served with cashew nuts; and braised tenderloin in Chianti.

Somerset Country Squire Tavern

10 Mangrove Bay Rd., Somerset Village. ☎ **441/234-0105.** Reservations not required. Main courses $18–$28. AE, MC, V. Daily 10am–1am. Bus: 7 or 8. BRITISH/SEAFOOD.

You'll pass through a moon-gate arch to reach the raised terrace of this waterside restaurant located in the center of the village. If you don't want to eat within the confines of the limestone blocks and hedges that ring the terrace, head to the interior dining room downstairs. The bill of fare ranges from British pub grub to fresh fish caught in local waters, or the traditional roast beef with Yorkshire pudding. Local Bermudian favorites, your best choices here, include curried mussel pie and fresh Bermuda tuna or wahoo. Look for the specialties of the day, but count on charbroiled and barbecued meals. Most of the food here is fairly routine, although the chef is especially proud of his Bermuda fish chowder, a tomato-based soup that some locals consider the best in the West End. Outdoor barbecues are often featured.

INEXPENSIVE

Freeport Gardens

At the Royal Naval Dockyard, 1 Freeport Rd. ☎ **441/234-1692.** Reservations not required. Main courses $7.50–$14 at lunch, $8.50–$35 at dinner. AE, MC, V. Daily 11am–11pm. STEAKS/SEAFOOD.

Set within a blue-shuttered, stone-sided cottage originally built during World War II, this is one of the most appealing of the restaurants within the Royal Naval Dockyards. Taken over in 1994 by German-born Ingo Roth, Freeport Gardens features a cozy, cedar-lined bar near the entrance, and a dining room with cedarwood beams and nautical touches. The menu is less formal—and somewhat less expensive—at lunchtime than at dinner, and it might include burgers, fish sandwiches, salads, pizzas, and steaks. Evening meals include fish-and-chips (usually concocted from tuna or wahoo), T-bone steaks, three different preparations of lobster, and such fish as panfried Bermuda rockfish with broiled garlic butter and white wine sauce and a

Check, Please! A Note on Service Charges

Although a service charge is usually added to restaurant bills (typically 10% to 15%), it's customary to leave something extra if the service has been good. However, this isn't necessary—in fact, there have been so many complaints about service in Bermudian restaurants that many diners find the 15% too generous. Be on the lookout for this scam: Some restaurants include the basic 15% service charge in the bill, leaving the service-charge line blank. Many diners unknowingly add another 10% to 15%, without realizing they've already paid for service. Scrutinize your bill carefully, and don't be shy about asking if you're not sure what's already been included.

choice of potatoes. Combination platters, with a sampling of meat, fish, and shellfish, are endlessly popular; diners dig right in with gusto.

Frog & Onion

The Cooperage, at the Royal Naval Dockyard. ☎ **441/234-2900.** Sandwiches, salads, and platters $5.50–$12 at lunch; main courses $12–$21.70 at dinner. MC, V. Daily 11:30am–3:30pm and 6–9:30pm. Bar (with snacks) daily noon–midnight. Closed Mon Dec–Feb. Bus: 8 or ferry from Hamilton. BRITISH.

Located in the former 18th-century cooperage (barrel-making factory) within the Royal Naval Dockyard, this is the most quintessential British pub in Bermuda. Its name derives from its Franco-Bermudian owners: French-born Jean-Paul Magnin (the Frog) and Bermuda-born Carol West (the Onion). You can sit back with a pint of English lager in the shadows of the cooperage's enormous fireplace. Many folks stay on to dine: At lunch there are sandwiches, salads, lasagna, bangers and mash, and such bar pies as sweet lamb and curry, steak and mussel, and vegetable and cheese. The dinner menu includes all of the lunchtime choices plus a variety of liver, lamb, beef, and chicken dishes. It's well-prepared and hearty fare. The portions are large—no one leaves here hungry.

4 Southampton Parish

VERY EXPENSIVE

✪ Newport Room

In the Southampton Princess, 101 South Shore Rd. ☎ **441/238-8000.** Reservations required. Jacket and tie requested but not required. Main courses $32–$39. AE, DC, MC, V. Daily 6:30–9:30pm (when the last orders are taken). Closed usually Dec to mid-Jan. Ferryboat from Hamilton. FRENCH.

The Newport Room is unequaled in its sumptuously understated decor, as well as in its French cuisine—it's among the best in Bermuda. The dining room, entirely paneled in teak and rosewood with nautical brass touches, evokes the expensive interior of a yacht. At the entrance you'll be greeted by a maître d' stationed beside a ship's compass. In the center of the room are exact miniature replicas of two of the winning sailboats from the Newport-to-Bermuda Race.

Settle into a leather armchair and prepare yourself for what might be your most memorable meal in Bermuda. The menu reads like a gourmet variation of *cuisine moderne,* including duck breast with cinnamon and fig sauce. The menu changes often, but all dishes are made from the freshest and best ingredients available. The personal attention and service and the carefully prepared and artfully presented dishes are complemented by a wide array of international wines, all served in Irish crystal.

☼ Waterlot Inn

At the Southampton Princess, Middle Rd. ☎ **441/238-8000.** Reservations required. Main courses $28–$42. AE, DC, MC, V. Daily 6:30–9:30pm. Closed Jan–Feb. Guests are shuttled from the hotel to this waterside inn. MEDITERRANEAN.

This is one of our all-time favorites for a special night out. The service is impeccable, and the culinary repertoire is inventive—doubly impressive given the large number of diners who shuttle through the dining room every evening.

About 300 years ago, merchant sailors unloaded their cargo directly into the basement of this historic inn and warehouse. Today, the best way to approach this inn is still by water, and that's precisely what many Bermudians do, mooring their sailing craft in its sheltered cove. Over the years the inn has attracted such guests as Mark Twain, James Thurber, Eleanor Roosevelt, and Eugene O'Neill. After the landmark building was devastated by a gas explosion in 1976, the Southampton Princess had it renovated, and today it's one of their gourmet restaurants.

You can enjoy a drink in an upstairs bar and be entertained by the resident classical pianist. After descending a white-balustraded colonial staircase, you'll be seated in one of three conservatively nautical dining rooms. Each is filled with captain's or Windsor chairs, oil paintings of old clipper ships, and lots of exposed wood. The bouillabaisse is about as good as it gets this side of the Riviera, although there are many other temptations as well. The veal chop served in sage-infused oil with young stuffed vegetables is an especially good choice. Occasionally we've settled happily for a plate of grilled Mediterranean vegetables, ranging from artichokes to eggplant.

EXPENSIVE

☼ Henry VIII

South Shore Rd. (between the Southampton Princess and the Sonesta Beach Resort). ☎ **441/238-1977.** Reservations required for dinner. Main courses $6–$14 at lunch, $18.50–$32 at dinner; Sun brunch $22.50 per person. Early-bird dinner (6–7pm) $25.50; fixed-price dinner $31.50. AE, DC, DISC, MC, V. Daily noon–2:30pm and 6–10pm. Bus: 7 or 8. ENGLISH/CONTINENTAL.

This pub/restaurant below Gibbs Hill Lighthouse looks rather gimmicky with its faux Tudor decor, but the food is exceptionally good—far superior to anything that was probably served to Henry VIII in his day. The food is worth a special trip. The restaurant is richly decorated with oak furnishings, brass railings, and period-style lighting fixtures.

Hot pub lunches include steak-and-kidney pie, mussel pie, and plain old hamburgers that are all far superior to the usual pub grub. The Sunday brunch is one of the most popular on the island. In the evening, the chef turns dishes such as a delectable broiled seafood combination and prime rib, both of which are terrific. Other notable beef dishes are the pepper steak, with a zesty flavor, and chateaubriand. Like a first-class London restaurant, the kitchen always prepares a classic mixed English grill. You also might want to drop by the split-level Oak Room Bar for some English draft beer and, in summer, nightly entertainment.

Lillian's

In the Sonesta Beach Resort, South Shore Rd. ☎ **441/238-8122.** Reservations recommended. Main courses $19–$45. AE, DC, MC, V. Daily 6–10pm. Closed Dec–Mar. Bus: 7. NORTHERN ITALIAN.

Many visitors to Southampton Parish head for one of the Sonesta's restaurants, including Lillian's, a glamorous art nouveau room with formal service. The menu is ambitious, including antipasti such as vegetable lasagna and house-smoked salmon (served with roasted pepper risotto cakes, fennel, and aioli); you might also begin with Tuscan-style white-bean soup made with spinach and Italian sausage. There are also good pizzas and succulent pastas, as either full or half courses. Main courses might include baked wahoo with grilled polenta, or roast Atlantic salmon with a fennel risotto. The roasted rack of lamb with vegetable lasagna is also noteworthy.

The Rib Room

In the Southampton Princess, 101 South Shore Rd. ☎ **441/238-8000.** Reservations recommended. Main courses $18.50–$30. AE, DC, MC, V. Daily 6:30–9:30pm (when the last orders are taken). Ferry from Hamilton. STEAKS/SEAFOOD.

One look at the menu and you'll think you're in one of London's finest chophouses. Many of the juicy and delectably tender beef dishes are broiled over charcoal. The broiled lamb chops are classic, or maybe you'll go all out for the roast prime rib of beef with Yorkshire pudding. For those who prefer fish, the chef will prepare the catch of the day. All dinners come with an extensive salad bar.

The Rib Room sits atop the resort's golf pro shop, near the tee-off point for the first hole. As you relax in upholstered armchairs, taking in the panoramic view from the windows, you might want to start your evening with a "Dark 'n Stormy," a black rum and ginger beer drink for the adventurous at heart.

The Sea Grape

In the Sonesta Beach Resort, South Shore Rd. ☎ **441/238-8122.** Reservations recommended. Main courses $23–$38; dinner buffet $25. AE, DC, MC, V. Daily noon–4pm and 7–10pm. Closed Dec–Mar. Bus: 7. PACIFIC RIM.

The Sea Grape, on an outdoor terrace by the sea, prides itself on its Pacific Rim menu. Generally, it includes calorie- and cholesterol-conscious foods with California-, Korean-, and Japanese-inspired sauces served on the side. Zesty appetizers range from spiced poached pineapple with coconut yogurt and candied ginger to grilled shrimp with a smoked bacon guacamole. Main dishes are often grilled and served with fresh chutneys, salsas, and yakisoba (wheat) noodles. Our favorite main course is sesame-crusted pork tenderloin. There's also usually a daily catch, market priced.

Whaler Inn

In the Southampton Princess, 101 South Shore Rd. ☎ **441/238-8000.** Reservations recommended. Main courses $8–$15 at lunch; $18–$27 at dinner. AE, DC, MC, V. Daily noon–2:30pm and 6:30–9:30pm. Closed Nov–Mar. Ferry from Hamilton. SEAFOOD.

This restaurant, perched atop a low cliff overlooking the rocks and pink sands that border the Atlantic near the Southampton Princess, is famous for its seafood. Its landscaped terraces sprout with clusters of sea grape, Norfolk Island pine, and padded iron armchairs; from here, you can watch the sunsets that redden the lapping waves of one of the island's most secluded beaches. Inside, the huge windows create an airy setting where the panoramic view is the main decor.

To whet your appetite, you might begin with baked oysters Rockefeller, Bermuda fish chowder, or something as exotic as roasted pumpkin potato gnocchi served with roasted sunflower seeds. The special main courses will be well-seasoned portions of whatever game fish the local fishers brought in that day, which might be yellowfin tuna, barracuda, shark, wahoo, or dolphin fish (mahimahi)—all excellently prepared, either broiled or sautéed in butter. Additional main courses may include a kettle of seafood prepared St. David's style (flavored with Outerbridge's Original Sherry Peppers and a glass of rum), mussels marinière, and a deep-fried fisher's platter, along with a panfried local fish with almonds and bananas. Desserts might include banana fritters with black-rum sauce, or Armagnac ice cream with prunes.

MODERATE

Tio Pepe

117 South Shore Rd., Horseshoe Bay. ☎ **441/238-1897.** Reservations recommended. Pizzas and pastas $11–$17.75, main courses $18.75–$26.75; lunch from $6.75. AE, MC, V. May–Sept daily 11am–10:30pm; off-season daily noon–10pm. Bus 7. ITALIAN/SPANISH.

Don't let the Spanish name fool you—the cuisine here is predominantly traditional Italian, although a few Spanish dishes are scattered throughout the menu. It's all fairly straightforward fare: Tio Pepe serves pizzas, pastas, and the classic cuisine of Italy in generous portions, all with a bit of Mediterranean pizzazz. Bermuda's local fish, as well as salmon and lobster, are also served; they too have subtle Italian flavors. The friendly atmosphere, the bountiful food, and the prices are right on target.

Tio Pepe caters to a Hamilton clientele who appreciate its proximity to the Southampton Princess Hotel and Horseshoe Bay Beach. Guests have the choice of sitting on a wide garden-view terrace or in one of three indoor dining rooms. Chianti bottles top off the red-and-green interior.

INEXPENSIVE

✪ Grandview Restaurant

On the grounds of the Port Royal Golf Course, Port Royal. ☎ **441/234-5037.** Reservations not necessary. Main courses $7–$22, fixed-price dinner $19.50. AE, MC, V. Daily 8am–9pm (to 6pm in winter). INTERNATIONAL.

Set within the clubhouse of the Port Royal Golf Course, overlooking the 9th and 18th holes, this restaurant has a friendly bar that's the perfect 19th hole. Outfitted with big windows and wicker furniture, it's wonderfully unpretentious, and its two-fisted, well-prepared food tastes wonderful after a day outdoors. The food is reminiscent of country-club fare you'd find at golf courses throughout North America, including catch of the day (prepared either panfried or Cajun), juicy steaks with all the fixings, burgers, and pastas. A more unique specialty is the Bermuda fish cakes served on hot cross buns. During the tournaments that are sometimes held here, expect mobs of fellow drinkers and diners; otherwise, the place is laid-back, fraternal, and relaxing.

Where to Put Together the Perfect Picnic & Where to Enjoy It

The kitchens of many major hotels will prepare a picnic lunch for you, but you need to request it at least a day in advance. If you walk along Front Street in Hamilton, you can order sandwiches at a cafe, plus a bottle of wine or mineral water at a local shop. If it's a weekday, the best place to buy picnic supplies is **The Hickory Stick** (see "City of Hamilton," later in the chapter).

If you enjoy picnicking and biking, you can do both in Sandys Parish. Start by going over Somerset Bridge (heading in the direction of Somerset Village), and continue along Somerset Road to **Fort Scaur Park,** where you'll enjoy a panoramic view of Ely's Harbour.

Another ideal location is **Spanish Point Park** in Pembroke, where you will find a series of little coves and beaches. Here you don't need to go to the trouble of packing a picnic basket, since a lunch wagon rolls around every day at noontime (except in winter). We also love to picnic at one of the island's best beaches, **Warwick Long Bay,** which has rest rooms at the western end for washing up beforehand.

✪ Wickets Brasserie & Cricket Club

In the Southampton Princess, 101 South Shore Rd. ☎ **441/238-8000.** "Healthy start" breakfast buffet $15 per person; main courses $7.50–$13.50 at lunch. AE, DC, MC, V. Daily 7–11am and noon–6:30pm. Ferry from Hamilton. INTERNATIONAL.

Outfitted like a British cricket club, this brasserie and bistro features a health-conscious breakfast buffet with low-sodium and high-fiber offerings, as well as one of the longest and most comprehensive lunch menus on the island. Standard menu items include deli-style sandwiches, soups, chowders, pastas, salads, and platters such as grilled steaks, pork chops, and veal. The most popular fish here is grilled grouper with citrus-butter sauce.

The restaurant, situated on the lower lobby level of the Southampton Princess, provides a scenic view over the hotel's swimming pool and the ocean beyond. Since it stays open all afternoon until 6:30pm, many Bermudians like to come here for a late lunch or early supper. The informal but traditional restaurant requests only that guests cover their bathing suits with a shirt. A children's menu is available.

5 Warwick Parish

MODERATE

Pawpaws Restaurant & Bar

87 South Shore Rd. ☎ **441/236-7459.** Reservations recommended. Main courses $6–$14.75 at lunch, $18.50–$25.50 at dinner. MC, V. Daily 11am–5pm and 5:15–10pm. Bar open until 1am. Bus: 7. CONTINENTAL/BERMUDIAN.

This family favorite about 3 miles west of Hamilton offers a varied and unusual menu at reasonable prices. With the aura and ambience of a European bistro, Pawpaws attracts everybody from those seeking an upscale dinner to the family with kids in tow. On the walls are murals of papaw (papaya) trees and other scenes, along with trellis work and a few paintings by local artists.

The lunch menu features sandwiches and salads, as well as the restaurant's signature dish, Pawpaw Montespan, made from green papaw, ground beef, and herbs. In the evening, one of the most deservedly popular dishes is the lobster ravioli in a cream-flavored basil sauce with strips of smoked salmon. Equally good is the seafood vol-au-vent. If you're yearning for island cuisine, sample the red snapper in banana sauce. You'll also find more classic dishes, including a tender pepper steak in a cognac cream sauce or leg of lamb steak marinated in herbs.

6 Paget Parish

VERY EXPENSIVE

✪ Fourways Inn Restaurant

1 Middle Rd. ☎ **441/236-6517.** Reservations necessary in summer (at least 1–2 days in advance). For men, jacket required, tie recommended. Main courses $8–$25 at lunch, $28–$68 at dinner. Sun brunch $33.50. AE, MC, V. Daily 11:30am–2:30pm and 6:30–9:30pm. Bus: 8. FRENCH/BERMUDIAN.

The Fourways Inn has become the best restaurant in Bermuda. Housed in a former coral, stone, and cedar 18th-century Georgian home, with interior mahogany beams, it has a traditional Bermudian character and a predominantly European staff that makes it a bit stuffy. You can dine either inside or out, depending on the season. Most evenings, there's a pianist playing, and the atmosphere is relaxed. The old kitchen, with its whitewashed fireplace, has been turned into the Peg Leg Bar.

Bermuda's most tempting selection of hot and cold hors d'oeuvres is served here, including pan-roasted bay scallops and scampi with ratatouille and a fresh basil puree. A limited but excellent choice of fish is offered nightly, including a lightly charcoal-grilled local tuna with braised scallions, sun-dried tomatoes, and sweet peppers that is perfection itself. The good life filters ever more sweetly into the rest of the exquisite cuisine, which is based on the best seasonal ingredients. The chef's signature dish consists of thin slices of tender veal served with a zesty citrus sauce. A fine selection of fresh vegetables is served nightly. A nonvegetarian acquaintance of ours came here once and ordered only vegetables; she was extremely pleased with their preparation and taste. To complement its ambitious menu, the Fourways has the finest wine cellar on the island. At lunch, expect sandwiches, several hot dishes, and a catch of the day.

EXPENSIVE

Café Lido

In the Elbow Beach Hotel, 60 South Shore Rd. ☎ **441/236-9884.** Reservations recommended. Main courses $19.75–$29.75 at dinner, $9.95–$19.95 for lunch. AE, MC, V. May–Nov daily noon–2:45pm and 6:30–10:30pm; Dec–Apr daily noon–2:30pm and 6:30–9:30pm. Bus: 1, 2, or 7. MEDITERRANEAN.

Set on the beachfront of the Elbow Beach Hotel, this well-recommended choice is divided into an outdoor terrace and an indoor dining room with big windows that fill it with lots of light. The ambience is dominated by shades of Bermuda pink and salmon, the chairs are comfortable enough to linger in, and you'll enjoy the selections from one of the most diverse menus on the island. We strongly recommend trying one of their specialty pastas—some of the best include homemade herb and pepper fettuccine with a sauce made from mushrooms, caramelized onions, and port wine reduction; homemade ravioli stuffed with asparagus and dried ricotta and served with a sage-flavored butter sauce and freshly grated Parmesan; and spinach and potato gnocchi in a sauce of Taleggio cheese and spicy Italian sausage. Follow this with a traditional veal scallopini. Or try the baby rack of lamb—sprinkled with sesame seeds, roast garlic, and double port sauce—that's so tender, small, and succulent that it's technically designated for just one diner, though this dish is often served for two. Grilled swordfish, salmon, saffron-flavored casseroles whose specific ingredients depend on the whims of the chef, and tenderloin of beef are also staples.

The Middleton Room

In Horizons and Cottages, South Shore. ☎ **441/236-0048.** Reservations required. Jacket and tie required for men. Fixed-price menu $55. No credit cards. Daily 12:30–3pm and 7:30–9pm. Bus: 7. INTERNATIONAL.

Set on a hilltop overlooking 30 acres of carefully landscaped grounds and golf course, this well-recommended restaurant lies in a much-enlarged building that was originally constructed as a private home in the 17th century. It's a member of the

---

Dressing the Part

Most of the upscale restaurants in Bermuda ask that men wear a jacket and tie for dinner; some restaurants dispense with the tie but require a jacket. When you're making reservations, it's always wise to ask what the dress code is before showing up. "Casual but elegant" dress is preferred at most Sunday buffets.

prestigious Relais & Châteaux association of hotels and restaurants around the world, and it's associated with a clubby and very expensive cottage colony, very private and discreet.

Within an interior lined with French windows and a color scheme of green and white, you'll enjoy the eclectic cuisine of French-born Carolline Bouton, whose food often encompasses influences from France and the Far East. Menus, served only as fixed-price meals, change daily and depend on the whims of the chef. Depending as they do on inventories of whatever fish, produce, or meats happen to be fresh and available in the larders that day, they've even included artfully arranged sushi as a foil for European-style main courses. Examples from past (and memorable) meals here have included an osso buco of ostrich, curried lamb in phyllo pastry, venison in port wine sauce, and fillets of marlin, snapper, or tuna. Midsummer diners usually appreciate the medley of chilled soups that is one of the restaurant's warm-weather trademarks. The restaurant's collection of wines has won the *Wine Spectator* international award 7 years in a row.

The Norwood Room

In the Stonington Beach Hotel, South Shore Rd. ☎ **441/236-5416.** Reservations required. Jacket and tie required for men in the evening. Main courses $7–$18 at lunch; fixed-price dinner $54. AE, DC, MC, V. Daily noon–2pm and 7–8:15pm. Bus: 7. CONTINENTAL.

The Norwood Room offers stately dining in a large sun-filled room, decorated in blue and soft yellow. The room is laced with wood beams and a halo of arched windows looking out over the well-maintained lawn and the ocean. The restaurant is part of a state-run hotel training institute (see chapter 4, "Accommodations"). Although the young staff is inexperienced, they're thoughtful and courteous, and they probably try harder than more jaded personnel. A pianist or harpist provides music in the evening.

The food is splendid, and each dish is prepared with care. We always choose the set menu, which is broadly continental. We once had tenderloin of pork stuffed with dried winter fruit in an exotic chile plum dressing; another time it was pan-seared duck breast in a tart orange sauce, flambéed with Gosling's Black Seal rum; and still another time it was grilled fillet of mahimahi (dolphin fish) with tiger shrimps, served over polenta and drizzled with a gingery Malaysian sauce. The chef also prepares a pasta of the day.

INEXPENSIVE

Paraquet Restaurant

South Shore Rd. (near the Elbow Beach Hotel). ☎ **441/236-9742.** Reservations not required. Breakfast special (until 11am) $7.20; sandwiches $3.10–$9.95; main courses $11.95–$21.50. No credit cards. Daily 7:30am–1:30am. Closed Feb. Bus: 2 or 7. BERMUDIAN.

Located near a major traffic junction on the south shore near the Elbow Beach Hotel, this unpretentious restaurant is at the center of an apartment cluster of the same name. From your table, you can see a circular formal flower garden, created by the Portuguese owners. Both the coffee-shop setting and menu—complete with lime-colored Formica and substantial home-style Bermudian fare—are straight out of the 1950s. This is the type of good, wholesome food that Ike used to enjoy in the White House. You'll find one of the largest sandwich menus on the island (both hot and cold), as well as omelettes, homemade soups (there's always a fish chowder of the day), and salads. You can order mixed platters with such ingredients as turkey breast and crabmeat, or such grilled dishes as T-bone steak, fried liver and onions, or roast half-spring chicken.

7 City of Hamilton (Pembroke Parish)

VERY EXPENSIVE

The Tiara Room

In the Hamilton Princess, 76 Pitts Bay Rd. ☎ **441/295-3000.** Reservations required. Jackets required, tie optional for men. Main courses $18–$52. AE, DC, MC, V. Daily 6:30–9pm. Bus: 7 or 8. CONTINENTAL.

The gourmet choice at the Hamilton Princess, the Tiara Room is elegant hotel dining at its finest. This modernized restaurant has tiara-shaped chandeliers and offers a panoramic view of Hamilton Harbour; dozens of flickering candles illuminate the fine crystal and heavy silver. Flambé dishes are a specialty here, adding a touch of theatricality to the decor. This is a great choice for a regal night on the town.

The cuisine is continental, and the menu often changes. The food here is actually better than it's been in years. The pastas are delectable, especially the lobster linguini or the seafood casserole with lobster, scallops, shrimp, and mussels in a saffron cream. If that sounds too rich, choose a broiled or panfried fresh grouper fillet, or even the fresh catch of the day. As in the classic English tradition, there's a roast in the evening (your captain will tell all about it). Some of the main dishes are those allegedly preferred by Queen Elizabeth II herself: grilled lamb chops, roast duckling (or chicken), and filet mignon. Classic specialty flambé desserts include baked Alaska and cherries jubilee for two.

Waterloo House

Pitts Bay Rd. ☎ **441/295-4480.** Reservations required at dinner. Jacket required, tie optional for men. Main courses from $18 at lunch, $26–$32 at dinner. Daily noon–2:30pm and 7–9:30pm. AE, MC, V. INTERNATIONAL.

At the edge of Hamilton Harbour, this former private home—now the most famous inn on Bermuda—is a Relais & Châteaux property; its dining facilities are open to the public. Terraced gardens, which descend to the water, are often the setting for waterside buffets. Guests dine by candlelight either outside on the harbor-front terrace or in the elegantly appointed, English-style dining room, where a fire roars in the fireplace on nippy evenings.

Some reports have suggested that the food has declined in quality, but that's not what we found on recent visits. A most discriminating reader from Virginia agrees, finding the food "absolutely fantastic—though somewhat expensive." She cited portions so large at lunch that she skipped dinner.

You might begin with a cedar-smoked duck breast with a dried cherry dressing, or else snails baked in new potatoes with sour cream. The soups served here are often innovative, such as a chilled island pumpkin soup or a wild berry soup. The best main dishes are fish or shellfish—perhaps salmon with crushed mustard seeds and a saffron grapefruit sauce, or Cajun scallops in a sweet-and-sour sauce with curried vegetables. The classics are still served, ranging from roast rack of lamb to peppered Angus steak, but there's always something unusual on the menu as well—perhaps quail with a honey, apple, and thyme sauce. Lunches include vegetarian specials, soups (such as a green gazpacho), salads, sandwiches, and several items from the grill, such as Bermuda codfish cakes with a tomato and pineapple salsa.

EXPENSIVE

Ascots

In the Royal Palms Hotel, 24 Rosemont Ave. ☎ **441/295-9644.** Reservations recommended. Main courses $10–$18 at lunch, $18–$29 at dinner. AE, MC, V. Mon–Fri and Sun noon–2:30pm and 6:30–10pm, Sat 6:30–10pm. Bus: 1, 2, 10, or 11. ITALIAN/FRENCH.

Dining in the City of Hamilton

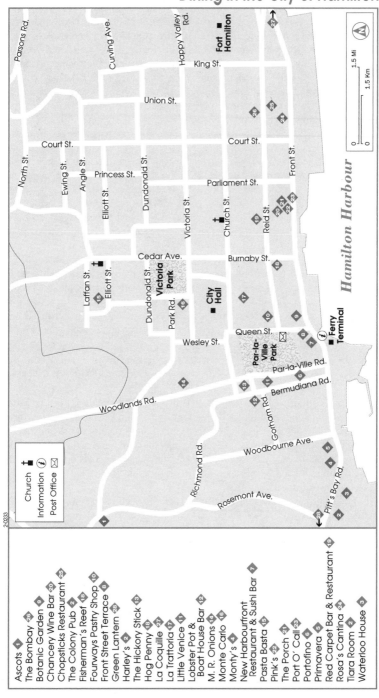

Ascots ❶
The Bombay ㉚
Botanic Garden ❾
Chancery Wine Bar ⑳
Chopsticks Restaurant ㉕
The Colony Pub ❷
Fisherman's Reef ⑯
Fourways Pastry Shop ⑩
Front Street Terrace ❽
Green Lantern ㉘
Harley's ❼
The Hickory Stick ⑬
Hog Penny ㉙
La Coquille ㉗
La Trattoria ⑭
Little Venice ㉖
Lobster Pot & Boat House Bar ⑫
M. R. Onions ⑥
Monte Carlo ㉓
Monty's ⑪
New Harbourfront Restaurant & Sushi Bar ❼
Pasta Basta ⑮
Pink's ❺
The Porch ㉑
Port O' Call ㉔
Portofino ❻
Primavera ❺
Red Carpet Bar & Restaurant ㊾
Rosa's Cantina ㉒
Tiara Room ❷
Waterloo House ❸

2-0233

Church ✝■
Information ⓘ
Post Office ⊠

This restaurant, in the Royal Palms Hotel, remains relatively undiscovered in spite of its tempting continental menu—but it deserves to be better known. Ascots is situated within a spacious house originally built around 1870, located in a residential neighborhood at the end of a Bermuda country lane at the edge of Hamilton. Before-dinner drinks are served from a large bar crafted from Bermuda cedar and brass in a setting of antique porcelain, Queen Anne armchairs, and Welsh pine that resembles a chintz-filled English country house. In the summer, candlelit tables are placed on the front porch, and sometimes beneath a tent in the garden.

Owner Claudio Vigilante, originally from San Remo, Italy, oversees the cuisine, which might include pasta Claudio, prepared at your table by the owner himself using sun-dried tomatoes, black olives, capers, onions, garlic, and "a family secret." The rest of the menu is based on classic techniques and first-rate ingredients. There's one of the best selections of hot and cold appetizers in Hamilton, ranging from a Mediterranean chicken salad with goat cheese to a fresh homemade ravioli filled with crabmeat and served in a smoked salmon and spinach cream sauce. Vegetarian dishes are available. Count on the chef's catch of the day, prepared as you like it, or try the blackened mahimahi (dolphin) with a tomato, pineapple, and lemon compote. If you prefer more traditional dishes, you might find the grilled sirloin steak with port glaze and roasted thyme polenta more suited to your taste. For dessert, the crepe Garibaldi (warm crepes filled with bananas and a chocolate hazelnut sauce and served with fresh berries and crème chantilly) is a good choice. Even more exciting are the flambé desserts; choose from Bermuda bananas with rum, crepes suzette, or seasonal berries with Frangelico and chocolate ice cream.

○ La Coquille

Pembroke Hall, 40 Crow Lane. ☎ **441/292-6122.** Reservations recommended. Main courses $8–$21 at lunch, $23.75–$30.75 at dinner. AE, MC, V. Daily noon–2:30pm and 6:30–10pm. Bus: 1, 2, 10, or 11. FRENCH/MEDITERRANEAN.

One of the most sophisticated French restaurants in Bermuda sits on the eastern extension of Front Street, in a dining room set within the Bermuda Underwater Exploration Institute. The decor isn't elaborate and overdone: Look for modern, clean lines and tones of blue. The staff, among the most polished in Bermuda, hails from France, Germany, Austria, and Italy. The upscale, carefully cultivated cuisine is European, vaguely Provençale—not very typical for Bermuda. The menu would be worthy of Paris or New York.

At lunchtime, expect a flavorful but relatively straightforward assortment of artfully presented sandwiches, grilled fish, and steaks. Evening meals are more elaborate and flamboyant. A worthy beginning is panfried foie gras with caramelized pears, served *en brioche* in a port wine reduction; or perhaps a very fresh, just-picked salad that mingles the best of Bermuda with Provence in the form of mesclun, pear tomatoes, local herbs, and kalamata olives. Two evening dishes of which the chefs are particularly proud include a gratin of scallops with saffron sauce, and a richly aromatic grilled semiboneless quail with wild boar sausages, served with porcini mushrooms, risotto pancakes, and roasted pearl onions. Especially succulent is a rack of lamb in a sun-dried tomato crust served with garlic-enriched whipped potatoes and sautéed baby artichokes.

Monte Carlo

9 Victoria St. (behind Hamilton's City Hall). ☎ **441/295-5453.** Reservations recommended. Main courses $10–$18 at lunch, $18–$25 at dinner. AE, MC, V. Mon–Fri noon–3pm; Mon–Sat 6–10:30pm. Bus: 1, 2, 10, or 11. CONTINENTAL/ITALIAN/MEDITERRANEAN.

This cheery restaurant celebrates the cuisines of southern France and Italy. Seating is within either of two dining rooms: Booths and banquettes in the outer room are

A Note on Hotel Dining

Many resort hotels require guests to take the modified American plan (MAP), or half-board arrangement of breakfast and dinner, in high season, from April to November. To escape the routine of eating in the same dining room every night, some hotels offer a "dine around" program, allowing you to dine at other hotels either on your MAP plan or at somewhat reduced prices. Ask about these arrangements when booking your hotel room.

ringed with a local artist's impressions of the countryside around Monaco; tables and chairs in the main dining room center around a brick-sided fireplace. The chefs prepare the best bouillabaisse in Hamilton; using Atlantic seafish, they achieve the savory style that's typical of Marseilles. One of the better dishes is fillet of tuna marinated in oil and herbs and grilled over charcoal. (The wahoo would be better served by this simple preparation, too; it's too much to top it with a lobster sauce.) The rack of lamb is tender and well seasoned with provençal herbs. Classic lamb chops appear with the flavoring of the Côte d'Azur, and the veal scaloppine is sautéed and served with sun-dried tomatoes and peppers on angel-hair pasta. Desserts are wheeled with a flourish on a trolley through the dining room.

New Harbourfront Restaurant & Sushi Bar

Front St. (between Queen St. and Par-la-Ville Rd.). ☎ **441/295-4207.** Reservations recommended. Main courses $9.75–$19.75 at lunch, $19–$29.75 at dinner. AE, DC, MC, V. Mon–Sat 11:30am–5:30pm and 6–10pm. Bus: 1, 2, 10, or 11. ITALIAN/SEAFOOD/SUSHI.

Front Street was once known only for pubs and fish-and-chips, but this restaurant has challenged its neighbors by offering some innovative continental dishes and even the town's best selection of sushi—no longer does fish have to be deep-fried in oil left over from last week! The cuisine here fairly bursts with flavors and aromas. If some dishes aren't as successful as others, at least the kitchen should be applauded for trying to wake up the sleepy taste buds of Hamilton. However, service remains sluggish and indifferent—one reader even dismissed it as a "classic tourist trap," but nevertheless commended the food.

For starters, the inevitable Bermudian fish chowder appears, but miso soup is also available. Of the pasta specialties offered, our pick is the lobster and rockfish ravioli served open-faced with a red pepper sauce. Fresh fish appears in a variety of ways, including "fisherman style," with shrimp, scallops, squid, mussels, and clams in a sun-dried tomato, mushroom, and wine sauce with angel-hair pasta. You might also try the shrimp and vegetable tower—vegetable ragout surrounded by grilled jumbo shrimp served on a champagne-leek sauce. The restaurant also offers poultry and meat, including a well-prepared sliced breast of duck served in an orange Curaçao and cumin-scented sauce with glazed red cabbage. Pastries and cakes are prepared daily, and a wide variety of homemade Italian ice cream is always available.

The spacious restaurant is on the second floor of an old Hamilton building across from the ferry terminal in the center of town. A balcony, which juts out over the street, has a limited number of tables and is quite popular in fair weather.

MODERATE

Chancery Wine Bar

Chancery Lane (between Reid and Front Sts.). ☎ **441/295-5058.** Reservations recommended. Main courses $10–$17 at lunch, $18–$25 at dinner. AE, MC, V. Mon–Sat noon–2:30pm; Mon–Thurs 6–10pm, Fri–Sat 6–10:30pm, Sun 7–10pm. Bar daily noon–1am. Bus: 1, 2, 10, or 11. CONTINENTAL.

This isn't the best restaurant in Hamilton, but in its limited, unpretentious way it succeeds admirably. Located in a street-level building whose vaulted ceiling and thick stone walls date from the early 1900s, this cozy and much-awarded wine bar offers a candlelit ambience very much like that of a European wine cellar. There's a trellis-covered courtyard in back with a handful of tables for alfresco dining. Oenophiles will appreciate the selection of vintages from around the world—more than 160 different wines. The dress code here is casual and the atmosphere relaxed. Since the menu changes monthly, you never know what to expect. There might be an unusual soup like chili potato, or perhaps a salmon, potato, and wild-mushroom strudel with Sevruga caviar. Main dishes are likely to include a tender rack of veal chop stuffed with sun-dried tomatoes; or medallions of pork, lamb, and beef tenderloin with a wild-mushroom ratatouille, basil, and balsamic vinegar sauce.

The Colony Pub

In the Hamilton Princess, 76 Pitts Bay Rd. ☎ **441/295-3000.** Reservations recommended for meals, not necessary for the bar. Lunch buffet $18.50 Mon–Sat, $19.75 Sun. Main courses at dinner $16.95–$29.95. AE, DC, MC, V. Daily 11:45am–2:30pm and 6:30–10pm. Bus: 7 or 8. INTERNATIONAL.

Many Hamilton locals like to drop in here for a drink and to soak up the atmosphere of old Bermuda, complete with nautical memorabilia and English overtones. Look for six beers on tap, including three (Spinnaker, Full Moon, and Wild Hog) brewed on Bermuda. If you happen to be here at lunchtime, you can check out the generous buffet, which is often frequented by local businesspeople.

Dinners are more lavish, and heartier, with an emphasis on chicken, seafood, and two-fisted beef dishes that include sometimes amazingly generous (25-oz.) portions of prime rib of beef. The restaurant, whose meat is flown in fresh three times a week, serves generous portions. Even if the restaurant doesn't meet its goal of having "the best meat anywhere outside the U.S.," customers are generally satisfied. The meat is fork tender, well flavored, and juicy. The huge baked potatoes are flown in from Idaho; there are also chicken selections. The most popular item is the 8-ounce filet mignon, with the 12-ounce New York strip running a close second. The catch of the day generally ranks as a popular third for more health-conscious diners. In the unlikely event you still have room for dessert, we recommend the chocolate brownie with cappuccino ice cream.

Fisherman's Reef

5 Burnaby Hill. ☎ **441/292-1609.** Reservations recommended. Main courses $18–$26; fixed-price lunch $15.95; early-bird dinner (6–7:30pm) $19.95. AE, DC, MC, V. Mon–Fri noon–2:30pm; daily 6–10:30pm. Bus: 1, 2, 10, or 11. SEAFOOD/BERMUDIAN.

Situated above the Hog Penny pub in the heart of Hamilton, Fisherman's Reef is a good choice for local seafood and typical island dishes. Its setting is predictably nautical, with a separate bar and cocktail lounge; dress is smart casual. You can order wahoo, one of Bermuda's most popular game fish, cut into steaks and topped with banana and bacon strips. Since we've never been fond of wahoo and banana, we usually order the Bermuda rockfish instead; it can be prepared in any of a half dozen ways. Our favorite is grilled and served with a sauce of Black Seal rum; others prefer it either blackened in the Cajun style or served in the Mediterranean fashion with herbs and shrimp. Also, in season, Bermuda guinea chicks (that is, small lobsters) are broiled on the half shell, and are they ever good (if only they weren't so expensive!). Ask the waiter about the daily catch—usually snapper, grouper, yellowtail, or shark—which can be panfried, broiled, or poached. Although most people come here for fish, the chef also prepares fairly standard meat courses such as pepper steak flambé, as well as a number of veal specials, including Oscar, marsala, and français. Banana fritters laced with black rum are a favorite dessert.

Harley's

In the Hamilton Princess, 76 Pitts Bay Rd. ☎ **441/295-3000.** Reservations recommended at dinner. Main courses $7.95–$14.95 at lunch, $21–$27 at dinner. AE, DC, MC, V. Apr–Nov Wed–Mon noon–3pm and 6–10pm. Closed Dec–Mar. Bus: 7 or 8. MEDITERRANEAN.

The food at this popular place used to be merely safe and predictable, but it's acquired some flair, making this restaurant a worthwhile choice even if you aren't a hotel guest. In warm weather, outdoor tables are moved close to the edge of the swimming pool, creating the effect of a flowering terrace on the Italian Riviera.

Many people who are shopping in Hamilton for the day like to drop by for lunch, when there's a large selection of "salad extravaganzas"; our favorite is the classic Caesar with grilled *goujons* (slices) of grouper. The catch of the day can also be grilled for you, and there are burgers galore, including one served "topless." Pizzas are also featured, and one part of the menu is reserved for kids. The dinner menu is significantly better, with a choice of pastas—the best is grilled salmon fillets on linguine. Many of the main dishes will bring back memories of sunny Italy, especially beef tenderloin with shrimp and chicken suprème served with a trio of sauces; or tender breasts of chicken with tomato, green pepper, olives, red onions, mushrooms, and fresh herbs.

La Trattoria

Washington Lane. ☎ **441/295-1877.** Reservations not necessary. Main courses $13.75–$24. AE, MC, V. Mon–Sat 11:30am–3pm; daily 5:30–10:30pm. Bus: 1, 2, 10, or 11. NEAPOLITAN/ITALIAN.

This family-oriented restaurant is tucked away on a narrow alleyway 2 blocks north of Hamilton's harborfront. (Look for it in the middle of the block bordered by Reid, Church, Burnaby, and Queen Streets.) There's not a single cutting-edge or glamorous thing about this place, and that's not what the loyal regulars are looking for. Instead, you'll find a decor straight out of old Naples, with checkered tablecloths in green, red, and white, and hanging Chianti bottles. The attentive, if somewhat harried, wait staff will bring you rather standard, well-flavored Italian food that arrives in generous portions. You'll find 10 kinds of pizza, and the kitchen is happy to create additional variations for you. Pastas include lasagna, spaghetti pescatore, and angel hair with shrimp, pesto, and sun-dried tomatoes. Veal can be ordered either parmigiana style or as *scaloppini al limone,* and there's a revolving array of fresh fish.

Little Venice

Bermudiana Rd. (between Par-la-Ville Rd. and Woodbourne Ave.). ☎ **441/295-3503.** Reservations recommended. $9.95–$18.95 main course at lunch, $12.95–$29.75 main course at dinner. AE, DC, MC, V. Mon–Fri 11:45am–2:15pm and 6–10pm, Sat–Sun 6–10pm. Bus: 1, 2, 10, or 11. ITALIAN/CONTINENTAL.

This is one of the most prominent Italian restaurants in Bermuda, a staple that has been here as long as anyone can remember. The owner (originally from Capri) is proud of his specialties, one of which is a savory *casseruola di pesce dello chef,* which consists of a medley of local seafood—including lobster, shrimp, mussels, clams, and several kinds of fish—cooked together with white wine, herbs, and tomatoes. Other choices include a well-flavored fish chowder, spaghetti with seafood, several veal dishes, and an array of pastas, including a superb homemade ravioli stuffed with spinach and ricotta cheese. If you have room for dessert, you might try the smooth zabaglione. Italian wines are featured, either in bottles or (less expensively) in carafes. An abbreviated menu is offered at lunchtime.

ⓘ Family-Friendly Restaurants

M. R. Onions *(see p. 116)*   M. R. Onions is one of the best family restaurants in the city of Hamilton. Everybody loves the barbecue chicken, ribs, and steak; there's also an array of burgers, which can't fail even with the fussiest kids.

Pink's *(see p. 121)*   This Hamilton restaurant is designed to serve the needs of the entire family weekdays until 4:30pm. Everything is available, from breakfast to hearty sandwiches, hot platters, and picnic baskets.

Rosa's Cantina *(see p. 122)*   This house of chili, burritos, fajitas, nachos, tacos, and enchiladas in the city of Hamilton has no equal on the island. The kids get balloons to help create a festive environment, as well as paper and crayons to keep them busy once they've been seated.

Wickets Brasserie & Cricket Club *(see p. 107)*   The children's menus at this popular choice at the Southampton Princess Hotel make this a great place to take the kids. If you arrive before 6:30pm, they can order their dinners from the lower-priced lunch menu.

✪ Lobster Pot & Boat House Bar

6 Bermudiana Rd. ☎ **441/292-6898.** Reservations recommended. Lunch main courses $6.75–$16.75; dinner main courses $18.50–$28.50. Lobster, at either lunch or dinner, can go as high as $40–$80 per person, depending on its size. AE, DC, MC, V. Mon–Fri 11:30am–3pm and 6–10:30pm, Sat 6–10:30pm. Bus: 1, 2, 10, or 11. SEAFOOD.

Set close to the Hamilton Princess Hotel, within a 5-minute drive from the heart of Hamilton, this is one of the best-recommended and most consistently popular restaurants on the island, a fixture since 1973. The Lobster Pot sports walls lined with cedarwood planks, brass and bamboo trim, and such underwater touches as fishnets, branches of coral, and sea fans. There's a bar near the entrance if you want a before-dinner drink, and a dining room behind it where menu items include both Maine and spiny Caribbean lobster, each prepared four ways. Fish sandwiches and platters of hogfish, wahoo, tuna, and rockfish, are prepared any way you want them; we prefer grilled versions with amandine, banana, or lemon-butter sauce. The all-around best start for a meal here is a cup or bowl of steaming Bermuda fish chowder, which emerges a savory brown color from the kitchen, enhanced with cherry peppers and shots of black rum. If you like it, you won't be alone—quarts of the stuff are hauled in frozen form back to the North American mainland by visitors who want to retrieve a portion of their Bermuda holiday someday.

M. R. Onions

Par-la-Ville Rd. ☎ **441/292-5012.** Main courses $9.75–$30; early-bird 3-course dinner $17.95. AE, DC, MC, V. Daily noon–1am; bar daily 11:30am–1am. Bus: 1, 2, 10, or 11. AMERICAN/BERMUDIAN.

The name of this popular restaurant and bar, a chicken-and-ribs kind of place, is a colloquialism: Bermudians are known as onions, and the "M. R." stands for "'em are," or "they are"; hence the name means "they are Bermudians." Resembling an Edwardian-era bar, the restaurant is filled with brass, potted palms, leaf-green walls, and oak trim; caricatures of many Bermudians hang on the walls. If you go early, plan to have a drink at the large rectangular bar that fills most of the front room. During happy hour (daily 5 to 7pm), M. R. Onions is a favorite rendezvous for office workers in the neighborhood. A new addition in the bar is a cybercafe, where you can surf the Web or simply stop by to check e-mail while enjoying a drink.

Well-prepared meals are served in both the bar and the dining room. Specialties include the house onion soup and fresh fish—including tuna, wahoo, rockfish, and mahimahi (dolphin fish)—which can be charbroiled, panfried, or served à la amandine or spicy Cajun blackened-style. Tasty barbecued chicken, ribs, burgers, and steak are also available. Maybe you'll even have enough room left for mud pie, cheesecake, or another creation from the dessert trolley. There's a no-smoking dining room.

The Porch

93 Front St. (between Burnaby and Parliament Sts.). ☎ **441/292-4737.** Reservations recommended. Main courses $7.75–$19 at lunch, $14–$25 at dinner. AE, MC, V. Mon–Sat 11am–10pm. Bus: 1, 2, 10, or 11. INTERNATIONAL.

Lined with bricks and aged paneling, this warmly decorated restaurant is housed in a century-old building. As the restaurant's name implies, it boasts a porch with a sweeping view over Hamilton's harbor; there are also an English-style pub and a wide outdoor terrace for dining in nice weather. (Navigate the stairs carefully as you climb up from Front Street, and be even more careful as you come down after having a drink or two.) Food is available throughout the place, even in the pub-style areas you might have thought were reserved only for drinking.

The menu offers routine fare, particularly veal and beef dishes, including prime sirloin steak (10 oz.), prime roast rib of beef with Yorkshire pudding, steak with shrimp, and even wild boar in season (a throwback to the days of the early settlers on Bermuda). Lunch features sandwiches, salads, fresh fish, crab cakes, burgers, and oysters. It's all quite competently prepared if straightforward. It's a nice place even to just drop by for a drink and soak up the atmosphere.

Port O'Call

87 Front St. ☎ **441/295-5373.** Reservations recommended at dinner. Main courses $7–$22 at lunch, $12–$28 at dinner; fixed-price early-bird dinner (Mon–Fri 5–6pm only) $16.75. AE, MC, V. Mon–Fri noon–2:30pm and 5–10pm, Sat 6–10pm. SEAFOOD/STEAKS.

Housed in a cedar- and brass-trimmed room reminiscent of the interior of an old-fashioned steamship, this restaurant specializes in fresh local fish, four different preparations of lobster, and steaks. If you're fond of lobster, consider the curried version that's served here, unless you'd rather opt for shrimp, or a surf-and-turf combination that might include your choice of various cuts of steak with either shrimp or lobster. Desserts are suitably caloric and include a choice of parfaits. If you're watching your wallets, maybe you'll go for one of the two-course, early-bird, set-price specials, favored even by local residents. During the off-season, if business is slow, the place might close earlier than the hours listed above, so call and check if you're planning on dining late.

Primavera

In Hamilton West, 69 Pitts Bay Rd. (between Front St. and the Hamilton Princess). ☎ **441/295-2167.** Reservations recommended. Main courses $10.75–$24 at lunch, $16.50–$28 at dinner. AE, MC, V. Tues–Fri 11:45am–2:30pm; daily 6:30–10:30pm. Bus: 7 or 8. ITALIAN.

Primavera has long been a staple on the dining scene, a good choice when you're tired of the traditional steak and seafood served almost everywhere else. The cuisine reflects all the regions of Italy, including Sicily, Sardinia, and Rome. We won't pretend that this is the best Italian food in Hamilton; many diners prefer to eat at Little Venice instead. But what you get here is the type of food that those old rat-packers like Dino and Frank used to prefer back when they were on the road: You might begin with a choice of either cold or hot antipasti (for example, a cold seafood salad or hot baked clams served in a marinara sauce), and follow it with soup (perhaps minestrone) or a salad (probably a Caesar). The array of pasta dishes includes tortellini primavera (the chef's surprise) and black ravioli with lobster, or a good chicken cacciatore or sautéed veal with fresh vegetables. Top off your meal with an Italian espresso or a frothy cappuccino. The service is impeccable.

Red Carpet Bar and Restaurant

In the Armoury Building, 37 Reid St. ☎ **441/292-6195.** Reservations recommended. Main courses $10.75–$18.75 at lunch, $17.75–$28.95 at dinner. AE, MC, V. Daily 11:30am–3pm and 6:30–10:30pm. Bar open until 1am. Bus: 1, 2, 10, or 11. ITALIAN/FRENCH/INTERNATIONAL.

Located in a 150-year-old building, Red Carpet serves many Italian dishes despite its English pub–style ambience. This place does a thriving lunch business, thanks to the many offices nearby. Later, after work, the bar (with its decor of darkly stained wood trim, dark-red carpeting, and dim lights) is a popular place for people to relax with a beer. Lunch offerings include sandwiches, cold platters, and a few hot dishes such as panfried fish (including Bermuda tuna and wahoo). Dinners feature a wider array such as veal scaloppine, veal marsala, chicken cacciatore, filet mignon, and New York strip sirloin; a variety of pasta dishes is also featured. Both Primavera and Little Venice serve better food, but your bill here will be more to your liking. What you get is quite good, familiar fare.

INEXPENSIVE

The Bombay

In the Rego Furniture Building, 75 Reid St. ☎ **441/292-0048.** Reservations required. Main courses $13.95–$22; fixed-price lunch $11.95. AE, MC, V. Mon–Fri noon–2:30pm; Mon–Sat 6–11pm. Bus: 1, 2, 10, or 11. INDIAN.

Just can't face another meal of grilled fish or steak? Indian cuisine might be just the thing to break up Bermuda's routine offerings. Authentic Indian dishes, the best on the island, are expertly prepared and served in this third-floor upstairs hideaway, where you can enjoy lunch or dinner in a relaxed atmosphere. Visitors from London or New York may be used to better Indian fare at home, but still, it's a nice change of pace. For lunch, there's "A Taste of India" buffet daily, with a variety of dishes ranging from mulligatawny soup to chicken, beef, lamb, and seafood served with a choice of sauces, in a spicy curry, or roasted in the tandoori oven. The Indian chefs will prepare your dishes with the mild, delicate tastes of coastal India if you prefer, but there are more fiery dishes to choose from if you like things spicy. There are lots of vegetarian options, of course, and even a handful of continental selections. Dress is smart casual.

Botanic Garden

In Trimingham's, 17 Front St. (between Reid and Queen Sts.). ☎ **441/295-1183.** Reservations not accepted. Soups and quiches $4.50; seafood salads $4.50–$5; sandwiches $4–$5. No credit cards. Mon–Sat 9:30am–4:30pm. Bus: 1, 2, 10, or 11. INTERNATIONAL.

Housed on the third floor of the most famous department store in Hamilton, this place attracts shoppers who know good value when they see it. It's an informal, self-service place, ideal for morning coffee or afternoon tea. The pastries, pies, and cakes are excellent, especially the banana bread and the gingerbread. An array of sandwiches is served as well.

✪ Chopsticks Restaurant

88 Reid St. ☎ **441/292-0791.** Reservations recommended. Main courses $6.75–$12 at lunch, $8.95–$20 at dinner. AE, MC, V. Mon–Fri noon–2:30pm; daily 5–11pm. Bus: 1, 2, 10, or 11. CHINESE.

Sooner or later, that craving for Chinese food rears its head. Although off the beaten track at the east end of Hamilton, Chopsticks offers some of Bermuda's best

Afternoon Tea, Island Style

Bermuda still observes the British tradition of afternoon tea. Many guests prefer to have afternoon tea at their own hotels, which provides a good opportunity to meet fellow guests. Others like to visit a variety of hotels for afternoon tea; all of the big resort hotels (including Elbow Beach, Marriott's Castle Harbour Resort, the Hamilton Princess, Sonesta Beach Resort, and the Southampton Princess) offer tea to guests and nonguests alike. Our favorites are the traditional teas served at the Hamilton Princess and Elbow Beach.

Tea is usually served daily from 3:30 to 5pm either indoors or out, depending on the weather. Dress is more casual than in London; men can wear Bermuda shorts and a shirt with sleeves, and women can appear in a simple cotton dress (swimwear, however, is frowned upon). You're always advised to call ahead and reserve (see chapter 4 for contact information).

Among restaurants and cafes, the two offering the best traditional afternoon tea are the **Botanic Garden** and **Fourways Pastry Shop** (**see above or see below tk.**)

Chinese and Thai food, including spicy soup, tangy pork ribs, and seafood. The chef specializes in Szechuan, Hunan, Thai, and Cantonese dishes, with an emphasis on fresh vegetables and delicate sauces. We love the excellent jade chicken, with spears of broccoli, mushrooms, and water chestnuts in a mild Peking wine sauce. Peking duck is served only for two, and it must be ordered 24 hours in advance. Seafood is also prominent on the menu, in dishes such as shrimp in lobster sauce. The best Thai dish is green curry chicken (chicken breast strips simmered with onions and bamboo shoots and served with fresh basil, coconut milk, and a green-curry paste); it can be prepared mild, spicy, or hot. Most of the dishes are the standard ones you'd find in any North American Chinese restaurant, including sweet-and-sour chicken or beef in oyster sauce. Some dishes, however, including the duck in red curry, have real flair. Vegetarians will find a haven here.

Fourways Pastry Shop
In the Washington Mall, Reid St. (at Queen St.). ☎ **441/295-3263.** Reservations not accepted. Tea or coffee $1.40; sandwiches $5.50 each; daily specials $8.75. MC, V (for purchases of $25 or more). Mon–Sat 8am–4:30pm. Bus: 1, 2, 10, or 11. PASTRIES/SANDWICHES.

This is one of Hamilton's most consistently crowded lunchtime venues, serving hundreds of office workers every day. Although the most popular choices are pastries, sandwiches, and endless cups of tea and coffee, they also offer at least three platters of the day that are full meals in themselves. Depending on what's available at the market on any particular day, daily specials might include lasagna with a side salad, savory breast of chicken with greens, or a platter of "deep-fried rice" with minced beef or pork.

Front Street Terrace
In the A. S. Cooper & Sons, Ltd., Building, 59 Front St. ☎ **441/296-5265.** Reservations not necessary. Lunch soups, salads, and platters $4–$15. MC, V. Daily 9am–4pm. Bus: 1, 2, 10, or 11. INTERNATIONAL.

Set within one of Hamilton's largest department stores, but managed independently, this ground-floor, waterfront bistro, set on an outdoor patio, attracts midday shoppers who enjoy healthy salads, sandwiches, soups, and platters. If you're caught in the rain, you can duck in here for shelter on the cedar-trimmed veranda.

The light-textured cuisine reflects international influences, always with special emphasis on healthy ingredients and avoiding chemical additives. All ingredients, including what goes into the rough-textured, six-grain bread, are organically and locally grown. Look for offerings such as jerk tuna sandwiches with a fresh pineapple/avocado mayonnaise; Thai chicken prepared in a sweet chili-flavored vinaigrette that's enhanced with fresh cilantro and mint and Asian greens; charcoal-grilled vegetable sandwiches served with fresh local goat cheese; and salads that include versions with fresh local avocados, tiger prawns, and three-pepper vinaigrette. The owner, Melanie Barnett, is proud of her collection of single malts.

Green Lantern

Serpentine Rd. at the junction of Pitts Bay Rd. ☎ **441/295-6995.** Reservations recommended. Main courses $7.50–$15. AE, MC, V. Mon–Tues and Thurs–Sat 9am–9pm; Wed 9am–3pm. Bus: 1, 2, 10, or 11. INTERNATIONAL.

One of the least pretentious restaurants in Bermuda might remind you of an upscale diner, with a homey-looking decor. The limited menu changes every day, though you'll always find some kind of fresh fish, roasted chicken, and roast beef. Depending on when you arrive, the menu might feature meatloaf and pork chops, lamb chops and stewed oxtail, or curried chicken and steak. No liquor is served at this restaurant, although the owners will indulge you if you want to bring in a bottle of something celebratory on your own. The setting, incidentally, is a century-old Bermudian house about a mile west of the city limits of Hamilton, whose outside is painted—guess what—a pale shade of green.

The Hickory Stick

2 Church St. (at Bermudiana Rd.). ☎ **441/292-1781.** Salads $3–$5.25; sandwiches and hot take-out platters $2–$5.50. No credit cards. Bus: 1, 2, 10, or 11. DELI.

Located near the rose-colored walls of the Hamilton Princess, the Hickory Stick is the most popular delicatessen and take-out restaurant in the city, serving 1,000 customers a day, including lots of office workers.

Although one section seems like a coffee shop (with scones, doughnuts, and morning coffee providing doses of caffeine for the neighborhood residents), most customers are attracted to the overstuffed sandwiches and take-out portions. Offerings include steaming portions of chicken Parmesan, barbecued spare ribs, and fish cakes. Even more popular, however, are the salads, sandwiches, and hot dogs, all of which can be wrapped up and carried away as picnic fare (they'll provide paper napkins and plastic knives, forks, and spoons on request). Advance telephone orders are accepted—a good idea if you don't want to wait for your order to be prepared.

Hog Penny

5 Burnaby Hill. ☎ **441/292-2534.** Reservations strongly recommended. Main courses $7.25–$17 at lunch, $8–$23 at dinner; fixed-price dinner (5:30–7:30pm) $23.50. AE, MC, V. Oct–Mar daily noon–3pm and 5:30–10pm, Apr–Sept daily 11:30am–3pm and 5:30–10:30pm. Bus: 1, 2, 10, or 11. ENGLISH/BERMUDIAN.

Bermuda's most famous pub, built and decorated in the British style with dark paneled rooms, is extremely popular, offering draft beer and ale to a crowd of visitors and locals. The decor consists of old fishing and farm tools, as well as bentwood chairs and antique mirrors. At lunch you can order pub specials (including shepherd's pie and seafood crepes) or a tuna salad. The kitchen prepares a number of passable curries, including chicken and lamb. Fish-and-chips and steak-and-kidney pie are the perennial favorites, and they are comparable to what you'd find in a London pub. Dinner is more elaborate; the menu might include a whole lobster (if available), a fresh fish of the day (perhaps Bermuda yellowfin tuna), and Angus beef (which is excellent). There's nightly entertainment from 9:30pm to 1am; dress is casual.

it's a big world.

And we've got the network to cover it.

Global
connection
with the AT&T
Network

AT&T direct service

...joy going to the corners of the earth? We're with you. With the ...orld's most powerful network, **AT&T Direct**® Service ...es you fast, clear connections from more countries than anyone,* ...d the option of an English-speaking operator. All it takes is ...ur AT&T Calling Card or credit card. And the planet is yours.

...OR A LIST OF **AT&T ACCESS NUMBERS**, TAKE THE ...TACHED WALLET GUIDE.

For
Travelers
who want more than
the Official Line

Monty's

75 Pitts Bay Rd. ☎ **441/295-5759.** Reservations not required. Sandwiches and burgers $4–$7.50; main courses $11.25–$22.50. AE, MC, V. Mon–Sat 7:30am–3pm and 5:30–10pm; Sun 7:30am–2:30pm. INTERNATIONAL.

Situated on the western waterfront road leading to the most congested part of Hamilton, this family-style choice is a simple, friendly place to sit down for a meal. The atmosphere is bright, airy, and very casual; many guests of the nearby Hamilton Princess head here.

Monty's serves a variety of dishes, with an emphasis on English and classic Bermudian fare. Hot dishes include bangers and mash, meat loaf with mashed potatoes, and curried chicken, as well as more exotic choices such as smoked salmon with mango sauce and pumpernickel bread. Also available is a selection of hot and cold sandwiches and burgers. This is also a great choice for breakfast if you're in the mood to venture out of your hotel in the early hours. Stop by on Sunday morning for the traditional Bermudian codfish-and-potatoes breakfast.

Pasta Basta

1 Elliott St. ☎ **441/295-9785.** Reservations not accepted. Salads $5; pastas $5.75 (half portion) or $9.75 (full portion). No credit cards. Mon–Sat 11:45am–11pm, Sun 5–11pm. Bus: 1, 2, 10, or 11. PASTA.

This is the larger of two restaurants with the same cafeteria-style pasta-and-salad combination. (The other, Pasta Pasta, is in St. George's; the slight difference in the spelling of its name has caused a lot of discussion.) In a rather summery setting, customers are offered two kinds of salad (tossed and Caesar) and about a dozen varieties of pasta. Served in full or half portions, pasta choices include two kinds of lasagna (one of which is meatless), plus a frequently changing array of pastas topped with a choice of meat, seafood, or vegetarian sauces. The daily special is likely to be shell-shaped pasta with sausage and onions in a pink sauce. This restaurant is a great place to fill up on quite decent food at a reasonable price—don't expect a lot more. *Note:* No wine, beer, or alcohol is served here, and local licensing laws do not permit you to bring your own drinks.

Pink's

55 Front St. ☎ **441/295-3524.** Breakfast croissant with coffee $2.75; salads, sandwiches, and hot take-out platters $3.25–$7; complete picnic boxes $20 per person. MC, V. Mon–Fri 7:30am–3:30pm, Sat 8:30am–3:30pm. Bus: 1, 2, 10, or 11. DELI.

Outfitted in pink and green, Pink's serves breakfast every day to hundreds of Hamilton's office workers. You can join them in the morning for fresh-made croissants and scones, or at lunch for well-stuffed sandwiches, the best and largest Caesar salads in Bermuda, and a rather unusual couscous salad. Also available are hot platters such as beef pies or summer chicken (drenched in a sauce of sour cream, yogurt, thyme, and orange juice). One of the greatest things about Pink's is its wide second-floor veranda—the longest porch along Front Street—where canopies protect the outdoor tables from the elements.

✪ Portofino

Bermudiana Rd. ☎ **441/292-2375.** Reservations recommended. Main courses $10.95–$24.95; pizzas $9.50–$13. AE, MC, V. Mon–Fri 11:30am–3:45pm; daily 6–11:45pm. Bus: 1, 2, 10, or 11. ITALIAN.

The warm and inviting decor of this trattoria, complete with hanging lamps, evokes northern Italy. You'll find well-prepared, reasonably priced specialties, including a classic minestrone; three kinds of spaghetti and fresh-made pastas, including lasagna, ravioli, and cannelloni; and 17 kinds of 9-inch pizzas. There are also such standard and familiar Italian dishes as Venetian-style liver, veal parmigiana, chicken cacciatore, and beefsteak pizzaiola. Your best bet is one of the freshly made specials posted daily. The kitchen is noted for its ice-cream desserts. There's a limited selection of Italian wines.

Rosa's Cantina

121 Front St. ☎ **441/295-1912.** Reservations required only on Fri and Sat. Main courses $11.50–$20.95; lunch from $7.95. AE, MC, V. Daily noon–1am. Bus: 1, 2, 10, or 11. TEX-MEX.

Head here for your Tex-Mex fix. You can fill up here on beef and chicken fajitas, zesty chili, nachos, tacos, enchiladas, and burritos (the largest on the island), accompanied by frozen margaritas to put the fire out. While the music of mariachi bands plays in the background, you might begin with a hearty and thick black-bean soup, and then move on to *carne asado* (mesquite grilled rib-eye steak)—a chef's specialty. The prices are reasonable, and the best place to sit is on the alfresco balcony.

8 Smith's Parish

EXPENSIVE

Inlet Restaurant

In the Palmetto Hotel, Harrington Sound Rd., Flatts Village. ☎ **441/293-2323.** Main courses $6–$20 at lunch, $19–$36 at dinner. AE, MC, V. Daily noon–2:30pm and 6:30–9pm; light snacks served in pub until 9:30pm. Bus: 10 or 11. INTERNATIONAL.

In creating this restaurant, the owners added a slope-roofed modern extension to a paneled lounge lined with Bermuda cedar. You can sit either near the big windows, which look out over the moon gate and the swimming pool, or in the darker and more intimate recesses of the back. For lunch, there's a selection of sandwiches and burgers; light snacks can be had outside on the patio in nice weather. The dinner menu is larger and more varied. You might start with a spinach or Caesar salad, or Bermuda fish chowder. An attempt has been made to lift dishes, such as the filet mignon in a red wine sauce or a baked Atlantic salmon under a nut crust, out of the ordinary. Seafood courses include a casserole of shrimp and scallops, or perhaps fresh Bermuda fish, broiled or panfried. Each of these dishes is well prepared and is probably your best bet.

9 Hamilton Parish

VERY EXPENSIVE

Mikado

In Marriott's Castle Harbour Resort, 2 South Rd. ☎ **441/293-2040.** Reservations required. Main courses $22–$40; sushi $4.75–$6.25 per order (usually 2 pieces). AE, DC, MC, V. Feb 11–Dec daily 6:30–9:30pm. Bus: 2 from St. George's. JAPANESE.

Located on the lower level of the Marriott (see chapter 4), this is the only real Japanese restaurant in Bermuda, although sushi is served at other places. You pass through lacquered gateways to reach a whimsically art deco version of a Japanese tea garden. For each group of eight diners, an experienced chef prepares teppanyaki-style cuisine; grills placed near each table permit you to watch him work. Rare imported fish mixed with very fresh local fish, such as wahoo, is prepared at the sushi bar. All the traditional Japanese specialties, including tempura, along with an aromatic sake, are available. You won't find any other place like this on Bermuda; for the island, it's unique.

A Note on Reservations

Nearly all major restaurants prefer that you make a reservation; many popular places require that you do so as far in advance as possible. Weekends in summer can be especially crowded. Some old Bermuda hands even make their reservations for the most popular spots before they leave home.

✪ Tom Moore's Tavern

Walsingham Lane, Walsingham Bay. ☎ **441/293-8020.** Reservations required. Jackets required for men at dinner. Main dishes $25–$37. AE, V. Daily 7–10pm. Closed Jan 5–Feb 2. Bus: 1 or 3. FRENCH/CONTINENTAL.

Bermuda's oldest restaurant, built in 1652 as a private home, is located on Walsingham Bay, near the Crystal Caves. It was visited in 1804 by the Irish romantic poet Thomas Moore, who wrote some of his verses here; he referred to a calabash tree that still stands some 200 yards from the tavern. This is the most famous dining room in Bermuda, having experienced many incarnations. The present tavern was opened in 1985 by two Italians, Bologna-born Bruno Fiocca and his Venetian partner, Franco Bortoli; it quickly became one of the island's most popular upscale restaurants. With its four fireplaces and darkened cedar walls, this landmark establishment serves classical French and Italian cuisine.

Seafood is a specialty. During the summer months, there's usually a tank of Bermuda lobsters outside. Local fish featured on the menu are likely to include rockfish and yellowtail; these may be your best bet. One reader wrote that he found the place "very expensive, but worth the price, as the service and atmosphere are both top-notch. The cuisine is not light, however. Extremely well-prepared meals contain very rich sauces." He's right; nevertheless, we'd like to recommend the chef's specialty: quail filled with goose liver, morels, and truffles, and then baked together in puff pastry. Two other recommendations are sautéed sweetbreads in a creamy basil sauce, and Latino-style jambalaya. The setting, the English silver, the German crystal, the Luxembourg china, and the general ambience contribute to a memorable visit.

MODERATE
Windsor Dining Room

At Marriott's Castle Harbour Resort, 2 South Rd. ☎ **441/293-2040.** Reservations required. Main courses $17–$26. AE, DC, MC, V. Mon, Wed–Thurs, and Sat 6–9pm. Closed Dec. Bus: 1. INTERNATIONAL/ITALIAN.

Despite its limited open hours, this is a nice, soothing spot to keep in mind. Amid a decor of forest green and burgundy, you'll enjoy a view over the harbor and the Marriott hotel's courtyard while perusing an Italian and international menu. Perhaps you'll choose a paella-like seafood risotto studded with mussels, shrimp, and chunks of lobster; pappardelle with portobello mushrooms, pepper, and garlic; grilled Bermuda swordfish with Kalamata olive-and-tomato relish; or grilled 8-ounce fillet of beef with a Parmesan-herb crust and Barolo wine glaze. Consider prefacing a meal here with a drink in the adjacent lounge bar, where music from a live piano adds to a clientele of mostly middle-aged diners.

INEXPENSIVE
✪ Bailey's Ice Cream & Food D'Lites Restaurant

At Wilkinson Ave. and Blue Hole Hill, Bailey's Bay. ☎ **441/293-8605.** Sandwiches $3–$4.75; ice cream $2 per scoop. No credit cards. Mon–Sat 11am–6pm, Sun 11am–7pm. Closed Dec–Feb. Bus: 1, 3, 10 or 11. ICE CREAM/SANDWICHES.

This ice-cream parlor, housed in a small Bermuda cottage, is just across from the Swizzle Inn (see below). For all-natural ice cream, there's no comparable spot in Bermuda—20 to 25 different flavors are made in the shop's 40-quart ice-cream maker. You can enjoy your Bermuda banana, coconut, white-chocolate cherries and chips, or other exotic-flavored ice cream at one of the outdoor tables. A sandwich nook, which uses fresh-baked bread for all sandwiches, is a popular attraction. Also featured are fresh-fruit ices, frozen yogurts, and natural juices—perfect on a hot, sunny day.

Halfway House Restaurant & Bar

8 North Shore Rd., Flatts Village. ☎ **441/295-5212.** Reservations not necessary. Main courses $12.50–$21.50. MC, V. Daily 11am–11pm. Bus: 1 or 3. INTERNATIONAL.

Named because of its position in the heart of Flatts Village, midway between Hamilton and St. George's (and about 6½ miles from either of them), this is a popular and unpretentious neighborhood bar and restaurant with a wide-ranging menu that includes virtually every North American–inspired specialty you can think of. You can get huge salads, burgers, pastas, curried pork and chicken dishes, and succulent versions of both Bermuda fish chowder and red-bean Portuguese soup. Fish is very fresh and is prepared in any of about four ways, including grilled, according to your tastes and preferences. Examples include rockfish, wahoo, swordfish, and the perennial favorite, panfried yellowtail snapper with parsley-flavored butter sauce.

Swizzle Inn

3 Blue Hole Hill, Bailey's Bay. ☎ **441/293-9300.** Reservations accepted only for parties of 5 or more. Main courses $5.75–$12 at lunch, $8.95–$23.95 at dinner. AE, MC, V. June–Sept daily 11am–3am, off-season daily 11am–midnight. Closed Mon Jan–Feb. Bus: 3 or 11. BERMUDIAN/ENGLISH.

The oldest pub in Bermuda—some 300 years old—and the home of the Bermuda rum swizzle lies west of the airport, near the Crystal Caves. Thousands of business cards and reams of graffiti cover the walls. All of the food is freshly prepared. The meaty Swizzleburger was voted best in Bermuda; other pub favorites include fish-and-chips, conch fritters, and shepherd's pie. These dishes are at least a notch above typical Bermudian pub grub. Popular among both Bermudians and visitors at lunch are the Bailey's Bay fish sandwich and onion rings. The larger and more varied dinner menu appeals to a variety of tastes and diets. Dining is available both inside and on the upper and lower patios; upstairs there's also a no-smoking room and a gift shop. A piano player entertains Tuesday to Sunday.

10 St. George's Parish

MODERATE

✪ Black Horse Tavern

101 St. David's Rd., St. David's Island. ☎ **441/297-1991.** Reservations recommended for parties of 4 or more. Main courses $8.50–$27. AE, MC, V. Tues–Sat 11am–1am, Sun noon–1am. Bus: 6. INTERNATIONAL/BERMUDIAN.

If you should land here, in a section of the island that Bermudians call "the country," you'll dine with the locals, many of whom maintain (with some justification) that this is the best place for "an authentic taste of Bermuda." It looks like a dusty-rose-colored private home, with green shutters and a glassed-in porch in the rear that looks over Smith's Sound. Over the years, the tavern has hosted many celebrities; a number of the guests arrive in yachts.

You might begin your meal with curried conch stew, shark hash (made with minced puppy shark), fish chowder, or curried mussels. Later choices include sandwiches, burgers, or perhaps a platter of fish-and-chips or chicken-and-chips.

Dining in St. George's

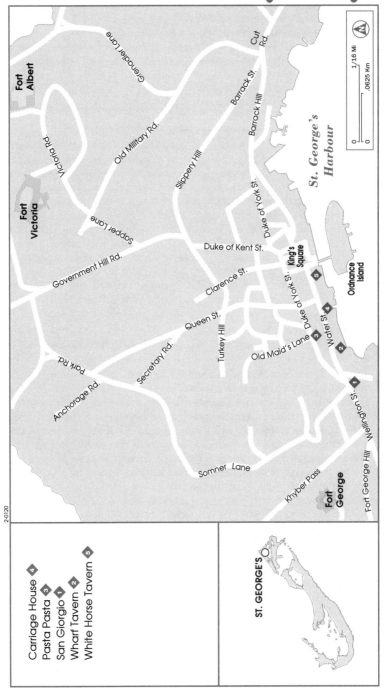

Carriage House ◆ 4
Pasta Pasta ◆ 3
San Giorgio ◆ 1
Wharf Tavern ◆ 2
White Horse Tavern ◆ 5

ST. GEORGE'S

2-0120

125

The chef also prepares a good sirloin steak and a chicken dinner. If your luck holds, the only Bermuda Triangle you'll encounter is a drink made here with pineapple juice, orange juice, black rum, and Bermuda gold liqueur. This place is more of a regular restaurant than the equally famous Dennis's Hideaway (see below).

Carriage House

22 Water St., Somers Wharf. ☎ **441/297-1730.** Reservations recommended. Main courses $9.75–$24.50 at lunch, $14.50–$29 at dinner; fixed-price lunch $18.75; 4-course early-bird special (5:30–6:45pm) $19.50; Sun buffet $26.50 per person. AE, DC, MC, V. Daily 11:30am–4:30pm and 5:30–9:30pm; Sun buffet brunch noon–2pm. Bus: 3, 10, or 11. STEAKS/SEAFOOD.

Housed in an old waterfront storehouse, the restored Carriage House specializes in beef and seafood, which you can enjoy on a terrace if the weather is right. It retains the 18th-century warehouse look with two rows of bare brick arches, spruced up with hanging baskets of greenery. Guests can choose to dine outdoors by the harborside. The chef specializes in prime rib, which is always cut to order (and priced according to size) and served with a ramekin of creamed horseradish in the British tradition. Other specialties include English lamb chops with rosemary, and tasty versions of Bermuda rockfish, black grouper, or snapper. Many dishes are well prepared, especially oven-roasted barbary duck breast and panfried steak Diane flambéed at your table with cognac. A different soup is offered every day. At lunch, there's a large selection of hamburgers, as well as sandwich platters, Bermuda fish chowder, pastas, soups, and oysters. The dessert choices are always excellent.

✪ Dennis's Hideaway

Cashew City Rd., St. David's Island. ☎ **441/297-0044.** Reservations required. Fixed-price dinners $15–$32.50, platters $21.50. No credit cards. Daily 10am–10pm. Bus: 3. SEAFOOD.

Dennis Lamb, a burly St. David's islander, is one of the treasures of Bermuda. So is his quaint little restaurant, located in the easternmost parish of St. George's. As you approach it (the cottage is accessible by land or sea), you're likely to see Dennis working in his garden in front (he grows the cabbage for his coleslaw and beets for pickling, among other things). He'll show you into his fisher's cottage, situated by one of the island's little coves. Once inside, you'll feel like you've left Bermuda and are visiting some little pocket-size country with its own distinctive personality.

Descended from whalers and pilots ("wooden ships and iron men"), Dennis and his son will offer you dishes that have otherwise virtually disappeared from Bermuda's restaurants, dishes that are normally available only in private homes today. For $32.50, he'll give you "the works": an array of dishes, including conch stew, mahimahi (dolphin fish), herb-flavored shark hash, shrimp, conch fritters— you name it (but please don't order the turtle, an endangered species). If you don't want to eat so much, ask for the $15 fish dinner.

This offbeat, informal ambience isn't for everyone. Some readers give it high marks, claiming they've made at least 20 pilgrimages here during their annual visits to Bermuda. However, some feel that we shouldn't send diners to "this grubby place." Thus, we would recommend Dennis's Hideaway only to the adventurous. You may bring your own wine. Don't dress up.

San Giorgio

Water St. (next to the Tucker House Museum). ☎ **441/297-1307.** Reservations recommended. Main courses $10.50–$17 at lunch, $16–$25 at dinner; pizzas and pastas $10–$14. MC, V. Mon–Sat noon–2:30pm and 6:30–10pm. Bus: 3, 10, or 11. ITALIAN.

This little restaurant is your best bet for Italian dining in the East End (though the Italian restaurants in Hamilton are better). The 150-year-old building was originally a private house and later served as the local telephone exchange for St.

George's; to reach it, you must climb a short flight of steps opposite Somers Wharf. Today, the bistro/trattoria is deliberately informal, with red-and-white-checked table-cloths, a casual dress code, and several artifacts commemorating San Giorgio and his dragon. Most guests begin with a selection of antipasto, which is fairly routine. There are several savory pasta dishes, including tortellini and a creamy lasagna. Among the main courses is an excellent breast of chicken sautéed with black-cherry-and-rum sauce, a hot shrimp salad, and a hot scallop salad. If it's on the menu, the regularly featured fresh broiled wahoo with lemon butter sauce might be your best bet.

Wharf Tavern

Somers Wharf. ☎ **441/297-1515.** Reservations recommended. Main courses $5.50–$16.50 at lunch, $8.50–$26.50 at dinner. MC, V. Daily 11am–11pm. Bar daily 10am–1am. Bus: 3, 10, or 11. SEAFOOD.

The Wharf Tavern is a nautically themed but modern restaurant located on the ground floor of a 200-year-old former warehouse. Only pedestrians are allowed nearby, which might account for the popularity of the porch and the window seats; there's also a darkly paneled bar area inside. The setting is more interesting than the food, which is just standard, but Bermudians have been eating and enjoying it for decades. Dinners might include curried mussels, Bermuda fish cakes with peas and rice, panfried or broiled rockfish, broiled wahoo, oysters on the half shell, steak-and-kidney pie, and a London-style mixed grill. All main courses are served with a salad and a "starch." During the summer months, entertainment is presented 7 nights a week beginning at 10pm (there's no cover charge). A children's menu is available.

White Horse Tavern

King's Sq. ☎ **441/297-1838.** Reservations accepted only for groups. Main courses $5.85–$25 at lunch, $9.25–$25 at dinner. MC, V. Restaurant daily 11:30am–4pm and 5:30–10pm; bar daily 11:30am–1am. Bus: 3, 10, or 11. BERMUDIAN.

St. George's oldest tavern may be the most popular in Bermuda; it's always jammed with visitors. This white building with green shutters has a restaurant and cedar bar with a terrace jutting into St. George's Harbour. In nice weather, guests usually prefer to sit on the terrace. The most popular item on the menu here is fish-and-chips (often overdone), cooked in the manner of St. David's Island. The Bermuda fish chowder is good, as are rum-drenched pork chops or grilled wahoo (the local catch). At lunch, there are Tavern burgers, fresh salads, and open-faced sandwiches. Finish off with the White Horse chocolate cake if you have room. Dress is casual, and enjoyable entertainment is often featured.

INEXPENSIVE

Pasta Pasta

York St., St. George's. ☎ **441/297-2927.** Reservations not accepted. Salads $5; pastas $5.75 (half portion), $9.75 (full portion). No credit cards. Mon–Sat 11:45am–11pm, Sun 5–11pm. Bus: 8, 10, or 11. PASTA.

This is the smaller and slightly less expensive of two Bermuda restaurants with the same owners and the same pasta-and-salad emphasis. (Its twin, listed separately under "City of Hamilton," has a slight difference in the spelling of its name.) Decorated in summery colors, this restaurant offers two kinds of salad (tossed and Caesar) and about a dozen types of pasta. There are two kinds of lasagna (one of which is meatless), served in full or half portions, and a frequently changing array of pastas topped with a choice of meat, seafood, or vegetarian sauces. Much of the pasta sold here is prepared for take-out. Yes, you will find better pasta elsewhere, but not in St. George's. No wine, beer, or alcohol is served here, and local licensing laws do not allow you to bring your own drinks.

6 Fun in the Surf & Sun

Although people visit Bermuda mainly to relax on its spectacular pink-sand beaches, the island also offers a wealth of activities, both onshore and off, for active travelers: In fact, its sports facilities are better than those found on most of the Caribbean or Bahamian islands.

The most popular outdoor pursuits in Bermuda are tennis and golf, but sailing ranks high, too. You'll find a fair number of tennis courts and renowned golf courses around the island where you may practice your swing, often with players of better-than-average ability. But if you hesitate to pick up a racket or golf club because you've neglected your game of late, fear not: Your Bermudian partner, on the court or on the links, would deem it quite improper to remark that your game was anything but superb; and if a word of friendly criticism is ever offered, be assured that it will be as gentle as the ocean breezes that sweep over the island.

Bermuda's waters are the clearest in the western Atlantic. Its reefs, shipwrecks—many in such shallow water they're even accessible to snorkelers—a variety of marine life and coral formations, and underwater grottoes make Bermuda ideal for scuba diving and snorkeling.

1 Beaches

Bermuda is one of the world's leading beach resorts. Its miles of pink shoreline are broken only now and then by cliffs that form sheltered coves. Many stretches have shallow, sandy bottoms for some distance out, making them safe for children and nonswimmers. Some beaches (usually the larger ones) have lifeguards; others do not. Public facilities in Bermuda are supervised by the Parks Division of the Department for Agriculture and Fisheries. Hotels and private clubs often have their own private beaches and facilities.

Although you'll find dozens of appropriate spots for sunbathing, swimming, and beachcombing, here's a listing of the island's most famous sands, arranged clockwise beginning with the south-shore beaches closest to the city of Hamilton.

✪ ELBOW BEACH

One of the most consistently popular beaches in Bermuda, Paget Parish's Elbow Beach incorporates almost a mile of (occasionally interrupted) pale pink sand, the edges of which are dotted with private homes and resort hotels. Because of the protective coral reefs that surround it, Elbow Beach is one of the safest on the island—and it's the family favorite. This is also the beach of choice among college students who vacation on Bermuda during spring break.

The Bermuda government provides lifeguards as a public service. The **Elbow Beach Hotel** (☎ **441/236-3535**) offers a variety of facilities and amenities, including sun chairs, changing rooms, showers, rest rooms, and beach towels distributed three times a day by beach attendants (all trained in water safety and lifeguard techniques); they're free for hotel guests but unfortunately off-limits to others. The hotel also rents paddleboats, sea kayaks, and "explorer boats" (surfboards with glass bottoms for underwater viewing) for around $15 per hour; snorkeling equipment for $15 per hour; and Italian-style cloth-sided beach cabanas for $75 per day. Take bus no. 2 or 7 from Hamilton.

✪ ASTWOOD COVE

This Warwick Parish public beach has no problem with overcrowding during most of the year thanks to its remote location, at the bottom of a steep and winding road that intersects with South Shore Road. Many single travelers and couples head here to escape the families with kids that tend to overrun beaches like Elbow in the high season. We like this beach for many reasons, one of them being that its cliffs in the background are home to Longtail bird nests. Although you'll find public rest rooms here, Astwood Beach doesn't have many facilities. An added advantage here, though, is nearby Astwood Park, a favorite picnic and hiking area. If you like your beaches small and secluded, make it Astwood. Take bus no. 2 or 7 from Southampton.

✪ WARWICK LONG BAY

Like Astwood Cove, this is one of the best places for people who want solitude and are trying to escape the family crowds. Unlike the sheltered coves of nearby Chaplin and Horseshoe Bays (see below), this popular beach features a half-mile stretch of sand, the longest on the island, which allows for either social interaction or plenty of space to yourself—whichever you prefer. Against a backdrop of scrubland and low grasses, the beach lies on the southern side of South Shore Park, in Warwick Parish. Despite the frequent winds, the waves are surprisingly small thanks to an offshore reef. Jutting above the water less than 200 feet from the shoreline is a jagged coral island that, because of its contoured shape, appears to be floating above the water's foam. There are rest rooms at the beach's western end, plus lots of parking; no other facilities are available. There are no lifeguards since the undertow is not very strong.

JOBSON'S COVE

Located in Warwick Parish, this beach has the feeling of a secret hideaway, thanks to pink sands, gentle waves, and calm waters. This is a horseshoe-shaped bay that opens to the ocean with a width of only 30 feet. Set adjacent to the much larger, much more prominent Warwick Long Bay, it's excellent for snorkeling, because waters stay at about 6 feet of depth for a long way out into the bay. There are no buildings along the water here, adding to the feeling of seclusion and peace.

STONEHOLE BAY

Set near Jobson's Cove in Warwick Parish, Stonehole Bay is more open and less sheltered than Jobson's, with a sandy shoreline that's studded with big rocks. It's almost never crowded, and wading is safe despite the fact that strong waves sometimes make the waters cloudy (less than ideal for snorkeling).

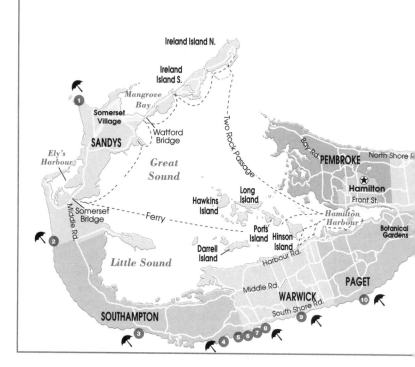

✪ CHAPLIN BAY

Straddling the boundary between Warwick and Southampton Parishes, this small but secluded beach disappears almost completely during storms or exceptionally high tides. Geologists come here to admire the open-air coral barrier that partially separates one half of the beach from the other. Chaplin Bay, like its more famous neighbor to the west, Horseshoe Bay (see below), lies at the southern extremity of South Shore Park. From Chaplin, you can walk over to use all the facilities and beach equipment available at Horseshoe, but you'll enjoy more solitude by basing yourself at this less-crowded beach than at the more active Horseshoe Bay. Take bus no. 7 from Hamilton.

✪ HORSESHOE BAY

With its long, curved strip of pink sand, the beach at Horseshoe Bay, on South Shore Road in Southampton Parish, is one of Bermuda's most famous beaches. That means

Achilles Bay ⑭	John Smith's Bay ⑫
Astwood Cove ⑨	Shelly Bay Beach ⑪
Chaplin Bay ⑤	Somerset Long Bay ①
Church Bay ③	Stonehole Bay ⑥
Elbow Beach ⑩	Tobacco Bay Beach ⑬
Fort St. Catherine's Beach ⑮	Warwick Long Bay ⑧
Horseshoe Bay ④	West Whale Bay ②
Jobson's Cove ⑦	

it's likely to be crowded, especially if cruise ships are in port. Although families flock here, Horseshoe Bay isn't the safest beach in Bermuda. Don't be fooled by the seemingly smooth surface; there can be dangerous undercurrents. If you're using the beach after a storm, be especially careful that you don't encounter a Portuguese man-of-war; they often wash up on the beach here in greater numbers than elsewhere on the island.

One superior advantage this beach has over others is the ✪ **Horseshoe Bay Beach House** (☎ **441/238-2651**), offering changing rooms, toilets, beach-gear rentals, and showers. It also serves snacks and sandwiches from 9am to 5pm daily. A lifeguard is on duty from May to September. *Insider's tip:* When you tire of the crowds at Horseshoe Bay, take one of the little trails that wind through the park nearby; they'll lead you to some secluded cove beaches, where you'll find more privacy. Our favorites are Port Royal Cove to the west and Peel Rock Cove and Wafer Rocks Beach to the east. You might also sneak over to Chaplin Bay to the east (see above). Take bus no. 7 from Hamilton.

✪ CHURCH BAY

Although this beach off West Side Road lies along Bermuda's southwestern edge, at the point in Southampton Parish where the island hooks off to the northeast (and where the waves pound the shore mercilessly), it's sheltered by rows of offshore reefs. Marine life abounds within the relatively calm waters, much to the delight of snorkelers. And if you're just planning to lounge in the sun, this is a great place to do it: The beach offers unusually deep-pink sands. There are toilets at the top of the hill near the parking area, but don't expect much in the way of facilities (unless some local entrepreneur decides to open a concession at the time of your visit). It's a great place for snorkeling, but rent your equipment before you get here. Take bus no. 2 or 7 from Hamilton.

✪ SOMERSET LONG BAY

Whenever offshore storms trouble the waters northwest of Bermuda, the water here is unsafe for swimming. Because its bottom isn't always sandy or of a consistent depth, many people feel this beach is better suited to beachcombing or long walks rather than actual swimming. Nevertheless, many single travelers favor this beach when they're looking for seclusion. The undeveloped parkland of Sandys Parish shelters it from the rest of the island, and the beach's crescent shape and length— about a quarter mile—make it unusual by Bermudian standards. You'll find rest rooms and changing facilities. We think this is one of the best places on Bermuda to watch the sunset. An added plus is the beach's proximity to the Bermuda Audubon Society Nature Reserve, where you can go for long walks and enjoy moments of solitude—except on weekends, when family picnics abound. You can take bus no. 7 from Hamilton, or approach Somerset Long Bay via Cambridge Road in Sandys Parish.

✪ SHELLY BAY

This beach of abundant pink sand is suitable for both families and those seeking solitude. Because it's not well-known, it's unlikely to be crowded, and its calm and shallow basin makes it safe for swimming. Off North Shore Road in Hamilton Parish, Shelly Bay lies within a cove whose encircling peninsula partially shelters it from mid-Atlantic waves. There are trees to sit under when the beach gets too hot, and at the beach house you can rent snorkeling equipment, lounge chairs, beach towels, and other items; there are also public rest rooms. Buses from Hamilton heading east along the north shore stop off here.

ST. GEORGE'S ISLAND

This island comprises *all* of St. George's Parish, the most easterly parish on Bermuda, site of the island's oldest community and the island's airport, plus lots of low-lying, sun-blasted scrublands. The entire island is connected to the other islands of Bermuda by a single bridge (the St. George Causeway), and once across it, you can escape the more congested parts of the island. St. George's Island has many beaches in its own right. They include Archilles Bay, Tobacco Bay, and Fort St. Catherine's Beach (formerly known as the Club Med beach), all of which are sandy, with clean bottoms. Waters of beaches on the south shore are a bit rougher than waters of beaches on the north shore.

One of the loveliest beaches of St. George's island is **Natural Arches Beach,** near Tucker Town, which is owned outright by the private Mid-Ocean Golf Club. Wave and wind erosion has worn away the limestone to a weird series of jagged rocks. Swimmers sunbathe near striking rock formations, a few of which have formed arches. The sea is relatively calm, the bottom is sandy, and the beach is inviting and geologically very interesting—but, unfortunately, enjoyed only by members of the club.

Also lovely and accessible to the public is ✪ **Tobacco Bay.** This East End family favorite used to be the beach for the now-defunct Club Med. It's the most popular beach on St. George's Island, especially among those who come for the day to visit the historic town of St. George's. With its broad open sands, Tobacco Bay looks more like beaches on the southern shore than those on the north side. Its pale pink sand is sheltered within a coral-sided cove just a short walk west of Fort St. Catherine and St. Catherine Beach. The major disadvantage here is that the beach is likely to be overrun with cruise-ship passengers; when they're in port, you may want to seek more secluded beaches such as nearby St. Catherine. You can get a suntan here and even go for a swim, but don't venture out too far; the currents are dangerously strong.

Look for the Tobacco Bay Beach House, Naval Tanks Hill, St. George's, which offers toilets, changing rooms, showers, and a snack bar. At beachfront kiosks you can rent flotation devices and snorkeling gear by the hour from May to September; stands also sell cold sodas and sandwiches (tuna, grilled cheese, and the like, as well as hamburgers, hot dogs, and french fries). Take bus no. 10 or 11 from Hamilton.

✪ JOHN SMITH'S BAY

This is the only public beach in Smith's Parish, and it tends to be popular with residents of Bermuda's eastern end more so than with visitors, who often don't know about it. It's ideal for those seeking solitude. Long, flat, wide, and rich with pale pink sand, this beach has a lifeguard from May to September. Some shallow areas make it ideal for snorkeling. There are toilet and changing facilities on-site. To get here, take bus no. 1 from Hamilton.

2 Snorkeling

Bermuda is known for the gin-clear purity of some of its waters, as well as for its vast array of coral reefs. If you're ready to explore the waters, all it takes are a snorkel, a mask, and fins—if you can swim, you can snorkel. If you'd like, a handful of Bermuda-based companies are ready, willing, and able to help you; otherwise, you can hit the water on your own.

The best places to go snorkeling are at any of the public beaches (see "Beaches," above). Many hotels that are right on the beach will either lend or rent you fins, masks, and snorkels, as well as advise you of the best sites in your area—you almost never have to travel far.

Die-hard snorkelers, some of whom visit Bermuda every year, prefer **Church Bay** to all other snorkeling spots on Bermuda. Church Bay lies on the south shore, west of the Southampton Princess Golf Course and Gibbs Hill Lighthouse; this little cove, which seems to be waiting for a movie camera, is carved out of coral cliffs and is well protected and filled with snug little nooks. Another advantage is that the reefs are fairly close to land. However, the seas can be rough (as is true anywhere in Bermuda), so we always advise caution.

At the eastern end of the south shore, **John Smith's Bay,** situated to the east of Spittal Pond Nature Reserve and Watch Hill Park, is another top spot, especially if your hotel is in the east. Even more convenient, especially for snorkelers staying at St. George's or at a hotel near the airport, is **Tobacco Bay,** directly north of St. George's Golf Course. Another good small snorkeling spot is **West Whale Bay;** it lies along the south shore at the west end of Southampton, west of the Port Royal Golf Course.

Walking Underwater

Helmet diving enjoys great popularity in Bermuda. Underwater walkers—clad in helmets that are fed air through hoses connected to the surface—stroll along the sandy bottom in water to depths of 10 to 12 feet.

Anybody can take part in this adventure, which was featured twice in *Life* magazine. These undersea walks among the coral reefs are safe for anyone from age 5 to 85, even nonswimmers. It's possible to walk underwater wearing your contact lenses or glasses, and you won't even get your hair wet. A helmet is placed on your shoulders as you climb down the ladder of the boat to begin your guided walk. An experienced guide personally conducts the tours. It's as simple as walking through a garden. On your helmet dive, you can feed dozens of rainbow-hued fish, which take food right from your hands. You'll also see sponges breathing and coral feeding.

You can arrange your undersea walk with Bermuda's original helmet diving company by contacting ✪ **Bermuda Bell Diving,** 5 North Shore Rd. (P.O. Box FL281), Flatts FL BX, Bermuda (☎ **441/292-4434**). A 50-foot boat, *Carioca,* leaves Flatts Village daily at 10am and 2pm. The underwater wonderland walk costs $48 per adult or $36 for children 5 to 12. Children under 5 aren't allowed. Bus no. 10 or 11.

The best snorkeling is from May to October, although snorkeling is a year-round pursuit. Snorkelers usually wear wet suits in winter, when the water temperature dips into the 60s. The waters of the Atlantic, which can be tempestuous at any time of the year, can be especially rough in winter. Therefore, winter snorkelers should head for the more sheltered waters of **Castle Harbour** and **Harrington Sound,** both on the East End, where you'll find bizarre coral formations, underwater caves, grottoes, and schools of brilliantly hued fish.

Some of the best snorkeling sites are accessible only by boat; you can swim to others, but it's usually a long way out. If you want to head out on your own, we suggest renting a small boat (see "Sailing," under "More Fun in the Water," below), some of which have glass bottoms. If you rent a boat, the rental company will advise you on where to go and not to go. There are countless wrecked boats on the many reefs that surround Bermuda. If you're not familiar with Bermuda's waters, you should stay in the sounds, harbors, and bays, especially in Castle Harbour and Harrington Sound. If you want to make a trip to the reefs, it's better to take one of the snorkeling cruises recommended below (also see "Scuba Diving," below).

For details on shallow wreck sites that are accessible to snorkelers, see "Scuba Diving," below.

Bermuda Water Sports

At Hamilton Parish. ☎ **441/293-2640.** Mid-Apr to Oct booking hrs. daily 9am–9pm. Bus: 10 or 11.

Friendly captain Paul Wakefield offers a glass-bottom snorkel cruise aboard a 60-foot motorized catamaran. The special design of this boat allows it to anchor in very shallow waters, which is ideal for novices or unsure swimmers. Priced at around $40 for a 3½-hour cruise, the cost includes free use of snorkeling equipment and the expertise of a crew that really knows the marine life of Bermuda's offshore reefs. There's a cash bar and a freshwater shower on board.

Bermuda Water Tours Ltd

Tours leave from the docks near Hamilton's Ferry Terminal. ☎ **441/236-1500.** Booking 24 hrs. a day. Bus: 1, 2, 10, or 11.

Capt. Bruce King offers three options. The shortest cruise, a 2-hour glass-bottom-boat cruise, costs $25 and departs daily at 10am. Another glass-bottom-boat cruise that also includes time for snorkeling can be arranged as well; the cost is $40.

Salt Kettle Yacht Charters

Salt Kettle, Paget Parish. ☎ **441/236-4863.** Booking 24 hrs. Ferryboat from Hamilton every 30 min.

Salt Kettle offers private sailing charters on a 55-foot sloop, *Bright Star,* a luxury yacht. To save money, you can join a sailing party aboard the yacht that lasts 3 hours and includes time for swimming and snorkeling. The party includes complimentary rum swizzles and soft drinks; the cost is $35 per person. The outfitter also rents private motor charters on its 35-foot *Magic Carpet* for sightseeing or snorkeling among the wrecks and reefs.

3 Scuba Diving

Diving in Bermuda isn't as dramatic as diving in the Cayman Islands, but it's great for novices, who can learn the fundamentals and go diving in about 20 to 25 feet of water on the same day as their first lesson. In general, Bermuda's reefs are still healthy despite talk about dwindling fish and dying coral formations. On occasion, in addition to the rainbow-hued schools of fish, you may even find yourself swimming with a barracuda.

Although scuba fanatics dive all year, the best diving months are May to October. The sea is the most tranquil at that time, and the water temperature is moderate (it averages 62°F in the spring and fall and 83°F in summer).

Weather permitting, scuba schools function daily, and all dives are overseen by fully licensed scuba instructors. Most dives are conducted from a 40-foot dive boat, and a wide range of dive sites are covered. Night dives and certifications are offered as well.

All dive shops display a map of wreck sites that you can visit—there are nearly 40 in all, the oldest of which dates back to the 17th century. Although it's believed that there may be a total of some 300 wreck sites, those that are mapped are the best known and in the best condition. Dive depths at these sites vary between 25 and 85 feet. Inexperienced divers may want to stick to the wreck sites off the western part of Bermuda, since these tend to be in more shallow waters—perhaps no more than about 32 feet. These shallow wreck sites are popular with snorkelers as well.

Many of the hotels have their own water-sports equipment. If yours doesn't, all of the outfitters below have equipment for rent.

Note: Spearfishing is not allowed within 1 mile of any shore, and spear guns are not permitted in Bermuda.

Blue Water Divers Co. Ltd

Robinson's Marina, Southampton. ☎ **441/234-1034.** Daily 7am–9pm. Bus: 6 or 7.

Bermuda's oldest and largest full-service scuba-diving operation offers introductory lessons and half-day dives for $91. Daily one- and two-tank dive trips cost $50 and $70, respectively. Snorkeling trips are $36 per half day. Full certification courses are available through PADI, NAUI, and SSI. All equipment is provided and reservations are necessary.

Fantasea Diving
Darrells Wharf, Harbour Rd., Paget Parish. ☎ **441/236-6339.**

Fantasea Diving is a year-round operation, specializing in wreck diving. It arranges daily dives at 8am and 1pm. Its "Discover Scuba" course costs $91 for 3½ hours. Its popular reef-wreck dive at various depths costs $50 for 3 hours. A two-tank dive may appeal to experienced divers who want to see wrecks and reefs; it lasts 4½ hours and costs $70. Finally, night dives, for experienced divers only, run $60. Snorkeling trips can also be arranged, and underwater cameras are available for rent to both scuba divers and snorkelers.

Nautilus Diving Ltd
At both the Southampton Princess and the Hamilton Princess. ☎ **441/238-2332** or 441/295-9485. Daily 8am–5:30pm.

This is one of the leading dive operators on the island, offering a "Discover Scuba" resort course ($99 for 3 hr.) that's quite popular. All dives are from a 40-foot boat. Its one-tank dive for $55 goes to reef or wreck sites, and a two-tank dive, including a view of a shipwreck and the exploration of a reef in 25 to 30 feet of water, costs $75 (equipment not included). This is a PADI, five-star center.

South Side Scuba Water Sports
At Sonesta Beach Resort, South Shore Rd., Southampton. ☎ **441/238-1833.** Call 1 day in advance, 8am–6pm. Closed 2 weeks in Feb or Mar. Bus: 7.

South Side Scuba is known for its daily two-tank wreck and reef dives, costing $75. A Resort Course lesson plus dive is $95. A single-tank dive goes for $50, and you can snorkel off the boat for $38. If you want to ride along as a nonparticipating passenger, the cost is $15. The company has two fully equipped, custom-built fiberglass dive boats with the latest approved safety gear. This is a NAUI- and PADI-affiliated dive center.

4 More Fun in the Water

FISHING
Bermuda is one of the world's finest fishing destinations, especially in light-tackle fishing. However, blue marlin catches have increased dramatically in recent years, and Bermuda can also add bill-fishing to its already enviable reputation. Fishing is a year-round sport in Bermuda, but it's best from May to November. No license is required.

You can obtain fishing information from the **International Game Fish Association's** representative for Bermuda, Tom Smith (☎ 441/238-0112). The **Bermuda Game Fishing Association,** P.O. Box HM 1306, Hamilton HM FX, Bermuda, is an advisory body that represents all the IGFA-affiliated clubs in Bermuda and serves as caretaker for all local records and world records held locally.

DEEP-SEA FISHING
Wahoo, amberjack, blue marlin, white marlin, dolphin, tuna, and other varieties of fish call Bermuda's warm waters home. A number of island outfitters offer the necessary equipment to help you fish for them; we've listed our favorite below.

Bermuda Sportsfishing
Creek View House, 8 Tulo Lane, Pembroke Parish HM 02, Bermuda. ☎ **441/295-2370.** Daily 7am–10pm. Bus: 1, 2, 10, or 11.

Bermuda Sportsfishing is run by the De Silva family, which has been in business for many years. They charge $650 for a half day of fishing and anywhere from $875 to

---

Anglers Aweigh: How to Make Your Big Catch a Winning One

The **Bermuda Game Fishing Tournament** is open to any angler who takes the time and trouble to fill out the tournament application at the time they catch a really big fish. No special license is required, but your catch will have to be weighed, and an affidavit to its weight signed by three witnesses. Special prizes are awarded each year for top catches of 17 species of game fish, based on a point system calibrated to the species of fish you catch. For more information on how to register the really big ones that didn't get away, contact the **Bermuda Department of Tourism,** Global House, 43 Church St., Hamilton HM 12, Bermuda (☎ **441/292-0023**).

$1,200 for a full day, depending on the size of the boat. Boats range in size from 34 to 46 feet.

REEF FISHING

Three major reef banks lie off Bermuda's shore, and they're likely to turn up such catches as greater amberjack, almaco jack, great barracuda, little tunny, Bermuda chub, gray snapper, yellowtail snapper, and assorted bottom fish. The closest one begins about a half mile offshore and stretches for nearly 5 miles. The Challenger Bank is about 14 miles offshore, and Argus Bank is the most distant, about 30 miles. Of course, the farther out you go, the more likely you are to turn up larger fish.

Several charter companies offer either half- or full-day charters. Arrangements can also be made through Bermuda Sportsfishing (see "Deep-Sea Fishing," above).

SHORE FISHING

Shore fishing turns up such catches as bonefish, palometa (pompano), gray snapper, and great barracuda. Locals and most visitors prefer shore fishing at Spring Benny's Bay or West Whale Bay; Great Sound and St. George's Harbour are other promising grounds. The activities director at your hotel can help make fishing arrangements for you.

PARASAILING

Bermuda Island Parasail Company
1 Darrell's Wharf, Paget. ☎ **441/232-2871.** Apr–Oct, daily 9am–5pm (7pm in summer).

This company offers harness-style Parasail rides that last approximately 7 to 10 minutes. Adults pay $50; children under 12 pay $35. Tandem rides are also available for $80. Your dry takeoff and landing will be on the Nordic 28, and you'll Parasail above Hamilton Harbor.

St. George's Parasail Water Sports Ltd.
Somers Wharf, St. George. ☎ **441/297-1542.** Apr–Oct Mon–Fri 9am–6pm, Sat–Sun 11am–5pm.

Parasailers soar above St. George's Harbor after taking off from the Krant Craft deck. Rides are single tandem and cost $50 per person for adults, or $35 for children under 12. Rides last approximately 8 minutes.

Skyrider Bermuda Ltd.
Royal Naval Dockyard, Sandys. ☎ **441/234-3019.** Apr–Oct daily 10am–5pm.

Skyrider takes a maximum of eight passengers into the Great Sound and northshore area for two-person chair Parasail rides. The 8-minute ride costs $40 for adults and $32 for children 12 and under. Boat passengers who do not Parasail pay $12.

SAILING

Bermuda is one of the world's sailing capitals. Sail-yourself boats are available on a 2-hour, half-day (4-hr.), or full-day (8-hr.) basis.

Bermuda Caribbean Yacht Charter

2A Light House Rd., Southampton Parish. ☎ **441/238-8578.** Daily 9am–5pm. Bus: 7 or 8.

You can charter a yacht with a licensed skipper at a number of places, including Bermuda Caribbean Yacht Charter. Offering a keen insight on the islands, the owner of the 35-foot ketch *Selina King,* Arthur Ransom, operates from April to November; he charges $350 for a half day (10am to 1pm and 1:30 to 4:30pm) or $600 for a full day for six passengers. Any additional person pays an extra $20.

✪ Blue Hole Water Sports

Grotto Bay Beach Hotel, 11 Blue Hole Hill, Hamilton Parish. ☎ **441/293-2915.** Daily 8:30am–5:30pm. Bus: 1, 3, 10, or 11.

This outfitter rents Windsurfers or Sunfish for $25 for the first hour, $10 for each additional hour. Sun Cats are available for $35 per hour. A wide range of other equipment is also on hand, including single and double kayaks.

✪ Mangrove Marina

Somerset Bridge, Ely's Harbour, Sandys. ☎ **441/234-0914.** Daily 8:30am–sunset.

Mangrove Marina is the best outlet for renting Boston whalers for island hopping on your own. A 13-foot Boston whaler (25 or 30 hp) carries four and costs $65 for 2 hours, $165 for 8 hours. Mangrove provides lots of extras, such as Bimini tops, special maps, a ladder, a viewing box, and a fish and coral ID card.

✪ Pompano Beach Club Watersports Centre

36 Pompano Beach Rd., Southampton Parish. ☎ **441/234-0222.** May–late Oct daily 7:30am–midnight.

This is one of the island's best outfitters, mainly because of its variety of modern boats. These include O'Brien Windsurfers, which hold one passenger, either novice or experienced; they rent for $12 per hour or $36 for 4 hours. One or two people can also rent an Aqua Finn sailboat or a Dolphin paddleboat for the same price. A one-person Buddy Board (a kayak-type boat with a viewing window) goes for $7 per hour; single-person kayaks go for $12 per hour. Two-person Sun Cats, which travel 6 m.p.h. and look like motorized lawn chairs, go for $35 per hour, or $25 per half hour.

WATERSKIING

You can water-ski in the protected waters of Hamilton Harbour, Great Sound, Castle Harbour, Mangrove Bay, Spanish Point, Ferry Reach, Ely's Harbour, Riddells Bay, and Harrington Sound. May to September, when the waters are usually calm, is the best time for waterskiing. Bermuda law requires that water-skiers be taken out by a licensed skipper. There are only a few boat operators for this sport, and charges fluctuate with fuel costs. Rates include the boat, skis, safety belts, and usually an instructor. Hotels and guest houses can assist with arrangements.

Bermuda Waterski Centre

Robinson's Marina, Somerset Bridge. ☎ **441/234-3354.** May–Sept daily 8am–7:30pm. Bus: 6 or 7.

Up to five people can water-ski from a specially designed Ski Nautique. Lessons are available. The charge is $60 for a half hour of skiing, $100 for an hour. This isn't a per-person charge—the rate is the same if it's for 1 or 10.

Blue Hole Water Sports

Grotto Bay Beach Hotel, Hamilton Parish. ☎ **441/293-2915.** May–Sept daily 8am–6pm, weather permitting. Closed Oct–Apr. Bus: 1, 3, 10, or 11.

This company takes up to five people on board a Barefoot Nautique. Rates run $40 for 15 minutes, $60 per half hour, or $95 for an hour (prices include a lesson).

5 Where to Play Some of the World's Best Golf

Since the first course was laid out on the island in 1922, golf has been one of Bermuda's most popular sports. It can be played year-round, but spring, fall, and early winter offer the best seaside golf conditions. You must arrange tee times at any of the island's eight courses in advance through the management of your guest house or hotel. Women's and men's clubs, either right- or left-handed, are available at each course, and most leading stores in Bermuda sell golf balls.

The Castle Harbour Hotel golf course is one of the most scenic courses on the island, whereas the Port Royal, designed by Robert Trent Jones, is a challenge to your golfing expertise. Two famous courses—the Mid Ocean Club at Tucker's Town and the Riddells Bay Golf and Country Club—are private, and introduction by a member is required before you can play there. Some luxury hotels can sometimes secure playing privileges at the Riddells Bay Golf and Country Club. One of the most photographed golf courses in Bermuda is at the Southampton Princess Hotel, where rolling hills and flowering shrubs add to the players' enjoyment.

The golf courses listed below that are part of hotel complexes also permit nonguests to use their facilities. All of these golf courses have pros, and you can take lessons if you wish.

Tournaments are held throughout the year, with top players participating. For information, contact the **Bermuda Golf Association,** P.O. Box HM 433, Hamilton HM BX, Bermuda (☎ **441/238-1367**).

✪ Belmont Golf & Country Club

Between Harbour and Middle Rd., Warwick Parish. ☎ **441/236-6400.** Daily 7am–5pm. Ferry from Hamilton.

A Scotsman, Emmett Devereux, designed this 18-hole, par-70, 5,777-yard course in 1923, and its layout has long been a challenge to golfers. All of the golfing magazines write of its par-5 11th hole, with a severe dogleg left and blind tee shot. It's sometimes difficult to finish uphill at number 18. Crystal caves under the turf sometimes cause the ball to roll unpredictably. In spite of these disadvantages, golf pros recommend the Belmont for beginning golfers; the first hole is said to be "confidence building." It's estimated that with a 9 or 10 handicap, golfers will shoot in the 70s at Belmont—but there are no guarantees. Most of the course is inland and, unlike many golf courses in Bermuda, this one provides few views of the Atlantic.

Warning: Gas carts are mandatory and cost $21 for 9 holes or $42 for 18 holes. Greens fees are $86 Monday to Friday, $91 on the weekend. A full set of golf clubs rents for $28. There's a dress code, which requires shirts with collars.

✪ Castle Harbour Golf Club

Tucker's Town, Hamilton Parish. ☎ **441/298-6959.** Daily 7:30am–6pm. Bus: 22.

This 18-hole, par-71, 6,440-yard course was designed by golf architect Charles Banks. This resort championship course features challenging tee shots; the first tee by the clubhouse is often compared to a "crow's nest" by golfing magazines. It gives you an immediate sense of what to expect with this course, which offers panoramic

Bermuda's Best Golf Courses

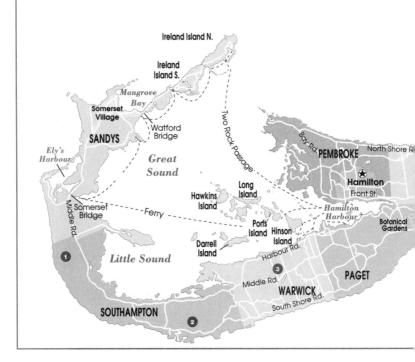

views of Castle Harbour's blue-green waters and the darker Atlantic beyond. As you look down over the fairway, you'll think you're seeing the course from a helicopter. Winds sweeping in from the Atlantic make it a constant challenge. Sometimes the greens are elevated, especially the 190-yard, par-3 13th hole, lying atop an embankment that rises about 100 feet. Golfers consider the 235-yard, par-3 18th hole as the hardest finishing hole on the island, especially if the Atlantic decides to send a wind out of the north just as you hit the ball. There aren't as many sand traps here as on other Bermuda courses.

This is one of the more expensive courses to play, but at least part of the money is used to maintain the best-kept greens on the island. Greens fees are $120 for 9 or 18 holes, plus $46 for the mandatory cart rental. From January to February, greens fees are lowered to $70. There are no caddies. A full set of clubs rents for $28. Golfers must wear shirts with collars, and no jeans or cutoffs.

Ocean View Golf Course

2 Barkers Hill Rd., Devonshire Parish. ☎ **441/295-9092.** Daily 7:30am–6:30pm. Bus: 2.

Airport ✈

| 0 | | 3 Mi |
| 0 | | 3 Km |

Belmont Hotel Golf & Country Club ③
Castle Harbour Golf Club ⑤
Ocean View Golf Course ④
Port Royal Golf Course ①
Southampton Princess Golf Club ②
St. George's Golf Club ⑥

This 9-hole course is par-35, 2,940 yards. Back in the 1950s, this was a club for African Bermudians; later, as other clubs started to admit black players, the course fell into disrepair. The government spent some $2 million vastly improving this course, but its old reputation lives on. In the center of Bermuda in Devonshire Parish, the course offers panoramic views of the ocean from many of its elevated tees. Many golfers consider the terrain unpredictable; that, combined with rambling hills, makes the course more challenging than it first appears. A few holes have as many as six tees. Winds from the Great Sound might have a greater effect on your score than you might think. The green on the 177-yard, par-3 5th hole has been cut into the coral hillside; since it's draped with semitropical vines, golfers sometimes have the eerie feeling that they're hitting the ball into a Bermudian cave.

Weekdays, this course tends to be the least crowded of any in Bermuda. However, as improvements continue to be made, this might change. Greens fees are $25 for 9 holes or $32 for 18 holes. "Sunset" golf, rounds that begin after 3:45pm, cost only $16 for 9 or 18 holes (or whatever you can fit in before closing). There are no caddies. Golf carts cost $18 for 9 holes or $36 for 18. Club rental is $20 for a full set. Dress code is shirts with collars—no jeans or "short shorts." Golf shoes are mandatory.

○ Port Royal Golf Course

Middle Rd., Southampton Parish. ☎ **441/238-9430.** Daily 7am–5pm. Bus: 7 or 8.

This is an 18-hole, par-71, 6,565-yard public course. Golf architect Robert Trent Jones designed the course, which is owned and operated by the Bermuda government, along the oceanside terrain. Jack Nicklaus might be found at the famous 16th hole, a favorite for photo layouts in golf magazines. Both the 16th and the 15th holes ring the craggy cliffs around Whale Bay; sometimes winds from the Atlantic taunt the golf balls that are hit from these tees. The 7th and 8th holes are a dogleg par-5 and a windy par-3, respectively.

Port Royal is so popular that some avid golfers reserve starting times a year in advance. Greens fees for 18 holes are $70 Monday to Friday and $80 on weekends. There are no caddies. A full set of clubs rents for $25, and handcarts rent for $9. Gas-powered carts go for $18 for 9 holes or $36 for 18 holes. The clubhouse, which overlooks the ocean and the 9th and 18th greens, boasts a bar and a restaurant serving breakfast, lunch, and dinner. Dress code is shirts with collars.

○ Southampton Princess Golf Club

101 South Shore Rd., Southampton Parish. ☎ **441/239-6952.** Daily 7am–sunset. Bus: 7 or 8.

On the grounds of one of the most luxurious hotels in Bermuda, this 18-hole, par-54, 2,684-yard course occupies not only the loftiest but also one of the most scenic settings on the island. Elevated tees, strategically placed bunkers, and plenty of water hazards make it a challenge; golfers have been known to use every club in their bag when the wind blows in from the Atlantic. Against the backdrop of the Gibbs Hill Lighthouse, the 16th hole was designed in a cup ringed by flowering bushes. The vertical drop on the 1st and 2nd holes is almost 200 feet. Even experienced golfers like to "break in" on this course before taking on some of Bermuda's more challenging ones. Because of the hotel's irrigation system, we've often found this course to be green while some of the others were experiencing a summer brownout.

Greens fees are $54 for 18 holes for hotel guests and $60 for visitors. There are no caddies. The charge for renting clubs is $20. Shirts with collars are required—no bathing suits or cutoffs are allowed.

○ St. George's Golf Club

1 Park Rd., St. George's Parish. ☎ **441/297-8067.** Apr–Sept Mon–Fri 8am–6pm, Sat–Sun 7:30am–6pm. Off-season Mon–Fri 7:45am–5:30pm, Sat–Sun 7:30am–5:30pm. Bus: 6, 8, 10, or 11.

Redesigned by Robert Trent Jones, this 18-hole, par-62, 4,043-yard course is the newest of the Bermuda government's courses. Lying on a headland at the northeastern tip of the island, it's within walking distance of St. George's. Links run along the hillsides, providing players with panoramic vistas of the ocean; winds coming in off the ocean will also have a significant effect on your game. On some of the par-3s, players need everything from a 9-iron to a driver to reach the green. The greens are the smallest on the island; some appear to be no more than 2 dozen feet across. The abundant salt air makes them slick.

This course isn't usually crowded at midweek. Greens fees for 18 holes are $43. There are no caddies. A full set of clubs rents for $18; gas golf carts go for $36 and handcarts for $7. You must wear either Bermuda-length shorts or slacks with a collared shirt—no jeans.

6 Other Outdoor Pursuits: Biking, Horseback Riding & Tennis

BIKING

With a year-round average temperature of 70°F, Bermuda is often ideal for bicycling. Not only is biking a great way to have fun and stay in shape, but it allows you to take a hands-on approach to your island sightseeing as well.

Most roadways are well paved and maintained. Although the island's speed limit is 20 m.p.h. for all vehicles, you should exercise caution when riding a bike or scooter on Bermuda's roads: They're narrow and winding, and car traffic, especially during the day, tends to be heavy. Most drivers are considerate of cyclists, but a car may approach suddenly without honking because the government discourages unnecessary horn honking. You might even be overtaken by fellow cyclists, since bicycle racing is one of the most popular local sports.

Much of the island's terrain consists of flat stretches, although the hills provide what the locals call "challenges." Some of these climbs are steep, especially the roads that run north and south along the island. The South Shore Road through Southampton and Warwick Parishes often leaves bikers huffing and puffing.

In spite of all the tourist brochures extolling the glories of bicycling in Bermuda, the truth is that the roads are not suitable for beginners. You might also need to give careful thought about where it might be safe for youngsters to ride.

RENTING A BIKE

Push-bikes (or pedal bikes), the term Bermudians use to distinguish bicycles from mopeds, are a popular form of transportation on the island. You can rent a bicycle on an hourly basis, for the day, or for the entire period of your Bermuda holiday. For information about cycle and scooter rentals, see "Getting Around," in chapter 3. All of the recommended shops also rent bicycles, and many hotels have them available for guest use, with or without a fee. Rental costs are generally $10 to $15 for the first day, and then $5 per day for each additional day. Both 3- and 10-speed bikes are usually available. It's always a good idea to call one of these rental shops as far in advance as possible, since demand is great, especially from April to October.

WHERE TO BIKE ON BERMUDA

Only the hardiest of cyclists set out to traverse the 21-mile length of Bermuda in 1 day. For most people, it's far better to focus on smaller sections of the island at different times. So, decide what interests you parish by parish and proceed from there. To save cycling time, you can take your bike aboard various ferries (you can carry your bike on board for free) then begin cycling once you reach your desired destination.

Some of the most interesting cycling trails are in **Devonshire and Smith's Parishes.** The hills throughout these areas will guarantee that you'll get your exercise for the day, and the beautiful landscapes will make all of your efforts worthwhile. **Spittal Pond,** a wildlife sanctuary with bike paths running along seaside cliffs, is one of the most rewarding destinations for cyclists. Another good choice for beginning riders is the Bermuda Railway Trail (see below).

If you're a real demon on a bike, you can go farther west and experience the challenge of pumping up to **Gibbs Hill Lighthouse,** the oldest cast-iron lighthouse in the western hemisphere. The panoramic view from the foot of the lighthouse is well worth the effort.

For Birders in Pursuit of the Fork-Tailed Flycatcher

There's a group of local bird-watching enthusiasts in Bermuda, but not many organized tours are offered. Visiting bird-watchers should make arrangements for tours with local enthusiasts, who can greatly increase their chance of seeing some rare birds (Bermuda is home to some 40 species of eastern warblers alone). The island's vast array of feathered friends includes everything from the heron to the fork-tailed flycatcher; there's even the rare cahow, a gray-and-white petrel.

Visiting birders should pick up a copy of David Wingate's *Check List and Guide to the Birds of Bermuda* or Eric Amos's *A Guide to the Birds of Bermuda,* both of which are available at local bookstores. You might also want to contact **David Wingate,** a conservation officer for the Bermuda government, directly at ☎ **441/297-2623** or **Eric Amos** at ☎ **441/236-9056.** They occasionally, but not always, give advice over the phone about the island's best retreats, walkways, and hideaways.

You can also contact the **Bermuda Audubon Society,** P.O. Box HM 1328, Hamilton HM FX, Bermuda (☎ **441/235-5513**), for information about any organized field trips that might be scheduled while you're in Bermuda.

If you'd like to combine a picnic with your bicycle outing, head for **Sandys Parish.** First cross Somerset Bridge, the smallest drawbridge in the world, and then pedal along Somerset Road to Fort Scaur Park. Once here, you can relax and admire the view of Ely's Harbour while enjoying your picnic.

Another interesting bicycle option is the ✪ **Bermuda Railway Trail** (see chapter 8), which is restricted to bicyclists and pedestrians. The Railway Trail can be divided into seven sections, each of which has its own character. It's up to you to decide how much of the trail you'd like to cover in 1 day, and which sections you'd like to focus on.

The trail begins in Sandys Parish, where the Gilbert Nature Reserve and the Heydon Trust Estate provide contrasting views of rural Bermuda. The first part of the trail ends at Somerset Bridge.

The second section of the trail begins as you cross into Southampton Parish, where you'll get a sense of 19th-century Bermudian life. Southampton includes much of Bermuda's 500 acres of arable land, as well as examples of traditional manor houses.

As it enters Warwick Parish, the trail skirts Little Sound and then passes through an allspice forest. Near the island's central area, the West End's woodlands and fields become dotted with Bermuda's traditional old houses, some still featuring domed water tanks and old stone butteries.

The trail then rises above Paget Marsh, a National Trust Nature Reserve, which includes Bermuda's oldest palmetto forest and a wide variety of bird life. The tour of Paget Parish ends with a ride through a 450-foot-long railway tunnel, partially covered with the thick roots of a rubber tree.

Picking up beyond Hamilton, Bermuda's capital city, the trail leads to Palmetto House, built in the shape of a cross and virtually unchanged since the 1700s.

After traversing a cricket "pitch," or field, while it takes you from Devonshire into Hamilton Parish, the trail then edges the wild coastline along Bailey's Bay.

The final section of the trail is in St. George's Parish, where the windswept coast is rocky and rugged. The mariner's landmark of Sugarloaf Hill offers a panoramic seascape and views of the historic seafaring town of St. George's.

HORSEBACK RIDING

Lee Bow Riding Centre

1 Tribe Rd., Devonshire Parish. ☎ **441/236-4181.** Daily 9am–5pm; reserve 1 day in advance. Bus: 3.

Lee Bow is especially geared for children ages 6 to 18, although riders of all ages are accommodated, often in small groups of no more than four. Instruction is available. Trail rides of 1 or 1½ hours are $35 and $50, respectively. Lesson costs vary.

Spicelands Riding Centre

Middle Rd., Warwick Parish. ☎ **441/238-8212.** Call at least 1 day in advance, 9am–5pm, to make arrangements. Bus: 8.

Spicelands offers trail rides for $50 per person per hour, regardless of the ride. The popular early-morning ride, a 1½-hour jaunt, is followed by a continental breakfast. From May to September, evening rides are offered Monday to Friday.

TENNIS

Nearly all the big hotels, and many of the smaller ones, have courts, most of which can be lit for night play. It's best to bring your own tennis clothing and sneakers with you to Bermuda, since a tennis outfit may be required. Tennis outfits no longer have to be white; colored tennis togs, so popular in America, also arrived in Bermuda some time ago.

Each of the facilities listed below has a tennis pro on duty, and lessons can be arranged. In case you didn't come prepared, you can rent racquets and buy balls at each place.

Elbow Beach Hotel

60 South Shore Rd., Paget Parish. ☎ **441/236-3535.** Call for bookings daily 9am–5pm. Bus: 1, 2, or 7.

The Elbow Beach Hotel has five LayKold courts (one for lessons only). Hotel guests are charged $8 to play here; others pay $12. Lessons cost $30 for 30 minutes or $60 for 1 hour. Racquets can be rented for $5, and balls are $6 per can of three.

Government Tennis Stadium

Cedar Ave., Pembroke Parish. ☎ **441/292-0105** to reserve a court or to arrange lessons. Mon–Fri 8am–10pm, Sat–Sun 8am–7pm. Bus: 1, 2, 10, or 11.

There are three clay and five Plexicushion courts here. Charges to play are $8 per adult and $4 per junior. An extra $8 is charged for playing at night on one of the three lit courts. Tennis attire is mandatory. Racquets rent for $5 per day; balls cost $6 per can.

Port Royal Club

Off Middle Rd., Southampton Parish. ☎ **441/238-9070.** Daily 7:30am–midnight. Bus: 7 or 8.

The Port Royal golf course has four Plexipave courts. Daytime play is $10 per person per hour; it's an additional $4 to play at night. Although the courts are open late, you must call before 6:30pm for reservations.

Southampton Princess

101 South Shore Rd., Southampton Parish. ☎ **441/238-1005.** Daily 8am–7pm. Bus: 7 or 8.

This resort has Bermuda's largest tennis-court layout, with 11 Plexipave courts, although none is lit for night play. Hotel guests pay $10 per hour and nonguests pay $12 per hour. Rackets rent for $6 per hour, and balls cost $6 per can.

Exploring Bermuda's Natural Wonderlands

The National Trust in Bermuda has wisely protected the island's nature reserves. If you play by the rules—that is, don't disturb animal life or take plant life for a souvenir—you can explore many of these natural wonderlands. They're one of the most rewarding reasons to visit Bermuda, if you enjoy nature trails.

The best and largest of these is ✪ **Spittal Pond Nature Reserve** in Smith's Parish. Birders, especially from September to April, are drawn to the reserve to see herons, ducks, flamingos, terns, and many migratory fowl (the latter can't be seen after March). This 60-acre untamed seaside park is always open to the public with no admission charge. **The Department of Parks** (☎ **441/236-4201**) offers guided tours of the refuge. Tours are free and are offered primarily from November to May; call for schedule and additional information.

The island abounds with other places of natural wonder. Craggy formations shaped over the centuries out of limestone and coral dot the beaches along the southern coast, with towering cliffs forming a backdrop. The best of these is **Natural Arches,** one of the most photographed sights in Bermuda. Two limestone arches, which took nature centuries to carve, rise 35 feet above the beach. This natural attraction is signposted almost at the end of South Shore Road, directing you to Castle Harbour Beach.

7 Spectator Sports

In this tradition-bound British colony, the most popular spectator sports are cricket, soccer, field hockey, and the not terribly genteel game of rugby. As you might expect, boating, yachting, and sailing are also popular. In this tradition-bound British colony, the most popular spectator sports are cricket, regattas, soccer, field hockey, and the not terribly genteel game of rugby. The Bermuda Department of Tourism can provide dates and venues for upcoming events; see "Visitor Information," in chapter 2, for contact information before you go, and "Orienting Yourself: The Lay of the Land," in chapter 3, for information once you've arrived. Also see the "Bermuda Calendar of Events," in chapter 2.

CRICKET

Far more Bermudians have memorized this terribly British sport's arcane rules than you might have imagined. If you arrive in midsummer (the game's seasonal high point), you'll probably see several regional teams practicing on cricket fields throughout the island. Each match includes enough pageantry to remind participants of the game's imperial antecedents and enough conviviality (picnics, socializing, and chitchat among the spectators) to give you a real feel for Bermuda.

The **Cup Match Cricket Festival,** the year's most important cricket event, takes place in late July or early August, when playoffs between Bermuda-based and visiting teams are scheduled at the **St. George's Cricket Club,** Willington Slip Road (☎ **441/297-0374**), and at the **Somerset Cricket Club,** Broome Street, off Somerset Road (☎ **441/234-0327**). Throughout the rest of the year, these organizations keep in close touch with the various cricket-related activities throughout the island.

FIELD HOCKEY

One of the great women's competitive sports is field hockey, played with curved wooden mallets. Each team—usually clad in knee socks and either shorts or kilts—

tries to drive a small white ball into the opposing team's net. Bermuda has several teams that compete against one another on Sunday afternoons between October and April at the **National Sports Club,** Middle Road, Devonshire Parish (☎ **441/ 236-6994**). Admission is usually free.

GOLF TOURNAMENTS

Bermuda offers some of the finest all-around golfing terrain in the world. Part of this is because of the climate, which supports lush driving ranges and putting greens. In addition, the ever-present golfers play at surprisingly high levels. Golf tournaments are held throughout the year, culminating in the annual, much-publicized **Bermuda Open** in early October. Both amateurs and professionals are welcome to vie for one of the most sought-after golfing prizes in the world.

HORSE RACING

If you're part of the horse-loving set, check to see what events may be taking place at the **National Equestrian Centre,** Vesey Street, Devonshire Parish (☎ **441/ 234-0485**). From September to Easter, harness races are staged about twice a month. One of the major equestrian events is held in October: the FEI/Samsung Dressage Competition and Show-Jumping. More details are available from the **Bermuda Equestrian Federation,** P.O. Box DV 583, Devonshire DV BX, Bermuda (☎ and fax **441/234-0485**). If you can't reach this organization on the phone (which is quite likely), ask at the tourist office or check the local newspaper for news of events.

RUGBY

A blend of American-style football and European soccer, this rough-and-tumble game has many Bermudian fans; the island has several hotly competitive teams. Rugby players—completely devoid of protective padding—seem to revel in this violent sport. The Easter Rugby Classic, attracting teams from throughout the British Commonwealth, is the final event in the island's rugby season, which runs from September to April. The venue for virtually every rugby game in Bermuda is at the **National Sports Club,** Middle Road, Devonshire Parish (☎ **441/236-6994**).

SOCCER

This fast-paced game is attracting increasing numbers of fans on both sides of the Atlantic. Bermudians view soccer as an important part of elementary education and therefore actively encourage this sport for children and teenagers. In early April, teams from countries around the Atlantic and Caribbean compete for the Diadora Youth Soccer Cup, with players in three age divisions. Games are held on various fields throughout the island. More accessible to spectators at other times, however, are the many games among high-school athletic teams, held regularly throughout the year.

YACHTING

Bermuda has never hesitated to capitalize upon its geographical position in the mid-Atlantic to lure the yachting crowd. The yacht-racing season runs every year from March to November, with most races scheduled on weekends and taking place within the relatively calm waters of Bermuda's Great Sound. Although it can be confusing to watch these races from land because of the shifting sight lines, the best land vantage points include Spanish Point, the islands northeast of Somerset, and Hamilton Harbour. Even better views are available from the decks of privately owned boats that anchor near the edge of the racecourse. Despite the confusion of newcomers who watch these carefully choreographed regattas, the sight of a fleet of racing craft with spinnakers and pennants aloft is always exciting.

In late June, Bermuda is the final destination in two of the most important annual yacht races: the **Annapolis-Bermuda Race** and the even more prestigious **Newport-Bermuda Race.** Both provide enough visual distraction and maritime pageantry to keep you enthralled. Participating yachts range from 30 to 100 feet in length, and their skippers are said to be among the most dedicated in the world.

Around Halloween, the autumn winds propel dozens of less exotic racing craft through the waters of the Great Sound. These compete in a series of one-on-one playoffs for the **King Edward VII Gold Cup International Match Racing Tournament.**

The island's yachting events are by no means limited to the above-mentioned international competitions. Bermuda's sheltered bays and windswept open seas provide year-round enticement for anyone who has ever wanted to experience the thrill of a snapping jib and taut mainsail. See "Sailing," under "More Fun in the Water," above, for details on yacht charters.

Even though a large number of people live on this small island, you should never feel crowded. There are no billboards or neon signs, and relatively few cars to spoil the rolling countryside. The island's houses for the most part seem to fit quite naturally into the landscape.

Bermuda is divided into nine parishes (or counties): Sandys Parish (in the far western end of the island); Southampton Parish; Warwick Parish; Paget Parish (which has the greatest concentration of hotels); Pembroke Parish (home to the city of Hamilton, seat of the Bermudian government); Devonshire Parish; Smith's Parish; Hamilton Parish (not to be confused with the city of Hamilton); and St. George's Parish (at the far eastern end of the island), which includes the U.S. naval air base and the little island of St. David's. In the early days, these districts—which encompass about 21 square miles—were called "tribes." By the beginning of the 18th century, the term "Tribe Road" was used for the boundaries between parishes. Pembroke, because it encloses the city of Hamilton, is the largest parish in population; St. George's has the largest land area.

Because of the island's small size, it's easy to get to know the island parish by parish. From the western tip of Somerset to the eastern end of St. George's, there's much to see, by bike, ferry, bus, or taxi. You'll need plenty of time, though, since the pace is slow. Cars and any other motorized vehicles, such as mopeds, can travel at a maximum speed of 15 m.p.h. in Hamilton and St. George's, 20 m.p.h. outside these towns. The speed limits are rigidly enforced, and there are severe penalties for any violations.

Many guidebooks are fond of pointing out that you can't get lost in Bermuda. Don't believe them! Along the narrow, winding roads, originally designed for the horse and carriage, you can get lost (several times), especially if you're looking for an obscure guest house on some long-forgotten lane. But don't worry, you won't stay lost for long. Bermuda is so narrow that if you keep going in either an easterly or a westerly direction, you'll eventually come to a main road. At its broadest point, Bermuda is only about 2 miles wide. The principal arteries are the North Shore Road, the Middle Road, and the South Shore Road, so you'll usually have at least some indication as to what part of the island you're in.

If you're visiting for the first time, you'll want to follow the tourist route, basically the equivalent of visiting New York and seeing the

Statue of Liberty and the Empire State Building: the Aquarium, Devil's Hole, and cruise-boat outings. But a different experience unfolds for visitors on a second, third, or fourth visit to Bermuda. Once you've done all the "must-sees," you'll want to walk around and make discoveries on your own. The best parishes for walking are Somerset, St. George's, and Hamilton.

But don't fill your days with too much structured sightseeing. You'll want time to lounge on the beach and play in the water or hit the links, and to enjoy moments like sitting by the harbor in the late afternoon, enjoying the views as the yachts glide by. Absorbing Bermuda's beauty in your own time and at your own pace, and stopping to chat with the occasional islander, is really the point.

In this chapter we'll go on a do-it-yourself tour, taking in Bermuda parish by parish. Also consider taking one or more of the walking tours described in chapter 8.

1 What to See If You Don't Have Much Time: The Island's Highlights

THE TOP ATTRACTIONS

Although Bermuda is a small island, you really can't see much of it in a day or two. If you have more time, you may want to explore it methodically, parish by parish. That's what we'll do in this chapter—visit each parish's attractions in detail, heading west to east. If your time is limited, however, you may want to consider heading straight for the following highlights (for details, see the appropriate parish section in this chapter):

- A walking tour of historic St. George's town (see chapter 8).
- A walking tour of the city of Hamilton, Bermuda's largest city and the seat of its government (see chapter 8, and if you want to combine shopping and sightseeing, also check out chapter 9).
- A fascinating ode to Bermuda's nautical heritage housed in a 19th-century fortress: the Bermuda Maritime Museum, at the Royal Naval Dockyard on Ireland Island in Sandys Parish.
- The Bermuda Aquarium, Museum & Zoo, a wonderful complex located along North Shore Road across Flatts Bridge in Hamilton Parish.
- A guided tour of spectacular Crystal Caves, including crystal-clear Cahow Lake, in Hamilton Parish.
- The 18th-century mansion known as Verdmont in Smith's Parish, which stands on property once owned by the man who left Bermuda to found a colony called South Carolina.
- Fort Hamilton, a massive Victorian fortification overlooking the city of Hamilton and its harbor ("The City of Hamilton" walking tour in chapter 8 will take you there).
- The Botanical Gardens, a Shangri-La in the mid-Atlantic, located on South Shore Road in Paget Parish.
- Gibbs Hill Lighthouse in Southampton Parish, the oldest cast-iron lighthouse in the world.
- Southampton Parish's Horseshoe Bay Beach, the most photographed of the pink sandy beaches of Bermuda (see "Beaches," in chapter 6).
- Paget Parish's Elbow Beach, Bermuda's top stretch of sand for fun in the surf and sun.

HIGHLIGHTS FOR ARCHITECTURE LOVERS

All of Bermuda should interest the architecture lover. Mark Twain wrote of the whiteness of Bermuda houses and roofs: "It is exactly the white of the icing of a cake, and has the same emphasized and scarcely perceptible polish. The white of marble is modest and retiring compared with it . . . clean-cut fanciful chimneys— too pure and white for this world—that will charm one's gaze by the hour." For more details and lore, see the appendix.

THE TOWN OF ST. GEORGE'S

The town of St. George's—the oldest and most historic settlement on the island— is likely to hold the greatest fascination for architecture buffs (also see chapter 8 for a walking tour).

The **Old State House,** constructed in 1620, is the oldest stone house in Bermuda. The governor at the time of its erection, Nathaniel Butler, believed he was building the house in an Italianate style. He ordered the workmen to use a combination of turtle oil and lime as mortar. This established a style for subsequent buildings in Bermuda.

Many architects have wanted to finish the **Unfinished Cathedral,** reached via Blockade Alley. Construction was launched in 1874; but then a schism developed in the church and then there was no money to continue the project. To this day, it remains unfinished—hence, the name.

The **Old Rectory,** now a private residence, was built by a former pirate in 1705. Located on Broad Alley, it's distinguished by its Dutch doors, chimneys, shutters, and what's called a "welcoming arms" staircase.

From an architectural point of view, one of the most intriguing structures in St. George's is **St. Peter's Church,** on Duke of York Street. This is the oldest Anglican Church in the western hemisphere, dating from 1620. It was constructed to replace an even older structure (from 1612) that had been poorly built from posts and palmetto leaves. A storm destroyed that church in 1712. The present St. Peter's was rebuilt and enlarged in 1713. In 1833, the galleries on each side of the church were added. The section around the triple-tiered pulpit is believed to be the oldest part of the structure, dating from the 1600s. The first governor of the island, Richard Moore, ordered construction of the dark red Bermuda cedar altar in 1615. It's the oldest surviving piece of woodwork from the colonial period.

Tucker House, on Water Street, was built of native limestone. The house is furnished in an interesting manner, mostly with pieces from the mid-1700s and early 1800s.

SMITH'S PARISH

Another notable architectural monument in Bermuda is **Verdmont,** situated on Verdmont Lane in Smith's Parish. Dating from around 1710, it was once owned by a wealthy shipowner, as well as the founder of the colony of South Carolina. There have been many other owners throughout its long history, including an American Loyalist, John Green, who fled from Philadelphia to Bermuda at the end of the Revolutionary War. Built to resemble an English manor house, Verdmont has a striking double roof and a quartet of large chimneys. Each room has its own fireplace. The style of the sash windows was once fashionable in certain English manor houses.

Attractions Around the Island

Admiralty House Park 15
Bermuda Aquarium, Museum & Zoo 21
Bermuda Arts Centre 2
Bermuda Craft Market 2
Bermuda Historical Society Museum 11
Bermuda Maritime Museum 1
Bermuda National Gallery 11
The Bermuda National Trust Museum 26
Bermuda Perfumery 22
Birdsey Studio 13
Botanical Gardens 14

Bridge House Gallery 26
Carriage Museum 26
Cathedral of the Most Holy Trinity 1
Christ Church 9
Crystal Caves 23
Deliverance 25
Devil's Hole Aquarium 20
Fort St. Catherine 27
Fort Scaur 6
Gates Fort 24
Gibbs Hill Lighthouse 7

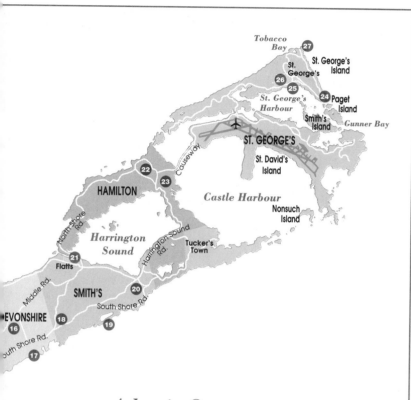

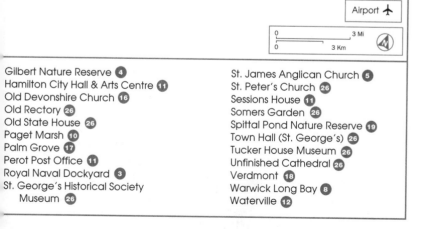

Gilbert Nature Reserve ④
Hamilton City Hall & Arts Centre ⑪
Old Devonshire Church ⑯
Old Rectory ㉖
Old State House ㉖
Paget Marsh ⑩
Palm Grove ⑰
Perot Post Office ⑪
Royal Naval Dockyard ③
St. George's Historical Society
   Museum ㉖

St. James Anglican Church ⑤
St. Peter's Church ㉖
Sessions House ⑪
Somers Garden ㉖
Spittal Pond Nature Reserve ⑲
Town Hall (St. George's) ㉖
Tucker House Museum ㉖
Unfinished Cathedral ㉖
Verdmont ⑱
Warwick Long Bay ⑧
Waterville ⑫

2 Letting Others Show You Their Bermuda

You can more or less explore Bermuda on your own. But if you'd prefer some help from island-born and -bred residents, it's available.

OFFSHORE TOURS

Bermuda Island Cruises, East Broadway Marina, Pembroke Parish (☎ 441/292-8652), offers a number of cruises that will show you the island. Monday to Saturday the company gives 2-hour glass-bottom-boat tours of Bermuda's famous reefs and shipwrecks. The cruises, which include commentary by a knowledgeable guide, leave at 10am from Hamilton Harbor. The cost is $25 for adults, $12.50 for children 6 to 12.

The Pirate Party Night at Hawkins Island evening cruise includes a buffet dinner, music from the Island Fever Band, a Hot Spice Limbo show, and a complimentary bar. The cost is $75 per adult, half price for children 7 to 12, free for children 6 and under. Children under 18 must be accompanied by a parent. Departures are at 7pm on Tuesday, Wednesday, Friday, and Saturday, returning at 10:30pm.

Bermuda Island Cruises tours can be booked over the phone at the number above, or at various hotel tour desks.

Bermuda Water Tours Ltd., P.O. Box 1572, Hamilton (☎ 441/236-1500), offers 2- and 4-hour trips, most of which include a visit to the sea gardens, where you can see the wonders of coral reefs and fish through the glass bottom of the boat. Also available are a variety of water trips, ranging from 2-hour sea-garden tours to snorkeling. You can call 24 hours a day for information.

ENVIRONMENTAL TOURS

To study climate change and the greenhouse effect, the **Bermuda Biological Station for Research,** a U.S. nonprofit organization, has been given a $500,000 grant by the U.S. National Science Foundation to study the carbon cycle. The Bermuda Biological Station has collected the world's most comprehensive data on the oceanographic absorption of human-released carbon dioxide, since it has tracked carbon dioxide levels for more than 40 years over a 13-mile area southeast of Bermuda. The station has also compiled an extensive record on acid rain in the North American atmosphere.

You can learn firsthand what these scientists are studying at the station by taking a free 90-minute guided tour of the grounds and laboratory in St. George's. Guides explain what scientific studies are being conducted in Bermuda and how they relate to the overall world environment. They also discuss the island's natural areas, including the coral reefs, protected by strict conservation laws, and how humans have produced changes in the fragile ecological environment.

The special educational tours, offered at 10am on Wednesday, are conducted by trained volunteers and by scientists who are actually carrying out the study projects. Visitors should assemble before 10am in the Biological Station's Hanson Hall. For more information, contact the **Bermuda Biological Station for Research,** 17 Biological Lane, Ferry Reach, St. George's (☎ 441/297-1880).

3 Sandys Parish

Sandys Parish is one of the real beauty spots on the island. If you're looking for a place to just wander about and get lost on a summer day, this lovely parish is well worth your time. Fort Scaur and the Royal Naval Dockyard on Ireland Island are

⭐ Frommer's Favorite Bermuda Experiences

Strolling Bermuda's Pink Sands. The pink-sand beaches are reason enough to come to the island. Find your favorite cove (perhaps Whale Bay, Astwood Cove, or Jobson's Cove), and stroll aimlessly at dawn, at twilight, or whenever your fancy dictates.

Cycling Across the Land. On a rented bicycle, or maybe a moped built for two, explore Bermuda from end to end. Start in St. George's in the East End and go all the way to the Royal Naval Dockyard in the West End, or vice versa. You don't necessarily have to do this in 1 day, however.

Following the Deserted Railway Trail. As you follow this intermittent trail from one end of the island to the other, you'll view panoramic seascapes, see exotic flora and fauna, and hear the soothing sounds of the island's bird life.

Touring by Horse and Buggy. No one has ever improved on this old-fashioned method of sightseeing and shopping along Hamilton's Front Street. Or, better yet, go on a 2-hour shopping tour of Somerset Village in the West End.

Viewing Bermuda from Gibbs Hill Lighthouse. Climb the 185 steps of the oldest cast-iron lighthouse in the world for one of the greatest views of the Atlantic Ocean. Springtime visitors may be lucky enough to see migrating whales beyond the shore reefs.

the major attractions here; if you're pressed for time, skip the Gilbert Nature Reserve and St. James' Anglican Church.

To explore this tip of the fishhook of Bermuda, it's best to take a ferry (the fare is $3.75); the trip from Hamilton to Watford Bridge takes 45 minutes. You can take your bike aboard the ferry free (there's a $3.50 charge for scooters and mopeds). Ferries also stop at Cavello Bay, Somerset, and the Royal Naval Dockyard. The **Visitors Service Bureau** is at the Royal Naval Dockyard (☎ **441/234-3824**), across from the ferry terminal. From May to October, hours are Monday to Friday from 9am to 5pm and Sunday from 11am to 4pm (closed Sat); off-season hours are Monday to Friday from 9:30am to 2pm and Sunday from 11am to 3pm.

✪ Scaur Hill Fort Park

Ely's Harbour, Somerset Rd. ☎ **441/236-5902**. Free admission. May–Oct daily 9am–4pm; Nov–Apr daily 10am–4:30pm. Closed Christmas and New Year's Day. Bus: 7 or 8 from Hamilton.

On the highest hill in Somerset, Fort Scaur was part of a ring of fortifications constructed in the 19th century, during a period of troubled relations between Britain and the United States. Intended as a last-ditch defense line for the Old Royal Naval Dockyard, the fort was skillfully constructed, taking advantage of the land contours to camouflage its presence from detection at sea. The fort has subterranean passages and a dry moat that stretches across the land from Ely's Harbour to Great Sound.

The World's Smallest Drawbridge

After leaving Fort Scaur, you can continue over the much-photographed 17th-century **Somerset Bridge,** the world's smallest drawbridge. When it's open for marine traffic, the space between the spans is a mere 22 inches at road level—just large enough for the mast of a sailboat to pass through.

Open to visitors since 1957, Fort Scaur has become one of Somerset's most popular tourist attractions. The fort has panoramic views of Ely's Harbour and Great Sound; using the free telescope, you'll see such faraway points as St. David's Lighthouse and Fort St. Catherine. The fort is encompassed by 22 acres of parkland filled with interesting trails, picnic areas, a rocky shoreline for fishing, and a public dock. Picnic tables, benches, and rest rooms are available.

Gilbert Nature Reserve

Somerset Rd. ☎ **441/236-6483.** Free admission. Daily sunrise–sunset. Bus: 7 or 8 from Hamilton.

In the center of the island lies the Gilbert Nature Reserve, 5 acres of unspoiled woodland. It bears the name of the family that owned the property from the beginning of the 18th century until 1973, when it was acquired by the Bermuda National Trust (in conjunction with the Bermuda Audubon Society).

St. James' Anglican Church

90 Somerset Rd. ☎ **441/234-0834.** Free admission. Daily 8am–6pm. Bus: 7 or 8 from Hamilton.

This is one of the most beautiful churches in Bermuda. It was constructed on the site of a structure that was destroyed by a hurricane in 1780. The present church was built 9 years later. A unique feature is the altar, which faces west instead of the customary east; this happened because a road to the west of the church was inadequate, so a new road was cut through to the east side of the church. The north and south aisles of the church were added in 1836, the entrance gate in 1872, and the spire and chancel in 1880. The church was struck by lightning in 1939 but was restored shortly thereafter.

IRELAND ISLAND & THE OLD ROYAL NAVAL DOCKYARD

The ✪ **Old Royal Naval Dockyard,** with its Bermuda Maritime Museum, is the number-one tourist attraction on the island. Even if you plan to skip all the other sights above and spend all your precious Bermuda time on the pink sandy beaches, try to schedule at least a half day to check it out.

The Royal Naval Dockyard has been transformed into a park, with Victorian street lighting and a Terrace Pavilion and bandstand for concerts. When this dockyard, which had been on British Admiralty land, was sold to the Bermudian government in 1953, it marked the end of British naval might in the western Atlantic. A multimillion-dollar cruise-ship dock has been built, and a tourist village has emerged in this historic area; today, vendors can be found pushing carts filled with food, dry goods, and local crafts. There's a full-service marina with floating docks, along with a marina clubhouse and showers. The area also houses the Bermuda Maritime Museum, the Neptune Theatre, the Crafts Market, and the Bermuda Arts Centre.

Ferries from Hamilton stop at Ireland Island, at the extreme west end of Bermuda, once each hour from 7am to 6pm. The fare is $3.75 each way. Buses (no. 7 or 8) leave Hamilton for the Royal Naval Dockyard Monday to Saturday every 15 minutes from 6:45am to 11:45pm. The trip takes 1 hour and costs $3.75 for adults, $1 for children 5 to 15; children 4 and under ride free. Note: Bus fares are accepted by the drivers in coins only.

Bermuda Arts Centre

4 Freeport Rd. ☎ **441/234-2809.** Free admission. Daily 10am–5pm.

Works by local artists are featured in this gallery, with exhibits changing about every 6 weeks. An eclectic range of original art and prints are for sale. Local artists in residence now include a cedar sculptor, a watercolorist, and a silversmith/jewelry maker.

Especially for Kids

Bermuda is a great destination for the entire family. Most resorts offer specific children's activities and special family packages. Most of the larger properties also give Mom and Dad an opportunity to spend some time alone by offering baby-sitting services for minimal fees.

Even more important, Bermuda offers a wide range of activities that will keep the kids going all day long. They include sailing, waterskiing, snorkeling, and glass-bottom-boat trips from April to October; tennis; visits to museums and caves; and a wide array of walking tours. Here are some of Bermuda's top sights and activities for kids:

Bermuda Aquarium, Museum & Zoo *(see p. 165)*   This complex offers kids a wonderful introduction to the undersea world. Handheld cassette tapes let you listen to a history of marine life while visiting live exhibits of Bermuda's native fish.

Bermuda Maritime Museum *(see p. 157)*   Everyone in the family takes equal delight in seeing the exhibits of Bermuda's nautical history in this authentic Victorian fortress museum.

Bermuda Railway Trail *(see p. 182)*   This nature walk, with strolls overlooking the seashore and along quiet, tree-lined alleyways, is suitable for the entire family. You can pick up the 21-mile trail at many points and explore as many sections as you prefer, according to your stamina and interests.

Devil's Hole Aquarium *(see p. 165)*   This aquarium near Harrington Sound, founded in 1834, was the first established attraction in Bermuda. Kids toss baited but hookless lines to feed fish and turtles in this natural marine environment.

Crystal Caves *(see p. 165)*   Two boys chasing a runaway ball in 1907 discovered an enormous cavern surrounded by an underground lake. Easily navigable walkways take parents and kids down into the caverns of the Crystal Caves in Hamilton Parish.

Undersea Walk *(see. p. 134)*   Your kids can explore the ocean floor on their own—all they need is an underwater helmet and a little guidance. Following a predive educational lecture aboard the ship, kids of all ages can walk along the ocean floor for face-to-face encounters with friendly sea creatures.

Horseback Riding *(see p. 145)*   The Lee Bow Riding Stables are well equipped for taking younger riders out to explore the island on the back of a friendly horse.

Bermuda Craft Market

In the Cooperage Building, 4 Freeport Rd. ☎ **441/234-3208.** Free admission. Daily 9:30am–5pm.

This is the place to watch local artists at work and to buy their wares, which make ideal take-home gifts. Established in 1987, it offers items made from Bermuda cedar, candles, clothing, dolls, fabrics, hand-painted goods, jewelry, metal and gem sculpture, needlework, quilts, shell art, glass panels, and woven-cane goods, among other things.

Bermuda Maritime Museum

Old Royal Naval Dockyard. ☎ **441/234-1418.** Admission $7.50 adults, $6 seniors and students, $3 children 5–18 (4 and under free); family ticket $15 for 2 adults and up to 5 children. Apr–Nov daily 9:30am–4:30pm; Dec–Mar daily 10am–4:30pm. Closed Christmas.

Stepping Back into the Ice Age

Bermuda has one of the highest concentrations of limestone caves in the world. Most of this cave-making activity began during the Pleistocene Ice Age. As early as 1623, the adventurer Capt. John Smith complained that he had encountered "vary strange, darke, cumbersome caves."

In Bermuda, nature's patient, relentless underground sculpting is a dream world for even the casual spelunker. Deep in the majestic silence of the earth's interior, you can roam in caverns of great stalactites and stalagmites of Gothic grandeur, and of delicacy and beauty. This awesome underground has been the inspiration for creative achievements as diverse as Shakespeare's *The Tempest* and Henson Associates' "Fraggle Rock" Muppets.

You can visit Crystal Caves on guided tours; the cave complex is located along Harrington Sound Road in Hamilton Parish (see p. 165 for more information).

Located in a large 19th-century fortress built by convict labor, this museum exhibits artifacts, models, and maps pertaining to Bermuda's nautical heritage. The fortress's massive buildings of fitted stone, with their vaulted ceilings of English brick, are alone worth a visit. So are the 30-foot defensive ramparts; the underground tunnels, gun ports, and magazines; and the water gate and pond for entering by boat from the sea. Exhibits in six large halls illustrate the island's long, intimate connection with the sea—from Spanish exploration to 20th-century ocean liners, from racing dinghies to practical fishing boats, from shipbuilding and privateering to naval exploits.

The museum's most famous exhibit is in the 1837 Shifting House, which opened in 1979. Here, you can see such artifacts as gold bars, pottery, jewelry, silver coins, and other items recovered from 16th- and 17th-century shipwrecks, including some earthenware and pewter that belonged to the English settlers on their way to Jamestown aboard the Sea Venture (wrecked in 1609). Most visitors come here to gaze at the Tucker Treasure. A well-known local diver, Teddy Tucker, made a significant find in 1955 when he discovered the wreck of the San Antonio, a Spanish vessel that had gone down off the coast of Bermuda in a violent storm in 1621. One of the great treasures of this find, the Pectoral Cross, was stolen in 1975 just before Queen Elizabeth II officially opened the museum. The priceless original cross was replaced by a fake. To this day, the original cross has never been recovered, and its mysterious disappearance is still the subject of much discussion.

As you enter the Parade Ground at the entrance to the museum, you'll notice a 10-foot-high figure of King Neptune. This comes from the HMS *Irresistible,* recovered when the ship was broken up in 1891; it has now been duplicated in Indiana limestone. The Queen's Exhibition Hall houses general maritime exhibits, including those on navigation, whaling, and cable and wireless communications. A "Bermuda in Five Hours" exhibit focuses on Pan American's early "flying boats." The building itself was constructed in 1850 for the purpose of storing 4,860 barrels of gunpowder.

The Forster Cooper Building (from 1852) illustrates the history of the Royal Navy in Bermuda, including the Bromby Bottle Collection. This exhibit was opened in 1984 by Princess Margaret. The Boatloft houses part of the museum's boat collections, including the century-old fitted dinghy *Victory,* the 17-foot *Spirit of Bermuda,* and the *Rambler,* the only surviving Bermuda pilot gig. On the upper floor, the original dockyard clock, which is still working, chimes the hours and the quarter hours.

4 Southampton Parish

All visitors pass through Southampton for the beaches, if for no other reason. Many prefer to stay here. Even if you're not staying here, it's worth a journey over to see the view from Gibbs Hill Lighthouse—there's no finer panorama in all of Bermuda.

✪ Gibbs Hill Lighthouse

Gibbs Hill, Lighthouse Rd. (between South Shore and Middle Rd.). ☎ **441/238-0524.** Admission $2.50, free for children under 5. Daily 9am–4:30pm. Bus: 7 or 8 from Hamilton.

Southampton's main attraction is this lighthouse, built in 1846. It's the oldest cast-iron lighthouse in the world. Although there's a 185-step climb to the top, the panoramic view of Bermuda and its shoreline from the outlook balcony makes the climb worthwhile. The lighthouse keeper will explain the workings of the machinery. If you visit in the spring, you may spot migrating whales beyond the south-shore reefs.

5 Warwick Parish

This parish has little in the way of sightseeing attractions, but it is a place of natural beauty. Visitors come here mostly for the sandy beach, Warwick Long Bay, on South Shore Road; it's one of the finest in Bermuda (see "Beaches," in chapter 6, for details). Nearby, you can visit Christ Church, across from the Belmont Hotel on Middle Road. Built in 1719, it's one of the oldest Scottish Presbyterian churches in the New World.

Warwick is also the site of some of the best golf and horseback riding in Bermuda; again, see chapter 6 for specifics.

6 Paget Parish

On every visit to Bermuda, we always schedule a long stopover at the Botanical Gardens, which are worth the trip, even if you're staying in the East End. Once you're here, it's also worthwhile to look at Waterville, one of the oldest houses in Bermuda. You could cap your visit with a walk through unspoiled Paget Marsh, although you might skip it if you've already seen Spittal Pond (see "Smith's Parish," below).

The Birdsey Studio

5 Stowe Hill. ☎ **441/236-6658.** Bus: 8 from Hamilton.

Original artwork, watercolors, and oils are sold by Jo Birdsey Lindberg, daughter of the island's best-known artist, Alfred Birdsey (1912 to 1996). An experienced painter herself, she continues a family tradition by producing and showing her work at this studio in a garden setting. Her impressionistic style is seen in compositions ranging from landscapes of Bermuda to architectural and nautical themes. Prices range from $50 to $700. Also available are note cards reproduced from paintings by Alfred Birdsey. Studio hours are Monday to Friday from 10:30am to 1pm March to July and September to November (or else by appointment).

✪ Botanical Gardens

Point Finger Rd. (at South Shore Rd.). ☎ **441/236-4201.** Free admission. Daily sunrise–sunset. Bus: 1, 2, or 7. If you're on a bike or moped, turn left off Middle Rd. onto Tee St.; at Berry Hill Rd., go right; about ½ mile farther on the left is the signposted turnoff to the gardens; take a right fork to the parking lot on the left.

This 36-acre landscaped park, maintained by the Department of Natural Resources, is one of Bermuda's major attractions, with hundreds of flowers, shrubs, and trees all clearly identified along the pathways. Attractions include collections of hibiscus and subtropical fruit, an aviary, banyan trees, and even a garden for the blind. It's best to take one of the 90-minute walking tours that depart at 10:30am on Tuesday, Wednesday, and Friday from the visitor center; the cafe here sells sandwiches and salads (soup and chili in winter).

Paget Marsh

Middle Rd. ☎ **441/236-6483.** Free admission. Mon–Fri 9am–5pm by special arrangement. Bus: 8 from Hamilton.

Paget Marsh comprises 25 acres of unspoiled native woods and marshland, with vegetation and bird life of ecological interest. Since it's a fully protected area with few trails, prospective visitors should call the number given above to make special arrangements and obtain a map from the Bermuda National Trust.

Waterville

5 The Lane (Harbour Rd.), at Pomander Rd. ☎ **441/236-6483.** Free admission. Mon–Fri 9am–5pm. Bus: 7 or 8 from Hamilton.

Built before 1735, this is one of the oldest houses in Bermuda; it was home to seven generations of the prominent Trimingham family. From the cellar storage rooms of this house in 1842, James Harvey Trimingham started the business that was to become Trimingham Brothers—now one of Bermuda's finest Front Street department shops. Waterville is now the headquarters of the Bermuda National Trust, housing its offices and reception rooms. Major renovations were undertaken in 1811, and the house has been restored in this period's style. The two main rooms have also been furnished in this period, mainly with Trimingham family heirlooms specifically bequeathed for use in the house. Waterville is just west of the Trimingham roundabout, quite close to the city of Hamilton.

7 Pembroke Parish & the City of Hamilton

The ideal way to see the city of Hamilton and its parish, Pembroke, for the first time is to sail in through Hamilton Harbour, past the offshore cays.

In 1852, the cornerstone was laid for the Hamilton Hotel, Bermuda's first hotel, which was completed in 1863. It survived until 1955, when it was destroyed by fire. When the Hamilton Princess opened in 1887, it overshadowed the Hamilton Hotel and became the hotel of choice for the island. Over the years it has had a colorful history, especially when it was taken over by Allied agents during World War II.

If Princess Louise were to visit Bermuda today, she would probably stay at **Government House,** which stands on North Shore Road and Langton Hill. The residence of the governor of the island, it's not open to the public (you can view the spacious grounds by applying to the governor's aide-de-camp). This Victorian home has housed many notable guests, including Queen Elizabeth II and Prince Philip, as well as Prince Charles, Sir Winston Churchill, and Pres. John F. Kennedy. The saddest moment for Government House was in 1973, when Gov. Sir Richard Sharples and his aide, Capt. Hugh Sayers, along with the governor's dog, Horsa, were assassinated while they were walking on the grounds. This tragedy led to a state of emergency in Bermuda.

While touring Pembroke Parish, visitors are fond of looking at **Black Watch Well,** located at the junction of North Shore Road and Black Watch Pass. Excavated by a detachment of the Black Watch Regiment, the well was ordered to be dug in 1894, when Bermudians were suffering through a long drought.

Another choice spot to visit is **Admiralty House Park,** lying off North Shore Road at the point where it merges with Spanish Point Road. In the 1800s this scenic area formed the estate of John of Dunscombe, who later became lieutenant governor of Newfoundland. After the property was sold to the British military in 1816, a house was erected here to offer accommodations for the commanding British admiralty, who worked at the naval base at the Dockyard. Over the years the house was rebuilt several times, including in the 1850s when a series of subterranean tunnels was added, plus a number of galleries and caves carved into the cliffs above the sea. By 1951 the Royal Navy withdrew, and the house was torn down except for a ballroom which still remains. You can explore the parklike grounds today, and even find a sheltered beach at Clarence Cove with good swimming.

THE CITY OF HAMILTON

Hamilton has been the capital of Bermuda since 1815 and was once known as the "Show Window of the British Empire." Both Mark Twain and Eugene O'Neill, who lived in places that opened onto Hamilton Harbour, cited its beauty.

Named for a former governor, Henry Hamilton, Hamilton was incorporated as a town in 1793. Because of Hamilton's central location and its large, protected harbor, it was chosen as the island's new capital in 1815, replacing St. George's. Since Hamilton encompasses a total of only 182 acres of land, most visitors explore it on foot.

Today Hamilton is the hub of the island's economy; however, long before it became known as the "showcase of the Atlantic," it was a modest outlet for the export of Bermuda cedar and fresh vegetables.

The city of Hamilton is actually more popular for its shops and restaurants than for its attractions. Hamilton boasts the largest number of restaurants and bars in Bermuda, especially on or near Front Street. These restaurants charge a wide range of prices, and there are many English-style pubs if you'd like to go on a pub crawl. Although there is a huge conglomeration of bars, religion isn't neglected—there are also 12 churches within the city limits, one or two of which merit a sightseeing visit.

If you'd like to go sightseeing here, it's better to take our walking tour (see chapter 8) for an overall view. The only sights that truly merit interior visits are Fort Hamilton (seen on the walking tour), the Bermuda Historical Society Museum, and the Bermuda National Gallery. You can safely skip the rest if you're pressed for time.

A stroll along **Front Street** will take you by some of Hamilton's most elegant stores, but you'll want to branch off into the little alleyways to check their shops and boutiques. If you get tired of walking or shopping (or both), you can go down to the docks and take one of the boats or catamarans waiting to show you the treasures of Little Sound and Great Sound.

On certain days you may be able to see locals buying their fresh fish—the part of the catch that hasn't already been earmarked for restaurants—right from the fishers who sell the catch of the day at the **Front Street docks.** Although rockfish is the most abundant, you'll also see snapper, grouper, and many other species.

Hamilton should be seen not only from land, but also from the water; try to make time for one of the frequent boating tours of the harbor and its coral reefs. If you're visiting from other parishes, the ferry will let you off at the western end of Front Street, which is ideal if you'd like to drop by the Visitors Service Bureau and pick up a map. It's located near the Ferry Terminal. The staff here also provides information and helpful brochures; hours are 9am to 4:45pm Monday to Saturday.

To return to the parishes of Paget, Warwick, and Sandys, ferries leave daily between 6:50am and 11:20pm. On Saturday and Sunday, there are fewer departures.

Opposite the Visitors Service Bureau stands the much-photographed **"Bird Cage,"** where you used to be able to see a police officer directing traffic. Such a sight is rare now. For many years, visitors wondered if the traffic director was for real or placed there for tourist photographs.

Nearby is Albouy's Point, site of the Royal Bermuda Yacht Club, founded in 1844. The point, named after a 17th-century professor of "physick," is a public park overlooking Hamilton Harbour.

All of the sights listed below are reachable via bus no. 1, 2, 10, or 11.

Bermuda Historical Society Museum

13 Queen St., Par-la-Ville Park. ☎ 441/295-2487. Free admission. Mon–Sat 9:30am–3:30pm.

After leaving the harbor, proceed up Queen Street to the public library and the Bermuda Historical Society Museum, which has a collection of old cedar furniture, antique silver, early Bermuda coins (hog money), and ceramics that were imported to Bermuda by early sea captains. You'll see the sea chest and navigating lodestone of Sir George Somers, whose flagship, the *Sea Venture*, became stranded on Bermuda's reefs in 1609. You'll also find portraits of Sir George and Lady Somers, as well as models of the ill-fated *Sea Venture*, along with models of *Patience* and *Deliverance*.

The museum is located in Par-la-Ville Park on Queen Street. It was designed by William Bennett Perot, Hamilton's first postmaster (from 1818 to 1862), who was somewhat eccentric. As he delivered mail around town, he is said to have placed letters in the crown of his top hat in order to preserve his dignity.

Bermuda National Gallery

City Hall, 17 Church St. ☎ 441/295-9428. Admission $3 adults; free for children under 16. Mon–Sat 10am–4pm. Tours Tues, Thurs, Fri at 1pm.

Located in the east wing of City Hall, the Bermuda National Gallery is the home of the Masterworks Foundation Bermudiana Collection, with works by such artists as Georgia O'Keeffe, Winslow Homer, Charles Demuth, Albert Gleizes, Ogden Pleissner, and Jack Bush. The Masterworks Foundation was established in 1987 to return to the island works of art that depict Bermuda and to exhibit them. The gallery is also home to the Hereward T. Watlington Collection, which includes 15th- to 19th-century paintings by such masters as Reynolds, Gainsborough, and de Hooch. The gallery also displays smaller paintings and watercolors collected by the Bermuda Archives and National Trust.

While a National Gallery for Bermuda was long overdue, Bermuda's humid climate and damaging sunlight made it necessary to build a gallery with proper climate control and lighting. As a result, the Bermuda Fine Art Trust was developed and incorporated by an Act of Parliament in 1982. In 1988, the Hon. Hereward T. Watlington bequeathed his collection of European paintings to the people of Bermuda on the condition that they be housed in a European-standard climate-controlled environment. The Corporation of Hamilton offered the use of the East Exhibition Room of City Hall and made a financial contribution toward the construction of a proper facility.

Cathedral of the Most Holy Trinity (Bermuda Cathedral)

Church St. ☎ 441/292-4033. Free admission to cathedral; admission to cathedral tower $3 adults, $2 seniors and children. Cathedral daily 7:15am–5pm and for Sun services; tower Mon–Fri 10am–3pm.

The Bermuda Cathedral is the so-called "mother" church of the Anglican diocese in Bermuda. It became a cathedral in 1894 and was formally consecrated in 1911. The building features a reredos, stained-glass windows, and ornate carvings. If you have the stamina, climb the 157 steps to the top of the tower for a panoramic view of Hamilton and the harbor.

Hamilton City Hall & Arts Centre

17 Church St. ☎ **441/292-1234.** Free admission. City Hall: Mon–Fri 9am–5pm. Bermuda Society of Arts: Mon–Sat 10am–4pm.

The City Hall, also home of the Bermuda Society of Arts, is an imposing white structure with a giant weather vane and wind clock to tell maritime-minded Bermudians which way the wind is blowing. Completed in 1960, the building is the seat of Hamilton's municipal government. The theater on the first floor is the venue for stage, music, and dance productions throughout the year and is also the main site of the Bermuda Festival. The Bermuda National Gallery (see above) is also here.

Since 1956, the Bermuda Society of Arts has encouraged and provided a forum for contemporary Bermuda artists, sculptors, and photographers. Its gallery, with ever-changing exhibitions, displays the work of local and visiting artists. Although their goals are often shared, this society is a separate entity from the newer Bermuda National Gallery.

Perot Post Office

Queen St., at the entrance to Par-la-Ville Park. ☎ **441/292-9052** or 441/295-5151, ext. 1192. Free admission. Mon–Fri 9am–5pm.

Bermuda's first stamp was printed in this landmark building. Beloved by collectors from all over the world, the stamps—signed by Perot, Bermuda's first, rather eccentric postmaster—are priceless. It's said that Perot and his friend Heyl, who ran an apothecary, conceived the first postage stamp to protect the post office from cheaters. People used to stop off at the post office and leave letters, but not enough pennies to send them. The postage stamps were printed in either black or carmine.

Philatelists can purchase contemporary Bermuda stamps in this same post office. For its 375th anniversary, Bermuda issued a series of stamps honoring its discovery in 1609. One stamp portrays the admiral of the fleet, Sir George Somers, along with Sir Thomas Gates, the captain of the *Sea Venture.* Another depicts the settlement of Jamestown, Virginia, which was on the verge of extinction when Sir George and the survivors of the Bermuda shipwreck finally arrived with supplies late in 1610. A third shows the *Sea Venture* stranded on the coral reefs of Bermuda. Yet another shows the entire fleet, originally bound for Jamestown, leaving Plymouth, England, on June 2, 1609.

Sessions House

21 Parliament St. ☎ **441/292-7408.** Free admission. Mon–Fri 9am–12:30pm and 2–5pm.

This Italian Renaissance–style structure was originally built in 1819. Its clock tower was added in 1887 to commemorate the Golden Jubilee of Queen Victoria. The House of Assembly meets on the second floor from November to May, and visitors are permitted in the gallery (call the above number to learn when meetings are scheduled). On the lower level, the chief justice presides over the Supreme Court.

8 Devonshire Parish

If you're passing through Devonshire, consider a stopover at the following attractions.

Old Devonshire Parish Church

Middle Rd. ☎ **441/236-3671.** Free admission. Daily 9am–5:30pm. Bus: 2.

A major attraction of the parish is the Old Devonshire Parish Church, which is believed to have been built on this Middle Road site in 1624, although the present foundation dates from 1716. An explosion virtually destroyed the church on Easter in 1970, but it was reconstructed. Today the church is very tiny, almost resembling a vicarage rather than a church. Some of the church's contents survived the blast, including its silver from 1590, which may be the oldest on the island. The church, designed by Sir George Grove and built of limestone, has an early English-style high-pitched roof. The Old Devonshire Parish Church stands northwest of the "new" Devonshire Parish Church, which dates from 1846.

Palm Grove

38 South Shore Rd. No phone. Free admission. Mon–Thurs 8:30am–5pm. Bus: 1.

This private estate, 2½ miles east of Hamilton, is one of the delights of Devonshire Parish. It's famous for its pond with a relief map of Bermuda in the middle of it. Each parish is an immaculately manicured grassy division. The site, which has well-landscaped flower gardens, opens onto a view of the sea.

9 Smith's Parish

Even if you're staying in remote Sandys Parish in the West End, the 18th-century mansion of Verdmont is worth a detour, as the good folks at Michelin say. If you're in the area, Spittal Pond Nature Reserve also merits some attention.

Spittal Pond Nature Reserve

South Shore Rd. ☎ **441/236-6483.** Free admission. Daily sunrise–sunset. Bus: 1 or 3.

Follow the rather steep Knapton Hill Road west to South Shore Road, turning at the sign for Spittal Pond, Bermuda's largest wildlife sanctuary. The most important of the National Trust's open spaces, it occupies 60 acres and has about 25 species of waterfowl, which can be seen annually from November to May. Visitors are asked to stay on the scenic trails and footpaths provided. Bird-watchers in particular like to visit in January, when as many as 500 species of birds can be observed wintering on the pond.

✪ Verdmont

6 Verdmont Lane, Collectors Hill. ☎ **441/236-7369.** Admission $3 adults, $2 children 6–18, free for children 5 and under. Tues–Sat 10am–4pm. Bus: 1 from Hamilton or St. George's.

This 18th-century mansion is of special significance to Americans who are interested in colonial and Revolutionary War history. It stands on property that was owned in the 17th century by William Sayle, who left Bermuda to found South Carolina on the American mainland and then become its first governor. The house was built before 1710 by John Dickinson, a prosperous ship owner who was also speaker of the House of Assembly in Bermuda from 1707 to 1710. Verdmont passed to Mr. Dickinson's granddaughter, Elizabeth, who married the Hon. Thomas Smith, collector of Customs. Their oldest daughter, Mary, married Judge John Green, a Loyalist who came to Bermuda in 1765 from Philadelphia. During and after the American Revolution, Green was judge of the Vice-Admiralty Court and had the final say on prizes brought in by privateers. Many American ship owners lost their vessels because of his decisions. The house, which is now administered by the National Trust, contains many antiques, china, and portraits, along with the finest cedar stair balustrade in Bermuda.

10 Hamilton Parish

Even if your sightseeing time is very limited, try to budget at least a half day for Hamilton Parish. It has some of the most intriguing attractions on the island, notably the Bermuda Aquarium, Museum & Zoo, plus Crystal Caves and Leamington Caves. If you have time for only one of these caves, we recommend Crystal Caves. However, if you've seen some of the great caves of America or

Europe, or even beyond, you may find Bermuda's caves a lesser thrill. While you're in the neighborhood, and if you have time, you might also check out the Bermuda Perfumery.

✪ Bermuda Aquarium, Natural History Museum & Zoo

North Shore Rd., Flatts Village. ☎ **441/293-2727.** Admission $8 adults, $4 children 5–12, free for children under 5. Daily 9am–4:30pm. Closed Christmas Day. Bus: 10 or 11 from Hamilton or from St. George's. From Hamilton, follow Middle Rd. or North Shore Rd. east to Flatts Village; from St. George's, once over the causeway, follow North Shore Rd. or Harrington Sound Rd. west to Flatts Village.

This complex is home to a wide collection of tropical marine fish, turtles, harbor seals, and other forms of sea life. In the museum you'll see exhibits on the geological development of Bermuda, deep-sea exploration, and humpback whales. The complex also has a zoo with Galapagos tortoises, alligators, and monkeys, along with a collection of birds, including parrots and flamingos.

The 140,000-gallon–tank North Rock Exhibit allows visitors to enter an exhibit to experience a coral reef washed by ocean surge. The tank houses a living coral reef, as well as reef and pelagic fish species. The tank holds the first living coral exhibit on this scale in the world, made possible by the Aquarium, Museum & Zoo's success in the science of coral husbandry.

There's parking for cycles and cars across the street from the aquarium.

Bermuda Perfumery

212 North Shore Rd., Bailey's Bay. ☎ **441/293-0627.** Free admission. Apr–Oct Mon–Sat 9am–5pm, Sun 10am–4pm; Nov–Mar Mon–Sat 9am–4:30pm. Closed Sun in winter. Bus: 1 or 3.

Lili Perfumes are made here. On guided tours, visitors can see the perfume-making process, including the old method of extracting scents from native flowers. Among the fragrances produced are passion flower, Bermuda Easter lily, and oleander jasmine. A small botanical garden with a seating area and walkways provides an attractive resting place. You can also visit the orchid house, which contains more than 500 varieties of orchids, and the nature trail, which passes through a large area of the property that is planted with tropical flowers, shrubs, and trees. The perfumery also has a gift shop.

✪ Crystal Caves

8 Crystal Caves Rd., off Wilkinson Ave., Bailey's Bay. ☎ **441/293-0640.** Admission $6 adults, $3 children 5–11, free for children 4 and under. Daily 9:30am–4:40pm. Closed Dec–Jan. Bus: 1 or 3.

This network of subterranean lakes, caves, and caverns is composed of translucent formations of stalagmites and stalactites; the setting includes the crystal-clear Cahow Lake. Discovered in 1907, the Crystal Caves are reached by a sloping path and a few steps; at the bottom, about 120 feet below the surface, is a floating causeway that follows the winding cavern, where hidden lights illuminate the interior. All tours through Crystal Caves are guided. Using a lighting system, the guides make silhouettes and are fond of pointing out the similarity to the skyline of Manhattan. If you suffer from claustrophobia, you might find the space too tight here.

Devil's Hole Aquarium

92 Harrington Sound Rd. ☎ **441/293-2072.** Admission $5 adults, $3 children 5–12, 50¢ children 4 and under. Daily 9:30am–4:30pm. Bus: 1 or 3.

The pool of this former cave is fed by the sea through a half mile of subterranean passages. A natural aquarium open to the public since 1834, it's stocked with some 400 individual fish, including moray eels, sharks, giant groupers, and massive green turtles. Visitors can tempt the pond's inhabitants with baited but hookless lines.

11 St. George's Parish

A great way to explore this historic town is by following the "Historic St. George's Town" walking tour in chapter 8.

THE TOWN OF ST. GEORGE'S

King's Square, also called Market Square or King's Parade, is the center of life in St. George's. The square is the site of the colorful **White Horse Tavern,** where you may want to stop for a drink after your tour of the town.

The street names in St. George's also evoke its history. Petticoat Lane (sometimes called Silk Alley) got its name when two recently emancipated slave girls were said to have paraded up and down the lane rustling their new and flamboyantly colored silk petticoats. Barber's Lane is also named for a former slave. It honors Joseph Hayne Rainey, a freedman from the Carolinas who fled to Bermuda aboard a blockade runner during the Civil War. He became a barber in Bermuda until the end of the war. At its conclusion he returned to the United States and was elected to Congress, becoming the first black member of the House of Representatives during Reconstruction.

St. George's branch of the **Visitors Service Bureau** is located on King's Square (☎ **441/297-1642**); it's open Monday to Saturday from 9am to 4pm in summer, and Monday to Saturday from 9:30am to 2pm in winter (Nov to Mar). Here you can get a map and any information you might need before setting out to explore. The bureau is opposite the Town Hall.

If you're really rushed for time, don't worry that you're missing out if you skip interior visits to all the sights previewed below. It's the entire town of St. George's, with its quaint streets and old buildings, that forms the three-star attraction here, not any one particular monument. If you have time to visit only one attraction's interior, make it St. Peter's Church. Otherwise, just wander around, do a little shopping, and soak in the atmosphere.

All the attractions below can be reached via bus no. 1, 3, 8, 10, or 11 from Hamilton.

The Bermuda National Trust Museum

At the Globe Hotel, King's Sq. ☎ **441/297-1423.** $4 adults, $2 children 7–18, free for children 6 and under. Mon–Sat 10am–4pm, Sun 1–4pm. Closed Christmas.

This was once the Globe Hotel, headquarters of Maj. Norman Walker, the Confederate representative in Bermuda; today it houses relics from the island's involvement in the American Civil War, but from a Bermudian perspective. St. George's was the port from which ships carrying arms and munitions ran the Union blockade. A replica of the Great Seal of the Confederacy is fitted to a Victorian press so that visitors can emboss copies as souvenirs. There's also a video presentation, *Bermuda: Centre of the Atlantic,* tracing the island's early history.

Bridge House Gallery

1 Bridge St. ☎ **441/297-8211.** Free admission. Mon–Sat 9:30am–5:30pm, Sun noon–4pm. Mid-Jan to mid-Feb Wed and Sat only, 11am–4pm.

This long-established gallery displays antiques and collectibles, old Bermudian items, original paintings, Bermuda-made crafts, and a studio belonging to Jill Amos Raine, a well-known Bermuda watercolor artist. The house was constructed in the mid–17th century and was home to several of the colony's governors. Its most colorful owner was Bridger Goodrich, a Loyalist from Virginia, whose privateers once blockaded Chesapeake Bay. So devoted was he to the king that he also sabotaged

That'll Teach You!

Right on King's Square you'll see a pillory and stock. Honeymooners like to be photographed in them today, but in earlier times they were used in deadly earnest. Victims were sometimes placed in the pillory for a certain number of hours—sometimes with one ear nailed to the post! Criminals were burned on the hand or branded, fined in tobacco, nailed to the post, or declared "infamous." Often, they had their ears cut off or were forced to "stand in a sheet on the church porch."

The list of offenses for which Bermudians were punished in the early 1600s offers a glimpse into the social life of the time. Along with such "usual" crimes as treason, robbery, arson, murder, and "scandal," punishable offenses included concealing finds of ambergris, exporting cedarwood, railing against the governor's authority, hiding tobacco, being "notorious cursers and swearers," leading an "uncivil life and calling her neighbor an old Bawd and the like," neglecting to receive Holy Communion, acting in any stage play of any kind whatsoever, and playing at unlawful games such as dice, cards, and ninepins.

Bahamian vessels trading with the American colonies. The building is named Bridge House because a bridge used to stand over a muddy creek (it's filled in now).

Deliverance

Ordnance Island. ☎ **441/297-1459.** Admission $3 adults, $1 children under 12. Apr–Oct daily 9am–6pm; Nov–Mar call for opening hrs.

Across from St. George's town square and over a bridge is Ordnance Island, where visitors can see a full-scale replica of *Deliverance,* a pinnace (small sailing ship) constructed in 1609 by the shipwrecked survivors of the *Sea Venture* to carry them on to Virginia. A tape recording guides visitors through the ship. Alongside *Deliverance* is the ducking stool, a replica of the horrible contraption used in 17th-century witch trials; it's demonstrated on Wednesday and Thursday at noon.

Adventures Enterprises owns *Deliverance* and also runs sightseeing and snorkeling adventures aboard its boat, *ARGO.* Bermuda's only high-speed tour boat, *ARGO* takes passengers along the barrier reef, the south-shore beaches, the historic forts, and the billionaires' mansions at Tucker's Town. *ARGO* was custom-built to allow access to the most beautiful parts of the island where larger vessels can't gain entrance. Call for details, which change seasonally.

Old Rectory

At the head of Broad Alley, behind St. Peter's Church. ☎ **441/236-6483.** Free admission; donations are appreciated. Nov–Mar Wed noon–5pm.

Built by a reformed pirate in 1705, this charming old Bermuda cottage was later inhabited by Parson Richardson, who was nicknamed the "Little Bishop." Now a private home, it's administered by the Bermuda National Trust.

Old State House

Princess St. ☎ **441/292-2480.** Free admission. Wed 10am–4pm or by appointment.

Behind the Town Hall is Bermuda's oldest stone building, the Old State House, constructed with turtle oil and lime mortar in 1620. Unless some special event is taking place here, you might settle for a look at the exterior of this building and then press on with your day's events. There isn't that much to see today in spite of the building's landmark status. The Old State House, where meetings of the legislative council once took place, was eventually turned over to the Freemasons of St. George's. The government asked the annual rent of one peppercorn and insisted on

Special Places Where You Can Be Alone

Bermuda is so popular for such a small island—but that doesn't mean that you can't escape the crowds and find peace and serenity in a lovely spot, hopefully with someone you love.

Sandys Parish   Visitors don't seem to spend a lot of time here; but for wandering about, getting lost, and finding enchanting little vistas, Sandys is without equal in Bermuda. At the point where Daniel's Head Road meets Cambridge Road, paths will take you to Somerset Long Bay Park, where you can go for a swim to refresh yourself. After that, take one of the unmarked trails to the Bermuda Audubon Society Nature Reserve, a gem of nature. The place is often deserted weekdays, but families like to come here on weekends; on occasion, we've had it all to ourselves. When the white-eyed vireos and the bluebirds call to you from fiddlewood trees, you'll really feel close to nature.

Southampton Parish   In this windswept, tourist-trodden parish, you'd think there was no place where you could find solitude. Not so! Signposted from Middle Road, a trail goes a half mile down to the entrance to Seymour's Pond Nature Reserve. Under the management of the Bermuda Audubon Society, this 2½-acre site attracts the occasional birder, as well as romantic couples looking for a little privacy. Just past the pond, you'll spot pepper trees and old cedars that escaped the blight; you might encounter bluebirds and an egret or two as well. After traversing Cross Church Road, you'll come upon the old Bermuda Railway Trail, where in summer you can see fennel growing wild. In the distance are panoramic views of shipwreck-clogged Black Bay and Five Star Island.

Warwick Parish   With its beautiful pink-sand beaches, sea-bordering parklands, natural attractions, and winding country lanes, this is one of the most charming Bermuda parishes for exploring and escaping the crowds. Even many longtime local residents haven't seen some of the beauty spots of this parish. The

the right to hold meetings here upon demand. The Masonic Lodge members, in a ceremony filled with pageantry, still turn over one peppercorn in rent to the Bermuda government every April. (Peppercorns were sometimes a form of payment in the old days. In the late 18th century, for example, two small islands off King's Square were sold for a peppercorn apiece. In 1782, Henry Tucker bought Ducking Stool Island, and in 1785, Nathaniel Butterfield bought Gallows Island; several years later Simon Fraser purchased both for 100 peppercorns and made them into one island, today's Ordnance Island.)

For those who have never witnessed the 45-minute spectacle of the annual **rent payment,** it begins around 11am with the gathering of the Bermuda Regiment on King's Square and the subsequent arrival of the premier, mayor, and other dignitaries, all amid the bellowing introductions of the town crier. As soon as all the principals have taken their places, a 17-gun salute is fired as the governor and his wife make a grand entrance in their open horse-drawn landau. His Excellency inspects a military guard of honor, while the Bermuda Regiment Band plays. The stage is, of course, now set for the presentation of the peppercorn, which sits on a silver plate atop a velvet cushion. Payment is made in a grand and formal manner, after which the Old State House is immediately used for a meeting of Her Majesty's Council.

place to head for here is Warwick Pond, a sanctuary for several rare species of birds. Administered by the Bermuda National Trust, it's open daily from sunrise to sunset. You can reach it by following the Bermuda Railway Trail until you come to Tribe Road No. 3; climb this road for a few hundred yards before it takes a dip down a hill to the pond. You might spot the occasional birder in search of a kiskadee blue heron or a cardinal. The pond, fed by a subterranean channel bringing in water from the sea, reminds us of Thoreau's Walden Pond.

✪ **St. David's Island**   Part of St. George's Parish, St. David's is Bermuda "the way it was." Virtually unknown to the ordinary visitor, it awaits your discovery. This is real down-home Bermuda—it's said that some St. David's islanders have never even visited "mainland" Bermuda. You can begin your walk at Great Head Park in the eastern part of St. David's, to the southeast of the local cricket fields; at the end of the parking lot, follow the trail into a wooded area filled with cherry trees and palmettos. After about 250 yards, bear right at the fork. Eventually you'll spot St. David's Lighthouse, an octagonal red-and-white tower in the distance to the southwest. The trail forks left until you come to a ruined garrison with a panoramic sea view; it's one of the remotest, loveliest spots on the island—and, chances are, you'll have it all to yourself.

Devonshire Parish   This parish, off the beaten track, is home to some real beauty spots—if you're adventurous enough to seek them out. Old Devonshire Church on Middle Road is a landmark; almost directly across the road lies the wilds of Devonshire Marsh, a natural water basin still in an untamed state. You'll also find two nature reserves, Firefly and Freer Cox Memorial, here on some 10 acres of marshland. The Bermuda Audubon Society has set aside this protected area as a bird sanctuary for many endangered wild birds; you can also see some of the most unusual plants of Bermuda, including orchids. The marsh is always open to the public.

St. George's Historical Society Museum

3 Featherbed Alley. ☎ **441/297-0423.** Admission $4 adults, $1 children 16 and under. Mon–Fri 10am–4pm.

Located in a home built around 1700, this museum contains an original 18th-century Bermuda kitchen complete with utensils from that period. Other exhibits include a 300-year-old Bible, a letter from George Washington, and Native American ax heads (some early settlers on St. David's Island were Native Americans, mainly Pequot).

✪ St. Peter's Church

Duke of York St. ☎ **441/297-8359.** Free admission, but donations appreciated. Daily 10am–4:30pm and for Sun services (guide available Mon–Sat).

From King's Square, head east to Duke of York Street, where you'll find St. Peter's Church, believed to be the oldest Anglican place of worship in the western hemisphere. The original church, built by colonists in 1612 almost entirely of cedar with a palmetto-leaf thatch roof, was almost completely destroyed by a hurricane in 1712. Some of the interior, including the original altar from 1615 (still used on a daily basis), was salvaged, and the church was rebuilt in 1713. It has been restored many times since then, providing excellent examples of the architectural styles of the 17th to the 20th centuries. The tower was added in 1814. On display in the vestry is a silver communion service given to the church by King William III in 1697. Before the Old State House was built, the colony held public meetings in the church. The first assize convened here in 1616, and the first meeting of Parliament was held in 1620. The church has Sunday and weekday services.

Some of the tombstones in the Graveyard of St. Peter's (entrance opposite Broad Alley) are more than 3 centuries old; many tombs mark the graves of slaves. Here you'll also find the grave of Midshipman Richard Dale, an American who was the last victim of the War of 1812. The churchyard also holds the tombs of Gov. Sir Richard Sharples and his aide, Capt. Hugh Sayers, who were murdered while strolling on the grounds of Government House in 1973.

Somers Garden

Duke of York St. ☎ **441/297-1532.** Free admission. Daily 9am–5pm.

The heart of Sir George Somers was buried here in 1610; a stone column perpetuates the memory of Bermuda's founder. The garden was opened in 1920 by the Prince of Wales (later King Edward VIII, and then the duke of Windsor, after he abandoned the throne to marry his true love, American Wallis Simpson).

Town Hall

7 King's Sq. ☎ **441/297-1532.** Free admission. Mon–Sat 10am–4pm.

Officers of the Corporation of St. George's, headed by a mayor, meet in the Town Hall, located near the Visitors Service Bureau. There are three aldermen and five common councillors. The Town Hall has a collection of Bermuda cedar furnishings, along with photographs of previous mayors.

Tucker House Museum

5 Water St. ☎ **441/297-0545.** Admission $3 adults, $2 children 6–18, free for children under 6. Mon–Sat 10am–4pm.

This was the home of the well-known Tucker family of England, Bermuda, and Virginia. It displays a notable collection of Bermudian furniture, portraits, and silver. Also in the Tucker House is the Joseph Rainey Memorial Room, where this African-American refugee (mentioned above) of the Civil War practiced barbering. A new exhibit on the ground floor traces the archaeological history of the site.

Unfinished Cathedral

Blockade Alley.

After leaving Somers Garden, head up the steps to the North Gate, which opens onto Blockade Alley. The structure here is known as the "folly of St. George's." The plan was that this cathedral, begun in 1874, would replace St. Peter's. But the planners ran into money problems and then a schism developed; as if that weren't enough, a storm swept over the island, causing considerable damage to the structure. Result: the Unfinished Cathedral.

HISTORIC FORTS THAT NEVER SAW MUCH ACTION

From its earliest days, St. George's has been fortified, and although it never saw much military action, reminders of those former days are interesting to explore. Located on the outskirts of town, the forts can be reached via Circular Drive. As forts go, these two are of relatively minor interest unless, of course, you're a fort buff—in that case, be our guest. If you have time for only one fort in Bermuda, Fort Hamilton on Happy Valley Road is the most intriguing (see "The City of Hamilton" walking tour in chapter 8 for details).

Along the coast is Building Bay, where the shipwrecked victims of the *Sea Venture* built their vessel, the *Deliverance,* in 1610.

Fort St. Catherine

15 Coot Pond Rd. ☎ **441/297-1920.** Admission $5 adults, $2 for children under 12. Daily 10am–4:30pm. Closed Christmas.

Towering above the beach where the shipwrecked crew of the *Sea Venture* came ashore in 1609 is Fort St. Catherine, completed in 1614 and named for the patron saint of wheelwrights and carpenters. The fortifications have been upgraded over the years. The last major reconstruction took place from 1865 to 1878, so the fort's appearance today is largely the result of work done in the 19th century.

Now that the fort is a museum, visitors first see a series of dioramas, "Highlights in Bermuda's History." Museum figures are used to depict various activities that took place in the magazine of the fort, restored and refurnished as it was in the 1880s. Large Victorian muzzle-loading cannons can be seen on their original carriages. In the keep, which served as the living quarters of the fort, you can see information on local and overseas regiments that served in Bermuda, a fine small-arms exhibit, a cooking-area display, and an exhibit of replicas of England's crown jewels. There's a short audiovisual show on St. George's defense systems and the forts of St. George's.

Gates Fort

Cut Rd. No phone. Free admission. Daily 10am–4:30pm.

Gates Fort was built in 1609 by Sir Thomas Gates, one of the original band of settlers on the *Sea Venture.* Gates was governor-designate for the colony of Virginia.

8 Island Strolls

You can cover much of Bermuda, especially the harbor city of Hamilton and the historic town of St. George's, on foot. Indeed, if you had the time, you could walk or bike through all of the parishes and visit the major attractions of each. But most visitors would rather devote their vacation time to less-taxing pursuits, such as relaxing on the beach or playing a leisurely game of golf. If you're interested in seeing the island's sights, however, do consider taking at least one of the walking tours suggested below.

WALKING TOUR 1
The City of Hamilton

Start: The Visitors Service Bureau/Ferry Terminal. (You might want to take an orientational ferry ride around the inner harbor first; that way, you'll get an overview of Hamilton before concentrating on specific landmarks or monuments. You could also end your tour with a ferry ride.)

Finish: Fort Hamilton.

Time: 2½ hours.

Best Time: Any sunny day.

Worst Time: When cruise ships are anchored in Hamilton Harbour.

Begin your tour along the harbor front at the:

1. **Visitors Service Bureau/Ferry Terminal.** Pick up some free maps and brochures of the island here.

From the bureau, you'll emerge onto Front Street, Hamilton's main street and principal shopping area. Before 1946, there were no automobiles here, but today its busy traffic includes small automobiles (driven only by Bermuda residents), buses, mopeds, and bicycles. You'll also see horse-drawn carriages, which are the most romantic (and the most expensive) way to see Hamilton.

The docks behind the Ferry Terminal are where you'll find the ferries to the parishes of Warwick and Paget; for details on their attractions, see chapter 7. You can also take a ferry across Great Sound to the West End and Somerset.

Walk directly south of the Ferry Terminal toward the water, taking a short side street between the Visitors Service Bureau and the large Bank of Bermuda. You'll come to:

Walking Tour—The City of Hamilton

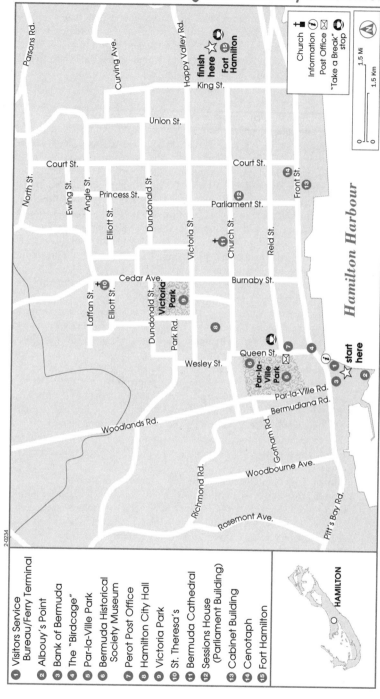

Legend:
- Church
- Information
- Post Office
- "Take a Break" stop

1. Visitors Service Bureau/Ferry Terminal
2. Albouy's Point
3. Bank of Bermuda
4. The "Birdcage"
5. Par-la-Ville Park
6. Bermuda Historical Society Museum
7. Perot Post Office
8. Hamilton City Hall
9. Victoria Park
10. St. Theresa's
11. Bermuda Cathedral
12. Sessions House (Parliament Building)
13. Cabinet Building
14. Cenotaph
15. Fort Hamilton

HAMILTON

2-0234

2. **Albouy's Point,** a small grassy park with benches and trees that open onto a panoramic vista of the boat- or ship-filled harbor. Nearby is the Royal Bermuda Yacht Club, an elite rendezvous for both the Bermudian and the American yachting set—including lots of the rich and famous—since the 1930s. To use the word *royal* in its name, special permission had to be given by Prince Albert, Queen Victoria's consort, in London. The club sponsors the widely televised Newport-Bermuda Yacht Race.

   After taking in the view, walk directly north, crossing Point Pleasant Road, to the:

3. **Bank of Bermuda,** which you can visit Monday to Friday from 9:30am to 3pm. On its mezzanine you can see Bermuda's most extensive coin collection—there's at least one sample of every coin minted in the United Kingdom since the reign of King James I in the early 17th century. Many Spanish coins used in colonial days are also on display. You'll also see the most famous Bermudian money, the first coins ever minted on the island, called "hog money." In use since the early 1600s, the hog coin is stamped on one side with the ill-fated *Sea Venture* and on the other side with a wild hog, the main source of food (excepting fish) for the early settlers. Look for an 1887 £5 piece depicting Queen Victoria; its issuance led to a protest throughout the British Empire, when critics claimed that the queen's small crown made her look foolish.

   Upon leaving the bank, head east along Front Street to the point where it intersects with Queen Street. This is the site of the:

4. **"Birdcage,"** the most photographed sight in Bermuda. Here you'll sometimes find a police officer directing traffic; if the "bobbie" is a man, he's likely to be wearing regulation Bermuda shorts. The traffic box, which was named after its designer, Michael "Dickey" Bird, stands at Heyl's Corner, which in turn is named for an American southerner, J. B. Heyl, who operated a nearby apothecary in the 1800s.

   Continue north along Queen Street until you reach:

5. **Par-la-Ville Park,** which was once a private garden attached to the town house of William B. Perot, the first postmaster of Bermuda, who designed the gardens in the 19th century. He collected rare and exotic plants from all over the globe, including an Indian rubber tree, which was seeded in 1847. Mark Twain wrote that he found the tree "disappointing" in that it didn't bear rubber overshoes and hot-water bottles.

   Also opening onto Queen Street at the entrance to the park is the:

6. **Bermuda Historical Society Museum,** 13 Queen St., which is also the Bermuda Library. It's filled with curiosities, including cedar furniture, collections of antique silver and china, hog money, Confederate money, a 1775 letter from George Washington, and other artifacts. The library has many rare books, including a 1624 edition of John Smith's *General Historie of Virginia, New England and the Somers Isles.* If you'd like to rest and catch up on your reading, you'll also find a selection of current local, as well as British, newspapers and periodicals here.

   Next door is the:

7. **Perot Post Office,** which was run by William Perot from 1818 to 1862. It's said that he'd go down to collect the mail from the clipper ships but would put it under his top hat in order to maintain his dignity. As he proceeded through town, he'd greet his friends and acquaintances by tipping his hat, thereby delivering their mail at the same time. He started printing stamps in 1848. A Perot stamp is extremely valuable today since only 11 are known to still exist; several are owned by Queen Elizabeth II. The last time a Perot stamp came on the market, in 1986, it fetched $135,000.

Continue to the top of Queen Street, then turn right onto (

8. Hamilton City Hall, 17 Church St., which dates from 19
a white tower. The bronze weather vane on top is a replica o
traits of the queen and paintings of former island leaders a
The Bermuda Society of Arts holds frequent exhibitions at
collection of stamps is also on display here.

TAKE A BREAK   The **Fourways Pastry Shop,** on the ground floor of
a shopping and office complex at Washington Mall and Reid Street (☎ **441/
295-3263**), serves the most irresistible pastries in town. You can also order ice
cream, tartlets, quiches, and croissant sandwiches, along with espresso and cappuccino. (For a complete review, see chapter 5.)

In back of Hamilton City Hall, opening onto Victoria Street, lies:

9. Victoria Park, a cool, refreshing oasis frequented by office workers on their
lunch break. It features a sunken garden, ornamental shrubbery, and a Victorian
bandstand. The 4-acre park was laid out in honor of Queen Victoria's Golden
Jubilee in 1887. Outdoor concerts are held here in summer.

Cedar Avenue is the eastern boundary of Victoria Park. If you follow it north
for 2 blocks, you'll reach:

10. St. Theresa's, a Roman Catholic cathedral that's open daily from 8am to 7pm
and for Sunday services. Dating from 1927, its architecture was inspired by the
Spanish Mission style. It's one of a half dozen Roman Catholic churches in
Bermuda; its treasure is a gold-and-silver chalice—a gift from Pope Paul VI when
he visited the island in 1986.

After seeing the cathedral, retrace your steps south along Cedar Avenue until
you reach Victoria Street. Cedar Avenue now becomes Burnaby Street; continue
south on this street until you come to Church Street and then turn left. A short
walk along this street (on your left) will bring you to the:

11. Bermuda Cathedral, or the Cathedral of the Most Holy Trinity as it is sometimes called. This is the seat of the Anglican Church of Bermuda, and it towers
over the city skyline. Its style is neo-Gothic, characterized by stained-glass windows and soaring arches. The lectern and pulpit duplicate those of St. Giles in
Edinburgh, Scotland.

Leave the cathedral and continue east along Church Street to the:

12. Sessions House (Parliament Building), on Parliament Street, between Reid and
Church Streets. It's open to the public Monday to Friday from 9am to 12:30pm
and 2 to 5pm. It's best to go on Friday when you can see political action,
Bermuda style, from the Visitors' Gallery. The speaker is attired in full wig and a
flowing black robe. The Parliament of Bermuda is the third oldest in the world,
after Iceland's and England's.

Continue to walk south along Parliament Street until you approach Front
Street, where you should turn left toward the:

13. Cabinet Building, between Court and Parliament Streets. The official opening
of Parliament takes place here in late October or early November. Wearing a
plumed hat and full regalia, the governor makes his "Throne Speech." If you visit
on a Wednesday, you'll see the Bermuda Senate in action. The building is open
Monday to Friday from 9am to 5pm.

In front of the Cabinet Building is the:

14. Cenotaph, a memorial to Bermuda's dead in World War I (1914 to 1918) and
World War II (1939 to 1945). In 1920, the Prince of Wales laid the cornerstone.

⌐ater, in 1936, as King Edward VIII, he would abdicate to marry an American divorcée, Wallis Simpson, and later still, during World War II, as the duke of Windsor, he would serve as governor of The Bahamas.) The landmark is a replica of the Cenotaph in London.

Continue east along Front Street until you reach King Street; then head north until you come to Happy Valley Road. Go right on this road until you see the entrance (on your right) to:

15. **Fort Hamilton,** an imposing old fortress on the eastern outskirts of Hamilton. The duke of Wellington ordered its construction to protect Hamilton Harbour. Filled with underground passageways and complete with a moat and 18-ton guns, the fort was outdated before it was even completed, and it never fired a shot. It does, however, offer panoramic views of the city and the harbor; it's worth a trip just for the view. In summer, try to be here at noon, when the kilted Bermuda Isles Pipe Band performs a skirling ceremony on the green, accompanied by dancers and drummers.

WINDING DOWN   After your stroll, wind down with some old-fashioned tea at the **Fort Hamilton Tea Shoppe** (no phone), where you can also order light refreshments.

WALKING TOUR 2
Historic St. George's Town

Start: King's Square.
Finish: Somers Wharf.
Time: 2 hours (not counting the time you spend inside the buildings).
Best Time: Any sunny day except Sunday, when much is closed.
Worst Time: When a cruise ship is anchored in the harbor.

At the east end of the island, St. George's was the second English town to be established in the New World (after Jamestown in Virginia). For the history buff, it holds more interest than Hamilton.

We'll begin the tour at:

1. **King's Square,** also known as Market Square and King's Parade, is the very center of St. George's. Only about 200 years old, it's not as historic as St. George's itself. This was formerly a marshy part of the harbor—at least when the shipwrecked passengers and crew of the *Sea Venture* first saw it. At the water's edge stands a branch of the Visitors Service Bureau, where you can pick up additional information on the area. On the square you'll notice a replica of the pillory and stocks that were formerly used to punish criminals—and, in many cases, the innocent (you could be severely punished here for such alleged "crimes" as casting a spell over your neighbor's turkeys).

From the square, head south across the small bridge to:

2. **Ordnance Island,** jutting into St. George's Harbour. The British army once stored gunpowder and cannons here, but today the island houses the *Deliverance,* a replica of the vessel that carried the shipwrecked *Sea Venture* passengers on to Virginia. Alongside the vessel is a ducking stool, a contraption used in 17th-century witch trials.

Walking Tour—Historic St. George's Town

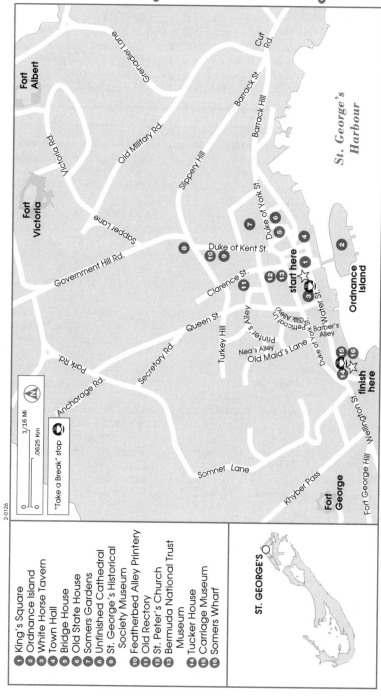

St. George's Harbour

Fort Albert

Fort Victoria

Grenadier Lane

Cut Rd.

Barrack St.

Barrack Hill

Old Military Rd.

Slippery Hill

Victoria Rd.

Sapper Lane

Government Hill Rd.

Duke of Kent St.

Duke of York St.

Clarence St.

Queen St.

Secretary Rd.

Park Rd.

Turkey Hill

Printer's Alley

Nea's Alley

Old Maid's Lane

Duke of York St. (Silk Alley)

Petticoat Ln.

Barber's Alley

Water St.

start here

finish here

Ordnance Island

Fort George

Fort George Hill

Wellington St.

Khyber Pass

Anchorage Rd.

Somner Lane

"Take a Break" stop

0   1/16 Mi
0   .0625 Km

2-0126

ST. GEORGE'S

1 King's Square
2 Ordnance Island
3 White Horse Tavern
4 Town Hall
5 Bridge House
6 Old State House
7 Somers Gardens
8 Unfinished Cathedral
9 St. George's Historical Society Museum
10 Featherbed Alley Printery
11 Old Rectory
12 St. Peter's Church
13 Bermuda National Trust Museum
14 Tucker House
15 Carriage Museum
16 Somers Wharf

177

Retrace your steps across the bridge to King's Square. On the waterside stands the:

3. White Horse Tavern, a restaurant jutting out into St. George's Harbour. Consider the tavern as a possible spot for lunch later (for a review, see chapter 5). But for now, we'll focus on its history: It was once the home of John Davenport, who came to Bermuda in 1815 to open a dry-goods store. Davenport was a bit of a miser; upon his death, some £75,000 in gold and silver was discovered stashed away in his cellar.

Across the square stands the:

4. Town Hall, near the Visitors Service Bureau. This is the meeting place of the corporation governing St. George's. It has antique cedar furnishings and a collection of photographs of previous lord mayors. *Bermuda Journey,* a multimedia audiovisual presentation, is shown here several times a day.

From King's Square, head east along King Street, cutting north on Bridge Street. There you'll come to the:

5. Bridge House, 1 Bridge St. Constructed shortly after 1700, this was once the home of several governors of Bermuda. Furnished with 18th- and 19th-century antiques, it's now home to an art gallery and souvenir shop.

Return to King Street and continue east to the:

6. Old State House, which actually opens onto Princess Street, at the top of King Street. This is the oldest stone building in Bermuda, dating from 1620, and it was once the home of the Bermuda Parliament. It's the site of the ancient Peppercorn Ceremony, in which the Old State House pays the government "rent" of one peppercorn annually. See chapter 7 for details on seeing this grand ceremony.

Continue your stroll down Princess Street until you come to Duke of York Street and the entrance to:

7. Somers Gardens. The heart of Sir George Somers, the admiral of the *Sea Venture,* is buried here. The gardens, featuring palms and other tropical plants, were opened in 1920 by the Prince of Wales.

Walk through Somers Gardens and up the steps to the North Gate onto Blockade Alley. If you look up the hill, you'll see what is known as "the folly of St. George's," the:

8. Unfinished Cathedral, which was intended to replace St. Peter's (see below). Work began on the church in 1874 but eventually came to an end; the church was beset by financial difficulties and a schism in the Anglican congregation.

After viewing the ruins, turn left onto Duke of Kent Street, which leads down to the:

9. St. George's Historical Society Museum, at the intersection of Featherbed Alley and Duke of Kent Street. An example of 18th-century architecture, the house has a collection of Bermudian historical artifacts and cedar furniture.

Around the corner on Featherbed Alley is the:

10. Featherbed Alley Printery, which has a working replica of the type of printing press invented by Johannes Gutenberg in Germany in the 1450s.

Go up Featherbed Alley and straight onto Church Street. At the junction with Broad Lane, look to your right to see the:

11. Old Rectory, at the head of Broad Alley, behind St. Peter's Church. Now a private home but administered by the National Trust, it was built in 1705 by a reformed pirate. You can go inside only on Wednesdays from noon to 5pm.

After seeing the Old Rectory, go through the back of the churchyard entrance, opposite Broad Alley, to reach:

12. St. Peter's Church. The church's main entrance is on Duke of York Street. This is believed to be the oldest Anglican place of worship in the western hemisphere.

In the churchyard, you'll see many headstones, some 300 years old. The assassinated governor, Sir Richard Sharples, was buried here. The present church was built in 1713, with a tower added in 1814. Across the street is the:

13. **Bermuda National Trust Museum.** When it was the Globe Hotel, this was the headquarters of Major Norman Walker, the Confederate representative in Bermuda. It was once a hotbed of blockade-running.

   As you continue west along Duke of York Street, you'll reach Barber's Lane, which honors Joseph Hayne Rainey. A former slave from South Carolina, Rainey and his French wife fled to Bermuda at the outbreak of the Civil War. He became a barber in St. George's but eventually returned to South Carolina, where in 1870 he was elected to the U.S. House of Representatives—the first African American to serve in Congress.

   Nearby is Petticoat Lane, also known as Silk Alley. The name dates from the 1834 emancipation, when two former slave women who'd always wanted silk petticoats like their former mistresses finally got some—and then paraded up and down the lane to show off their new finery.

   Continue west until you reach:

14. **Tucker House,** which opens onto Water Street. This was the former home of a prominent Bermudian family, whose members have included an island governor, a treasurer of the United States, and a captain in the Confederate Navy. The building houses an excellent collection of antiques, including silver, portraits, and cedar furniture. One room is devoted to memorabilia of Joseph Hayne Rainey.

   Diagonally across from the Tucker House is the:

15. **Carriage House,** 22 Water St., Somers Wharf (☎ **441/297-1730**), a former waterfront storehouse that's an excellent place for lunch. You can sample sandwich platters along with the famous Bermuda fish chowder. Soups, salads, and juicy burgers are also available. (See the complete review in chapter 5.)

   End your tour across the street at:

16. **Somers Wharf,** a multimillion-dollar waterfront restoration project that now includes shops, restaurants, and taverns.

WALKING TOUR 3
Sandys Parish

Start: Somerset Bridge.
Finish: Somerset Long Bay Park.
Time: 7 hours.
Best Time: Any sunny day.
Worst Time: When the weather's bad.

Sandys (pronounced "sands"), the far western parish of Bermuda, consists of Somerset Island (the largest and southernmost), as well as Watford, Boaz, and Ireland islands. When Bermudians cross into Somerset via Somerset Bridge, they say they are "up the country."

   The area is characterized by craggy coastlines, beaches, nature reserves, fisher's coves, old fortifications, winding lanes, and sleepy villages. All of Sandys's major attractions lie along the main road from Somerset Bridge to the Royal Naval Dockyard, which is at the end of Ireland Island.

   Although we are classifying this as a walking tour, you may want to rent a bicycle or moped to help you cover the longer stretches.

From the center of Hamilton, you can take a ferry to Somerset. Check the schedule: Some boats take only 30 minutes to get here, whereas others take up to an hour. The longer trip will give you a more leisurely opportunity to enjoy the waters of Bermuda's Great Sound. You can bring your cycle or moped aboard the ferry. You can also see the West End by public bus (for details, see "Getting Around," in chapter 3).

To begin the tour, take the ferry from Hamilton to:

1. **Somerset Bridge,** which links Somerset Island with the rest of Bermuda. It was among the first three bridges to be constructed in Bermuda in the 1600s, and it's said to be the smallest drawbridge in the world—its opening is just wide enough to accommodate a sailboat mast. Near the bridge you can take a look at the old Somerset Post Office and see an 18th-century cottage known as Crossways.

Next, walk up Somerset Road about 75 yards to the entrance to the:

2. **Railway Trail,** which is open only to pedestrians, cyclists, and bikers. This trail follows the path of old "Rattle and Shake," the Bermuda Railway line that once ran the entire length of the island. Since you may not want to walk the whole railway trail (although some hearty visitors do just that), it might interest you to know that this particular section of the trail—between Somerset Bridge and Sound View Road—is one of its most attractive. Parts of the trail open onto the coast, affording panoramic vistas of the Great Sound.

The trail goes across the parkland of Fort Scaur (see below), with its large moat. If you're here around noontime, you might want to consider this as a picnic spot. If you can spend all day in Somerset (which we highly recommend), you might also want to take time out for a swim before returning to your walking or cycling.

Follow the signposts to:

3. **Fort Scaur,** which covers 22 acres and opens onto Somerset Road. In the 1870s, the British feared an attack from the United States, so they built this fort on the highest hill in Somerset to protect Her Majesty's Royal Naval Dockyard. A huge dry moat was cut right across Somerset Island. You can wander at leisure around this fort, which proved unnecessary, since the feared invasion never materialized. If you stand on the ramparts, you'll be rewarded with a marvelous view of Great Sound. Through a telescope, you can see such distant sights as St. David's Lighthouse and Fort St. Catherine in the east end of Bermuda. If you follow the eastern moat all the way down to the Great Sound shore, you'll find ideal places for swimming and fishing.

After exploring the surrounding Scaur Hill Fort Park, resume your walk along the railway track and continue north for more than a mile until you come to Sound View Road. Turn right and stroll along this sleepy residential street, which has some of the finest cottages in Bermuda.

Continue around a wide arc, passing Tranquillity Hill and Gwelly and Saltsea Lanes. When you come to Scott's Hill Road, take a right and go about 85 yards to East Shore Road. At the first junction, take a little road, Cavello Lane, which branches off to the right; it will take you to:

4. **Cavello Bay,** a sheltered cove and a stopping point for the Hamilton ferry. Wait for the next ferry and take it (with your cycle or moped) either to Watford Bridge or directly to the:

5. **Royal Naval Dockyard.** There's so much to see here, you could spend an entire afternoon. The dockyard is a sprawling complex encompassing 6 acres of Ireland Island. The major attraction here is the:

6. **Bermuda Maritime Museum,** which was opened by Queen Elizabeth II in 1975. There's an exhibit of Bermuda's old boats, documenting the island's rich

Walking Tour—Sandys Parish

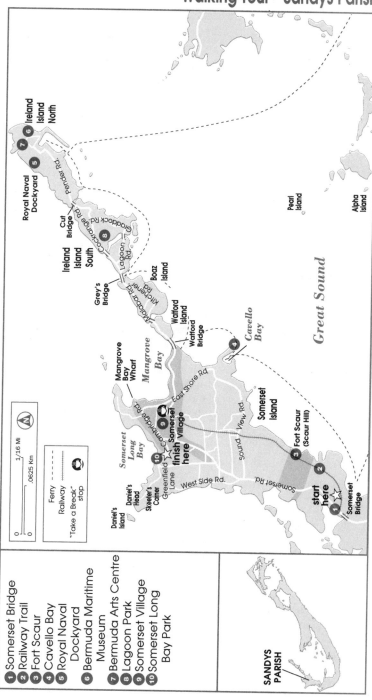

Somerset Bridge
Railway
"Take a Break" stop
Ferry

1/16 Mi
.0625 Km

Ireland Island North

Royal Naval Dockyard

Pender Rd.

Cut Bridge

Cockrange Rd.

Graddock Rd.

Ireland Island South

Lagoon Rd.

Grey's Bridge

Boaz Island

Kitchner Rd.

Maldrab Rd.

Watford Island

Watford Bridge

Cavello Bay

Great Sound

Pearl Island

Alpha Island

Mangrove Bay Wharf

Mangrove Bay

Somerset Island

East Shore Rd.

View Rd.

Fort Scaur (Scaur Hill)

Sound

Somerset Long Bay

Cambridge Rd.

finish here
Somerset Village

Greenfield Lane

West Side Rd.

Somerset Rd.

Daniel's Head

Skeeter's Corner

Daniel's Island

start here

Somerset Bridge

1. Somerset Bridge
2. Railway Trail
3. Fort Scaur
4. Cavello Bay
5. Royal Naval Dockyard
6. Bermuda Maritime Museum
7. Bermuda Arts Centre
8. Lagoon Park
9. Somerset Village
10. Somerset Long Bay Park

SANDYS PARISH

181

Rattle & Shake: The Bermuda Railway Trail

One of the most unusual sightseeing adventures in Bermuda is following the Bermuda Railway Trail (or parts thereof), which stretches for 21 miles along the old railroad right-of-way across three of the interconnected islands that make up Bermuda. This rail-line construction may have been one of the most costly ever on a per-mile basis. Opened in 1931, the Bermuda Railway ceased operations in 1948: Once the island's main source of transportation, the train eventually gave way to the automobile.

Before setting out on this trek, arm yourself with a copy of the *Bermuda Railway Trail Guide,* obtainable at the Bermuda Department of Tourism in Hamilton or at the Visitors Service Bureau in Hamilton or St. George's. You're now ready to hit the trail of the old train system that was affectionately called "Rattle and Shake." There are many ways to explore the trail: horseback, bicycle, moped, or the ever-trusty feet.

Although the line covered 21 miles stretching between St. George's in the east and Somerset in the west, a 3-mile stretch has been lost to roads in and around the capital city of Hamilton. For the most part, however, the trail winds along an automobile-free route, permitting some views of Bermuda not seen by the general public since the end of World War II.

In the West End of Bermuda, the trail begins near the Watford Bridge, but there are many convenient points of access. In the East End, it's most convenient to pick up the trail on North Shore Road.

Along the way, you'll see something of the 5-acre Gilbert Nature Reserve. You'll also view some of the rare Bermuda cedar, which nearly vanished as a result of the blight that struck the island in the early 1940s. There's also much greenery and semitropical vegetation along the trail, such as the poinsettia, oleander, and hibiscus. You can also see and visit Fort Scaur, the 1870s fortress in Sandys Parish. The tour of Sandys Parish, above, follows the detailed section of the route that includes Fort Scaur.

maritime history. You can cross a moat to explore the keep and the 30-foot-high defensive ramparts.

Across the street from the Maritime Museum is the Old Cooperage Building, site of the Neptune Cinema. Adjacent to the cinema is the Craft Market, which sells interesting items. Next door, call at the:

7. **Bermuda Arts Centre,** which was opened in 1984 by Princess Margaret. Showcasing the visual arts and crafts of the island, this nonprofit organization is staffed by volunteers.

From the dockyard, it's a long walk to Somerset Village, yet many people who have walked or cycled the distance feel that this was one of the highlights of their Bermuda trip. You'll find some of the best beaches here, so if you get tired along the way, take time out for a refreshing dip in the ocean.

Leave through the dockyard's south entrance, walking down Pender Road about a half mile. Cross Cockburn's Cut Bridge, heading for Ireland Island South. Go straight along Cockrange Road, which will take you to:

8. **Lagoon Park.** Enter the park as you cross over the Cut Bridge onto Ireland Island South. The park, which is crisscrossed by walking trails, has a lagoon populated with ducks and other wildfowl. There are places for picnicking in the park, which is free and open to the public.

To continue, cross Grey's Bridge to Boaz Island, and walk or cycle along Malabar Road. On your right you'll see the calm waters of Mangrove Bay. You'll eventually arrive at:

9. Somerset Village, one of the most charming in Bermuda. Only one road goes through the village. Although you could do some shopping here, most of the stores are just branches of larger stores in Hamilton.

TAKE A BREAK   **Somerset Country Squire Tavern,** 10 Mangrove Bay Rd. (☎ **441/234-0105**), is an English-style pub where you can order sandwiches or burgers, as well as such pub grub as steak-and-kidney pie or bangers and mash (sausages and mashed potatoes). The kitchen is also noted for its desserts. (For a complete review, see chapter 5.)

Follow Cambridge Road west to:

10. Somerset Long Bay Park, which is always open. Families like this park because of its good beach and shallow waters opening onto Long Bay. You can also picnic in the parkland. The nature reserve here is operated by the Bermuda Audubon Society, and the pond attracts migrating birds in both spring and autumn, including the Louisiana heron, the snowy egret, and the purple gallinule.

9 Shopping

Retailers on less prosperous islands have claimed that Bermuda's continuing popularity is the result of not only a superb climate, but also many years of skillful marketing. Indeed, no one has ever accused the Bermudians of not knowing how to sell their island—or their rich inventories of goods.

Bermuda, once widely hailed as a "showcase of the British Empire," is still that, at least in terms of variety of goods. Bermuda's retail scene draws upon its British antecedents today: Shopkeepers are generally both polite and discreet, with unusual and well-made merchandise. In addition, most retailers take full advantage of location—usually housing their shops within charming cottages or historically important buildings, making shopping even more fun. Even visitors who intend to do no more than window-shop are likely to break down and make a purchase or two.

In essence, shopping in Bermuda is about quality, not cheap prices. The low prices of yesterday have gone with the wind. Shops are faced with huge import tariffs, plus employer-related taxes; all of these high costs have had a ripple effect in the retail industry, leading to what some view as outrageously high prices. Once you're in Bermuda, it rarely pays to comparison shop. Prices are rather uniform: The price of a watch in a branch store in St. George's is likely to be exactly the same as in the main shop in Hamilton.

To find real bargains, you must shop harder and longer than before; you'll usually find them in the off-season (autumn and winter), when, with no uniformity, stores often reduce merchandise to make way for goods for the new season. But sales come and go year-round—there's no particular season, as in London. Keep an eye out for "sale" signs no matter when you're in Bermuda.

BERMUDA'S BEST BUYS

Most of Bermuda's best shops are along Front Street in Hamilton. Here, shopping is relaxed and casual. Among the choicest items are imports from Great Britain and Ireland, such as Shetland and cashmere sweaters, Harris tweed jackets, Scottish woolen goods and tartan kilts, and even fine china and crystal—many costing appreciably less than in their country of origin.

Because of a special "colony"-like arrangement Bermuda has with Great Britain, certain British goods can be cheaper here than in the United States thanks to lower import tariffs. Therefore, some frequent visitors take careful stock of their needs for porcelain, crystal, silverware, jewelry, timepieces, and perfume, perhaps anticipating a needed wedding gift several months in advance. The island is filled with merchandisers of fine tableware, including Royal Copenhagen, Wedgwood, and Royal Crown Derby. Crystal is also plentiful in Bermuda, with many of the finest manufacturers in Europe and North America providing wide selections of merchandise. For a fee, all of these items can be shipped, usually in well-wrapped packages that minimize breakage.

Liquor is also a good buy in Bermuda. U.S. citizens are allowed to bring back only 1 liter duty-free, but even adding U.S. tax and duty, you can save between 35% and 50% on liquor purchases, depending on the brand. Liqueurs offer the largest savings.

Antique lovers appreciate the fusion of the British aesthetic and mid-Atlantic charm that they find on Bermuda. The island has a wealth of antique engravings, 19th-century furniture, modern artwork, and handmade pottery and crafts available for sale in its antique shops, all of which could become elegant heirlooms. And anyone interested in carrying home a piece of Bermuda's nautical heritage is likely to find oversized ship's propellers, captain's bells, brass nameplates, scale models of the sailing ships of long ago, or maybe even an old-fashioned ship's steering wheel from a salvaged shipwreck. The island's wealth of antiques and collectibles is extraordinary.

Other good buys are "Bermudiana"—products made in Bermuda or manufactured elsewhere exclusively for local stores. They include cedarwood gifts, carriage bells, coins commemorating the 375th anniversary of the island's settlement, flower plates by Spode, pewter tankards, handcrafted gold jewelry, traditional-line handbags with cedar or mahogany handles, miniature cottages in ceramic or limestone, shark's teeth polished and mounted in 14-karat gold, decorative kitchen items, Bermuda shorts (of course), silk scarves, and watches with a map of Bermuda on their faces.

Although some items might be priced less than they are stateside, be aware that this isn't always the case—in fact, many, many items are overpriced. You should be familiar with prices on comparable goods back home before committing yourself to serious purchases.

1 The Shopping Scene

WHERE TO GO
THE CITY OF HAMILTON

The best and widest range of shopping choices is in the city of Hamilton (see "In the City of Hamilton," below). Although most shops are on Front Street, you may want to explore the back streets as well, especially if you're an adventurous shopper.

The Emporium on Front Street, a restored building constructed around an atrium, houses a number of shops, including jewelry stores. Windsor Place on Queen Street is another Bermuda-style shopping mall.

HISTORIC ST. GEORGE'S

The "second city" of St. George's also has many shops, stores, and boutiques, including branches of famous Front Street stores. King's Square, the center of St. George's, is filled with shops; the other major centers are Somers Wharf and Water Street.

SANDYS PARISH

Don't overlook the shopping possibilities of the West End either. Somerset Village in Sandys Parish has many shops. But of even greater interest may be the Royal

Naval Dockyard area on Ireland Island. Here you can visit the Craft Market, Island Pottery, and the Bermuda Arts Centre, where you'll see local artisans at work.

WHAT YOU SHOULD KNOW
STORE HOURS

Stores in Hamilton, St. George's, and Somerset are generally open Monday to Saturday from 9am to 5:30pm. When large liners are in port, stores sometimes stay open later, and sometimes on Sundays.

FINDING AN ADDRESS

Some Front Street stores post numbers on their buildings; others don't. Sometimes the number posted or used is the "historic" number of the building, which has nothing to do with the modern number. But somehow it all works out: You can always ask for directions, since most Bermudians are willing to help. Outside Hamilton, don't expect to find numbers on buildings at all, or even street names in some cases.

SALES TAX & DUTY

There's no sales tax in Bermuda, but it's not a duty-free island. Depending on which country you're returning to, you may have to pay duty. See "Entry Requirements & Customs," in chapter 2, for complete details.

Note: As with various countries and territories, including several in the Caribbean, Bermuda is covered by the U.S. law regarding "Generalized System of Preferences" status. That means that if at least 35% of an item has been crafted in Bermuda, you can bring it back duty-free, regardless of how much you spent. If you've gone beyond your $400 allotment, make a separate list for goods made in Bermuda. That will make it easier for Customs and, ultimately, for yourself.

"IN-BOND" (DUTY-FREE) SHOPPING

Goods such as liquor and cigarettes can be purchased at in-bond, or duty-free, prices—often at a savings of around 35%—and should be ordered several days in advance of your departure. You cannot consume these items in Bermuda; you must pick them up at the airport when you depart. They must be listed on your country's Customs Declaration Form. Liquor purchases should be made at one of the island stores, since the airport doesn't have an in-bond liquor store.

2 In the City of Hamilton
DEPARTMENT STORES

H. A. & E. Smith, Ltd.
35 Front St. ☎ **441/295-2288.**

This store has been selling top-quality merchandise since 1889, at substantial savings over U.S. prices. Smith's comprehensive stock includes sweaters for men and women (in cotton, cashmere, lambs wool, and Shetland), British cosmetics, and a collection from the top French parfumeurs. Smith's is noted for its selection of handbags, gloves, a very limited array of Liberty fabrics by the yard, and children's clothing. It also carries such merchandise as Fendi handbags from Italy, Burberrys rainwear from London, and Rosenthal china. A subsidiary, The Treasure Chest, across the street from the main store, carries a full line of French perfumes and gifts, plus souvenirs.

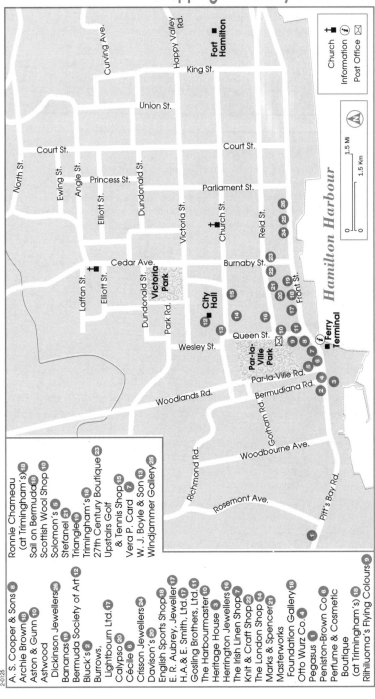

Shopping in the City of Hamilton

Church +■ Information ⓘ Post Office ⊠

1.5 Mi
1.5 Km

Hamilton Harbour

Streets and places:
Cunving Ave.
Happy Valley Rd.
Fort Hamilton
King St.
Union St.
Court St.
Court St.
North St.
Ewing St.
Angle St.
Princess St.
Parliament St.
Elliott St.
Dundonald St.
Victoria St.
Church St.
Reid St.
Cedar Ave.
Burnaby St.
Laffan St.
Elliott St.
Dundonald St.
Victoria Park
Park Rd.
City Hall
Front St.
Queen St.
Wesley St.
Par-la-Ville Park
Ferry Terminal
Par-la-Ville Rd.
Bermudiana Rd.
Woodlands Rd.
Gorham Rd.
Woodbourne Ave.
Richmond Rd.
Pitt's Bay Rd.
Rosemont Ave.

2-0125

A. S. Cooper & Sons ⑧
Archie Brown ⑱
Aston & Gunn ⑩
Astwood
Dickinson Jewellers ㉖
Bananas ⑲
Bermuda Society of Art ⑫
Bluck's ②
Burrows,
    Lightbourn Ltd. ⑰
Calypso ⑳
Cécile ⑥
Crisson Jewellers ㉔
Davison's ⑱
English Sports Shop ⑱
E. R. Aubrey, Jeweller ⑰
H.A.& E. Smith, Ltd. ⑰
Gosling Brothers, Ltd. ⑪
The Harbourmaster ⑩
Heritage House ③
Herrington Jewellers ⑯
The Irish Linen Shop ⑦
Knit & Craft Shop ㉒
The London Shop ⑭
Marks & Spencer ㉑
Masterworks
    Foundation Gallery ⑱
Otto Wurz Co. ④
Pegasus ①
Peniston-Brown Co ⑥
Perfume & Cosmetic
    Boutique
    (at Trimingham's) ⑱
Rihiluoma's Flying Colours ⑨

Ronnie Chameau
    (at Trimingham's) ⑱
Sail on Bermuda ⑱
Scottish Wool Shop ⑩
Solomon's ⑤
Stefanel ㉑
Triangle ⑲
Trimingham's ⑱
27th Century Boutique ㉓
Upstairs Golf
    & Tennis Shop ⑮
Vera P. Card ⑦
W. J. Boyle & Son ⑬
Windjammer Gallery ㉕

187

Marks & Spencer
7 Reid St. ☎ **441/295-0031.**

This branch of the famous British chain (sometimes oddly called "St. Michael") carries the same reliable quality merchandise as its sibling stores in the British Isles. You'll find men's, women's, and children's fashions in everything from resort wear to sleepwear, including lingerie. There are also well-tailored dresses and suits, dress shirts, blazers, and British-tailored trousers, as well as swimwear, toiletries, and English sweets and biscuits.

○ Trimingham's
37 Front St. ☎ **441/295-1183.**

Since 1842, Trimingham's has been Bermuda's largest department store, offering a full range of fine merchandise and featuring the largest selection of duty-free items on the island. Here, you'll find Bermuda's best selection of cosmetics and perfumes, including exclusives from Estée Lauder and Clinique. Waterford, Lenox, Portmeirion, and other fine china and crystal can be purchased at rates up to 30% off U.S. prices. Many lines of china and crystal can be delivered directly to your U.S. home. Fine jewelry is often a good buy here, and there is also a wide range of Bermuda shorts, cashmere sweaters, and polo shirts for sale.

GOODS A TO Z
ANTIQUES

Heritage House
2 Front St. W. ☎ **441/295-2615.**

Heritage House sells nautical prints, English antiques, old maps, modern porcelain, and the largest collection of fine art on the island. The store was completely overhauled in 1995, with many new gift items added, including one of the best collections of costume jewelry in town. Look for their large collection of "Halcyon Days" pillboxes.

○ Pegasus
Across from the Hamilton Princess, 63 Pitts Bay Rd. (at Front St. W.). ☎ **441/295-2900.**

Pegasus has a wide range of antique prints, engravings, and magazine illustrations. Owner Robert Lee and his wife, Barbara, scour the print shops of the British Isles to stock this unusual store. This is the best selection you'll find in Bermuda: The inventory is varied, with old maps of many different regions of the world, and more than 1,000 literary, sporting, medical, and legal caricatures from Vanity Fair. Most prints range from the late 1700s to the late 1800s and are carefully grouped according to subject. The authenticity of whatever you buy is guaranteed in writing. Prints run from $45 to $200, depending on the subject. The hand-colored engravings of birds, fruits, and flowers are worth framing and sometimes cost as little as $40 each.

The Lees also offer ceramic house signs, costing $100 and up, made at a small pottery in England. Each is unique, since the buyer chooses the design, after which the "house" and the house name or a number and street are hand-painted to specifications.

The shop also carries a wide range of English greeting cards, many with botanical designs. All maps, lithographs, and engravings are duty-free and will not affect your take-home quota.

ART

Bermuda Society of Arts
West Wing of City Hall, Church St. ☎ **441/292-3824.**

Loosely associated with the Bermudian government, and devoted to the exhibition of works by Bermuda-based artists, this store is one of the focal points of the arts scene in Bermuda. Set within the West Wing of Hamilton's City Hall (the island's Fine Arts Museum occupies the building's East Wing), it's the permanent home of the oldest arts society in Bermuda, an association of respected artists and art patrons that received a formalized seal of approval from Bermuda's Parliament in 1956. The site contains two separate exhibition areas, each of whose artwork changes every 2 to 3 weeks. Although themes range from the moderately avant-garde to the conservative, there are literally dozens of examples within any show of Bermudian landscapes, seascapes, or architectural renderings, any of which would make worthwhile souvenirs of your stay on the island. Except for copies of books and greeting cards by resident members of the society, the majority of artworks range from $80 to $3,500 each, and any of them can be packed for airplane transport off the island.

Windjammer Gallery
At Reid and King Sts. ☎ **441/292-7861.**

Housed in a coral cottage, this gallery exhibits paintings and bronze sculptures by local and international artists; it also carries an extensive selection of cards, prints, and limited editions. Adjacent to the gallery is the last private garden in the city, used for the display of sculpture and exhibitions. There's also a second gallery at 95 Front St. (☎ **441/292-5878**).

ARTS & CRAFTS

Masterworks Foundation Gallery
Bermuda House Lane, 97 Front St. ☎ **441/295-5580.**

Established in 1987 by a group of international philanthropists, this foundation showcases paintings by renowned European, Bermudian, and North American artists. Serving to some extent as the island's most visible arts center, it sponsors frequent art exhibitions, which have included works by Georgia O'Keeffe (who painted in Bermuda during the early 1930s), as well as seascapes by Winslow Homer and watercolors by artist Ogden Pleissner. The foundation also arranges guided art and architectural tours around the island and coordinates other artistic endeavors and exhibitions throughout the year.

Ronnie Chameau
At Trimingham's, 37 Front St. ☎ **441/295-1183,** ext. 344.

Noted local artist Ronnie Chameau, known throughout the island for her charming handmade dolls, crafts doll-shaped ornaments from such natural ingredients as banana leaves, hazelnuts, and grapefruit leaves, gathered from her own and her friends' gardens. Each ornament has a unique personality and comes individually boxed and gift-wrapped. The small dolls make great Christmas gifts, especially since they're all priced under $20. Ms. Chameau also makes dolls with historically authentic 19th-century costumes, as well as wooden Bermuda doorstops, each designed to look like a Bermuda cottage and priced at $65.

BEACHWEAR & SUNGLASSES

Bananas
Front St. W. (opposite the Bank of Bermuda). ☎ **441/295-8241.**

Bananas offers colorful, good-quality Bermuda signature items. You'll find T-shirts, jackets, beach bags, and beach umbrellas that will let your friends know where you've been.

Calypso

23–24 Front St. ☎ **441/295-2112.**

Calypso carries casual, fun fashions (including unusual garments from around the world) and the most comprehensive selection of swimwear in Bermuda. The shop also features Italian leather goods, espadrilles, hats, bags, pareos, Italian ceramics, and whimsical gift items; it's also the exclusive island retailer of Louis Vuitton luggage and accessories. There are branches at both the Southampton and the Hamilton Princess hotels, the Sonesta Beach Hotel, the Coral Beach Club, and the dockyard.

Sail on Bermuda

Old Cellar, Front St. ☎ **441/295-0808.**

A place where the locals shop, this store carries a unique collection of casual wear, bathing suits, and gifts. A recent poll indicated that shoppers found Sail on Bermuda to have the best T-shirts in Bermuda. A small addition, called "Shades of Bermuda," has the finest collection of sunglasses on the island.

CHINA & GLASSWARE

Also see Trimingham's under "Department Stores," above.

✪ A. S. Cooper & Sons

59 Front St. ☎ **441/295-3961.**

Bermuda's oldest and largest china and glassware store—family owned since 1897—offers a broad range of fine bone china, earthenware, and jewelry. Among the famous names represented are Minton, Royal Doulton, Belleek, Aynsley, Wedgwood, and Royal Copenhagen. The Crystal Room displays Orrefors, Waterford, Royal Brierley, and Kosta-Boda, among others. The Collector's Gallery is known for its limited editions of Bing & Grøndahl, Royal Doulton, and Lladró. A perfume department offers selections from the world's greatest perfumeries.

Bluck's

4 Front St. ☎ **441/295-5367.**

Established in 1844, Bluck's is well-known for carrying some of the finest names in china and crystal, including Royal Worcester, Spode, Aynsley, Royal Doulton, and Herend porcelain from Hungary. The choice in crystal is equally impressive: Kosta-Boda, Waterford, Baccarat, Daum, and, of course, Lalique, exclusive with Bluck's. Upstairs, you'll find the Antiques Room filled with fine English furniture, antique Bermuda maps, and an array of old English silver. Bluck's has branch shops on Water Street in St. George's and in the Southampton Princess.

FASHION

Also see "Beachwear & Sunglasses," above, and see "Shoes," "Sportswear," and "Woolens," below.

Aston & Gunn

2 Reid St. ☎ **441/295-4866.**

This shop sells the kind of career-oriented clothing preferred by professionals throughout the island. Although most of the clothing is for men (imported from Germany and Holland), there's a small women's department as well. In addition to the usual collection of shirts, ties, jackets, and suits, Aston & Gunn is the exclusive island distributor of Calvin Klein underwear.

Cécile

15 Front St. W. (near the Visitors Service Bureau and the Ferry Terminal). ☎ **441/295-1311.**

Well-stocked Cécile is a center for high fashion in Bermuda. They claim here that visiting one of Cécile's Bermuda shops is like calling upon the fashion capitals of the world—you'll find everything from German high fashion to Gottex swimwear. Its sweater and accessory boutique is also outstanding. Cécile has branches at the Southampton Princess and Marriott's Castle Harbour.

The London Shop
65 Washington Mall (at Church St.). ☎ **441/295-1279.**

This is the kind of store you might expect to find in an upscale neighborhood of London; it sells men's clothing by Pierre Cardin and a few other prominent designers. Sports jackets begin at $175, and a typical Pierre Cardin suit is priced at $300.

Stefanel
12 Reid St. ☎ **441/295-5698.**

This is the island's only outlet for the clothing of Carlo Stefanel, a well-known Italian designer. Stocking merchandise for both men and women, the store sells tropical-weight men's suits (in cotton and linen) and handmade skirts (some of them knit) with contrasting jackets for women. There's a stylish array of accessories as well. A line of clothing is also offered for infants and children.

Triangle
55 Front St. ☎ **441/292-1990.**

Catering to well-coifed, well-tailored women who travel, Diane Freis (pronounced *freeze*) specializes in easy-care chic but simple women's clothing. The garments, which are usually wrinkle free, tend to have mosaic-inspired patterns of boldly contrasting colors. The collection includes two-piece outfits, dresses, skirts, and evening jackets. Theoretically, none of the garments ever needs ironing. Although pricey, these clothes are generally less expensive than comparable clothing in North America.

27th Century Boutique
4 Burnaby St. (between Front and Church Sts.). ☎ **441/292-2628.**

Long known as a stylish and trend-setting shop, this boutique offers a selection of designer clothing, as well as silver costume jewelry and accessories. The European clothing is styled for women ages 13 and up: On our recent visit, a 16-year-old and a grandmother purchased the same shirt. The clothing is rather conservative and in good taste. The store also has a nice collection of shoes, for both men and women, from Canada and London.

GIFTS
Riihiluoma's Flying Colours
5 Queen St. ☎ **441/295-0890.**

This is everybody's favorite catchall emporium for inexpensive, impulse-purchase souvenirs and T-shirts with perky slogans. You'll also find paperweights, beach cover-ups, sarongs like actress Dorothy Lamour used to wear, key chains shaped like the island of Bermuda, and arts and crafts. The establishment's hard-to-spell name derives from the Finnish-born family that established it in 1937 and still manages it today.

Vera P. Card
11 Front St. ☎ **441/295-1729.**

Vera P. Card is known for its "gifts from around the world," including the island's largest collection of Lladró and Hummel figurines. Famous-name watches include

Nivada, Borel, and Rodania. The dinnerware collection features such famous names as Rosenthal, and the crystal department offers a wide assortment of Czech and Bohemian crystal, giftware, and chandeliers. Look for the "Bermuda Collection" of 14-karat gold jewelry. Other branches are located at 7 Water St. in St. George's, and at the Sonesta Resort and Marriott Castle Harbour hotels.

JEWELRY

Astwood Dickinson Jewellers
83–85 Front St. ☎ **441/292-5805.**

Here you'll find a treasure trove of famous-name watches, including Patek Philippe, Cartier, Tiffany, Tag Heuer, Tissot, Omega, and Swiss Army, plus designer jewelry, all at prices generally below U.S. retail. From its original Bermuda collection, you can select an 18-karat gold memento of the island. The outlet is also the agent for Colombian Emeralds International. There are also branches in the Walker Arcade and in the H. A. & E. Smith Department Store.

Crisson Jewellers
55 and 71 Front St. ☎ **441/295-2351.**

Crisson is the exclusive Bermuda agent for Rolex, Ebel, Seiko, Cyma, and Gucci watches, as well as other well-known makers. It also carries an extensive selection of fine jewelry and gems. Another branch is located on Queen Street, and there are also branches in several of the major hotels, including Marriott's Castle Harbour Resort, the Elbow Beach Hotel, the Sonesta Beach Resort, the Southampton Princess, and the Hamilton Princess.

E. R. Aubrey, Jeweler
19 Front St. W. (opposite the Ferry Terminal). ☎ **441/295-3826.**

This shop carries an extensive collection of gold chains, rings with precious and semiprecious stones, and charms, including the Bermuda longtail.

Herrington Jewellers
1 Washington Mall. ☎ **441/292-6527.**

A leading jewelry store in Hamilton, Herrington's offers a good selection of gold and silver jewelry. It's the authorized dealer for Citizen watches, sells Timex watches, and carries a vast selection of 14-karat gold chains and rings set with precious and semiprecious stones.

Solomon's
17 Front St. ☎ **441/292-4742.**

This is one of many jewelry stores that hawk their glittering wares to the cruise-going public, but some aficionados of the shopping scene consider it one of the most appealing. Don't expect a supermarket-style emporium with vast inventories: The site is small, select, and ever so polite, with a range of valuable stones set into mostly 18-karat gold settings, and to a lesser degree, platinum. You'll find it opposite the cruise-ship terminal on Front Street, in a position that makes it among the first to be spotted by cruise clients arriving for the first time in Bermuda.

LEATHER GOODS

The Harbourmaster
Washington Mall. ☎ **441/295-5333.**

This is your best bet for luggage and leather goods. The best buys here are goods from Colombia—often sold at prices 30% lower than in the United States. There are also more-expensive leather goods from Italy, such as handbags, along with an extensive collection of wallets, and nylon and canvas tote bags. The shop also stocks a number of travel accessories, including luggage carts. There's another branch in Hamilton at the corner of Reid and Queen Streets (☎ **441/295-4210**), which carries essentially the same merchandise.

LINENS
The Irish Linen Shop
31 Front St. (at Queen St.). ☎ **441/295-4089.**

At Heyl's Corner, near the "Birdcage" police officer, this shop stocks not only tablecloths of pure linen from Ireland, but also a large variety of other merchandise from Europe—everything from quilted place mats to men's shirts in French cotton from Souleiado of Provence. The owners go to Europe twice a year to bring back exceptional items such as Madeira hand embroidery and Belgian lace. You can often save as much as 50% over American prices by purchasing European linens in Bermuda.

LIQUOR & LIQUEURS
Burrows, Lightbourn Ltd.
87 Front St. ☎ **441/295-0176.**

This store has been in business since 1808. The maximum you can take from Bermuda is 1 liter of any spirits. Orders must be placed 24 hours before your departure, except on Sunday, when 48 hours' advance purchase is required. The store will deliver your liquor packages to the airport or to your ship. There are two locations in Hamilton, one in St. George's, one in Flatts Village, one in Paget and in Somerset, and one at the Royal Naval Dockyards on Ireland Island. Of course, you can also buy liquor to drink while in Bermuda.

Gosling Brothers, Ltd.
At Front and Queen Sts. ☎ **441/295-1123.**

This large competitor of Burrows, Lightbourn has been selling liquor in Bermuda since 1806. Here's where you can buy Gosling's Black Seal dark rum, perhaps one bottle to sample on the island and another as an in-bond purchase to take home with you. The bottle you drink on the island is likely to cost 50% more than the in-bond bottle. If you want to purchase liquor to take home for your duty-free allowance, you can arrange to have it sent to the airport. There's also another location, called the Black Seal Shop, at 69 Front St.

NEEDLEPOINT PATTERNS
Knit & Craft Shop
48 Reid St. ☎ **441/295-6722.**

This is the place to go if you knit, embroider, or crochet. The shop carries a large variety of needlepoint, crochet, and cross-stitch patterns with Bermudian themes, all of which are also available in kits, as well as craft supplies.

Factoid

You'll often find branches of Hamilton stores at major resorts. The prices—even the sales prices—are the same as those charged by their parent stores in Hamilton. The downside is that the selection is more limited. The good side is that these resort boutiques remain open on Sunday, when most stores in the city of Hamilton are shuttered.

PERFUMES
Peniston-Brown Co.
23 Front St. W. (opposite the Ferry Terminal). ☎ **441/295-0570.**

This shop carries almost all of the world's most popular perfumes. The shop's "fragrance specialists" will be happy to teach you something about the art of choosing and wearing perfume.

The Perfume and Cosmetic Boutique, Trimingham's
37 Front St. ☎ **441/295-1183.**

On the ground floor of Bermuda's largest department store is the island's most comprehensive emporium of prestigious fragrance and cosmetics lines—available at duty-free shop prices. Estée Lauder, Elizabeth Arden, Chanel, and Christian Dior are featured among Trimingham's beauty-care exclusives. Famous-name fragrance exclusives include Boucheron, Tiffany, and Issey Miyake.

SHOES
W. J. Boyle & Son
At Queen and Church Sts. ☎ **441/295-1887.**

In business since 1884, this shop offers footwear for men, women, and children. With the best collection in town, it specializes in brand-name footwear from England, Spain, Brazil, and the United States (including Clarks of England and Enzo Angiolini).

SILVER
Otto Wurz Co.
2 Vallis Building, 3–5 Front St. ☎ **441/295-1247.**

Otto Wurz is located at the western end of Front Street past the Ferry Terminal and the Bank of Bermuda, between Par-la-Ville and Bermudiana Roads. It specializes in articles made of silver, including jewelry, charms, and bracelets. One section of the store is devoted to gift items, such as pewter ware, cute wooden signs, and glassware, which the store can engrave.

SPORTSWEAR
Davison's
27 and 73 Front St. ☎ **441/292-2083.**

Sportswear with a Bermudian flair is the specialty at this emporium. Along with virtually anything you'd need to wear for almost any sport in Bermuda, it also carries accessories and sporting equipment. Almost anything you select here would be appropriate to wear at your local country club when you return home. Bags by Vera Bradley are also featured. Also available are culinary gift packages, including such items as Bermuda fish or clam chowder, fish-based sauces, and island herbs. In addition to the Front Street addresses, the store has other locations on the island: at the Clocktower in the Dockyard, on Water Street in St. George's, at the Southampton Princess, and at the Marriott Castle Harbour Resort.

Upstairs Golf & Tennis Shop
26 Church St. ☎ **441/295-5161.**

Everything you'll need for the tennis courts or the golf links is sold in this amply stocked store. For golfers, there's merchandise by Ping, Callaway, Titleist, and Lynx. Tennis enthusiasts will recognize products by Dunlop, Slazenger, and many others. There's also men's and women's rainwear from Scotland, which is suitable for Bermuda's rainy winters.

STAMPS
Perot Post Office

Queen St., at the entrance to Par-la-Ville Park. ☎ **441/292-9052** or 441/295-5151, ext. 1192. Mon–Fri 9am–5pm.

Bermuda's first stamp was printed in this landmark building. Beloved by collectors from all over the world, the stamps—signed by Perot, Bermuda's first, rather eccentric postmaster—are priceless. Philatelists can purchase contemporary Bermuda stamps in this same post office.

WOOLENS
Archie Brown

55 Front St. ☎ **441/295-2928.**

In business for more than half a century, this shop features sweaters for men and women in cashmere, cotton, lambs wool, and Shetland; for women, there are also matching skirts. Colors range from neutral to vibrant.

English Sports Shop

49 Front St. ☎ **441/295-2672.**

This shop, established in 1918, is one of the island's leading retailers of quality classic and British woolen goods for men, women, and children.

Scottish Wool Shop

7 Queen St. ☎ **441/295-0967.**

This shop carries a wide range of tartans for men, women, and children, all imported from Great Britain. Many woolen and cotton goods were made especially for this shop. There are women's accessories; children's toys; and Shetland, cashmere, lambs-wool, and cotton sweaters. Special orders can be placed for more than 500 tartan items.

3 Around the Island

As you leave Hamilton and tour the island, you may want to continue looking for typical Bermudian items at the shops listed below.

For other shopping suggestions, consider the Bermuda Craft Market and the Bermuda Arts Centre (see "Sandys Parish," in chapter 7). Those interested in Bermudian art might also want to visit the Birdsey Studio in Paget Parish (see "Paget Parish," in chapter 7).

SANDYS PARISH
IRELAND ISLAND
Bermuda Arts Centre at Dockyard

Museum Row, Royal Naval Dockyard, Ireland Island. ☎ **441/234-2809.**

Set within one of the stone-sided warehouses originally built by the British during their military tenure in Bermuda, this art gallery specializes in paintings, sculptures, and crafts by mostly Bermudian artisans. Not to be confused with the nearby Bermuda Crafts Centre, with which it is not associated, it's sponsored by a local foundation and, as such, strives for more than a purely commercial approach to art. Canvasses range in price from $50 to around $5,000, although several less-expensive craft items are also for sale. You never know if you'll be helped by a highly articulate staff member here, well versed in the nuances of the art being sold, or a newcomer who's much less sophisticated about the wares for sale here.

Island Pottery
Royal Naval Dockyard, Ireland Island. ☎ **441/234-3361.**

At this popular attraction, visitors can see Bermudian craftspeople at work. The spacious stone-built warehouse has a gift shop in one section and the workshop in the other. Artisans in traditional aprons toil over potter's wheels, turning out their wares. There's also a glassware artisan. Since the pottery is made in Bermuda, it's duty-free.

Kathleen Kemsley Bell
7 Seabright Lane. ☎ **441/236-3366.**

Mrs. Bell's work is displayed exclusively at the Bermuda Arts Centre at the dockyard. Working from her studio in Paget, she creates papier-mâché dolls with historically accurate, hand-stitched costumes. Each doll is signed as an original work of art. Mrs. Bell has sold top-of-the-line dolls, known for their expressive faces, to collectors in both Europe and North America. Prices begin at $275 and can go much higher. Mrs. Bell will work on commission; for this purpose, she can visit a buyer at any hotel. Call for an appointment.

SOMERSET
The Old Market
Main Rd., Mangrove Bay, Somerset Village. ☎ **441/234-0744.**

Occupying premises that date from 1827, the Old Market was formerly a private home. This unusual boutique offers everything from old coins, brass, and crystal to costume jewelry and casual clothes.

SOUTHAMPTON PARISH
Desmond Fountain Sculpture Gallery
On the mezzanine of the Southampton Princess, 101 South Shore Rd. ☎ **441/238-8840.**

Bermuda's most prominent sculptor, Desmond Fountain, has created some of the island's most visible public art. However, much of his work in recent years has been commissioned for upscale private homes and gardens around the world.

PAGET PARISH
Art House Gallery
80 South Shore Rd. ☎ **441/236-6746.**

The Art House specializes in original paintings and hand-signed lithographs by the Bermuda-born artist Joan Forbes. After studying in Massachusetts and Canada, she returned home to create watercolors and lithographs of Bermudian landscapes. Prices range from $10 to $50 for lithographs, and from $75 to $3,000 for original watercolors. Ms. Forbes also sells a variety of island-made craft and gift items.

HAMILTON PARISH
Bermuda Glass-Blowing Studio and Showroom
16 Blue Hole Hill. ☎ **441/293-2234.**

Bermuda's only glassblowing studio employs both locally trained Bermudians and European glassblowers. Although some of the studio's glass pieces have been commissioned, most of them have been inspired by cutting-edge developments in the art-glass world. Pieces on display in the showroom range in price from $5 to $1,000. The minimum commission accepted is usually in excess of $500.

ST. GEORGE'S PARISH

Bridge House Gallery
1 Bridge St., St. George's. ☎ **441/297-8211.**

Situated in one of the parish's oldest buildings—a two-story 18th-century building that was home to two of the island's governors and is now maintained by Bermuda's National Trust—this may be the best-stocked emporium on the island's East End. It carries a wide selection of antique and modern Bermudiana, including old lace, Christmas ornaments, imported English porcelain, antique maps, old bottles, post-cards, and unique mementos of Bermuda's unusual geography and history. One corner of the building has been set aside as the studio and sales outlet of local artist Jill Amos Raine. Since the gallery is actually a sightseeing attraction, it's also listed as such in chapter 7.

Carole Holding Studios
Town Sq., St. George's. ☎ **441/297-1833.**

Carole Holding is known and well respected for her skill in what might be Bermuda's most-loved art form: watercolor painting. Many of Ms. Holding's works depict the peace and serenity of Bermuda's homes and gardens. A few of her works were commissioned by individuals; more frequently, however, the subjects of her paintings came from her own imagination. Although Ms. Holding's works can be found in other gift shops around the island, most of them are in one of her three shops; there's one on Town Square in St. George's, one at 81 Front St. in Hamilton, and one at the Dockyards on Ireland Island.

Cow Polly
16 Water St., Somers Wharf, St. George's. ☎ **441/297-1514.**

Named after a rather unpleasant-looking fish that abounds in Bermuda waters, this upscale gift shop prides itself on its collection of unusual objects imported from virtually everywhere. The theme is aquatic designs, often inspired by fish and under-water mythology. Items for sale include hand-painted shirts, jackets, costume jewelry, and unusual neckties.

Frangipani
Water St., St. George's. ☎ **441/297-1357.**

This is a world of fun, color, and "dressy casual" fashion for women. You'll find a large selection of comfortable cottons, bright silks, and soft rayons, all with that island feeling. The store is known for its unusual merchandise, featuring exclusive island designs. There's also a fine collection of swimwear and unusual accessories.

Bermuda After Dark

Nightlife may not be Bermuda's main attraction, but there's a lot of it, even though it seems to float from hotel to hotel. Thus, it's hard to predict which pub or nightspot will have the best steel-drum or calypso band at any given time. Many of the local pubs feature sing-alongs at the piano bar, a popular form of entertainment in Bermuda. Most of the big hotels offer shows after dinner, with combos filling in between shows for couples who like to dance.

The island's visitor centers and most hotels distribute free copies of such publications as *Preview Bermuda, Bermuda Weekly,* and *This Week in Bermuda,* which will fill you in on the latest scheduled activities and events. There's also a calendar of events in the *Bermudian,* sold at most newsstands.

You can also tune in to the local TV station, which constantly broadcasts information for visitors, including details on cultural events and various nightlife offerings around the island. A local radio station, 1160 AM (VSB), broadcasts news of Bermuda cultural and entertainment events from 7am to 12:30pm daily.

1 The Club & Music Scene

PAGET PARISH

After Hours
117 South Rd. (past the intersection with Middle Rd.). ☎ **441/236-8563.**

The idea of an after-hours club in sleepy Bermuda, where many guests turn in at 9pm, seems incongruous. But there is such a place. Local night owls flock here for the good burgers and good times, downing food and drink until they're turned away at 4am. The club doesn't even open until midnight. It's a very popular spot in the early-morning hours with the locals, especially those who don't have to get up at 7am to report to work. The kitchen will also turn out well-stuffed sandwiches and curries for those late-night munchies.

SOUTHAMPTON PARISH

Henry VIII
South Shore Rd., Southampton Parish. ☎ **441/238-1977.** No cover. Bus: 7 or 8.

This restaurant (see the full review in chapter 5) is also a good bet for music and comedy. Piano playing and singing are often featured, and comedians join in fairly regularly. Performances begin at 9pm and last until the restaurant closes at 1am. The stage is visible from the pub and from one of the restaurant's three dining areas.

Neptune Club

At the Southampton Princess, 101 South Shore Rd., Southampton Parish. ☎ **441/238-8000.** Cover $6. Ferryboat from Hamilton.

The Neptune Club presents a vast array of talent Monday to Saturday nights. Depending on the season and availability of artists, you might catch a show featuring singers, dancers, or even a hypnotist. Acts usually begin about 9:30pm and continue, with breaks, until around midnight.

PEMBROKE PARISH (CITY OF HAMILTON)

The Club

Above Little Venice restaurant, Bermudiana Rd., Hamilton. ☎ **441/295-6693.** No cover. Bus: 1, 2, 10, or 11.

With its red velvet, mirrors, and brass, this club is sometimes favored by an older group of Bermuda business and professional people. It's located above the Little Venice restaurant, which has an understated mirrored entrance that reflects the two stone lions at its portals. Dress is smart casual. There are dancing and drinks. Open daily from 10pm to 3am.

The Gazebo Lounge

In the Hamilton Princess, 76 Pitts Bay Rd., Hamilton. ☎ **441/295-3000.** Cover $25. Bus: 7 or 8.

The Gazebo Lounge is Bermuda's premier location for a fun night of dinner and theater. Guests enjoy their meal in one of the Princess's dining rooms, then move into the bar/lounge to watch a 90-minute play performed by a local repertory company. Show schedules vary seasonally, but performances are usually staged every Thursday, Friday, and Saturday beginning around 9pm. Other nights, guests of the hotel and visitors can stop by the Colony Pub for drinks accompanied by piano music beginning at 9pm.

The Oasis Nightlife & The Rock Room

In the Emporium Building, 69 Front St., Hamilton. ☎ **441/292-4978.** Cover $10 Mon–Fri, $15 Sat–Sun includes entrance to both The Oasis Nightlife and The Rock Room. Bus: 3, 7, or 11.

One of the leading clubs on the island, The Oasis is reached by riding a glass-encased elevator to the third floor of a stylish commercial building in the center of Hamilton. It has been renovated in New York–warehouse style, and extensive work has improved the sound system and added lots of special-effects lighting. TV monitors are widely used throughout the nightclub to provide background video effects; the extensive music repertoire includes the latest Top 40 dance music. Top North American club bands complement local bands playing a variety of rock and blues in The Rock Room. Drink prices range from $5.50 to $6. The club is open daily from 9pm to 3am.

DEVONSHIRE PARISH

Clay House Inn

77 North Shore Rd., Devonshire Parish. ☎ **441/292-3193** for reservations. Cover $22.50 per person, including 2 drinks. Bus: 10 or 11.

Although calypso and steel-band music originated on islands south of Bermuda, this nightclub offers up those musical forms with panache. You're likely to be entertained in a folkloric celebration of island dances with both vocal and instrumental music; it's a carefully contrived package of Caribbean-style nostalgia. The shows are every Tuesday, Wednesday, and Thursday year-round; doors open at 10:30pm, and the show lasts until right after midnight. Friday and Saturday the club features reggae music from 10pm to 3am.

2 The Bar Scene

SANDYS PARISH

Frog & Onion
The Cooperage, Old Royal Naval Dockyard, Ireland Island. ☎ **441/234-2900.** No cover. Bus: 7 or 8.

Converted from an 18th-century cooperage, or barrel-making factory, this British-style pub lies within the Royal Naval Dockyard; see chapter 5 for a review of its restaurant. You can enjoy bar snacks throughout the afternoon and evening. Operated by a "frog" (a Frenchman) and an "onion" (a Bermudian), the pub is open March to November daily from noon to midnight.

PEMBROKE PARISH (CITY OF HAMILTON)

Casey's
25 Queen St. (between Reid and Church Sts.). ☎ **441/293-9549.** No cover. Bus: 1, 2, 10, or 11.

There's absolutely nothing flashy about this long and narrow room that locals seem to prefer as their favorite bar. The owner, Wesley Robinson, knows many of his clients and is an expert at mixing the house specialty, a Dark & Stormy, consisting of black rum with splashes of ginger beer. Look for yellowed photographs of old Bermuda and a carefully preserved, wall-mounted marlin caught by the owner in 1982. For reasons not known to anybody, Friday nights here are the most popular on the island, and the joint is overflowing. There's never any live music, and although no food is served, no one will mind if you bring your lunch in from any of the take-out facilities nearby. It's open Monday to Saturday from 10am to 10pm.

HAMILTON PARISH

Swizzle Inn
3 Blue Hole Hill, Bailey's Bay, Hamilton Parish. ☎ **441/293-9300.** No cover. Bus: 3 or 11.

The home of the Bermuda rum swizzle, this bar and restaurant lies west of the airport, near the Crystal Caves and the Bermuda Perfume Factory. You can order the Swizzleburger and fish-and-chips throughout the day; see chapter 5 for further details on dining here. In the old days, you might've run into Ted Kennedy here; now his present wife steers him to more sedate places. The tradition here is to tack your business card wherever you can find a spot, even the ceiling. Sports aficionados usually enjoy playing a game of darts. The jukebox plays both soft and hard rock. The inn is open daily from 11am to 1am, except in January and February, when it's closed on Mondays.

ST. GEORGE'S PARISH

Wharf Tavern
Somers Wharf, St. George's. ☎ **441/297-1515.** No cover. Bus: 1, 3, 10, or 11.

This is everybody's favorite spot in St. George's for knocking back glasses of tropical rum punch and talking of sailing the high seas. The tavern, housed in a converted warehouse from the 1700s, is also a good dining choice (see chapter 5 for

The Big Event: The Bermuda Festival

Bermuda's major cultural event is the Bermuda Festival, staged every January and February. Outstanding international classical, jazz, and pop artists come to Bermuda to perform, and major theatrical and dance performances from around the globe are staged. During the festival, performances are given every night except Sunday. Tickets for these events range in price from $20 to $35; some festival tickets are reserved until 48 hours before curtain time for visitors. Most performances are held at City Hall Theatre, City Hall, Church Street, Hamilton. For more information and reservations, contact the **Bermuda Festival,** P.O. Box 297, Hamilton HM AX, Bermuda (☎ **441/295-1291;** fax 441/295-7403).

further details), but you can come here just to drink, as many do. The bar is open daily from 10am to 1am.

3 The Performing Arts

You can order tickets for all of Bermuda's major cultural events through the **Box Office at the Visitors Service Bureau** in Hamilton (☎ **441/292-8572**) with your MasterCard, Visa, or American Express.

Note that although students and senior citizens are sometimes offered discounts to various entertainment events, such as performances of the Bermuda Philharmonic Society (see below), discount tickets aren't usually available for events.

CLASSICAL MUSIC

The **Bermuda Philharmonic Society,** conducted by Graham Garton, presents four regular concerts during the season. In addition, special outdoor **"Classical Pops" concerts** are presented on the first weekend in June in St. George's and at the Royal Naval Dockyard. Concerts usually feature the Bermuda Philharmonic orchestra and choir, along with guest soloists. You can get tickets and concert schedules from the **Harbourmaster,** Washington Mall (☎ **441/295-5333**). Tickets generally range from $18 to $20; seniors and students are often granted discounts, depending on the performance.

GOMBEY DANCING

Ask at the tourist office or call the box office (see above) to inquire if the gombey dancers will be performing during your stay. This is the island's single-most-important cultural expression of African heritage; once part of the slave culture, the tradition dates from the mid-1700s. This local dance troupe of highly talented men and women often performs at one of the big hotels (and on occasion aboard cruise ships for passengers) in winter. On all holidays, you'll see the gombeys dancing through the streets of Hamilton in their colorful costumes.

BALLET

The Bermuda Civic Ballet presents classical ballets at different venues on the island. On occasion a major European or American guest artist will appear with the troupe. The National Dance Theater of Bermuda also stages performances, both classical and modern, at venues around the island. Ask at the tourist office or call the box office (see above) to inquire if either troupe has any performances scheduled during your visit; prices vary with the performance.

MUSICAL THEATER

An all-volunteer organization based in Hamilton, the **Gilbert & Sullivan Society of Bermuda**, P.O. Box HM 3098, Hamilton HM NX (☎ **441/295-3218**), is known for producing at least one large-scale musical production per year. These days, only about 20% of their repertoire is based on the works of Gilbert and Sullivan; they've branched into such musicals as *Evita* and Sondheim's *A Little Night Music,* among others. The society performs at Hamilton's City Hall, on Church Street. Be warned that this is a small-scale, strictly volunteer organization; their sole production runs for 2 weeks at most, usually in October. They sometimes also contribute their talents to the Bermuda Festival in February (see box).

Bermuda is the only place outside of Cambridge where Harvard University's **Hasty Pudding Theatricals** are staged. Performances have been presented in Bermuda during College Weeks (in March and April) since the 1960s. They're staged at the City Hall Theatre on Church Street in Hamilton; call the box office at the Visitors Service Bureau (see above) for tickets, which cost about $25 each.

Appendix:
Bermuda in Depth

Welcome to an island of no pollution, no billboards, no graffiti, no litter, no rental cards, no unemployment (well, almost), no tolerance for drugs, no illiteracy (well, almost), and no nude or topless beaches. In a changing world, especially as evoked by those islands to the south in the Caribbean, Bermuda remains . . . well, Bermuda.

If there's a sore point among Bermudians today, it's their extreme desire to separate themselves from the islands of the Caribbean, and particularly from The Bahamas to the south. They often send angry letters to publishers of maps, reference sources, and travel guides claiming that Bermuda is *not* in the Caribbean. As one irate Bermudian put it, "You don't claim that Washington, D.C., is part of Dallas, Texas. They're the same distance apart that Bermuda is from the Caribbean."

Bermuda deliberately wants to distance itself from the islands of the Caribbean, many of which are plagued by economic, socioeconomic, and racial problems, including abject poverty. Unsavory businesses, money launderers, and tax evaders are not tolerated in Bermuda. Bermuda is promoting not just tourism, but its stellar reputation in banking and multinational business.

At the millennium, international business was positioning itself to overtake tourism as a primary source of revenue. With China's takeover of Hong Kong, Bermuda has persuaded some of the biggest names in world business to create official domiciles on the island. This trend actually began in the 1970s, when some Hong Kong businesspeople formed low-profile shipping, trading, and investment companies in Bermuda—companies that became, in essence, corporate cash cows. It's a trend that continues to significantly affect Bermuda's economy for the better.

When Britain surrendered Hong Kong to China in 1997, Bermuda became the largest British colony. A local businessman watched the televised ceremonies in which Britain handed over control, and was filled with glee: "All we can say is, Thank you very much Hong Kong, because here come the insurance companies and pension funds." By late 1998, nearly half of the companies listed on the Hong Kong Stock Exchange had established some sort of legal presence in Bermuda. Even some of the Chinese government's own holding companies have established a presence in Bermuda.

Amazingly, as tiny Bermuda faces the new millennium, it has emerged as the biggest and most prosperous of all the colonies, the bulk of which are now in the Caribbean. Actually, Britain prefers to call Bermuda and its other possessions "dependent territories" instead of colonies. (Technically, the sun still doesn't set over the diminished British Empire, because Britain still reigns over everything from the Falkland Islands to Gibraltar, from Diego Garcia Island in the Indian Ocean to the Pitcairn Islands in the South Pacific.)

And as aggressively as Bermuda is pursuing business, it's also more aware than ever of its fragile environment. There aren't too many Al Gores on the scene, but attention is being paid. Bermuda's population density is the third highest in the world, after Hong Kong and Monaco. Because the number of annual visitors is 10 times higher than the already-overcrowded population, Bermuda has had to take strong initiatives to protect its environment and its natural resources. These environmental protection laws take the form of stiff antilitter laws, annual garbage cleanup campaigns, automobile restrictions, cedar replanting (a blight in the 1940s and 1950s wiped out the native cedar trees), lead-free gasoline, a strict fishing policy, and other measures.

Along the shaky road to self-government, Bermuda had some ugly racial conflicts. Riots in 1968 gave way to the assassination in 1973 of the British governor. But that was a long time ago; today, Bermuda has the most harmonious race relations in this part of the world, far better than those in the United States, the Caribbean, and The Bahamas. Of course, there's still a long way to go, but Bermudians of African descent now have assumed important political, administrative, and managerial posts in every aspect of the local economy. Bermuda hasn't quite reached the point where the color of your skin is unimportant, but it has made more significant advancement toward that goal than its neighbors to the south.

As Bermuda faces the millennium, its average household income has risen to a healthy $68,500—contrast that with some of the less-fortunate islands in the south, many of which don't even have budgets to *compile* such statistics. On the downside, homes in Bermuda are at least three times the median cost of a house in the United States or Canada. Compared to Puerto Rico, Jamaica, and certainly Haiti, no one is really poor in Bermuda.

As a tourist destination, Bermuda has impeccable credentials. It was a resort long before Florida, Hawaii, Mexico, and many other places. Over the decades, it has successfully exploited its position in the northwest Atlantic between North America and Europe. By the late 1990s, it was even working to throw off its image as a staid resort, hoping to project a lively, more with-it atmosphere (although it has a long way to go in this department). The United States remains its largest market—about 86% of its visitors are Americans—but in recent years more and more visitors from Europe, the Far East, and the Near East can be seen dining, drinking, and shopping in Hamilton.

1 The Natural World: An Environmental Guide to Bermuda

Lying 570 miles east-southeast of Cape Hatteras, North Carolina, Bermuda is actually a group of some 300 islands, islets, and coral rocks clustered in a fishhook-shaped chain about 22 miles long and 2 miles wide at its broadest point. Together, the archipelago forms a landmass of about 21 square miles that's formally known as "the Bermudas."

Only 20 or so of the islands are inhabited. The largest one, called the "mainland," is Great Bermuda; about 14 miles long, it's linked to the other nearby major islands by a series of bridges and causeways. The capital of this archipelago, Hamilton, is situated on the mainland.

The other islands bear such names as Somerset, Watford, Boaz, and Ireland in the west, and St. George's and St. David's in the east. This chain of islands encloses the archipelago's major bodies of water, which include Castle Harbour, St. George's Harbour, Harrington Sound, and Great Sound. Most of the other smaller islands, or islets, lie within these bodies of water.

Bermuda is situated far north of the Tropic of Cancer, which cuts through the Bahamian archipelago. Bermuda is based on the upper parts of an extinct volcano, which may date from 100 million years ago. Through millennia, wind and water brought limestone deposits and formed the islands far from any continental landmass; today, the closest is the coast of the Carolinas. Bermuda is about 775 miles southeast of New York City, some 1,030 miles northeast of Miami, and nearly 3,450 miles away from London. It has a balmy climate year-round, with sunshine prevailing almost every day. The chief source of Bermuda's mild weather is the Gulf Stream, a broad belt of warm water formed by equatorial currents, whose northern reaches separate the Bermuda islands from North America and, with the prevailing northeast winds, temper the wintry blasts that sweep across the Atlantic from west and north.

The islands of Bermuda are divided, for administrative purposes, into several parishes. For a complete rundown of all the parishes, see "Orienting Yourself: The lay of the Land," in chapter 3.

MORE THAN ONIONS: THE ISLAND'S FLORA

Bermuda's temperate climate, abundant sunshine, fertile soil, and adequate moisture account for some of the most verdant gardens in the Atlantic. Some of the best of these, such as the Botanical Gardens in Paget Parish, are open to the public. Bermudian gardeners pride themselves on the mixture of temperate-zone and subtropical plants that thrive on the island, despite the salty air.

No matter how poor the soil in certain places, Bermuda is blessed with copious and varied flora. Examples include the indigenous sea grape, which flourishes along the island's sandy coastlines, preferring sand and saltwater to more arable soil; and the cassava plant, whose roots resemble the tubers of sweet potatoes. When ground into flour and soaked to remove a mild poison, these roots are the main ingredient for Bermuda's traditional Christmas pies. Also growing wild and abundant are prickly pears, aromatic fennel, yucca, and the Spanish bayonet, a spiked-leaf plant that bears, in season, a single white flower.

To the early colonial settlers, Bermuda's only native palm, the palmetto, proved particularly useful; its leaves were used to thatch colonial roofs. When crushed and fermented, the leaves produced a strong alcoholic drink called bibby, whose effects were condemned by the early Puritans. Its leaves were also fashioned into women's hats during a brief period in the 1600s, when they represented the height of fashion in London.

The banana, which flourishes today in Bermuda and constitutes one of its most dependable sources of fresh fruit, was introduced to the island in the early 1600s. It is believed that Bermudian bananas were the first to be brought back to London from the New World. They created an immediate sensation, leading to the cultivation of bananas in many other British colonies.

The plant that contributed most to Bermuda's renown was the Bermuda onion (*Allium cepa*). Imported from England in 1616, and later grown from seed brought from the Spanish and Portuguese islands of Tenerife and

Madeira, the Bermuda onion became so famous along the eastern coast of the United States that Bermudians themselves became known as "onions." Sadly, however, during the 1930s Bermuda's flourishing export trade in onions declined because of high tariffs, increased competition from similar species grown in Texas and elsewhere, and the limited arable land on the island.

Today, what you'll see decorating Bermuda's gently rolling landscapes are oleander, hibiscus, royal poinciana, poinsettia, bougainvillea, and dozens of other flowering shrubs and vines. Of the island's dozen or so species of morning glory, three are indigenous; they tend to grow rampant and over-whelm everything else in a garden.

CLOSE ENCOUNTERS WITH THE LOCAL FAUNA

AMPHIBIANS

Because of the almost-total lack of natural freshwater ponds and lakes, Bermuda's amphibians have adapted to seawater, or to slightly brackish water. Amphibians include the tree frog (*Eleutherodactylus johnstonei* and *Eleutherodactylus gossei*), whose nighttime chirping is sometimes mistaken by newcomers for the song of birds. Small and camouflaged by the leafy matter of the forest floor, you can spot the tree frog between April and November.

More visible are Bermuda's giant toads, or road toads (*Bufo marinus*), which sometimes reach the size of an adult human's palm. Imported from Guyana in the 1870s in the hope of controlling the island's cockroach pop-ulation, giant toads search out the nighttime warmth of the asphalt roads and are often crushed by cars in the process; they are especially prevalent after a soaking rain. The road toads are not venomous and, contrary to legend, they do not cause warts.

Island reptiles include colonies of harmless lizards, often seen sunning themselves on rocks until approaching humans or predators scare them away. The best-known species is the Bermuda rock lizard (*Eumeces lon-girostris*), also known as a skink, which is said to have been the only non-marine, nonflying vertebrate in Bermuda before the arrival of European colonists. Imported reptiles include the Somerset lizard (*Anolis roquet*), whose black eye patches give it the look of a bashful bandit, and the Jamaican anole (*Anolis grahami*), a kind of color-changing chameleon.

BIRD LIFE

Partly because of its ample food sources, Bermuda has an abundant bird population; many species nest upon the island's terrain during their annual migrations. Most of these birds arrive during the cooler winter months, usu-ally between Christmas and Easter. Serious birders have recorded almost 40 species of eastern warblers, which peacefully coexist with species of martin, doves, egrets, South American terns, herons, fork-tailed flycatchers, and even some species from as far away as the Arctic Circle.

Two of the most visible imported species are the cardinal, introduced during the 1700s, and the kiskadee. Imported from Trinidad in 1957 to control lizards and flies, the kiskadee has instead wreaked havoc on the island's commercial fruit crops.

The once-abundant eastern bluebird has been greatly reduced in number since the depletion of the cedar trees, its preferred habitat. Another bird native to Bermuda is the gray-and-white petrel, known locally as a cahow, which burrows for most of the year in the sands of the isolated eastern islands; the rest of the year it feeds at sea, floating for hours in the warm waters of the Gulf Stream. One of the most rarely sighted birds in the world—it was once regarded as extinct—the petrel is now protected by the Bermudian government.

Also native to Bermuda is the cliff-dwelling tropic bird, which can be recognized by the elongated plumage of its white tail. Resembling a swallow, it's the island's harbinger of spring, making its annual appearance in March.

Although the gardens and golf courses of many of the island's hotels attract dozens of birds, some of the finest bird-watching sites are maintained by either the Bermuda Audubon Society or the National Trust. Isolated sites known for sheltering thousands of native and migrating birds include Paget Marsh, just south of Hamilton; the Walsingham Trust in Hamilton Parish; and Spittal Pond in Smith's Parish.

SEA LIFE

In the deep waters off the shores of Bermuda, photographers have recorded some of the finest game fish in the world, including blackfin tuna, marlin, swordfish, wahoo, dolphin, sailfish, and barracuda. Also prevalent are bonefish and pompano, both of which prefer sun-flooded shallow waters closer to shore. Any beachcomber is likely to come across hundreds of oval-shaped chitons (*Chiton tuberculatus*), a mollusk that adheres tenaciously to rocks within tidal flats; locally, this mollusk is known as "suck-rock."

Beware of the Portuguese man-of-war (*Physalia physalis*), a floating colony of jellyfish whose stinging tentacles sometimes reach 50 feet in length. Give this dangerous and venomous marine creature a wide berth: Severe stings could require hospitalization. When it washes up on Bermuda beaches, usually between March and July, the man-of-war can sting even when it appears to be dead.

The most prevalent marine animal in Bermuda is responsible for the formation of the island's greatest tourist attraction, its miles of pale-pink sand. Much of the sand is composed of broken shells, pieces of coral, and the calcium carbonate remains of other marine invertebrates. The pinkest pieces are shards of crushed shell from a single-celled animal called foraminifer. Its vivid pink skeleton is pierced with holes, through which the animal extends its rootlike feet (*pseudopodia*), which cling to the underside of the island's reefs during the animal's brief life before it is washed ashore.

2 Life in the Onion Patch

GETTING TO KNOW "THE ONIONS"

Even though Bermuda isn't in the onion business the way it used to be, a true born-and-bred islander is still called an "Onion." That term dates from the turn of the century, when the export of Bermuda onions and Easter lilies to the U.S. mainland was one of the island's major sources of income.

The "Onions," a term that still carries a badge of pride, have their own unique lifestyle, and even their own vocabulary. For example, "Aunt Haggie's children" are frustrating, stupid people; "married by 10 parsons" is a reference to a woman with huge breasts; "backin up" means gay. You don't vomit in Bermuda, you "Go Europe." "Cockroach killers" (a term you may also hear in the American Southwest) are pointy-toed shoes. Although you'll rarely see it on local menus, the bream fish is called a "shit-bubbler."

Those who live on more-troubled islands to the south often look with envy upon the "Onions" of Bermuda, who have a much higher standard of living than Caribbean islanders do; they also pay no personal income tax and suffer from only a 7% unemployment rate. The literacy rate is high: An estimated 99% of females age 15 and older can read and write, as can 98% of all Bermudian males.

Today's 61,000 residents are mostly of African, British, and Portuguese descent. Bermuda's population density, one of the highest in the world, is about 3,210 per square mile. About 61% of the population is black, and 39% white. Many minority groups are represented, the largest and most established being the Portuguese; most, however, consist of islanders from the Caribbean or The Bahamas. Some Bermudians can even trace their ancestry back to the island's first settlers, and some to successful privateers and slaves.

Britain's influence in Bermuda is obvious in predominantly English accents, police who wear helmets like those of London bobbies, and cars that drive on the left. Schools are also run along the lines of the British system and provide a high standard of preparatory education. Children 5 to 16 years of age must attend school. The Bermuda College, which offers academic and technical studies, boasts a renowned hotel and catering program.

WHO'S MINDING THE STORE?

In essence, Bermuda is a self-governing dependency of Britain, with that country protecting its security and stability. The governor, appointed by the Queen, represents Her Majesty in the areas of external affairs, defense, and internal security.

By choosing to remain a British dependency, Bermuda rejected the trail that many former colonies in the Caribbean, including Antigua, blazed by declaring their independence. Even though they remain under the protection of the British umbrella, however, Bermudians manage their own day-to-day affairs. And ever since the people of Bermuda were granted the right to govern themselves in 1968, they have done so admirably well.

Bermuda has a 12-member cabinet headed by a premier. The elected legislature, referred to as the Legislative Council, consists of a 40-member House of Assembly and an 11-member Senate. Bermuda's oldest political party is the Progressive Labour Party, formed in 1963. In 1964, the United Bermuda Party was established and was the party in power until topped by Labour in 1998.

Bermuda's legal system is founded on common law. Judicial responsibility falls to the Supreme Court, headed by a chief justice in a powdery wig and robe. English law is the fundamental guide, and in court English customs prevail.

Each of the nine parishes into which the island is divided is managed by an advisory council. The capital, Hamilton, is located in Pembroke Parish. (For further details on the individual parishes, see "Orienting Yourself: The Lay of the Land," in chapter 3.)

TOURIST DOLLARS & NO INCOME TAX

Bermuda's political stability has proved beneficial to the economy, which relies heavily on tourism and foreign investment.

For much of the island's early history, the major industry was shipbuilding, made possible by the abundant cedar forests. But when, in the second half of the 19th century, wooden ships gave way to steel ones, the island turned to tourism. Today it's the country's leading industry, with annual revenues estimated at $450 million. Approximately 550,000 visitors come to Bermuda each year; an estimated 86% arrive from the United States, 4% from Britain, and 7% from Canada. Bermuda enjoys a 42% repeat-visitor rate.

Because Bermuda has enacted favorable economic measures, more than 6,000 international companies are registered here; these companies are engaged mostly in investment holding, insurance, commercial trading, consulting services, and shipping—but fewer than 275 companies are actually located on the island. The reason for this curious situation? Bermuda has no corporate or income tax.

The island's leading exports are pharmaceuticals, concentrates (primarily black rum and sherry peppers), essences, and beverages. Leading imports include foodstuffs, alcoholic beverages, clothing, furniture, fuel, electrical appliances, and motor vehicles. Bermuda's major trading partners are the United States, Great Britain, Canada, the Netherlands, and the Caribbean states.

3 History 101

THE EARLY YEARS The discovery of the Bermudas is attributed to the Spanish—probably the navigator Juan Bermúdez—sometime before 1511, for in that year a map was published in the *Legatio Babylonica* that included "La Bermuda" among the Atlantic islands. A little more than a century later, the English staked a claim to Bermuda and began colonization.

In 1609, the flagship of Admiral Sir George Somers, the *Sea Venture,* while en route to the colony at Jamestown, Virginia, was wrecked on Bermuda's reefs. The dauntless crew built two pinnaces (small sailing ships) and headed on to the American colony, but three sailors hid out and remained on the island. They were Bermuda's first European settlers. Just 3 years later, the Bermuda islands were included in the charter of the Virginia Company, and 60 colonists were sent there from England; St. George's Town was founded soon after.

Bermuda's status as a colony dates from 1620, when the first parliament convened (Bermuda's is the oldest parliament in continuous existence in the British Commonwealth). In 1684, Bermuda became a British Crown Colony under King Charles II. Sir Robert Robinson was appointed the colony's first governor.

Slavery became a part of life in Bermuda shortly after the official settlement. Although the majority of slaves came from Africa, a few were Native Americans. Later, Scots imprisoned for fighting against Cromwell were sent to the islands, followed in 1651 by Irish slaves. The fate of these bond servants, however, was not as cruel as that of plantation slaves in America and the West Indies. All slaves were freed by the British Emancipation Act of 1834.

Dateline

- **ca. 1511** Juan Bermúdez discovers Bermuda while sailing aboard the Spanish ship *La Garza.*
- **1609** The British ship *Sea Venture* is wrecked upon the reefs of Bermuda; all on board make it to shore safely and the settlement of Bermuda begins.
- **1612** The Virginia Company dispatches the *Plough* to Bermuda with 60 colonists on board. Richard Moore is appointed governor of Bermuda.
- **1620** The first Bermuda parliament session is held in St. Peter's Church, St. George's.
- **1684** The Bermuda Company's charter is taken over by the British Crown. Sir Robert Robinson is appointed the Crown's first governor of Bermuda.
- **1775** Gunpowder is stolen in St. George's and is shipped to the American colonies for use against the British.
- **1861** Bermuda becomes involved in the American Civil War when it runs supplies to the South to undermine the Union's blockade.
- **1919–33** Bermudians profit from Prohibition in the United States by engaging in rum-running.

continues

- **1940–45** Bermuda plays an important role in World War II counterespionage for the Allies.
- **1946** The a.utomobile is introduced in Bermuda.
- **1957** Great Britain withdraws militarily after 2 centuries of rule.
- **1963** Voter registration is open to all citizens.
- **1968** Bermudians are granted a new constitution that, while still protecting them under the umbrella of the British Commonwealth, now allows them to govern themselves.
- **1973** The governor, Sir Richard Sharples, and an aide are assassinated.
- **1979** Bermudians celebrate their own Gina Swainson as winner of the Miss World contest.
- **1987** Hurricane Emily causes millions of dollars' worth of damage; some 70 people are injured.
- **1990** Prime Minister Margaret Thatcher confers with Pres. George Bush in Bermuda.
- **1991** Prime Minister John Major meets with President Bush in Bermuda.
- **1995** Bermudians vote to maintain traditional ties with Britain.
- **1997** Pamela Gordon, 41, becomes island's first woman prime minister.

RELATIONS WITH AMERICA Bermuda established close links with the American colonies. The islanders set up a thriving mercantile trade on the eastern seaboard, especially with southern ports. The major commodity sold by Bermuda's merchant ships was salt from Turks Island.

During the American Revolution, trade with loyalist Bermuda was cut off by the rebellious colonies, despite the network of family connections and close friendships that bound them. The cutoff in trade proved a great hardship for the islanders, who, having chosen seafaring over farming, depended heavily on America for their supply of food. Many of them, now deprived of profitable trade routes, turned to privateering, piracy, and "wrecking" (salvaging goods from wrecked or foundered ships).

Britain's loss of its important American colonial ports led to a naval buildup in Bermuda. In the War of 1812, it was from here that ships and troops sailed in 1814 to burn Washington, D.C., and the White House.

Bermuda got a new lease on economic life during the American Civil War. The island was sympathetic to the Confederacy and, with approval of the British government, ran the blockade that the Union had placed on exports, especially of cotton, by the southern states. St. George's Harbour was a principal Atlantic base for the lucrative business of smuggling manufactured goods into Confederate ports and bringing out cargoes of cotton and turpentine.

When the Confederacy fell, so did Bermuda's economy. Seeing no immediate source of income from trading with the eastern states, the islanders turned their attention to agriculture and found that the colony's fertile soil and salubrious climate produced excellent vegetables. Portuguese immigrants arrived to farm the land, and soon celery, potatoes, tomatoes, and especially onions were being shipped to the New York market. So brisk was the onion trade that Hamilton became known as "Onion Town."

During Prohibition, Bermudians again profited by developments in the United States as they engaged in the lucrative business of rum-running. Although the distance from the island to the East Coast was too great for quick crossings in small booze-laden boats (as could be done from The Bahamas and Cuba), Bermuda nevertheless accounted for a good part of the alcoholic beverages transported illegally to the United States before the repeal of Prohibition in 1933.

A HOTBED OF ESPIONAGE Bermuda played a key role in World War II counterespionage for the Allies. The story of the "secret war" with Nazi Germany is told dramatically in William Stevenson's *A Man Called Intrepid*.

Beneath the Hamilton Princess Hotel, a carefully trained staff worked to decode radio signals to and from German submarines and other vessels operating in the Atlantic, close to the United States and the islands offshore. Unknown to the Germans, the British, early in the war, had broken the Nazi code through use of a captured German coding machine called "Enigma." The British also intercepted and examined mail between Europe and the United States.

Bermuda served as a refueling stop for airplanes flying between the two continents. While pilots were being entertained at the Yacht Club, the mail would be taken off the carriers and examined by experts. An innocent-looking series of letters from Lisbon, for example, often contained messages written in invisible ink. These letters were part of a vast German spy network. The British became skilled at opening sealed envelopes, examining their written contents, and then carefully resealing them.

The surreptitious letter-readers were called "trappers." Many of them were young women without any previous experience in counterespionage work, yet some performed very well. As Stevenson wrote, it was soon discovered that "by some quirk in the law of averages, the girls who shone in this work had well-turned ankles." A medical officer involved with the project even reported it as "fairly certain that a girl with unshapely legs would make a bad trapper." So, amazingly, the word went out that women seeking recruitment as trappers would have to display their gams.

During the course of their work, the trappers discovered one of the methods by which the Germans were transmitting secret messages: They would shrink a whole page of regularly typed text down to the size of a tiny dot and then conceal the dot under an innocuous-looking punctuation mark, such as a comma or period! The staff likened these messages with their secret-bearing dots to plum duff, a popular English dessert, for these "punctuation dots [were] scattered through a letter like raisins in the suet puddings." The term *duff method* then came to be applied to the manner in which the Germans were sending military and other messages through the mail.

When the United States entered the war, FBI agents joined the British in their intelligence operations in Bermuda.

BERMUDA COMES INTO ITS OWN In 1953, British prime minister Winston Churchill chose Bermuda, which he had visited during the war, as the site for a conference with U.S. president Dwight D. Eisenhower and the French premier. Several such high-level gatherings have followed in the decades since; the most recent one, between British prime minister John Major and U.S. president George Bush, took place in 1991.

Bermuda's increasing prominence led to changes in its relationships with Great Britain and the United States, as well as significant developments on the island itself. In 1957, after nearly 2 centuries of occupation, Britain withdrew its military forces, having decided to grant self-government to its oldest colony. The United States, however, under the Lend-Lease Agreement signed in 1941, and due to expire in 2040, continues to maintain a naval air station at Kindley Field, in St. George's Parish. Nearby, on Cooper's Island, the U.S. National Aeronautics and Space Administration operates a space-tracking system.

As Bermudians assumed greater control over their own affairs, they began to adopt significant social changes, but at a pace that did not satisfy some critics. Although racial segregation in hotels and restaurants ceased in 1959, schools were not integrated until 1971. Women received the right to vote in 1944, but the law still restricted suffrage only to property holders.

However, this law was rescinded in 1963, when voter registration was opened to all citizens.

During the rocky road to self-government, Bermuda was not without its share of problems. Serious rioting broke out in 1968, and British troops were called back to restore order. Then, in 1973, Sir Richard Sharples, the governor, was assassinated; in 1977, those believed to have been the assassins were themselves executed.

These events, however, which occurred at a time when several of the islands in the region as well as in the Caribbean were experiencing domestic difficulties, proved to be the exception rather than the rule. In the years since then, the social and political climate in Bermuda has been markedly calm—all the better for the island's economic well-being, since it encourages the industries on which Bermuda depends, including tourism.

In 1972, the Bermuda dollar gained its independence from the pound sterling; it's now pegged through gold to the U.S. dollar on an equal dollar-for-dollar basis.

During the 1990s, the political status of their island has once again become a hot topic among Bermudians. Some people feel it would be advantageous to achieve complete independence from Britain, whereas others believe it's in Bermuda's best interest to maintain its present ties to the Crown. In 1995, an independent referendum was conducted, and the majority of voters rejected a proposal to sever ties with Great Britain, preferring to maintain their current status.

In 1997, the governing party of Bermuda chose the daughter of a well-known civil rights leader as its prime minister. Pamela Gordon, former environment minister, was named to the post at the age of 41, the youngest leader in the island nation's 400-year-old history and the first woman to be prime minister. David Saul, the reigning prime minister, resigned in favor of a younger and more popular leader. In her first months in office, Ms. Gordon, a relative political newcomer, pledged to bridge differences between Bermuda's majority black population and its white business elite.

In that stated goal, at least based on election returns, she did not succeed. In November of 1998, the Progressive Labour Party, supported by many of Bermuda's blacks, ended 30 years of conservative rule by sweeping to is first victory in general elections. Although Ms. Gordon is black, as was most of her cabinet, her party was seen by many locals as "part of the white establishment."

The Labour Party's leader, also a woman, Jennifer Smith, became the new prime minister, claiming Bermuda's residents had met their "date with destiny." The Labour Party has moved more from the left to the center in recent years, and Ms. Smith has sought to reassure the island's white-led business community that it will be "business as usual" with her in power. The Labour Party made the economy an issue in the campaign, even though Bermuda residents are blessed with one of the highest standards of living in the world. Nevertheless, many island residents complain of declining education standards and a lack of affordable housing.

Frommer's Online Directory

by Michael Shapiro

Michael Shapiro is the author of *Internet Travel 101: How to Plan Trips and Save Money Online* (Globe Pequot).

Frommer's Online Directory is a new feature designed to help you take advantage of the Internet to better plan your trip. Section 1 lists some general Internet resources that can make any trip easier, such as sites for booking airline tickets. It's not meant to be a comprehensive list—it's a discriminating selection of useful sites to get you started. In section 2, you'll find some top online guides specifically for Bermuda.

1 Top Travel-Planning Web Sites

Among the most popular travel sites are online travel agencies. The top agencies, including Expedia, Preview Travel, and Travelocity, offer an array of tools that are valuable even if you don't book online. You can check flight schedules, hotel availability, car rental prices, or even get paged if your flight is delayed.

While online agencies have come a long way over the past few years, they don't *always* yield the best price. Unlike a travel agent, for example, they're unlikely to tell you that you can save money by flying a day earlier or a day later. On the other hand, if you're looking for a bargain fare, you might find something online that an agent wouldn't take the time to dig up. Because airline commissions have been cut, a travel agent may not find it worthwhile spending half an hour trying to find you the best deal. On the Net you can be your own agent and take all the time you want.

Online booking sites aren't the only places to book airline tickets—all major airlines have their own Web sites and often offer incentives, such as bonus frequent-flyer miles or Net-only discounts, for buying online. These incentives have helped airlines capture the majority of the online booking market. Here are the web sites for the major airlines flying to Bermuda:

American Airlines: www.aa.com
Delta Air Lines: www.delta-air.com
Continental Airlines: www.flycontinental.com
US Airways: www.usair.com
Air Canada: www.aircanada.ca
British Airways: www.britishairways.com

WHEN SHOULD YOU BOOK ONLINE?

Online booking is not for everyone. If you prefer to let others handle your travel arrangements, one call to an experienced travel agent

Factoid

Far more people look online than book online, partly due to fear of putting their credit cards through on the Net. Though secure encryption has made this fear less justified, there's no reason why you can't find a flight online and then book it by calling a toll-free number or contacting your travel agent. To be sure you're in secure mode when you book online, look for a little icon of a key (in Netscape) or a pad-lock (Internet Explorer) at the bottom of your Web browser.

should suffice. But if you want to know as much as possible about your options, the Net is a good place to start, especially for bargain hunters.

The most compelling reason to use online booking is to take advantage of last-minute specials, such as American Airlines' weekend deals or other Internet-only fares that must be purchased online. Another advantage is that you can cash in on incentives for booking online, such as rebates or bonus frequent-flyer miles.

Online booking works best for trips within North America—for international tickets, it's usually cheaper and easier to use a travel agent or consolidator.

Online booking is certainly not for those with a complex international itinerary. If you require follow-up services, such as itinerary changes, use a travel agent. Though Expedia and some other online agencies employ travel agents available by phone, these sites are geared primarily for self-service.

LEADING BOOKING SITES

Below are listings for the top travel booking sites. The starred selections are the most useful and best designed sites.

Cheap Tickets. **www.cheaptickets.com**
Essentials: Discounted rates on domestic and international airline tickets and hotel rooms.

Sometimes discounters such as Cheap Tickets have exclusive deals that aren't available through more mainstream channels. Registration at Cheap Tickets requires inputting a credit card number before getting started, which is one reason many people elect to call the company's toll-free number rather than booking online. Cheap Tickets actually regards this policy as a selling point, arguing that "lookers" who don't intend to buy will be scared off by its "credit card first" approach and won't bog down the site with their queries. If Cheap Tickets is serious about getting people to use its online booking service, it should abolish this credit card–first approach.. Despite its misguided credit card policy, Cheap Tickets is worth the effort because its fares can be substantially lower than those offered by its competitors.

✪ Expedia. **expedia.com**
Essentials: Domestic and international flights, hotel and rental car bookings; late-breaking travel news, destination features, and commentary from travel experts; deals on cruises and vacation packages. Free registration is required for booking.

Expedia makes it easy to handle flight, hotel, and car booking on one itinerary, so it's a good place for one-stop shopping. Expedia's hotel search offers crisp, zoomable maps to pinpoint most properties; click on the camera icon to see images of the rooms and facilities. But like many online databases, Expedia focuses on the major chains, such as Hilton and Hyatt, so don't expect to find too many one-of-a-kind resorts or B&Bs here.

Once you're registered (it's only necessary to do this once from each computer you use), you can start booking with the Roundtrip Fare Finder box on the home page, which expedites the process. After selecting a flight, you can hold it until midnight the

Take a Look at Frommer's Site

We highly recommend Arthur Frommer's Budget Travel Online (**www.frommers. com**) as an excellent travel-planning resource. Of course, we're a little biased, but you will find indispensable travel tips, reviews, monthly vacation giveaways, and online booking.

Subscribe to Arthur Frommer's Daily Newsletter (**www.frommers.com/ newsletters**) to receive the latest travel bargains and inside travel secrets in your mailbox every day. You'll read daily headlines and articles from the dean of travel himself, highlighting last-minute deals on airfares, accommodations, cruises, and package vacations. You'll also find great travel advice by checking our Tip of the Day or Hot Spot of the Month.

Search our Destinations archive (**www.frommers.com/destinations**) of more than 200 domestic and international destinations for great places to stay, tips for traveling there, and what to do while you're there. Once you've researched your trip, you might try our online reservation system (**www.frommers.com/ booktravelnow**) to book your dream vacation at affordable prices.

---

following day or purchase online. If you think you might do better through a travel agent, you'll have time to try to get a lower price. And you may do better with a travel agent because Expedia's computer reservation system does not include all airlines.

Expedia's World Guide, offering destination information, is a glaring weakness—it takes a lot of page views to get very little information. However, Expedia compensates by linking to other Microsoft Network services, such as its Sidewalk city guides, which offer entertainment and dining advice for many of the cities it covers.

Preview Travel. www.previewtravel.com
Essentials: Domestic and international flights, hotel and rental car bookings; Travel Newswire lists fare sales; deals on cruises and vacation packages. Free (one-time) registration is required for booking. Preview offers express booking for members but at presstime this feature was buried below the fold on Preview's reservation page.

Preview features the most inviting interface for booking trips, though the wealth of graphics involved can make the site somewhat slow to load. Use Farefinder to quickly find the lowest current fares on flights to dozens of major cities. Carfinder offers a similar service for rental cars, but you can only search airport locations, not city pick-up sites. To see the lowest fare for your itinerary, input the dates and times for your route and see what Preview comes up with.

In recent years Preview and other leading booking services have added features such as the Best Fare Finder: After Preview searches for the best deal on your itinerary, it will check flights that are a bit later or earlier to see if it might be cheaper to fly at a different time. While these searches have become quite sophisticated, they still occasionally overlook deals that might be uncovered by a top-notch travel agent. If you have the time, see what you can find online and then call an agent to see if you can get a better price.

With Preview's Fare Alert feature, you can set fares for up to three routes and you'll receive e-mail notices when the fare drops below your target amount. For example, you could tell Preview to alert you when the fare from New York to Bermuda drops below $250. If it does, you'll get an e-mail telling you the current fare.

Minor quibbles: When you search for a fare, hotel, or car (at least when we went to press), Preview launched an annoying little "Please Wait" window that gets in the way of the main browser window, even when your results begin to appear. The hotel search feature is intuitive, but the images and maps aren't as crisp as those at Expedia. Also: all sorts of extraneous information that's irrelevant to travelers is listed on the maps.

Note to AOL Users: You can book flights, hotels, rental cars and cruises on AOL at keyword: Travel. The booking software is provided by Preview Travel and is similar to Preview on the Web. Use the AOL "Travelers Advantage" program to earn a 5% rebate on flights, hotel rooms, and car rentals.

Priceline.com. www.priceline.com

Even people who aren't familiar with too many Web sites have heard about Priceline. com, which lets you "name your price" for domestic and international airline tickets. In other words, you select a route and dates, guarantee with a credit card, and make a bid for what you're willing to pay. If one of the airlines in Priceline's database has a fare that's lower than your bid, your credit card will automatically be charged for a ticket.

But you can't say when you want to fly—you have to accept any flight leaving between 6am and 10pm, and you may have to make a stopover. No frequent-flyer miles are awarded, and tickets are non-refundable and can't be exchanged for another flight. So if your plans change, you're out of luck. Priceline can be good for travelers who have to take off on short notice (and who are thus unable to qualify for advance purchase discounts). But be sure to shop around first—if you overbid, you'll be required to purchase the ticket and Priceline will pocket the difference.

Travelocity. www.travelocity.com

Essentials: Domestic and international flights, hotel and rental car bookings; deals on cruises and vacation packages. Travel Headlines spotlights latest bargain airfares. Free (one-time) registration is required for booking.

Travelocity almost got it right. Its Express Booking feature enables travelers to complete the booking process more quickly than they could at Expedia or Preview, but Travelocity gums up the works with a page called "Featured Airlines." Big placards of several featured airlines compete for your attention. If you want to see the fares for all available airlines, click the much smaller box at the bottom of the page labeled "Book a Flight."

Some have worried that Travelocity, which is owned by American Airlines' parent company AMR, directs bookings to American. This doesn't seem to be the case; I've booked there dozens of times and have always been directed to the cheapest listed flight, for example on Tower or ATA. But this "Featured Airlines" page seems to be Travelocity's way of trying to cash in with ads and incentives for booking certain airlines. (*Note:* It's hard to blame these booking services for trying to generate some revenue—many airlines have slashed commissions to $10 per domestic booking for online transactions so these virtual agencies are groping for revenue streams.) There are rewards for choosing one of the featured airlines. You'll get 1,500 bonus frequent-flyer miles if you book through United's site, for example, but the site doesn't tell you about other airlines that might be cheaper. If the United flight costs $150 more than the best deal on another airline, it's not worth spending the extra money for a relatively small number of bonus miles.

On the plus side, Travelocity has some leading-edge techie tools. Exhibit A is the Fare Watcher E-mail, an "intelligent agent" that keeps you informed of the best fares offered for the city pairs (round-trips) of your choice. Whenever the fare changes by $25 or more, Fare Watcher will alert you by e-mail. Exhibit B is Flight Paging. If you own an alphanumeric pager with national access that can receive e-mail, Travelocity's paging system can alert you if your flight is delayed.

FINDING LODGINGS ONLINE

While the services above offer hotel booking, it can be best to use a site devoted primarily to lodging because you may find properties that aren't listed on more general online travel agencies. Some lodging sites specialize in a particular type of accommodations, such as B&Bs, which you won't find on the more mainstream booking services. Other services, such as TravelWeb, offer weekend deals on major chain properties, which cater to business travelers and have more empty rooms on weekends.

All Hotels on the Web. www.all-hotels.com

Well, this site doesn't include *all* the hotels on the Web, but it does have tens of thousands of listings throughout the world. Bear in mind that each hotel listed has paid a small fee of ($25 and up) for placement, so it's not an objective list but more like a book of online brochures.

InnSite. www.innsite.com

B&B listings for inns in all 50 U.S. states and dozens of countries around the globe. Find an inn at your destination, have a look at images of the rooms, check prices and availability, and then send an e-mail to the innkeeper if you have further questions. This is an extensive directory of bed-and-breakfast inns, but only includes listings if the proprietor submitted one (note: it's free to get an inn listed). The descriptions are written by the innkeepers and many listings link to the inn's own Web sites, where you can find more information and images.

Places to Stay. www.placestostay.com

Mostly one-of-a-kind places in the U.S. and abroad that you might not find in other directories, with a focus on resorts. Again, listing is selective—this isn't a comprehensive directory, but can give you a sense of what's available at different destinations.

✪ TravelWeb. www.travelweb.com

TravelWeb lists more than 16,000 hotels worldwide, focusing on chains such as Hyatt and Hilton, and you can book almost 90 percent of these online. TravelWeb's Click-It Weekends, updated each Monday, offers weekend deals at many leading hotel chains. TravelWeb is the online home for Pegasus Systems, which provides transaction processing systems for the hotel industry.

LAST-MINUTE DEALS & OTHER ONLINE BARGAINS

There's nothing airlines hate more than flying with lots of empty seats (well, maybe they hate competition more, but that's another story). The Net has enabled airlines to offer last-minute bargains to entice travelers to fill those seats. Most of these are announced on Tuesday or Wednesday and are valid for travel the following weekend, but some can be booked weeks or months in advance. You can sign up for weekly e-mail alerts at airlines' sites (see above for a list), or check sites such as WebFlyer (see below) that compile lists of these bargains. To make it easier, visit a site (see below) that will round up all the deals and send them in one convenient weekly e-mail. But last-minute deals aren't the only online bargains—other sites can help you find value even if you can't wait until the eleventh hour.

✪ 1travel.com. www.1travel.com

Deals on domestic and international flights, cruises, hotels, and all-inclusive resorts such as Club Med.1travel.com's Saving Alert compiles last-minute air deals so you don't have to scroll through multiple e-mail alerts. A feature called "Drive a little using low-fare airlines" helps map out strategies for using alternate airports to find lower fares. And Farebeater searches a database that includes published fares, consolidator bargains and special deals exclusive to 1travel.com. *Note:* The travel agencies listed by 1travel.com have paid for placement.

✪ **Arthur Frommer's Budget Travel Online. www.frommers.com**
Budget travel strategies, a daily newsletter of travel deals, and features from the acclaimed magazine *Arthur Frommer's Budget Travel.* After scouring the planet for more than four decades in search of great travel bargains, Arthur Frommer has compiled much of the wisdom he's gained here. Click on "Research Destinations" to get the most bang for your buck in some 200-plus locales.

BestFares. www.bestfares.com
Budget seeker Tom Parsons lists some great bargains on airfares, hotels, rental cars and cruises, but the site is poorly organized. News Desk is a long list of hundreds of bargains, but they're not broken down into cities or even countries, so it's not easy trying to find what you're looking for. If you have time to wade through it, you might find a good deal. Some material is available only to paid subscribers.

Go4less.com. www.go4less.com
Specializing in last-minute cruise and package deals, Go4less has some eye-popping offers, such as off-peak Caribbean cruises for under $100 per day. The site has a clean design but the bargains aren't organized by destination. However, you avoid sifting through all this material by using the Search box and entering vacation type, destination, month, and price.

Moment's Notice. www.moments-notice.com
As the name suggests, Moment's Notice specializes in last-minute vacation and cruise deals. You can browse for free, but if you want to purchase a trip you have to join Moment's Notice, which costs $25.

Smarter Living. www.smarterliving.com
Best known for its e-mail dispatch of weekend deals on 20 airlines, Smarter Living also keeps you posted about last-minute bargains on everything from Windjammer Cruises to flights to Iceland.

✪ **WebFlyer. www.webflyer.com**
WebFlyer is the ultimate online resource for frequent flyers and also has an excellent listing of last-minute air deals. Click on "Deal Watch" for a round-up of weekend deals on flights, hotels and rental cars from domestic and international suppliers.

TRAVELER'S TOOLKIT

Seasoned travelers always carry some essential items to make their trips easier. Following is a selection of online tools to smooth your journey.

ATM LOCATORS

Visa (www.visa.com/pd/atm/)
MasterCard (www.mastercard.com/atm)
Find ATMs in hundreds of cities in the U.S. and around the world. Both include maps for some locations and both list airport ATM locations, some with maps. Remarkably, MasterCard lists ATMs on all seven continents (there's one at Antarctica's McMurdo Station). Tip: You'll usually get a better exchange rate using ATMs than exchanging traveler's checks at banks.

OTHER HELPFUL SITES

Intellicast. www.intellicast.com
Weather forecasts for all 50 states and cities around the world. Note that temperatures are in Celsius for many international destinations, so don't think you'll need that winter coat for your next trip to Athens.

Handy Tip

While most people learn about last-minute weekend deals from e-mail dispatches, it can be best to find out precisely when these deals become available and check airlines' Web sites at this time. To find out when deals become available, check the pages devoted to these deals on airlines' Web pages. Because these deals are limited, they can vanish within hours, sometimes even minutes, so it pays to log on as soon as they're available. An example: Southwest's specials are posted at 12:01 am Tuesdays (Central time). So if you're looking for a cheap flight, stay up late and check Southwest's site at that time to grab the best new deals.

The Travelite FAQ. www.travelite.org
Tips on packing light, choosing luggage, and selecting appropriate travel wear.

Universal Currency Converter. www.xe.net/currency
See what your dollar or pound is worth in more than a hundred other countries.

U.S. Customs Service Traveler Information. www.customs.ustreas.gov/travel/ index.htm
Wondering what you're allowed to bring in to the U.S.? Check at this thorough site, which includes maximum allowance and duty fees.

2 The Top Web Sites for Bermuda

ISLAND GUIDES
Check these sites to get updated on what's going on in Bermuda.

Always Dreaming of Bermuda. pweb.netcom.com/~mike143/Bermuda.html
A "virtual tour" and endearing collection of amateur photos taken by a Bermuda lover, with a nice set of links to other Bermuda Web sites.

For AOL members:
  AOL International: Bermuda
  Keyword: Bermuda
The perfect place for AOL members to get the latest news about Bermuda's attractions, including updates from Reuters and Bermuda newspapers, chat rooms, message boards, even an audio file of Bermuda's national anthem. Sign up for a free newsletter to keep you posted on breaking developments.

Bermuda Business. www.bermudabusiness.com
Excellent shopping listings.

Bermuda Chamber of Commerce. www.bermudacommerce.com
Business information and links to tourism offices.

✪ **Bermuda Department of Tourism. www.bermudatourism.com**
The best thing about Bermuda's official tourism site is its extensive calendar of events. Drop in before you leave home to see what's going on during the dates of your stay. You can also e-mail questions to the tourism office.

Bermuda Government Ferry Service. www.travelfacts.com/tfacts/htm/berferry/ ferry.htm
See ferry routes mapped out between Somerset, Paget, and Warwick, and learn about fares and schedules. A pulldown menu at the top of the page makes it easy to get timetables.

⚙ **Bermuda Online. bermuda-online.org**
An up-to-date calendar of events, cruise ship schedules, dining advice (with tips on local specialties), and local radio and television guide. There's also airport information and transportation tips, as well as aerial photos of the islands.

Bermuda Vacation Guide. www.keyguide.com
News about Bermuda's attractions, weather forecasts, and tips from locals to help you plan your vacation. You can also post a question in the online forum (electronic bulletin board) and sign up for an occasional e-mail dispatch that will keep you informed about the latest developments in Bermuda tourism.

Bermuda Yellow Pages. www.bermudayp.com
Search for businesses by name or keyword, or browse through categories. Click on "Menu Guide" to see Bermuda's top attractions located on a map.

Public Transport Bermuda. www.bermudabuses.com
Fares and schedules for Bermuda's buses as well as charter reservation information.

TravelFacts: Bermuda. www.travelfacts.com/tfacts/htm/ber/berdest.htm
An excellent calendar of events and extensive listings (with photos) covering tours, attractions, dining, shopping, and lodging. The copy is written by the businesses, so consider this a collection of online brochures rather than an editor's selection.

NEWSPAPERS & MAGAZINES

Bermuda Gazette. www.accessbda.bm/gazette.htm
News headlines, updated daily, let you know what's going on. Includes classifieds.

⚙ **Bermuda Sun. www.bermudasun.org**
News, sports, opinion, entertainment, and real estate classifieds from this twice-weekly newspaper (published Wednesdays and Fridays). Also includes restaurant reviews and links to hundreds of other sites related to Bermuda.

Hey Bye! www.bermudaonion.com
An online magazine listing top activities by month. It includes readers' picks of their favorites on the island—nicely designed with an interactive forum where you can ask questions, and a virtual island photo tour (with more than 200 images).

The Washington Post: Bermuda. www.washingtonpost.com/wp-srv/inatl/ longterm/worldref/country/bermuda.htm
Sure it's a very long Web address, but you may find it worth the trouble to get the latest Bermuda news from the Post and Associated Press.

Bermuda-L Email List. www.fes.uwaterloo.ca/u/kmayall/Bermuda/bda-l.intro. html
Information on how to sign up for an e-mail list that deals exclusively with messages about Bermuda. Read others' messages to the lists or send an e-mail yourself. You'll receive a copy of every e-mail written to the list, a nice way to get an insiders' view of the island before your trip.

ACTIVITIES & ATTRACTIONS

⚙ **Bermuda Aquarium, Museum and Zoo. www.bamz.org**
Find out when the seals are fed, learn about continuing exhibitions, and see your options for getting there (why not take the ferry?). While you're at it, have an advance peek at the Bermuda Ecotour, Biodiversity Project, and even some turtle studies. This is a well-designed site and will whet your appetite for the real thing.

Bermuda Arts Centre at Dockyards. www.bermuda.bm/artcentre
Check the schedule of exhibits of original artwork by local artists who reflect the diverse creativity of the art community in Bermuda.

Bermuda Festival. www.bermudafestival.com
Running from mid-January until late February, the festival includes music, theater and even Chinese acrobats. The Web site offers a schedule and advance ticket ordering.

Bermuda International Film Festival. www.bermuda.bm/filmfestival/index2.html
Held during April, this two-week festival includes little-known but worthy films from the U.S. and around the world. Find out what's playing and learn about the filmmakers at this extensive site.

Bermuda Musical & Dramatic Society. www.bmds.bm
The society stages six to eight plays a year; see if a show is playing during your trip.

✪ **Bermuda Underwater Exploration Institute. www.buei.org**
The institute is dedicated to sharing the ever-increasing knowledge of ocean life with Bermuda's people and visitors. Learn about current exhibitions, films, slideshows, and lectures. Be advised, though, that this site can take some time to load; on the home page, choose the low-tech option to avoid getting bogged down in heavy graphics.

Fish Bermuda. www.fishbermuda.com
Though the ultimate aim of this site is to lure you to sign up for a fishing charter, it's a great reference for learning about what fish bite during different seasons (click on the "Mako" link). Also includes a weather forecast, fishing report, and links to other fishing sites.

✪ **Tall Ships 2000. www.tallships2000.bm**
A flotilla of the world's most majestic tall sailing ships is scheduled to race into Bermuda June 9-12, 2000. This site includes a schedule, events, and a course map for the race that begins in England, stops in Bermuda, heads up to Boston, and then ends in Amsterdam.

Undersea Adventures in Bermuda. www.hartleybermuda.com
Learn all about underwater helmet diving (the air is pumped from the boat above so you don't have to carry tanks). Any questions? Send an e-mail to the proprietors.

Index

See also separate Accommodations and Restaurants indexes below.
Page numbers in italics refer to maps.

GENERAL INDEX

ACCOMMODATIONS

RESTAURANTS

FROMMER'S® COMPLETE TRAVEL GUIDES

FROMMER'S® DOLLAR-A-DAY GUIDES

Australia from $50 a Day	Hawaii from $70 a Day	New Zealand from $50 a Day
California from $60 a Day	Ireland from $50 a Day	Paris from $85 a Day
Caribbean from $70 a Day	Israel from $45 a Day	San Francisco from $60 a Day
England from $70 a Day	Italy from $70 a Day	Washington, D.C.,
Europe from $60 a Day	London from $85 a Day	from $60 a Day
Florida from $60 a Day	New York from $80 a Day	

FROMMER'S® PORTABLE GUIDES

Acapulco, Ixtapa & Zihuatanejo	Dublin	Puerto Vallarta, Manzanillo & Guadalajara
Alaska Cruises & Ports of Call	Hawaii: The Big Island	San Diego
Bahamas	Las Vegas	San Francisco
Baja & Los Cabos	London	Sydney
Berlin	Maine Coast	Tampa & St. Petersburg
California Wine Country	Maui	Venice
Charleston & Savannah	New Orleans	Washington, D.C.
Chicago	New York City	
	Paris	

FROMMER'S® NATIONAL PARK GUIDES

Family Vacations in the National Parks	National Parks of the American West	Yellowstone & Grand Teton
Grand Canyon	Rocky Mountain	Yosemite & Sequoia/ Kings Canyon
		Zion & Bryce Canyon

FROMMER'S® GREAT OUTDOOR GUIDES

New England	Southern California & Baja
Northern California	Washington & Oregon

FROMMER'S® MEMORABLE WALKS

Chicago	New York	San Francisco
London	Paris	Washington D.C.

FROMMER'S® IRREVERENT GUIDES

Amsterdam	London	New Orleans	Seattle & Portland
Boston	Los Angeles	Paris	Vancouver
Chicago	Manhattan	San Francisco	Walt Disney World
Las Vegas			Washington, D.C.

FROMMER'S® BEST-LOVED DRIVING TOURS

America	Florida	Ireland	Scotland
Britain	France	Italy	Spain
California	Germany	New England	Western Europe

THE COMPLETE IDIOT'S TRAVEL GUIDES

Boston	Ireland	Paris
Chicago	Las Vegas	San Francisco
Cruise Vacations	London	Spain
Planning Your Trip to Europe	Mexico's Beach Resorts	Walt Disney World
Florida	New Orleans	Washington, D.C.
Hawaii	New York City	

THE UNOFFICIAL GUIDES®

SPECIAL-INTEREST TITLES

WHEREVER YOU TRAVEL, *H*ELP IS NEVER FAR AWAY.

From planning your trip to providing travel assistance along the way, American Express® Travel Service Offices are always there to help you do more.

Bermuda

HAMILTON
Meyer Agencies Ltd. (R)
35 Church Street
(441) 295-4176

SANDYS
Meyer Agencies Ltd. (R)
Dockyard Terrace
(441) 234-2992

ST. GEORGE'S
Meyer Agencies Ltd. (R)
Somers Wharf
(441) 297-1616

Meyer Agencies Ltd. (R)
Bermuda International Airport
(441) 293-5375

do more AMERICAN EXPRESS
Travel
www.americanexpress.com/travel

American Express Travel Service Offices are found in central locations throughout Bermuda.